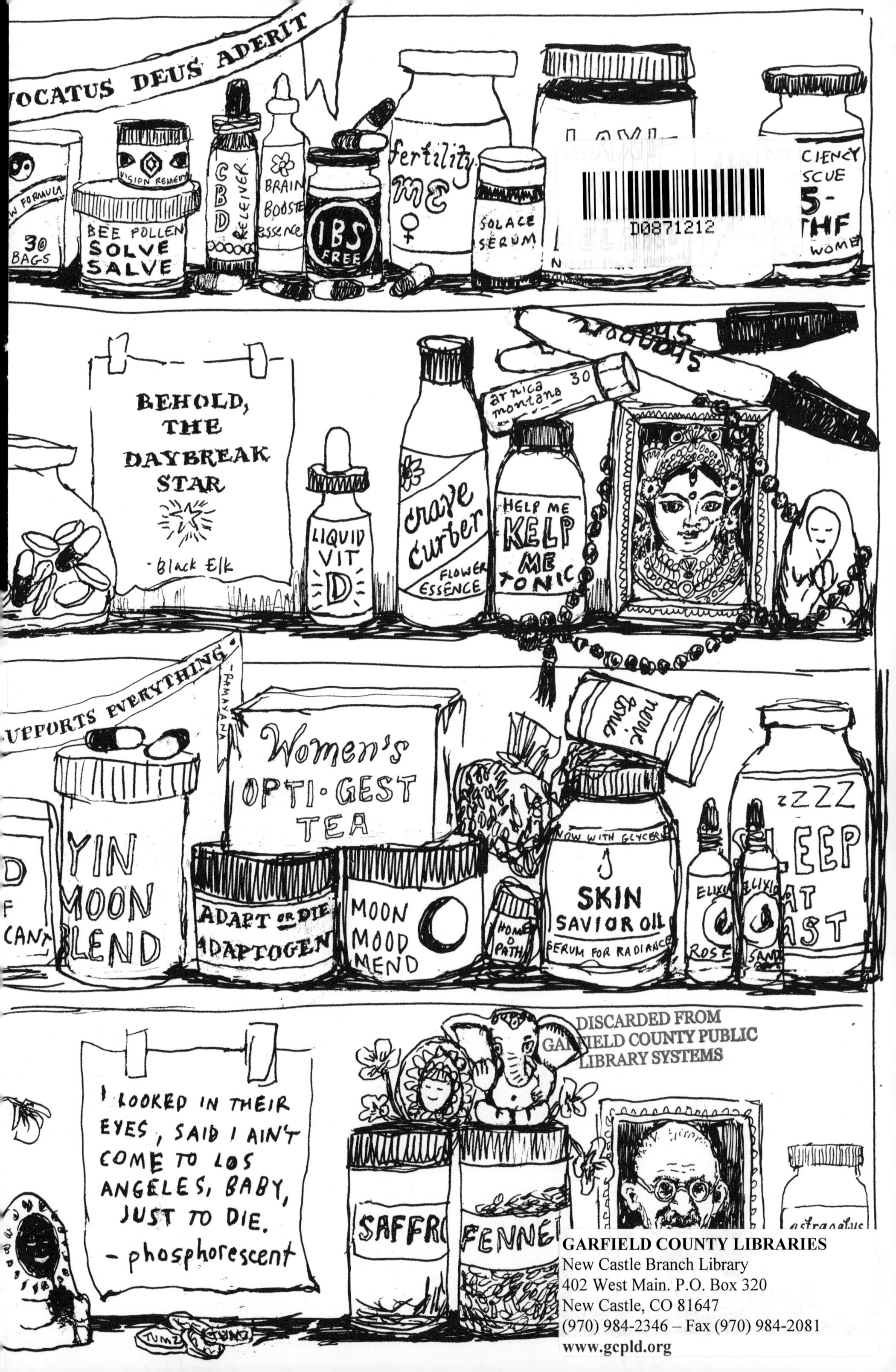
VOCATUS DEUS ADERIT
30 BAGS
VISION REMEDY
BEE POLLEN
SOLVE SALVE
CBD RELEIVER
BRAIN BOOSTER ESSENCE
IBS FREE
fertility ME
SOLACE SERUM
BEHOLD, THE DAYBREAK STAR
-Black Elk
LIQUID VIT D
crave curber
FLOWER ESSENCE
arnica montana 30
HELP ME KELP ME TONIC
SUPPORTS EVERYTHING
-RAMAYANA
Women's OPTI·GEST TEA
YIN MOON BLEND
ADAPT OR DIE ADAPTOGEN
MOON MOOD MEND
NOW WITH GLYCERIN
SKIN SAVIOR OIL
SERUM FOR RADIANCE
zZZZ
I LOOKED IN THEIR EYES, SAID I AIN'T COME TO LOS ANGELES, BABY, JUST TO DIE.
- phosphorescent
astragalus

BLOSSOMS & BONES
DRAWING A LIFE BACK TOGETHER

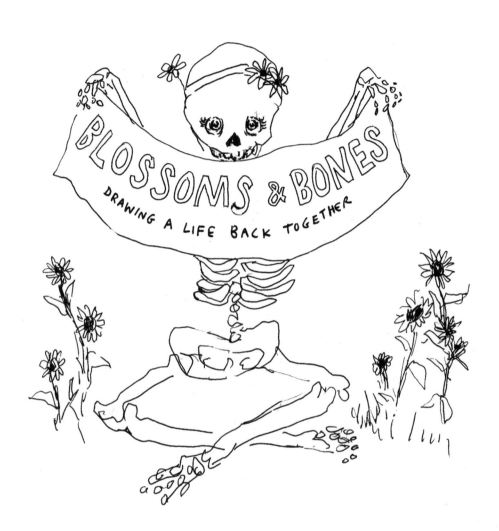

KIM KRANS

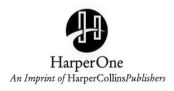

HarperOne
An Imprint of HarperCollins*Publishers*

HarperOne

"Statement" reprinted from Collected Poems: 1936-1976.
Copyright © 1976 by Robert Francis. Published by the
University of Massachusetts Press.

HarperCollins books may be purchased for educational,
business, or sales promotional use. For information
please email the special markets department at
SPsales@harpercollins.com.

HarperCollins website: http://www.harpercollins.com

Designed by Kim Krans & Su Barber

ISBN 978-0-06-298638-2

20 21 22 23 24 LEO 10 9 8 7 6 5 4 3 2 1

FIRST EDITION

Library of Congress Cataloging-in-Publication Data

Names: Krans, Kim, author.
Title: Blossoms & Bones : Drawing a Life Back
Together / kim krans.
Description: First Edition.
San Francisco, CA : HarperOne, [2020]

Identifiers:
LCCN 2019033519 (print)
LCCN 2019033520 (ebook)
ISBN 9780062986382 (hardcover)
ISBN 9780062986399 (ebook)

Subjects:
LCSH: Krans, kim. | Authors, American—21st century-
-Biography—Comic books, strips, etc. | Graphic novels.

Classification:
LCC PN6727.K686 246 2020 (print)
LCC PN6727.K686 246 2020 (ebook)
DDC 741.5/973 [B]—dc23

LC record available at https://lccn.loc.gov/2019033519
LC ebook record available at https://lccn.loc.gov/2019033520

THIS BOOK IS DEDICATED TO MICHAEL MEADE

thank you for telling that one story
that one time

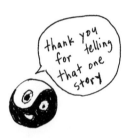

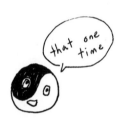

INTRODUCTION

Written April 23, 2019

THIS STORY WAS WRITTEN OVER A PERIOD OF ONE-MONTH. I ASSIGNED MYSELF THE DAILY TASK OF "DRAWING THE FEELING" AFTER ABOUT SIX MONTHS OF NEGOTIATING WHAT WAS QUICKLY DEVELOPING INTO A MID-LIFE EATING DISORDER. NOTHING SEEMED TO HELP MY SYMPTOMS. DOCTORS, FRIENDS, TEACHERS TOLD ME THAT IT WOULD PASS AS SOON AS THE BIG LIFE TRANSITIONS I WAS GOING THROUGH ~~WOULD~~ PASSED. I WANTED TO BELIEVE THEM. I WASN'T THE EATING DISORDER "TYPE." I WAS TOO SMART, TOO CONFIDENT, TOO SAVVY TO BE INVOLVED IN SUCH THINGS. NOT ME. NOT FOOD. NOT IN THIS LIFETIME. AT A YOUNG AGE I SENSED MY MOM'S FIXATION ON FOOD. EMOTIONAL EATING. I CAME TO RECOGNIZE ITS SIGNS & SYMPTOMS FROM ACROSS OUR HUMBLE MIDWEST TABLE: HIDING, NIBBLING, SECONDS THEN SECRET THIRDS. IT WAS A SPELL THAT PLAGUED MY AUNTS, MY MOM'S FRIENDS, MY GRANDMA. NOT ME, DECIDED. NOT IN THIS LIFETIME. NOT THIS WOMAN. SO I STAYED SKINNY. I DIDN'T CARE MUCH ABOUT FOOD. I DISCIPLINED MYSELF & AVOIDED THE HOOKS. I JUDGED OTHER WOMEN AS PART OF MY RESISTANCE TRAINING. I'M NOT LIKE THEM. I'M SEPARATE.

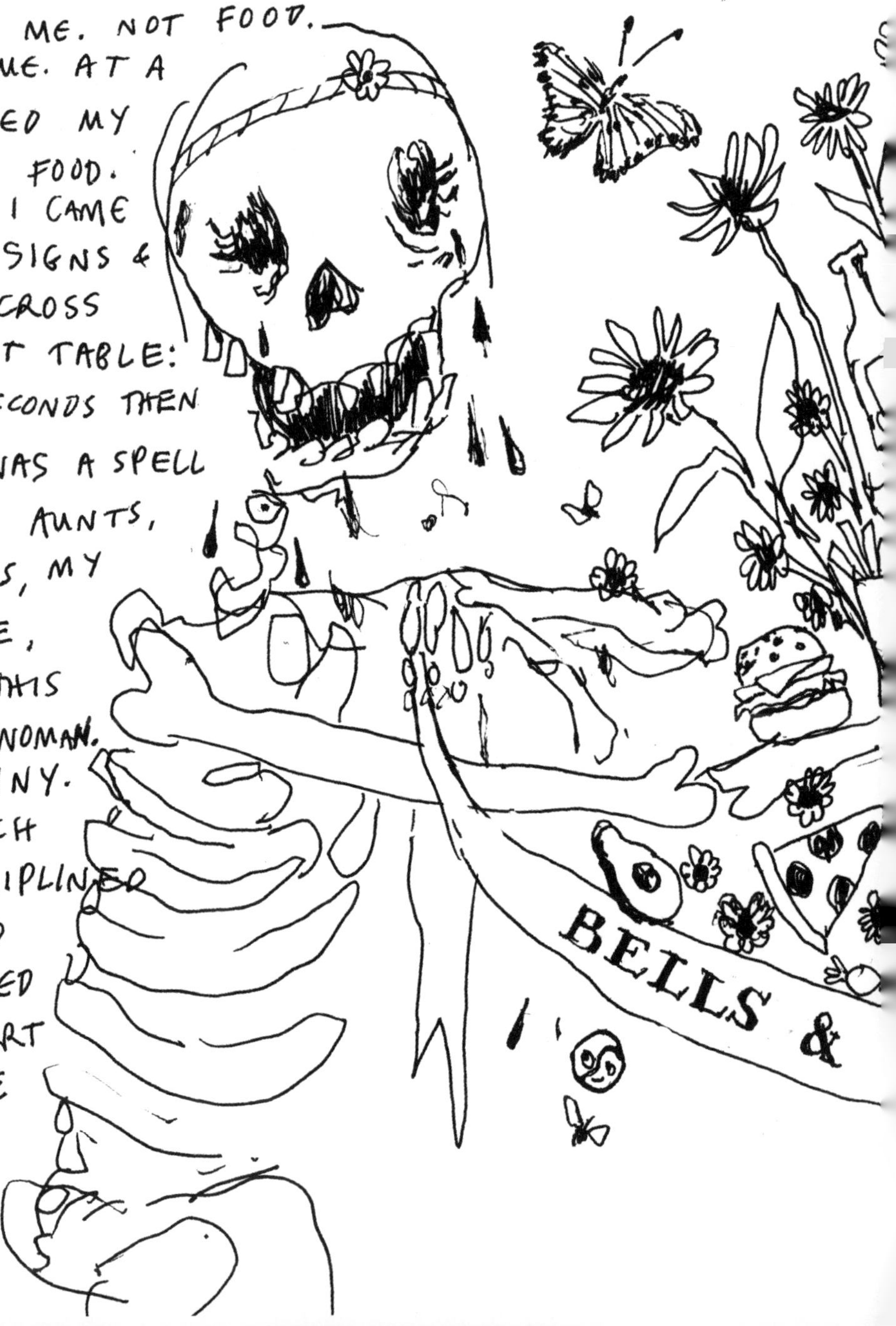
BELLS &

MY FIRST THIRTY-EIGHT YEARS PASSED THIS WAY, KEEPING A TIGHT BUT RELATIVELY BANAL REIN ON MY EATING HABITS. I WAS THIN & HEALTHY. THAT WAS THAT. IT WASN'T A THING. THEN LIFE TOSSED ME, AS IT TENDS TO DO, A SERIES OF UNFORESEEN CHANGES. SOON AFTERWARDS, THE "THING" THAT I CONVINCED MYSELF "WASN'T A THING," BECAME A "THING." SIMPLY PUT, I COULD NOT STOP EITHER EATING OR NOT EATING. I WOKE UP & WENT TO BED THINKING ABOUT FOOD. I ATE THINGS THAT WERE FROZEN, IN THE TRASH, IN OTHER PEOPLE'S CUPBOARDS, ALL IN SECRET, ALL IN SHAME. I COULD NOT RECOGNIZE MY BODY, MY THOUGHTS, OR MY ACTIONS. NOR COULD I CONTROL THEM. BEFORE MY EYES I WAS BECOMING ONE OF THE WOMEN I HAD SO COLDLY & CONSISTENTLY REJECTED. AFTER SIX, EIGHT, TEN MONTHS OF THIS (GIVE OR TAKE A JUICE CLEANSE) I DECIDED NO ONE COULD HELP ME EXCEPT THE FEELING ITSELF. IT WAS POWERFUL & BEYOND MY CONTROL. THEREFORE, IT COULD BECOME SOMETHING BIG. I DECIDED TO LET THE FEELING OUT OF THE CLOSET. AT THE TIME I HAD A RETURN FLIGHT BOOKED FROM NEW YORK CITY TO LOS ANGELES. I HAD JUST TAUGHT A SERIES OF WORKSHOPS ON CREATIVITY AND SPIRITUALITY IN WHICH I INSPIRED THE AUDIENCE WITH PAINFULLY WELL-FORMED BELLS & WHISTLES, & THEN RETURNED TO MY HOTEL ROOM TO SWALLOW

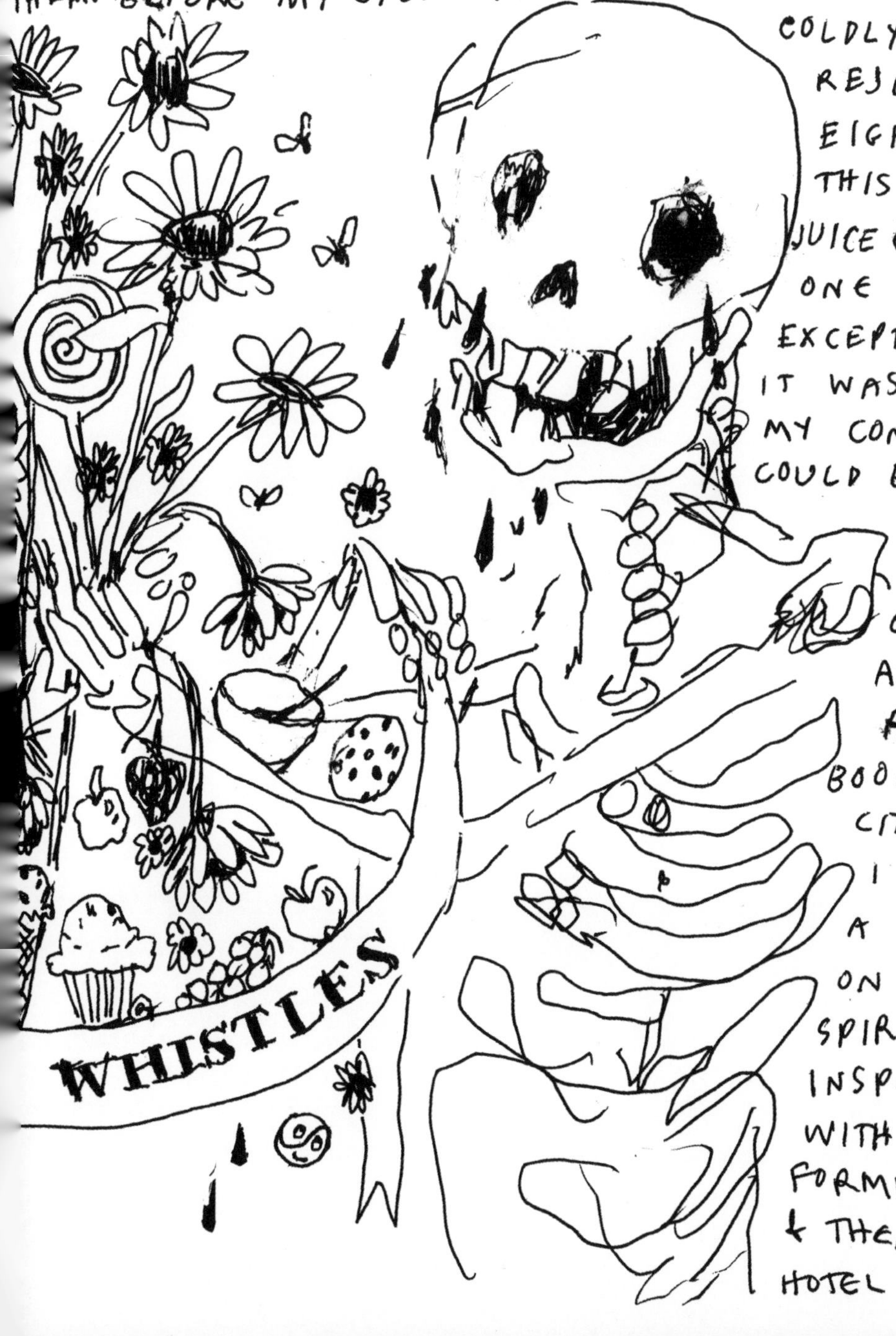
WHISTLES

MYSELF IN ONE, TWO, OR THREE ICE CREAM SANDWICHES,
THEN TWO BAGS OF CHIPS, A PACKAGE OR SO OF FANCY ROASTED
NUTS, PERHAPS CHOCOLATE, THEN SLEEP. THEN BREAKFAST. I WAS A SUCCESSFUL
WOMAN. NO ONE SUSPECTED SUCH BEHAVIOR. ~~AFTER ONE WEEK~~ MY FLIGHT BACK
TO LA LOOMED ON THE HORIZON. WAS I TO GO BACK TO THAT
BEACH BUNGALOW, WHERE I BINGED ON THE FLOOR, THEN THREW OUT
EVERYTHING EDIBLE WITHIN REACH, JUICE-FASTED FOR ONE WEEK,
THEN ORDERED TAKEOUT FROM MULTIPLE LOCATIONS IN ORDER TO
NOT APPEAR SUSPICIOUSLY HUNGRY? CRAWLING? EATING? FALLING?
I NEVER GOT ON THAT FLIGHT TO LOS ANGELES. NEVER WENT BACK.
I CANCELLED A FIVE-DAY SOLD-OUT WORKSHOP AT ONE OF THE
MOST PICTURESQUE & ICONIC RETREAT CENTERS IN THE COUNTRY.
"BUT THE OCEAN WILL SOOTHE YOUR WOES, KIM, " I THOUGHT, "JUST
TEACH. ~~YOU~~ YOU CAN'T CANCEL."
BUT I COULDN'T TEACH A LIE.
THE BELLS & WHISTLES WERE BROKEN.
I WENT TO PORT AUTHORITY BUS TERMINAL & BOARDED A
BUS TO A SMALL TOWN IN THE POCONOS WHERE AN ASHRAM
I HAD ONCE FREQUENTED SAT TUCKED AWAY IN THE HILLS.
I SAT IN THE SHRINE & CRIED. I SNUCK FOOD FROM
THE RESIDENTS' FRIDGE. BY THE SECOND WEEK I WAS
READY TO DRAW — TO LET THE FEELING BECOME A VISIBLE
PALPABLE THING. RATHER THAN ME TELLING IT WHAT TO
DO, I DECIDED TO LISTEN. NO MORE DIETS. ONLY ART.
AND SO, EACH DAY I WOKE AT DAWN AND ASKED TO
BE OF SERVICE TO THIS "THING." THIS FUCKING GNARLY,
TERRIFYING, ALL CONSUMING, TANGLED, FORCEFUL, DEVASTATING
"THING." THE ONE I'D SPENT MY LIFE DESPISING. THE
ARTIST WITHIN ME KNEW IT WANTED TO BECOME SOMETHING
AND SO IT BEGAN... DAY BY DAY... TO SPEAK & DRAW
ITSELF INTO BEING. I DID MY BEST TO LET IT.
IT IS IMPORTANT TO MENTION THAT NOTHING WITHIN THIS
BOOK WAS PRE-PLANNED, SKETCHED OUT, OR STRATEGIZED.
THE EDITS MADE HAVE BEEN EXCEEDINGLY MINIMAL, AND

ONLY TO SERVICE LEGIBILITY. I FELT IT WAS OF UTMOST IMPORTANCE THAT YOU COULD SENSE THE INTELLIGENCE OF THE FEELING ITSELF, AND ITS DESIRE TO BECOME A STORY. TO THOSE OF YOU WHO HAVE STRUGGLED OR ARE STRUGGLING WITH A SIMILAR "THING,"* KNOW THAT I AM WITH YOU, SITTING RIGHT NEXT TO YOU, ON THIS DAY AND ALL DAYS. I WILL NEVER AGAIN TURN MY BACK OR JUDGE A SINGLE SPECK OF CHOCOLATE THAT GRACES YOUR LIPS. I'M WITH YOU ON THE FLOOR, AT THE TABLE, TOILET, & FRIDGE. THERE'S NO GOING BACK TO SEPARATE. TO THOSE OF YOU AT THE ASHRAM WHO SUPPORTED ME WITH OR WITHOUT KNOWING IT, I CANNOT THANK YOU ENOUGH.

TOGETHER, WE LIFTED UP THE MOUNTAIN OF PERFECTION TO REVEAL AN ENTIRE ECOSYSTEM OF EMOTION UNDERNEATH. A NEW PARADIGM. A NEW FAMILY.

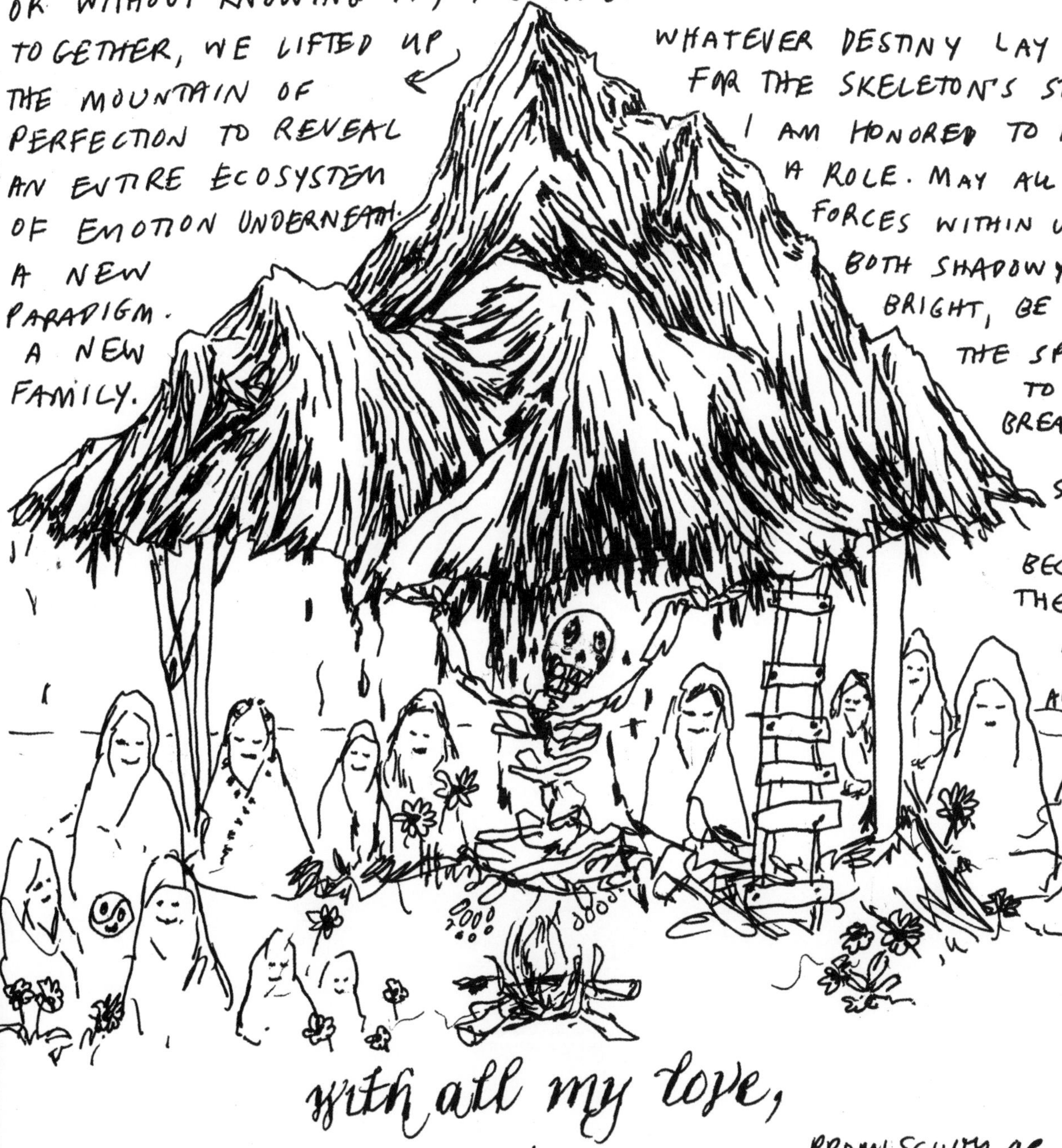

WHATEVER DESTINY LAY AHEAD FOR THE SKELETON'S STORY, I AM HONORED TO PLAY A ROLE. MAY ALL THE FORCES WITHIN US, BOTH SHADOWY & BRIGHT, BE GIVEN THE SPACE TO BREATHE, TO SPEAK, TO BECOME THEMSELVES. NOW & ALWAYS.

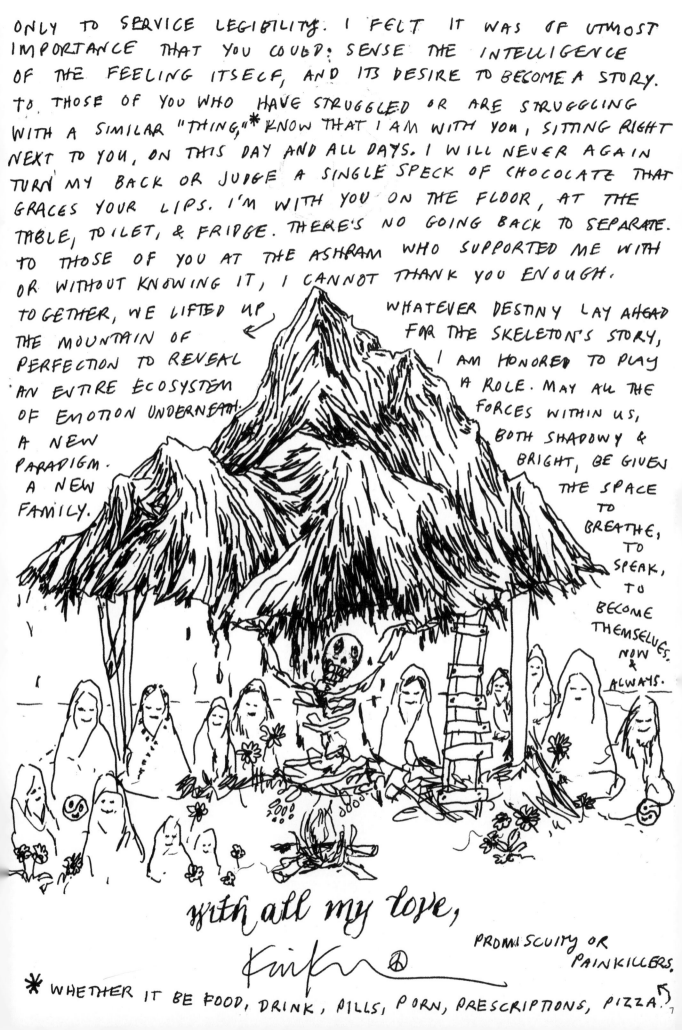

with all my love,

Kirk ☮

* WHETHER IT BE FOOD, DRINK, PILLS, PORN, PRESCRIPTIONS, PIZZA, PROMISCUITY OR PAINKILLERS.

INTRODUCTION *part two*

MAY 25, 2019

IT'S NO SURPRISE, LOOKING BACK, THAT 30 DAYS WAS NOT ENOUGH. HOW COULD IT BE? SIFTING, SORTING, MENDING, TENDING — THESE THINGS TAKE TIME. TIME & SPACE, TIME & SPACE, TIME & SPACE... THE TRUE REMEDIES FOR OUR MODERN AILS. AND SO THE 30 DAYS BECAME 40 WHICH IS ALSO NO SURPRISE, AS 40-DAY PRACTICES HAVE THEIR OWN ESOTERIC LINEAGE THROUGHOUT THE SPIRITUAL TRADITIONS OF OUR WORLD. "AUSPICIOUS," SOME SAY; "BLESSED," OTHERS SAY. WHO KNOWS IF IT'S TRUE. [redacted] FOR BLOSSOMS & BONES, IT'S JUST WHAT ENDED UP HAPPENING.

BUT SINCE 40-DAY PRACTICES SHOW UP IN KUNDALINI YOGA, IN JUDAISM, IN CHRISTIANITY, IT'S WORTH PONDERING FOR A MOMENT WHAT IT'S ALL ABOUT. I CAN TELL YOU FROM EXPERIENCE THAT 40 DAYS HAS A VERY PARTICULAR QUALITY. IT'S JUST ENOUGH TIME TO LOSE YOURSELF IN SOMETHING WITHOUT <u>FULLY</u> LOSING YOURSELF IN IT. YOU LET GO INTO A NEW PRACTICE, POSSIBILITY, PARADIGM. SOME BILLS GO UNPAID, THE VOICEMAILS PILE UP, THE HAIRCUT IS PUT OFF BUT ONLY FOR AWHILE. IT'S THE KIND OF GENTLE DISRUPTION, A LOOSENING, THAT CAN BRING NEW LIFE INTO BEING.

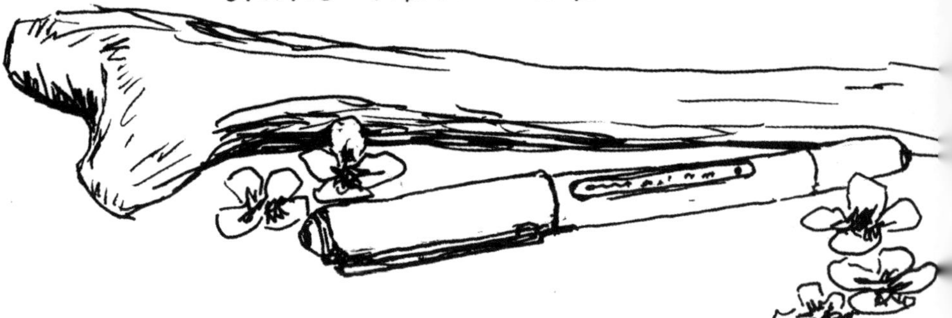

LIKEWISE, IT'S THE PERFECT AMOUNT OF TIME TO GIVE OTHERS A DOSE OF CURIOSITY (ESPECIALLY AT AN ASHRAM). "WHAT IS SHE DOING?" "WHAT KIND OF BOOK IS IT?" "BUT WHAT IS IT ABOUT?" "WHO IS SHE?" EYEBROWS RAISE, THE RUMOR MILL CHURNS.... AND IF THIS PROJECT WERE TO GO ON FOR EVEN ONE MORE DAY IT WOULD CROSS THE FINE LINE BETWEEN PUBLIC & PRIVATE, BETWEEN A PRACTICE & A PERFORMANCE.

ALL THIS TO SAY — TODAY IS MY LAST DAY OF "DRAWING THE FEELING." THIS I HAVE TRIED TO DO WITH ALL THE COURAGE I COULD MUSTER.

I RETURN NOW TO LIFE ON EARTH.
INSTEAD OF DRAWING EVERY MORNING I WILL WALK TO THE POND AND WATCH THE BEAVER WHO IS BUSY IN THE DAWN MIST.
OR PERHAPS I WILL SLEEP IN.

THE WORLD WAITS FOR ME.
AS IT DOES FOR YOU.

MAY WE BELONG FULLY
TO THE WORLD
AND
FULLY TO THE LAND
OF BLOSSOMS & BONES.

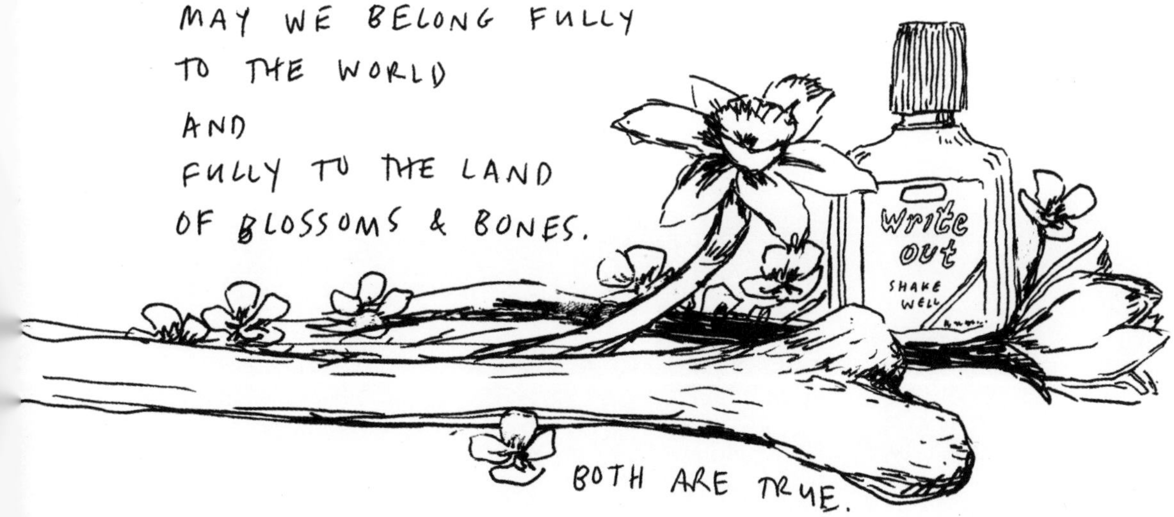
write out
SHAKE WELL

BOTH ARE TRUE.
BOTH ARE HOME.

Kim

APRIL 15, 2019

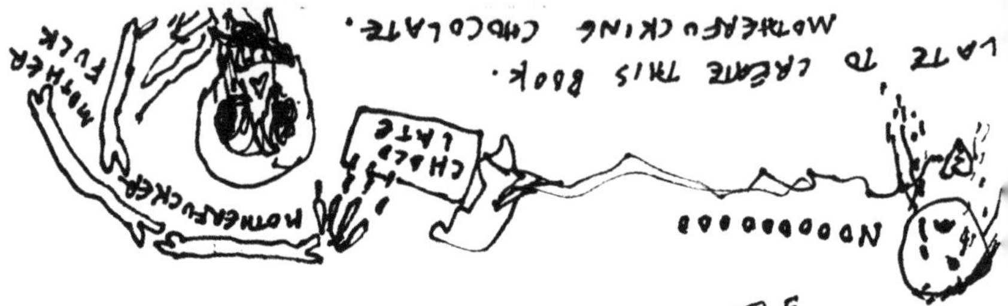
LATE TO CREATE THIS BOOK.
MOTHERFUCKING CHOCOLATE.
MOTHER FUCKER
MOTHERFUCKER
CHOCO LATE
NOOOOOOOOOOO

IT'S TAX DAY.

A NEW PROJECT BEGINS.

30 DAYS

A MONTH WITH THE STOMACH, (NO, THATS NOT THE RIGHT ~~NAME~~ TITLE)

A MONTH WITH THE HEART (NOPE. NICE TRY.)

THIRTY DAYS WITH AN EATING DISORDER (GETTING CLOSER)

A MONTH [redacted] OF BINGE DRAWINGS (MAYBE.)

[redacted] THE EATING DISORDER DRAWINGS (CLOSE)

~~CREATIVE~~ (MAYBE YOU SHOULD DRAW THE THING FIRST & ASK IT WHAT ITS NAME IS. THAT WOULD BE SHOWING UP, IN THE WAY THE WHOLE PROJECT INTENDS. SO, MAYBE... BE QUIET FOR A SEC AND SEE WHAT WANTS TO HAPPEN.)

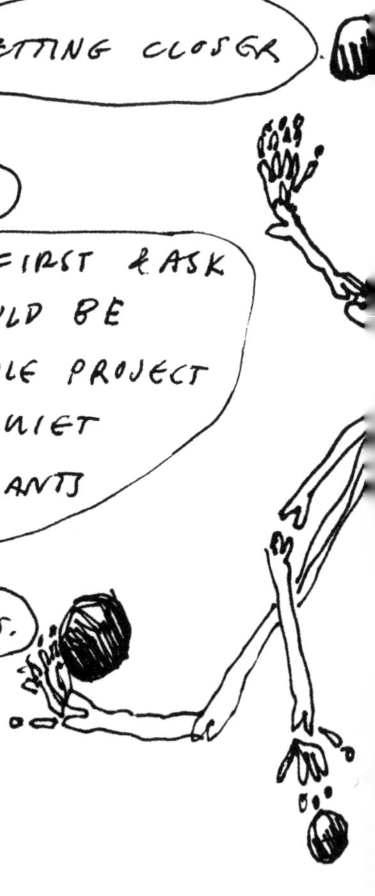

JUST START DRAWING IT RIGHT NOW? (YES.)

WITH NO PLAN? (YES)

WITHOUT A WAY TO (FRAME IT? YES. MANAGE IT? YES. PRESENT IT? YES.)

JUST DRAW THE FEELING? (YES.)

IT MAKES ME FEEL SICK JUST THINKING ABOUT THAT. (IT'S OK)

I'M ALREADY ASHAMED. (IT'S OK)

IT MAKES ME WANT TO EAT. (PERFECT. OF COURSE IT DOES. DRAW THE FEELING.)

AFTER I EAT? (NO, NOW)

MY MOUTH IS WATERING WITH SHAME. (WHOA, LOOK AT THAT TITLE!)

NO WAY. (OK, YOU'RE RIGHT. TOO INTENSE. BUT ONE WILL EMERGE. YOU'LL SEE.)

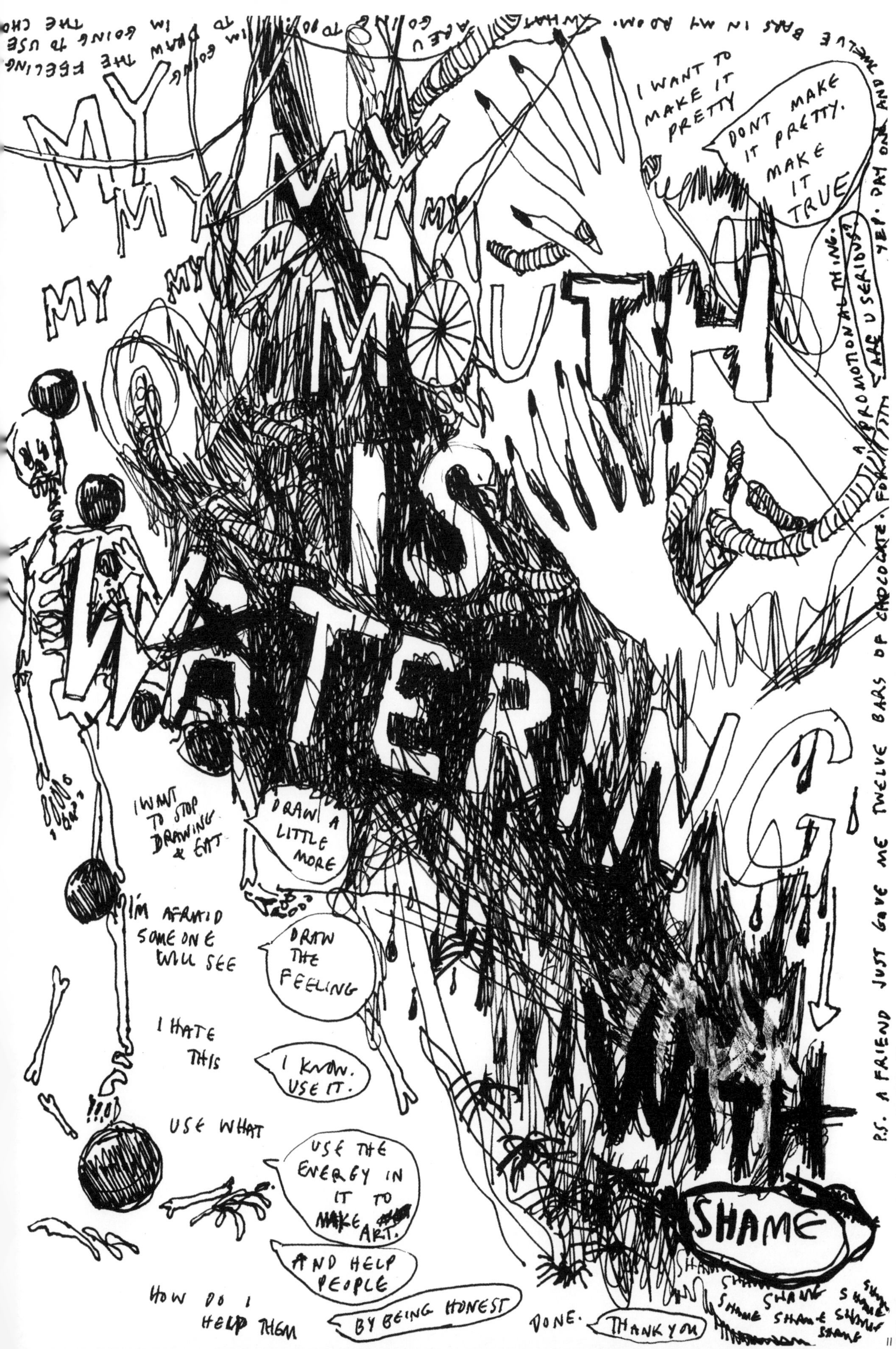
MY MY MY MY MY MY MY
MY MOUTH IS WATERING WITH SHAME
I WANT TO MAKE IT PRETTY
DONT MAKE IT PRETTY. MAKE IT TRUE
I WANT TO STOP DRAWING & EAT
DRAW A LITTLE MORE
I'M AFRAID SOMEONE WILL SEE
DRAW THE FEELING
I HATE THIS
I KNOW. USE IT.
USE WHAT
USE THE ENERGY IN IT TO MAKE ART.
AND HELP PEOPLE
HOW DO I HELP THEM
BY BEING HONEST
DONE.
THANK YOU
SHAME SHAME SHAME SHAME SHAME SHAME SHAME SHAME
P.S. A FRIEND JUST GAVE ME TWELVE BARS OF CHOCOLATE. FOR A PROMOTIONAL THING.
ARE U SERIOUS?!
YEP. PAY ONE AND TWELVE BARS IN MY ROOM.
WHAT ARE U GOING TO DO?
IM GOING TO DRAW THE FEELING
IM GOING TO USE THE CHO

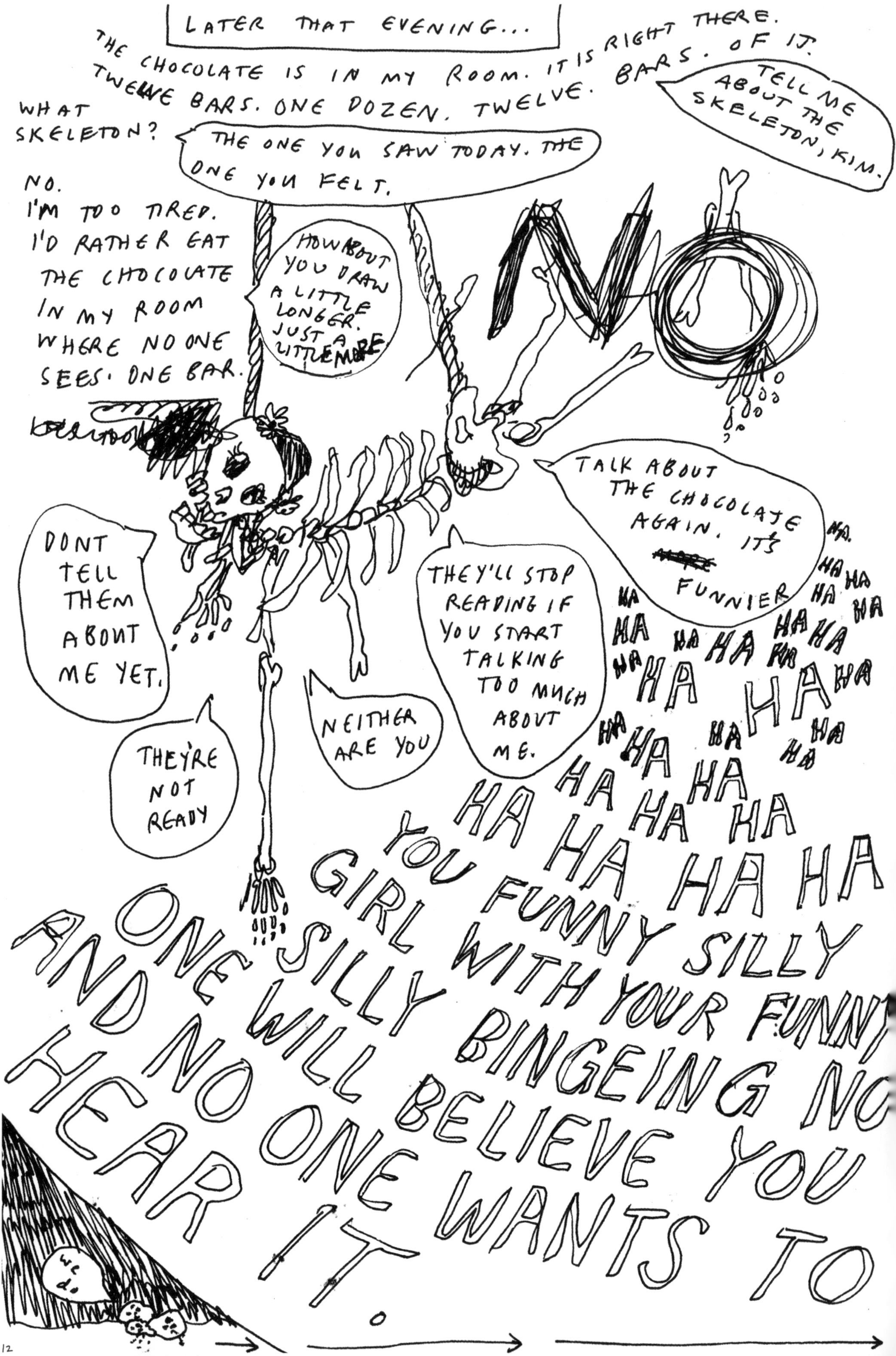
LATER THAT EVENING...
THE CHOCOLATE IS IN MY ROOM. IT IS RIGHT THERE. TWELVE BARS. ONE DOZEN. TWELVE. BARS. OF IT.
TELL ME ABOUT THE SKELETON, KIM.
WHAT SKELETON?
THE ONE YOU SAW TODAY. THE ONE YOU FELT.
NO. I'M TOO TIRED. I'D RATHER EAT THE CHOCOLATE IN MY ROOM WHERE NO ONE SEES. ONE BAR.
HOW ABOUT YOU DRAW A LITTLE LONGER. JUST A LITTLE MORE
NO
TALK ABOUT THE CHOCOLATE AGAIN. IT'S FUNNIER
DONT TELL THEM ABOUT ME YET.
THEY'RE NOT READY
NEITHER ARE YOU
THEY'LL STOP READING IF YOU START TALKING TOO MUCH ABOUT ME.
HA HA HA HA HA HA HA HA HA HA HA HA HA HA HA HA HA HA HA HA HA HA HA HA HA HA HA HA HA HA
YOU FUNNY SILLY GIRL WITH YOUR FUNNY SILLY BINGEING NO ONE WILL BELIEVE YOU AND NO ONE WANTS TO HEAR IT.
we do

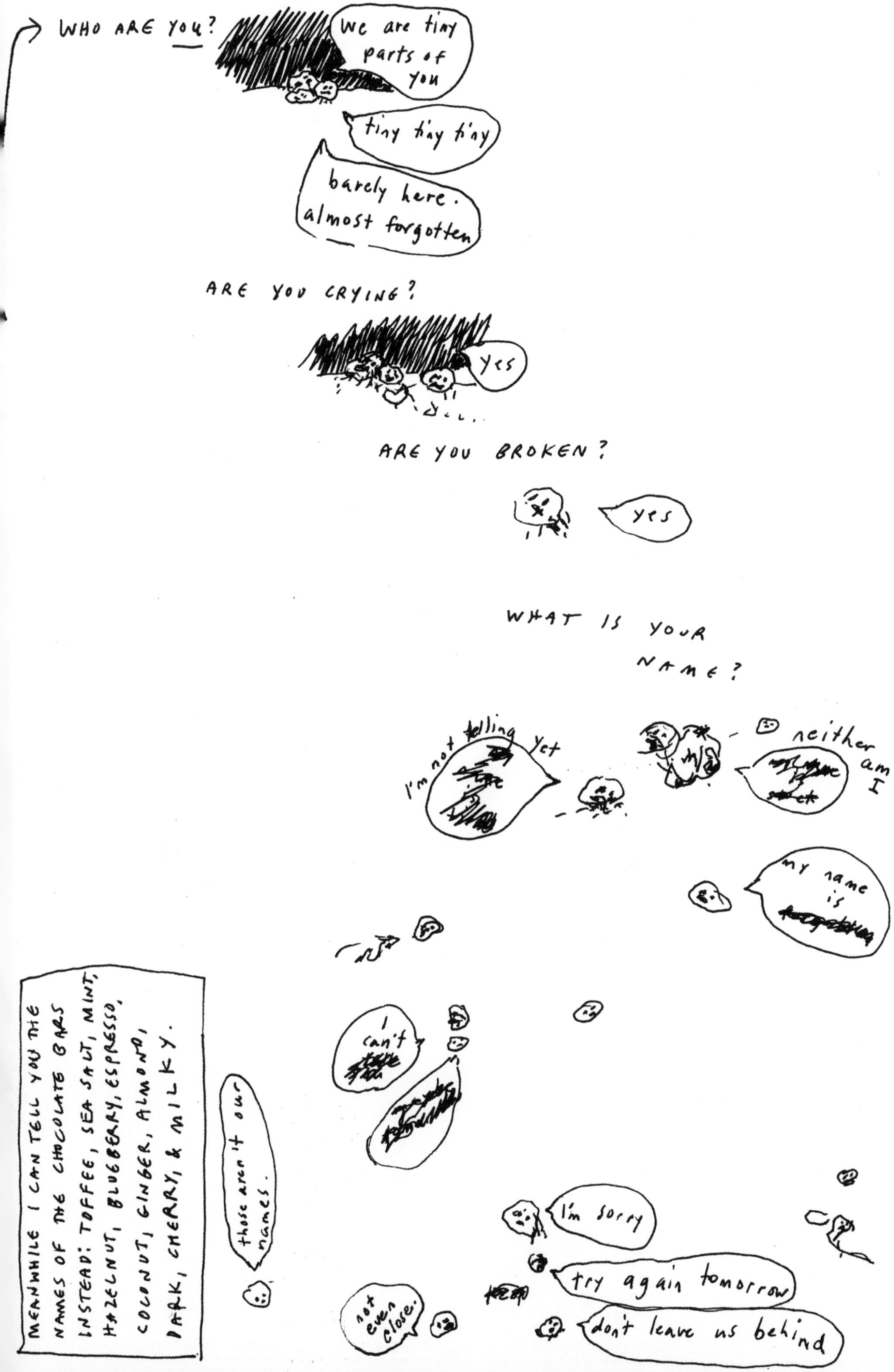

WHO ARE YOU?
We are tiny parts of you
tiny tiny tiny
barely here. almost forgotten
ARE YOU CRYING?
yes
ARE YOU BROKEN?
yes
WHAT IS YOUR NAME?
I'm not telling yet
neither am I
my name is
I can't
MEANWHILE I CAN TELL YOU THE NAMES OF THE CHOCOLATE BARS INSTEAD: TOFFEE, SEA SALT, MINT, HAZELNUT, BLUEBERRY, ESPRESSO, COCONUT, GINGER, ALMOND, DARK, CHERRY, & MILKY.
those aren't our names.
not even close.
I'm sorry
try again tomorrow
don't leave us behind

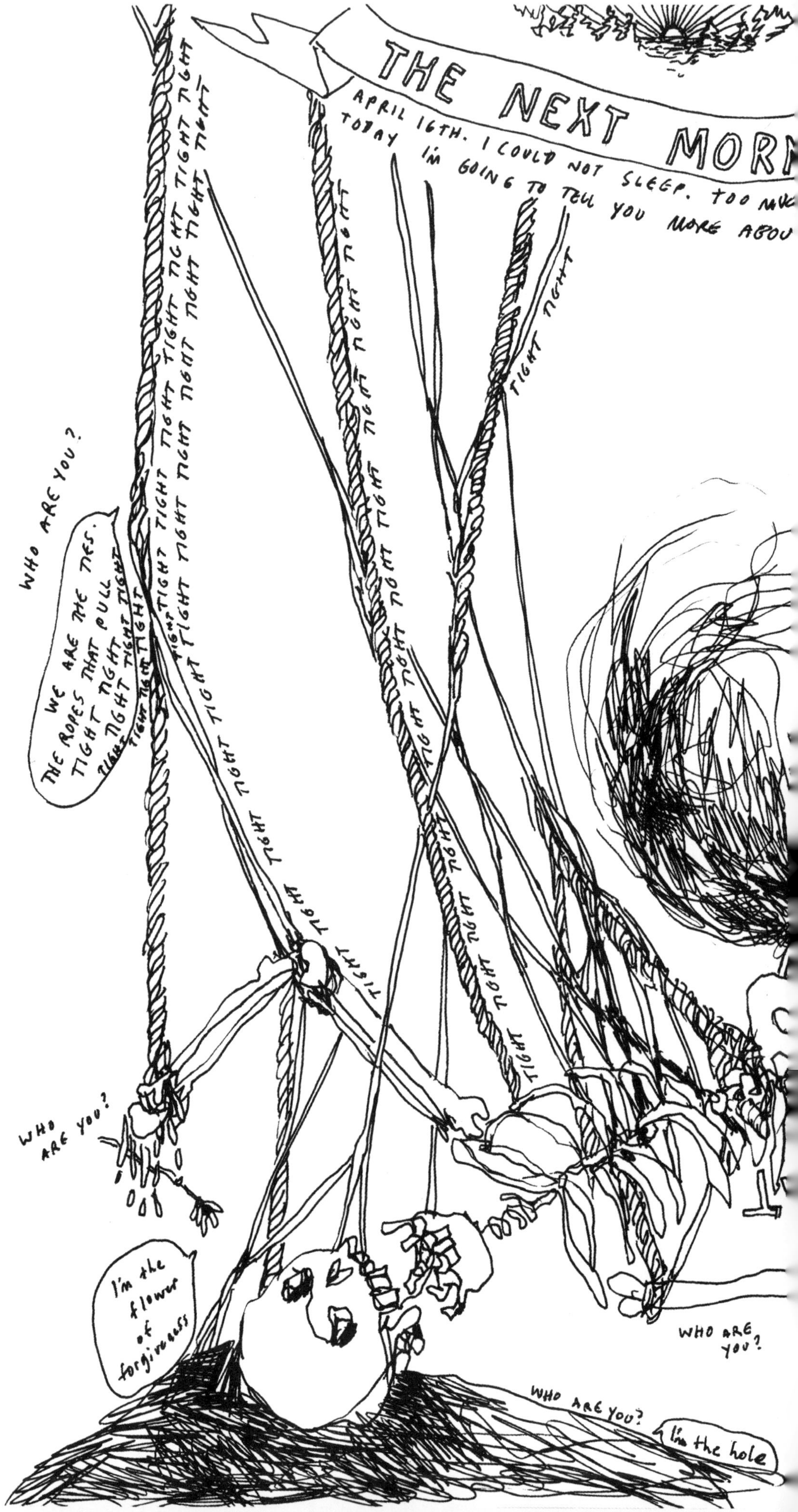
THE NEXT MORN
APRIL 16TH. I COULD NOT SLEEP. TOO MUC
TODAY I'M GOING TO TELL YOU MORE ABOU
WHO ARE YOU?
WE ARE THE TIES. THE ROPES THAT PULL TIGHT TIGHT TIGHT
WHO ARE YOU?
I'm the flower of forgiveness
WHO ARE YOU?
WHO ARE YOU?
I'm the hole

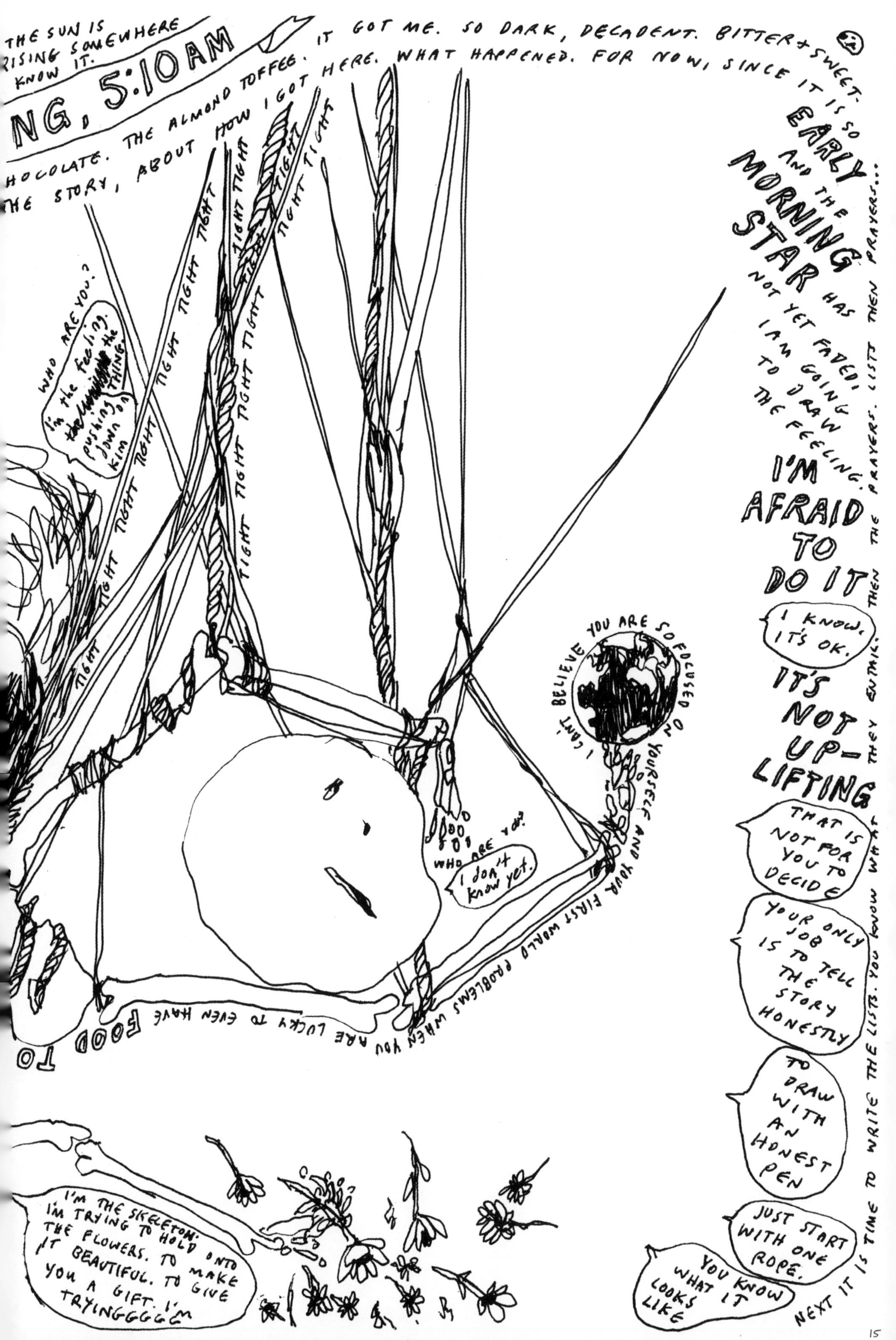
THE SUN IS RISING SOMEWHERE KNOW IT.
NG, 5:10 AM
IT GOT ME. SO DARK, DECADENT. BITTER + SWEET.
HOCOLATE. THE ALMOND TOFFEE.
THE STORY, ABOUT HOW I GOT HERE. WHAT HAPPENED. FOR NOW, SINCE IT IS SO EARLY AND THE MORNING STAR HAS NOT YET FADED, I AM GOING TO DRAW THE FEELING.
I'M AFRAID TO DO IT
I KNOW. IT'S OK.
IT'S NOT UP-LIFTING
THAT IS NOT FOR YOU TO DECIDE
YOUR ONLY JOB IS TO TELL THE STORY HONESTLY
TO DRAW WITH AN HONEST PEN
JUST START WITH ONE ROPE.
YOU KNOW WHAT IT LOOKS LIKE
NEXT IT IS TIME TO WRITE THE LISTS. YOU KNOW WHAT THEY ENTAIL. THEN THE PRAYERS. LISTS THEN PRAYERS...
WHO ARE YOU?
I'm the feeling pushing the THING down on Kim
TIGHT TIGHT TIGHT TIGHT TIGHT TIGHT TIGHT TIGHT TIGHT TIGHT TIGHT TIGHT TIGHT TIGHT
I CAN'T BELIEVE YOU ARE SO FOCUSED ON YOURSELF AND YOUR FIRST WORLD PROBLEMS WHEN YOU ARE LUCKY TO EVEN HAVE FOOD TO
WHO ARE YOU?
I don't know yet.
I'M THE SKELETON. I'M TRYING TO HOLD ONTO THE FLOWERS. TO MAKE IT BEAUTIFUL. TO GIVE YOU A GIFT. I'M TRYINGGGGG

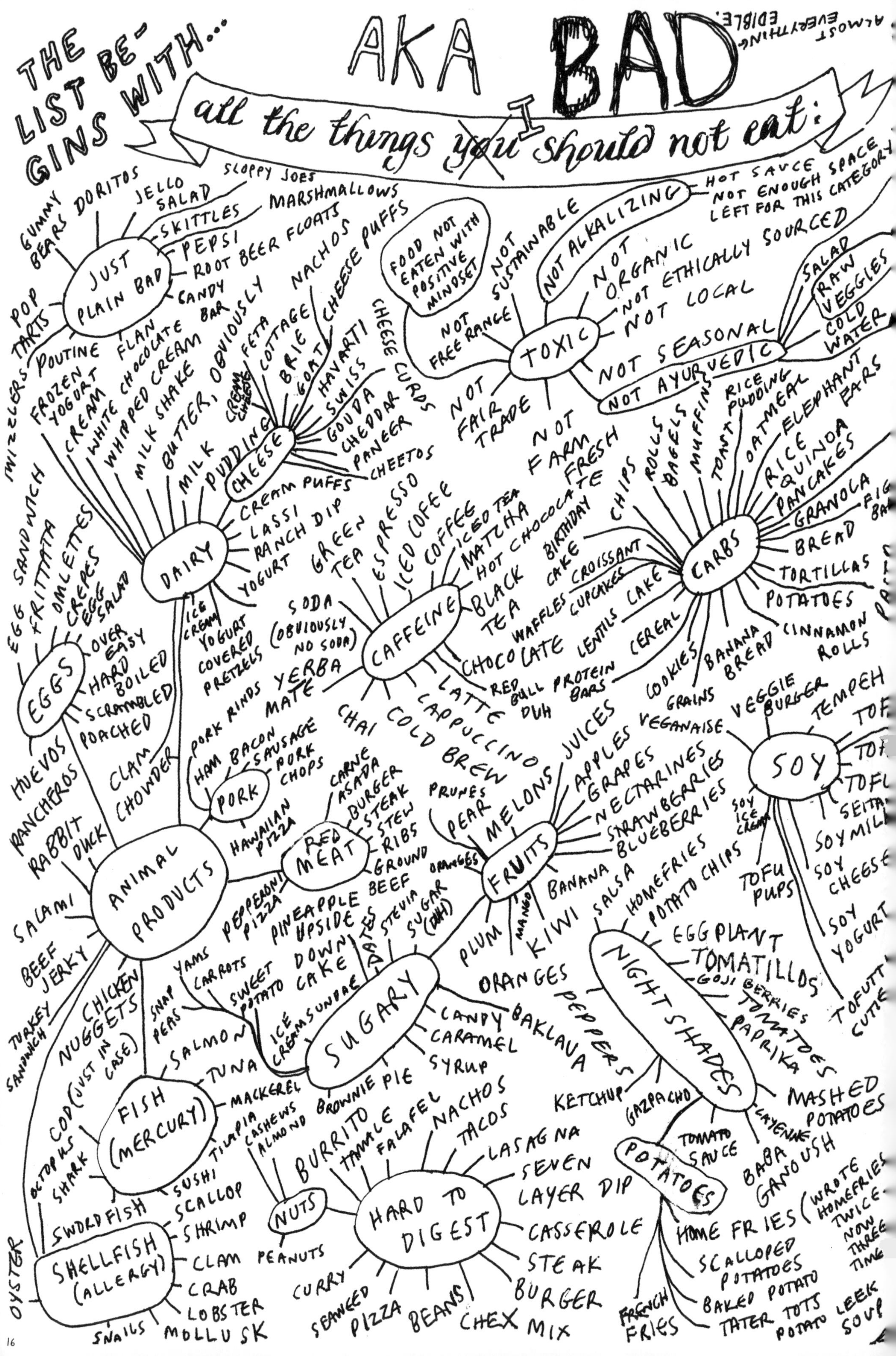
THE LIST BEGINS WITH...
AKA BAD
ALMOST EVERYTHING EDIBLE.
all the things you I should not eat:
JUST PLAIN BAD
GUMMY BEARS
DORITOS
JELLO SALAD
SLOPPY JOES
SKITTLES
MARSHMALLOWS
PEPSI
ROOT BEER FLOATS
CANDY
POP TARTS
TWIZZLERS
POUTINE
FLAN
FROZEN YOGURT
CREAM
WHITE CHOCOLATE BAR
WHIPPED CREAM
MILK SHAKE
BUTTER, OBVIOUSLY
NACHOS
CHEESE PUFFS
CHEESE
FETA
COTTAGE
BRIE
GOAT
CREAM CHEESE
HAVARTI
SWISS
GOUDA
CHEDDAR
PANEER
CHEESE CURDS
CHEETOS
PUDDING
MILK
DAIRY
CREAM PUFFS
LASSI
RANCH DIP
YOGURT
ICE CREAM
YOGURT COVERED PRETZELS
EGGS
EGG SANDWICH
FRITTATA
OMLETTES
CREPES
EGG SALAD
OVER EASY
HARD BOILED
SCRAMBLED
POACHED
HUEVOS RANCHEROS
CLAM CHOWDER
PORK RINDS
PORK
HAM
BACON
SAUSAGE
PORK CHOPS
HAWAIIAN PIZZA
RED MEAT
CARNE ASADA
BURGER
STEAK
STEW
RIBS
GROUND BEEF
PEPPERONI PIZZA
ANIMAL PRODUCTS
RABBIT
DUCK
SALAMI
BEEF JERKY
TURKEY SANDWICH
CHICKEN NUGGETS
COD (JUST IN CASE)
FISH (MERCURY)
SALMON
TUNA
MACKEREL
TILAPIA
OCTOPUS
SHARK
SUSHI
SWORDFISH
SHELLFISH (ALLERGY)
OYSTER
SCALLOP
SHRIMP
CLAM
CRAB
LOBSTER
SNAILS
MOLLUSK
CAFFEINE
SODA (OBVIOUSLY NO SODA)
GREEN TEA
ESPRESSO
ICED COFFEE
COFFEE
ICED TEA
MATCHA
HOT CHOCOLATE
BLACK TEA
CHOCOLATE
RED BULL DUH
YERBA MATE
CHAI
COLD BREW
CAPPUCCINO
LATTE
FOOD NOT EATEN WITH POSITIVE MINDSET
TOXIC
NOT SUSTAINABLE
NOT ALKALIZING
HOT SAUCE
NOT ENOUGH SPACE LEFT FOR THIS CATEGORY
NOT ORGANIC
NOT ETHICALLY SOURCED
NOT LOCAL
NOT SEASONAL
NOT AYURVEDIC
SALAD
RAW VEGGIES
COLD WATER
NOT FREE RANGE
NOT FAIR TRADE
NOT FARM FRESH
CARBS
BIRTHDAY CAKE
CROISSANT
CUPCAKES
WAFFLES
LENTILS
CAKE
CEREAL
PROTEIN BARS
COOKIES
GRAINS
BANANA BREAD
CINNAMON ROLLS
POTATOES
TORTILLAS
BREAD
GRANOLA
FIG BARS
PANCAKES
QUINOA
RICE
OATMEAL
ELEPHANT EARS
RICE PUDDING
TOAST
MUFFINS
BAGELS
ROLLS
CHIPS
PASTA
SOY
VEGGIE BURGER
TEMPEH
TOFU
SEITAN
SOYMILK
SOY CHEESE
SOY YOGURT
TOFUTTI CUTIE
SOY ICE CREAM
TOFU PUPS
FRUITS
JUICES
APPLES
VEGANAISE
GRAPES
NECTARINES
STRAWBERRIES
BLUEBERRIES
MELONS
PEAR
PRUNES
ORANGES
BANANA
KIWI
MANGO
PLUM
SALSA
HOMEFRIES
POTATO CHIPS
NIGHT SHADES
EGGPLANT
TOMATILLOS
GOJI BERRIES
TOMATOES
PAPRIKA
PEPPERS
MASHED POTATOES
CAYENNE
BABA GANOUSH
TOMATO SAUCE
GAZPACHO
KETCHUP
POTATOES
HOME FRIES (WROTE HOMEFRIES TWICE NOW THREE TIMES)
SCALLOPED POTATOES
BAKED POTATO
TATER TOTS
POTATO LEEK SOUP
FRENCH FRIES
SUGARY
PINEAPPLE UPSIDE DOWN CAKE
DATES
STEVIA
SUGAR (DUH)
YAMS
CARROTS
SWEET POTATO
SNAP PEAS
ICE CREAM SUNDAE
CANDY
CARAMEL
SYRUP
BAKLAVA
BROWNIE PIE
NUTS
CASHEWS
ALMOND
PEANUTS
HARD TO DIGEST
BURRITO
TAMALE
FALAFEL
NACHOS
TACOS
LASAGNA
SEVEN LAYER DIP
CASSEROLE
STEAK
BURGER
CHEX MIX
BEANS
PIZZA
SEAWEED
CURRY

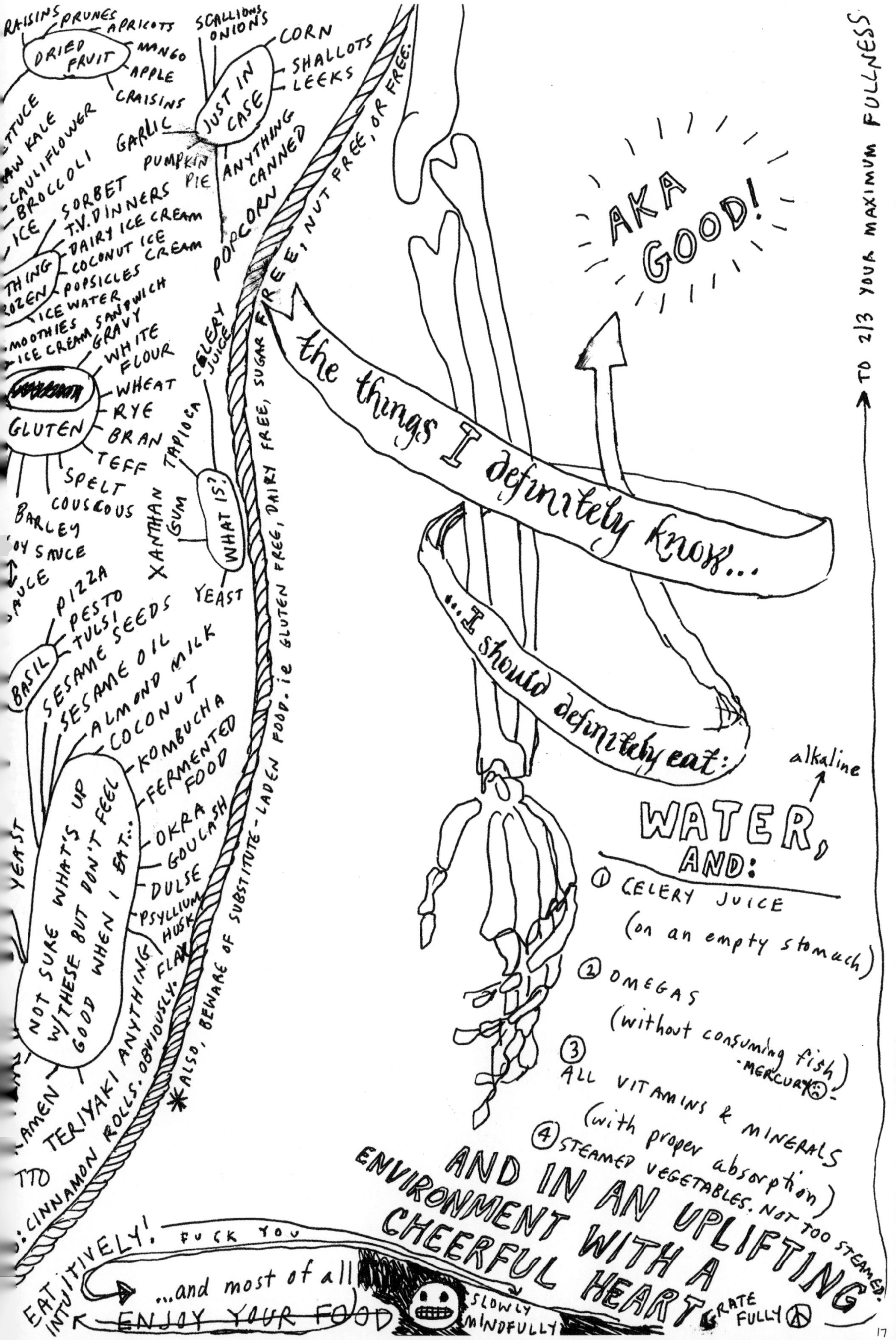

RAISINS
PRUNES
APRICOTS
DRIED FRUIT
MANGO
APPLE
CRAISINS
SCALLIONS
ONIONS
JUST IN CASE
CORN
SHALLOTS
LEEKS
ANYTHING CANNED
GARLIC
PUMPKIN PIE
POPCORN
TTUCE
W KALE
CAULIFLOWER
BROCCOLI
ICE
SORBET
T.V. DINNERS
DAIRY ICE CREAM
COCONUT ICE CREAM
THING ROZEN
POPSICLES
ICE WATER
ICE CREAM SANDWICH
MOOTHIES
ICE CREAM
GRAVY
GLUTEN
WHITE FLOUR
WHEAT
RYE
BRAN
TEFF
SPELT
COUSCOUS
BARLEY
OY SAUCE
SAUCE
CELERY JUICE
TAPIOCA
WHAT IS?
XANTHAN GUM
YEAST
BASIL
PIZZA
PESTO
TULSI
SESAME SEEDS
SESAME OIL
ALMOND MILK
COCONUT
KOMBUCHA
FERMENTED FOOD
OKRA
GOULASH
DULSE
PSYLLIUM HUSK
FLAX
NOT SURE WHAT'S UP W/THESE BUT DON'T FEEL GOOD WHEN I EAT...
YEAST
AMEN
TERIYAKI ANYTHING
CINNAMON ROLLS. OBVIOUSLY.
TTO
*ALSO, BEWARE OF SUBSTITUTE-LADEN FOOD. ie GLUTEN FREE, DAIRY FREE, SUGAR FREE, NUT FREE, OR FREE.
the things I definitely know...
...I should definitely eat:
AKA GOOD!
TO 2/3 YOUR MAXIMUM FULLNESS
alkaline
WATER, AND:
① CELERY JUICE (on an empty stomach)
② OMEGAS (without consuming fish -MERCURY☹)
③ ALL VITAMINS & MINERALS (with proper absorption)
④ STEAMED VEGETABLES. NOT TOO STEAMED.
AND IN AN UPLIFTING ENVIRONMENT WITH A CHEERFUL HEART
GRATEFULLY ☮
EAT INTUITIVELY!
FUCK YOU
...and most of all
ENJOY YOUR FOOD
SLOWLY
MINDFULLY

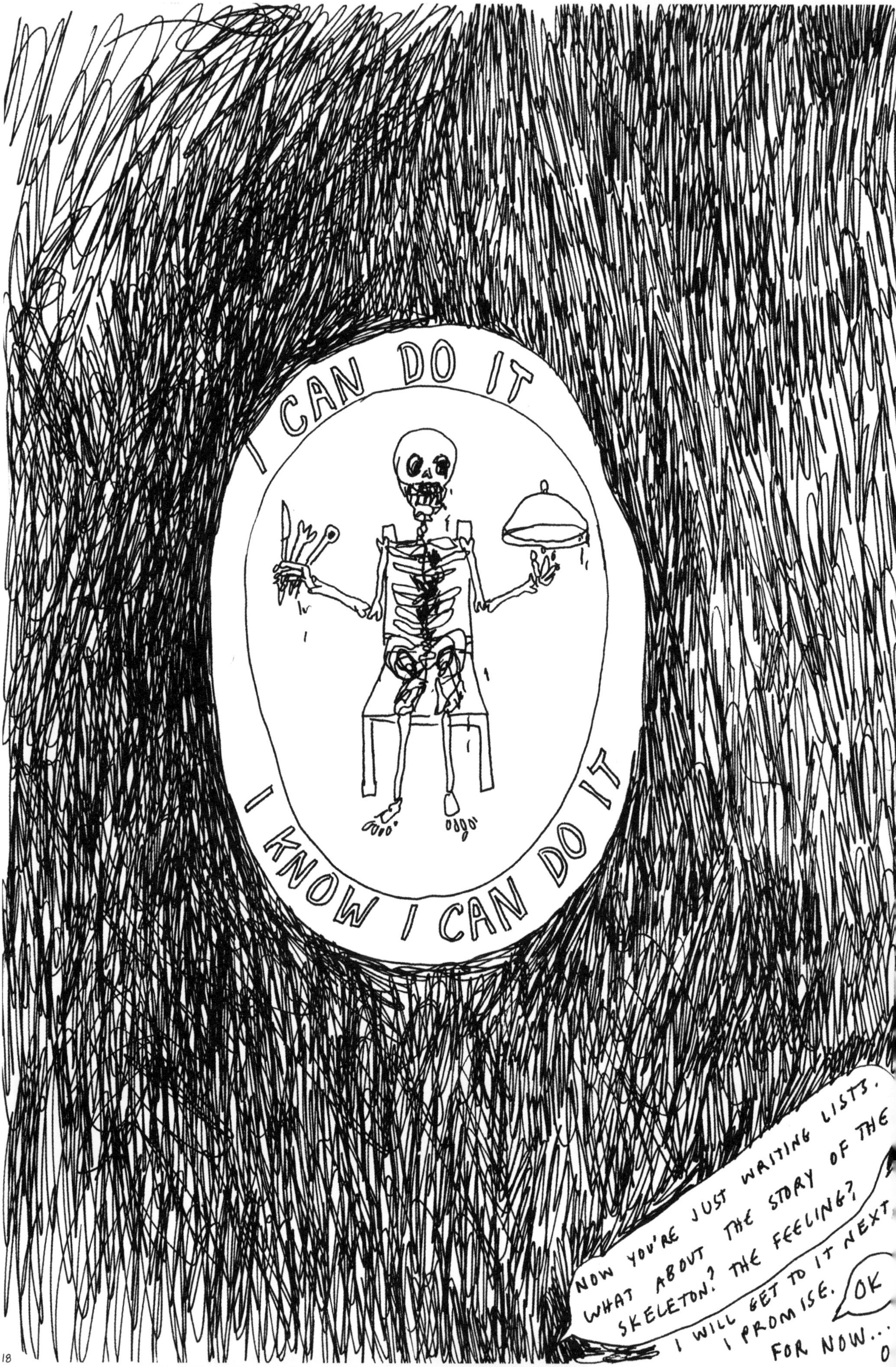
I CAN DO IT
I KNOW I CAN DO IT
NOW YOU'RE JUST WRITING LISTS. WHAT ABOUT THE STORY OF THE SKELETON? THE FEELING?
I WILL GET TO IT NEXT I PROMISE.
OK
FOR NOW...

THINGS
THAT
FEEL
GOOD:

SUNSHINE

SPACE

WALKS

NATURE

TREES

FRIENDS

MUSIC

OATMEAL

WARM
MILK

TEA

BEING HONEST

SAVASANA

WATER

LIGHT

ORE
LIST:

and...

tenderness

THANK GOD
FOR THAT LAST PAGE,
THE TENDER ONE
WITH THE FLOWERS. (WHY?)
BECAUSE IT'S BEAUTIFUL!
A NECESSARY BREAK,
A GLIMMER OF HOPE,
A REMINDER THAT THERE'S
MORE, OR THAT IT'S NOT JUST
ALL LIKE THIS. (LIKE WHAT?)
UGLY. EMBARRASSING.
DISGUSTING. SELFISH.
SHAMEFUL.

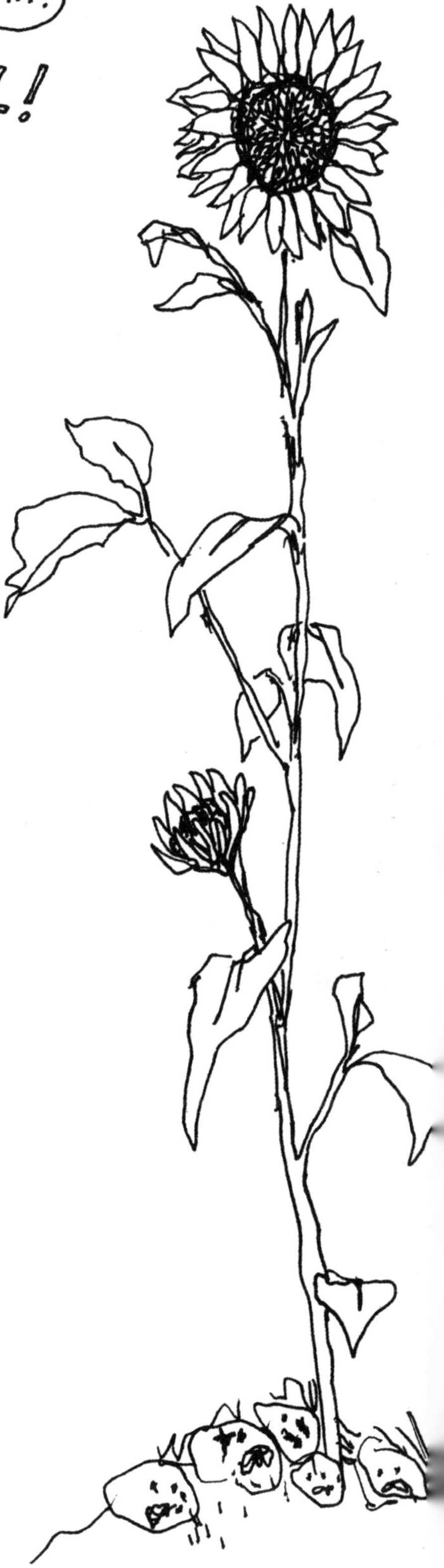

(WHAT ELSE?)

HIDDEN.
TRIVIAL.
IMAGINED.
SELF-MADE.
ATTENTION SEEKING
LOVE SEEKING
I CAN'T EVEN CONCENTRATE
ENOUGH TO FIND THE WORDS (WHY?)
BECAUSE I ATE SO MUCH CHOCOLATE.
THE TOFFEE BAR FOR SWEET,
THE SALTY ONE TO FOLLOW,
THEN BACK TO SWEET WITH CHERRY,
THEN TO COCONUT,
I WANT TO BARF DARK CHOCOLATE.
I GAVE FOUR BARS AWAY. I HAVE TO
THROW OUT THE REST. PATHETIC.
I'VE NEVER BEEN LIKE THIS BEFORE. (LIKE WHAT?)
OUT OF CONTROL. UNABLE TO STOP. (REALLY? ARE YOU SURE?)
I AM SURE. UP UNTIL NOW I COULD KEEP EVERYTHING IN ORDER. EVERYTH

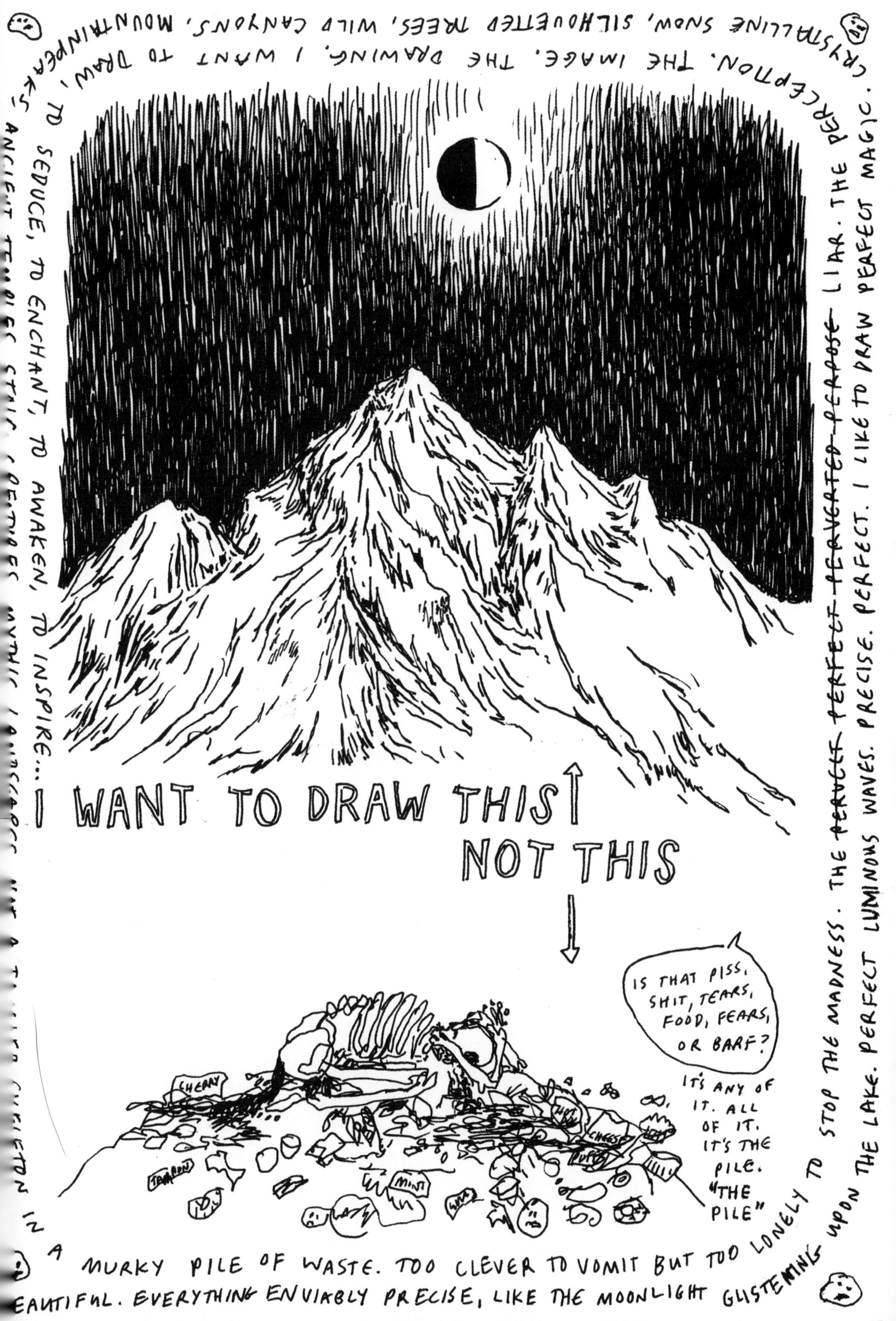
STOP THE MADNESS. THE ~~PERVECT~~ ~~PERFECT~~ ~~PERVERTED PERPOSE~~ LIAR. THE PERCEPTION. THE IMAGE. THE DRAWING. I WANT TO DRAW, TO SEDUCE, TO ENCHANT, TO AWAKEN, TO INSPIRE...
UPON THE LAKE. PERFECT LUMINOUS WAVES. PRECISE. PERFECT. I LIKE TO DRAW PERFECT MAGIC.
CRYSTALLINE SNOW, SILHOUETTED TREES, WILD CANYONS, MOUNTAINPEAKS'
ANCIE.T TE... MYTHIC ... SKELETON IN
A MURKY PILE OF WASTE. TOO CLEVER TO VOMIT BUT TOO LONELY TO
EAUTIFUL. EVERYTHING ENVIABLY PRECISE, LIKE THE MOONLIGHT GLISTENING
I WANT TO DRAW THIS
NOT THIS
IS THAT PISS, SHIT, TEARS, FOOD, FEARS, OR BARF?
IT'S ANY OF IT. ALL OF IT. IT'S THE PILE. "THE PILE"
CHERRY
MINT
CHEESE

KIM, NOW IS NOT THE TIME FOR MAJESTIC MOUNTAINS. NOW IS THE TIME TO SIFT THROUGH THE PILE OF SHIT. TELL MY STORY. I AM READY. PLEASE. NOW. IT IS

TIME. I AM READY TO TELL. THEY ARE READY TO LISTEN.

NO. THAT'S ENOUGH FOR TODAY. WE HAVE GONE FAR ENOUGH. IT CAN WAIT.

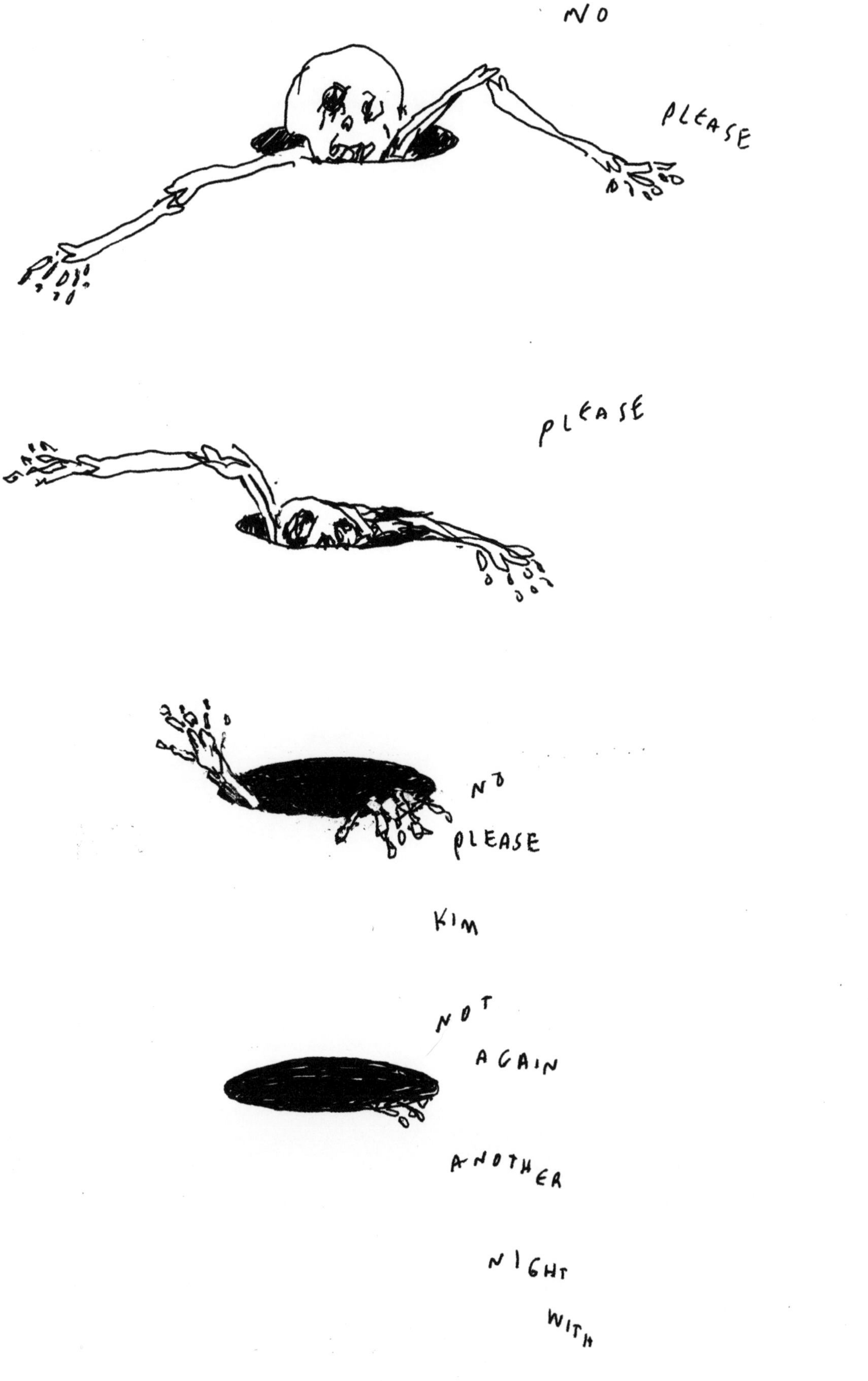
NO
PLEASE
PLEASE
NO
PLEASE
KIM
NOT
AGAIN
ANOTHER
NIGHT
WITH
THE
HOLE INSIDE.

IT'S APRIL 17TH. I PROMISED MYSELF I'D DO THIS PROJECT FOR 30 DAYS STRAIGHT. DRAW THE FEELING, SEE WHAT HAPPENS. BUT NOT TODAY. I WANT TO QUIT. I WANT TO LEAVE THE STORY, THE HOLE, THE SKELETON. I CAN'T GET TO THE BOTTOM OF IT & NEVER WILL. IT'S BEYOND ME. BEYOND MY POWER & MY VISION. A PRAYER CAME TO ME IN THE SHRINE THIS MORNING. I WILL WRITE IT HERE. I WILL DRAW IT SIDEWAYS, SO YOU ALWAYS KNOW WHICH ONES THE PRAYERS ARE. THEY ARE NOT THE STORY. THEY ARE WHAT GETS US THROUGH THE STORY WHEN THE STORY COULD SWALLOW US ~~WHOLE~~ ALIVE.

HOLDING →

OUR LIGHTSABER AT OUR HEART.

← NE GO,

GREAT SPIRIT, MY NAME IS KIM. I AM ONE OF YOUR MANY CHILDREN. IN ME YOU HAVE PLACED THE LIGHT OF A THOUSAND SUNS, A FLAME TO SHINE UPON THE SACRED AND THE MUNDANE, THE INTRICATE DETAILS

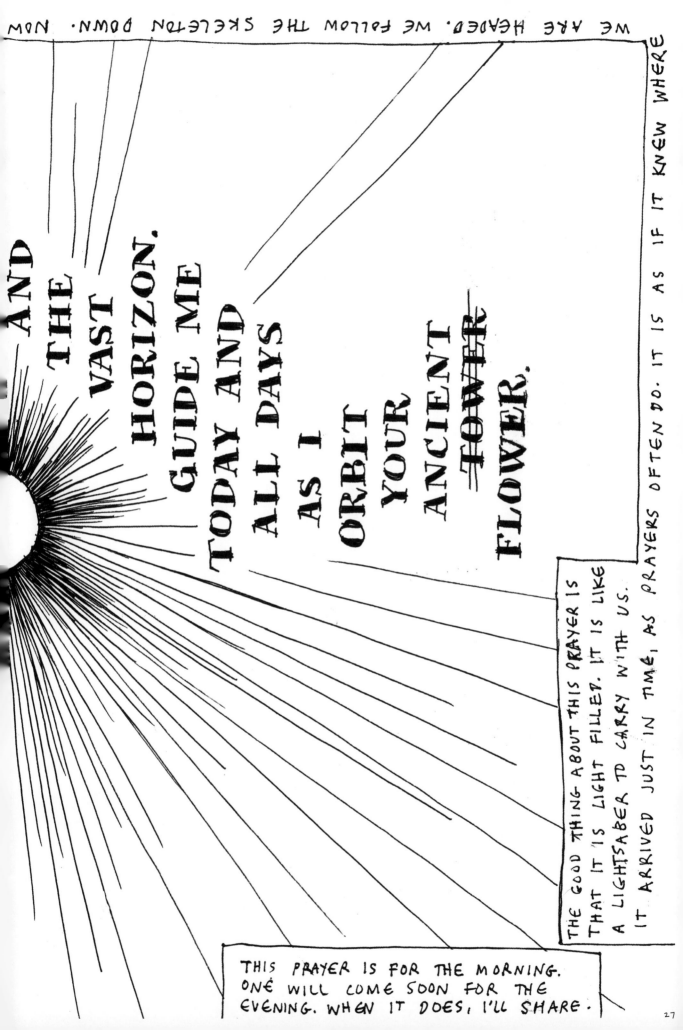

AND
THE
VAST
HORIZON.
GUIDE ME
TODAY AND
ALL DAYS
AS I
ORBIT
YOUR
ANCIENT
~~TOWER~~
FLOWER.

THE GOOD THING ABOUT THIS PRAYER IS THAT IT IS LIGHT FILLED. IT IS LIKE A LIGHTSABER TO CARRY WITH US. IT ARRIVED JUST IN TIME, AS PRAYERS OFTEN DO. IT IS AS IF IT KNEW WHERE WE ARE HEADED. WE FOLLOW THE SKELETON DOWN. NOW

THIS PRAYER IS FOR THE MORNING. ONE WILL COME SOON FOR THE EVENING. WHEN IT DOES, I'LL SHARE.

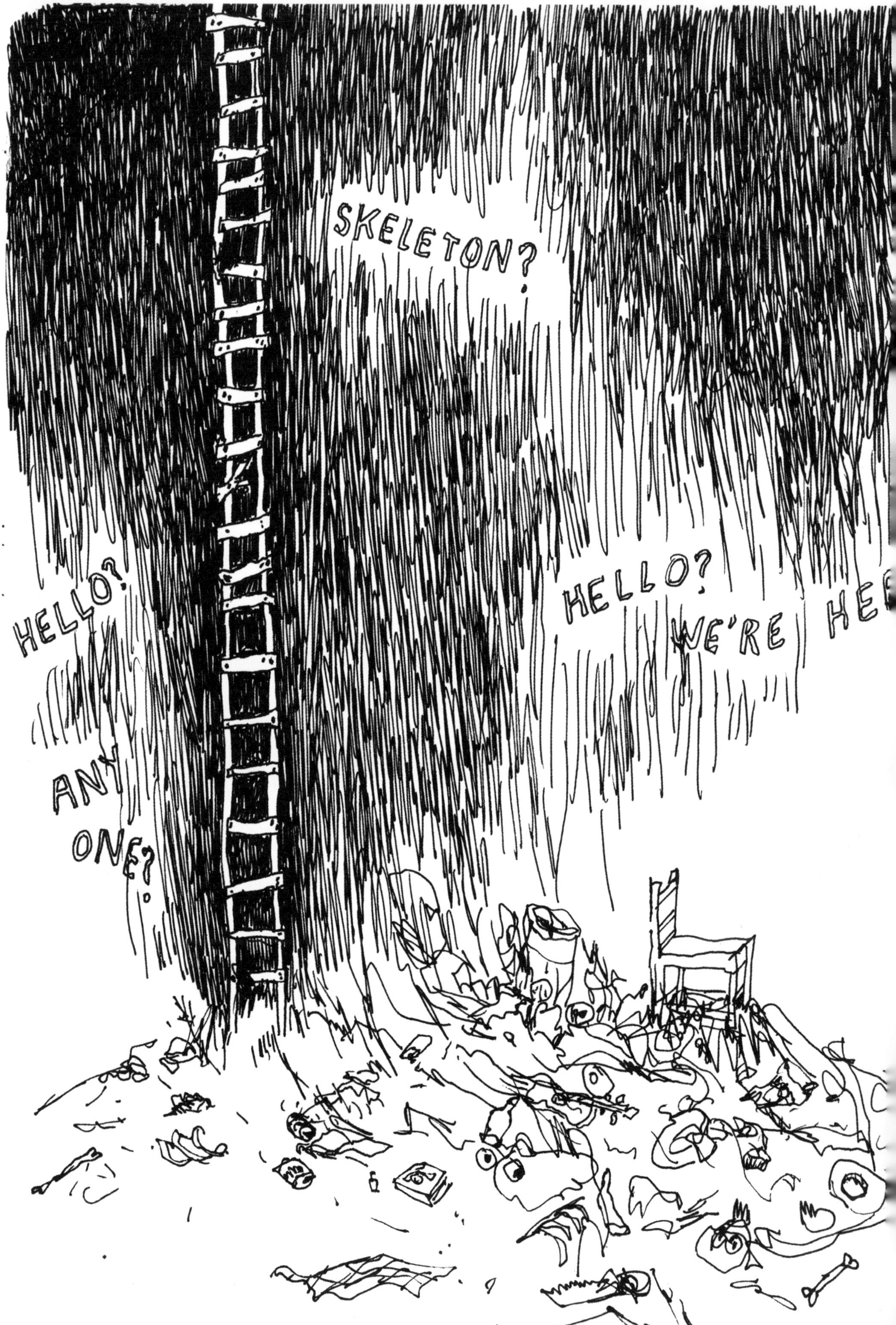
SKELETON?
HELLO?
ANY
ONE?
HELLO?
WE'RE

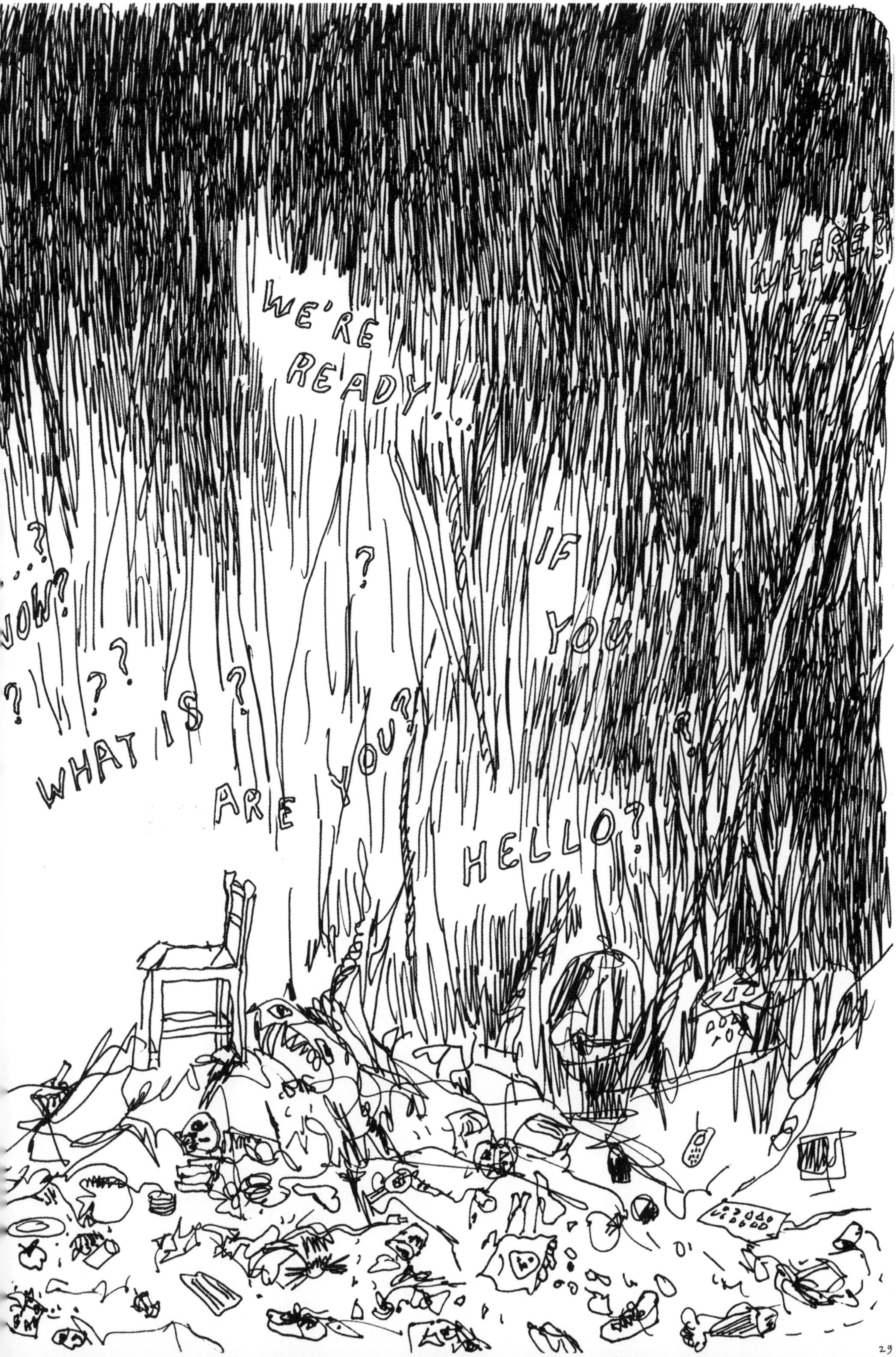
WE'RE READY...
WHERE
IF YOU
NOW?
WHAT IS ?
ARE YOU?
HELLO?

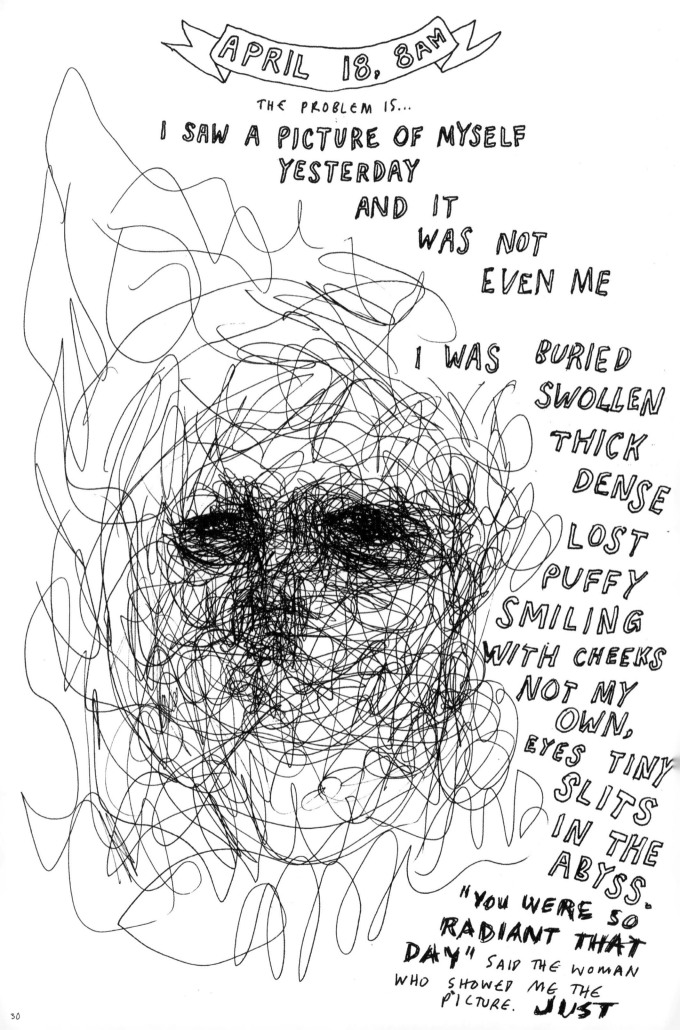

APRIL 18, 8AM

THE PROBLEM IS...

I SAW A PICTURE OF MYSELF
YESTERDAY
AND IT
WAS NOT
EVEN ME

I WAS   BURIED
SWOLLEN
THICK
DENSE
LOST
PUFFY
SMILING
WITH CHEEKS
NOT MY
OWN,
EYES TINY
SLITS
IN THE
ABYSS.

"YOU WERE SO
RADIANT THAT
DAY" SAID THE WOMAN
WHO SHOWED ME THE
PICTURE. JUST

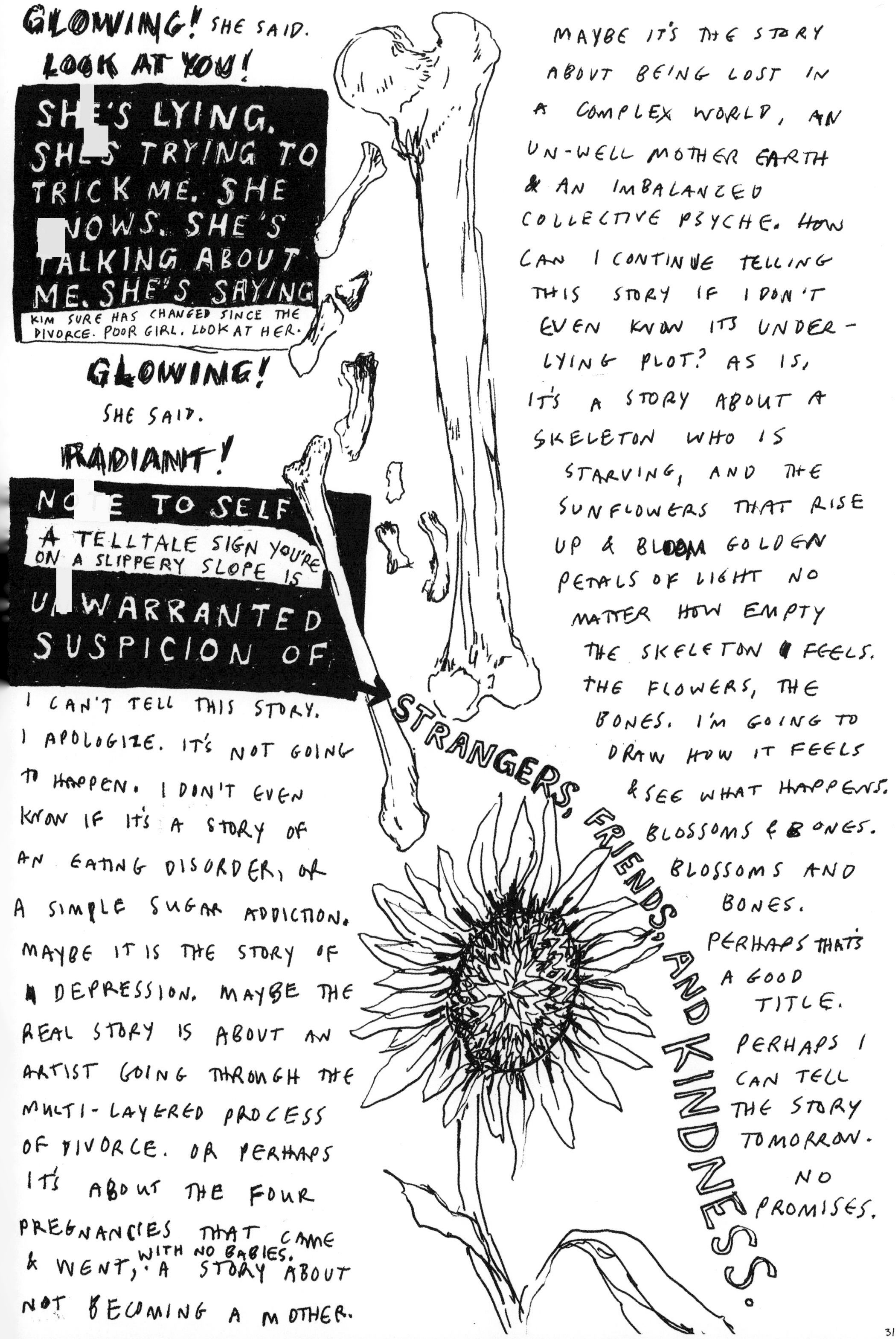
GLOWING! SHE SAID.
LOOK AT YOU!
SHE'S LYING. SHE'S TRYING TO TRICK ME. SHE KNOWS. SHE'S TALKING ABOUT ME. SHE'S SAYING
KIM SURE HAS CHANGED SINCE THE DIVORCE. POOR GIRL. LOOK AT HER.
GLOWING!
SHE SAID.
RADIANT!
NOTE TO SELF
A TELLTALE SIGN YOU'RE ON A SLIPPERY SLOPE IS
UNWARRANTED SUSPICION OF
STRANGERS, FRIENDS, AND KINDNESS.
I CAN'T TELL THIS STORY. I APOLOGIZE. IT'S NOT GOING TO HAPPEN. I DON'T EVEN KNOW IF IT'S A STORY OF AN EATING DISORDER, OR A SIMPLE SUGAR ADDICTION. MAYBE IT IS THE STORY OF A DEPRESSION. MAYBE THE REAL STORY IS ABOUT AN ARTIST GOING THROUGH THE MULTI-LAYERED PROCESS OF DIVORCE. OR PERHAPS IT'S ABOUT THE FOUR PREGNANCIES THAT CAME & WENT, WITH NO BABIES. A STORY ABOUT NOT BECOMING A MOTHER.
MAYBE IT'S THE STORY ABOUT BEING LOST IN A COMPLEX WORLD, AN UN-WELL MOTHER EARTH & AN IMBALANCED COLLECTIVE PSYCHE. HOW CAN I CONTINUE TELLING THIS STORY IF I DON'T EVEN KNOW ITS UNDERLYING PLOT? AS IS, IT'S A STORY ABOUT A SKELETON WHO IS STARVING, AND THE SUNFLOWERS THAT RISE UP & BLOOM GOLDEN PETALS OF LIGHT NO MATTER HOW EMPTY THE SKELETON FEELS. THE FLOWERS, THE BONES. I'M GOING TO DRAW HOW IT FEELS & SEE WHAT HAPPENS. BLOSSOMS & BONES. BLOSSOMS AND BONES. PERHAPS THAT'S A GOOD TITLE. PERHAPS I CAN TELL THE STORY TOMORROW. NO PROMISES.

perhaps it looks like this:
↓
(THE COVER)

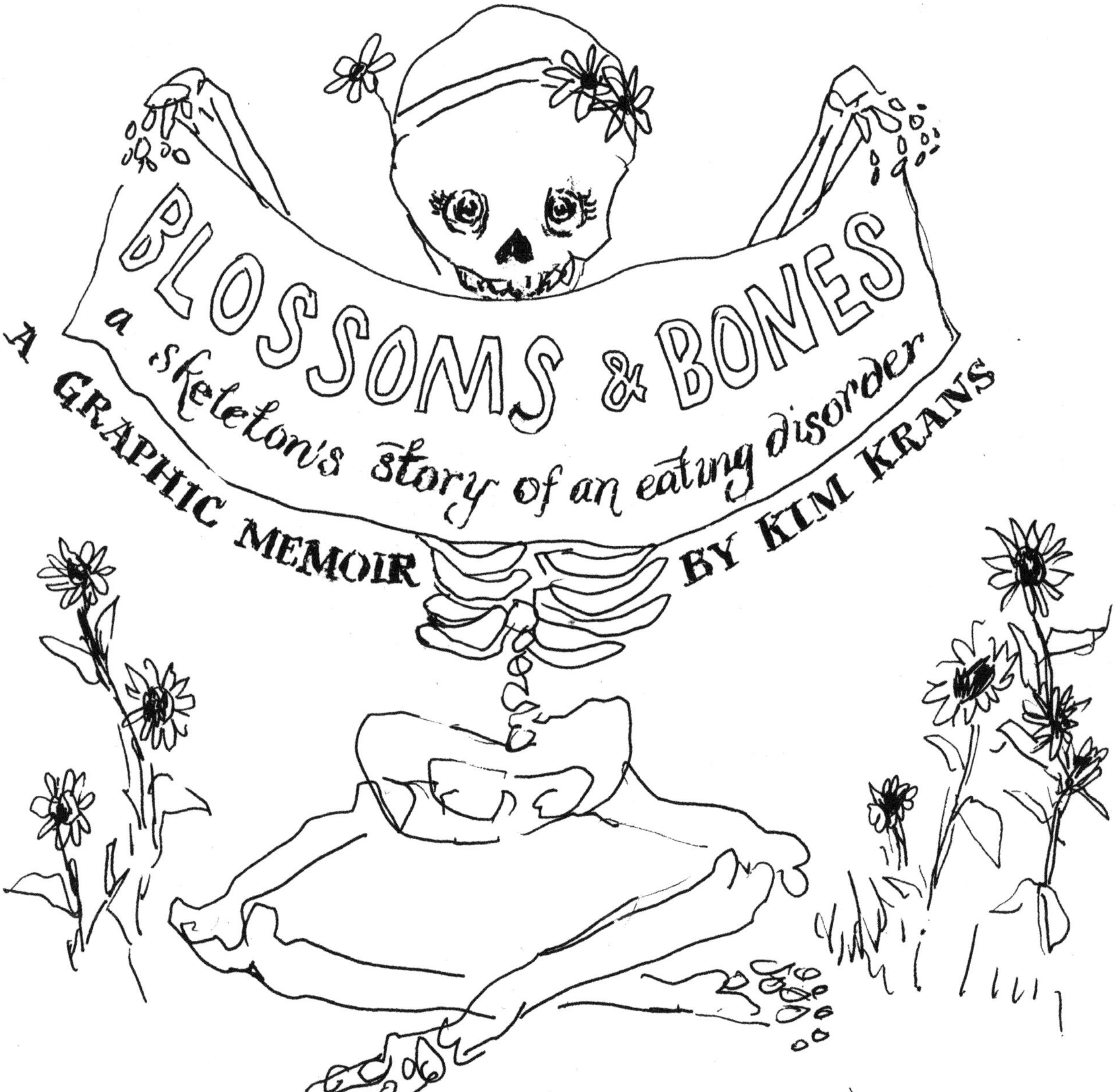
BLOSSOMS & BONES
a skeleton's story of an eating disorder
A GRAPHIC MEMOIR BY KIM KRANS

OR
AN ARTIST'S STORY OF RECOVERY

OR
A PSYCHEDELIC STORY OF A STARVING SKELETON IN A WORLD OF CHAOTIC CONSUMPTION

OR...
THE STORY OF A STARVING SKELETON IN A WELLNESS-OBSESSED WORLD

OR
A STARVING SKELETON IN AN ADDICTED WORLD

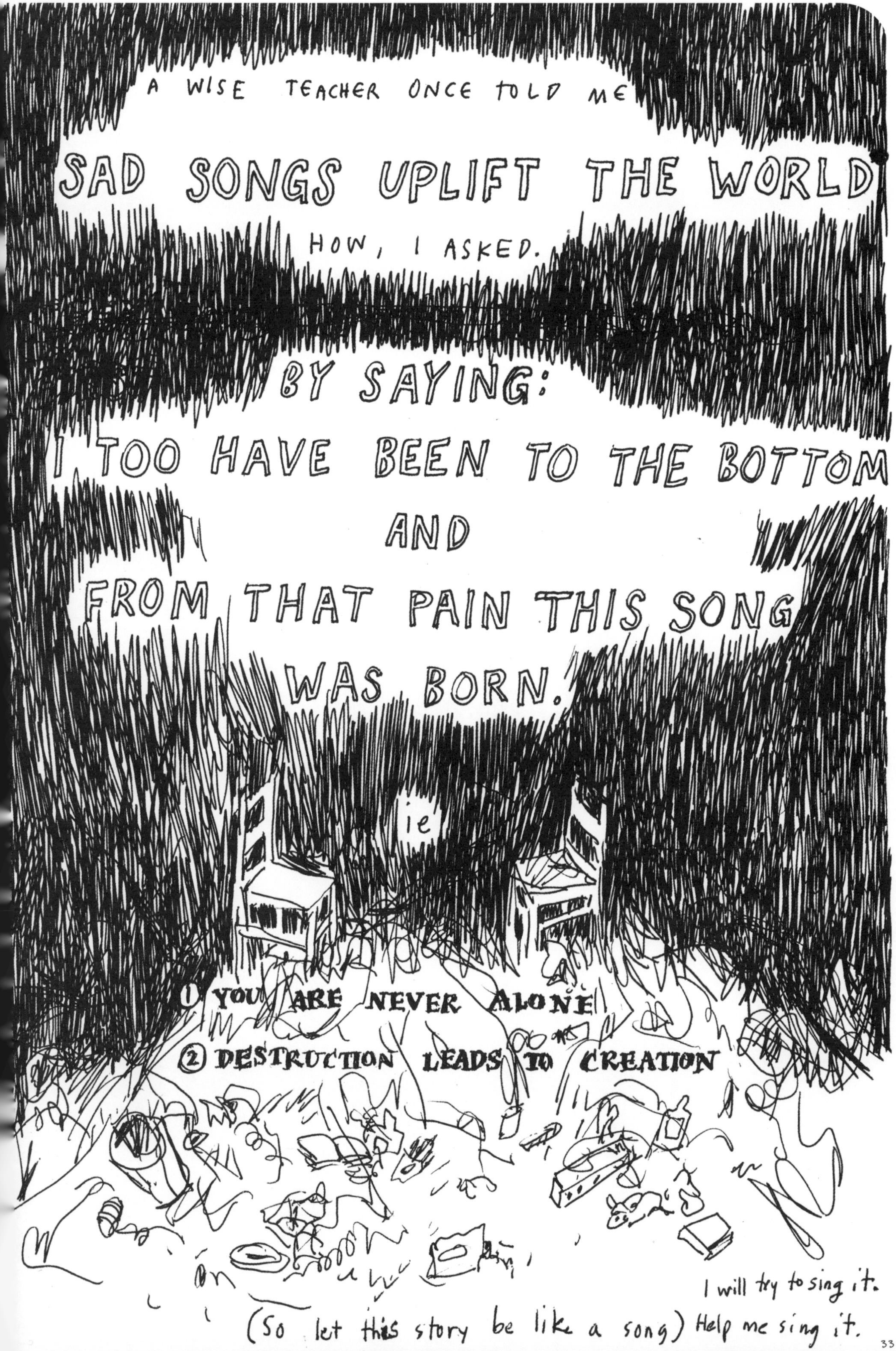
A WISE TEACHER ONCE TOLD ME
SAD SONGS UPLIFT THE WORLD
HOW, I ASKED.
BY SAYING:
I TOO HAVE BEEN TO THE BOTTOM
AND
FROM THAT PAIN THIS SONG
WAS BORN.
ie
① YOU ARE NEVER ALONE
② DESTRUCTION LEADS TO CREATION
(So let this story be like a song)
I will try to sing it.
Help me sing it.

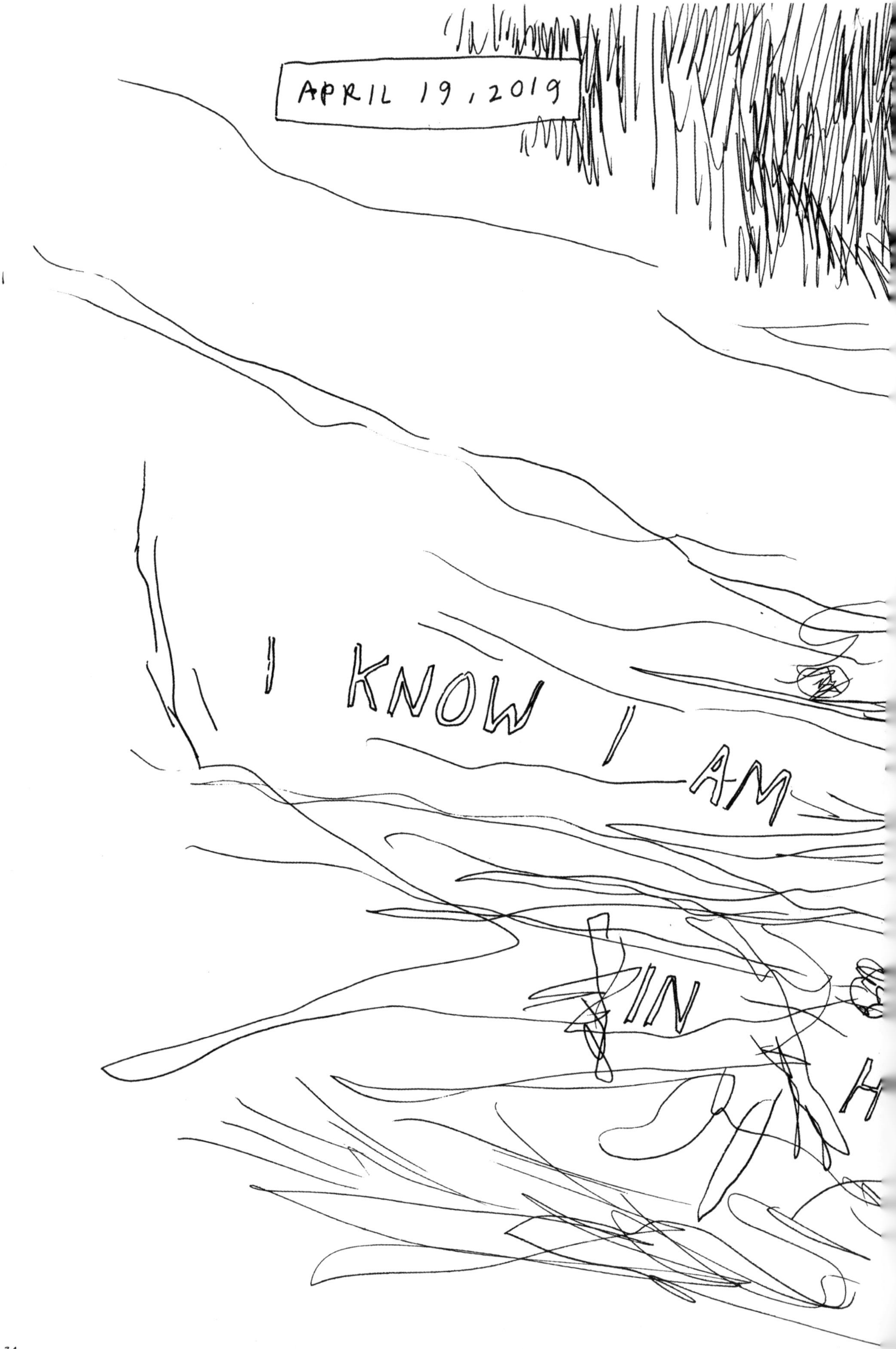
APRIL 19, 2019
I KNOW I AM
IN H

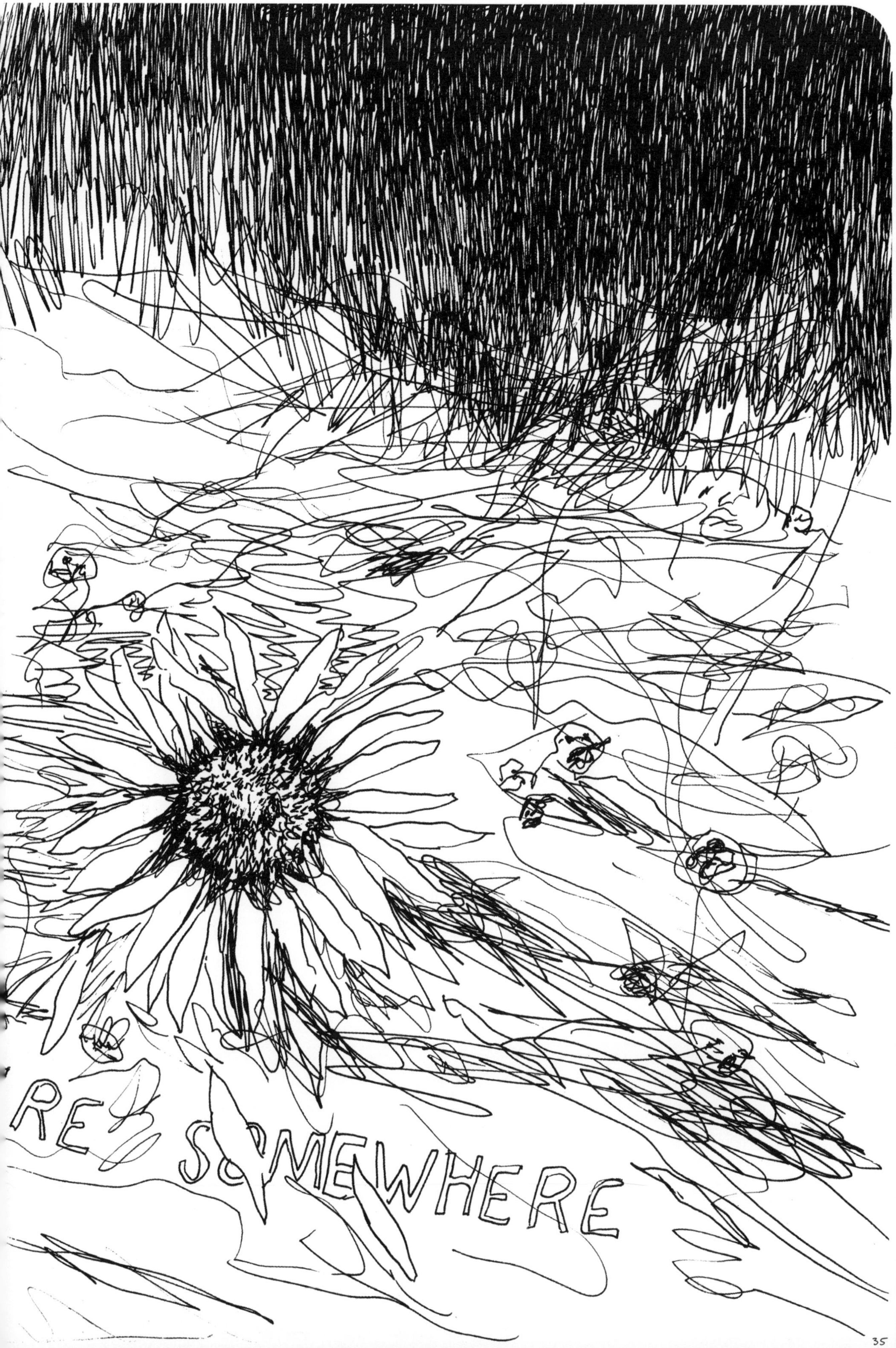
RE SOMEWHERE

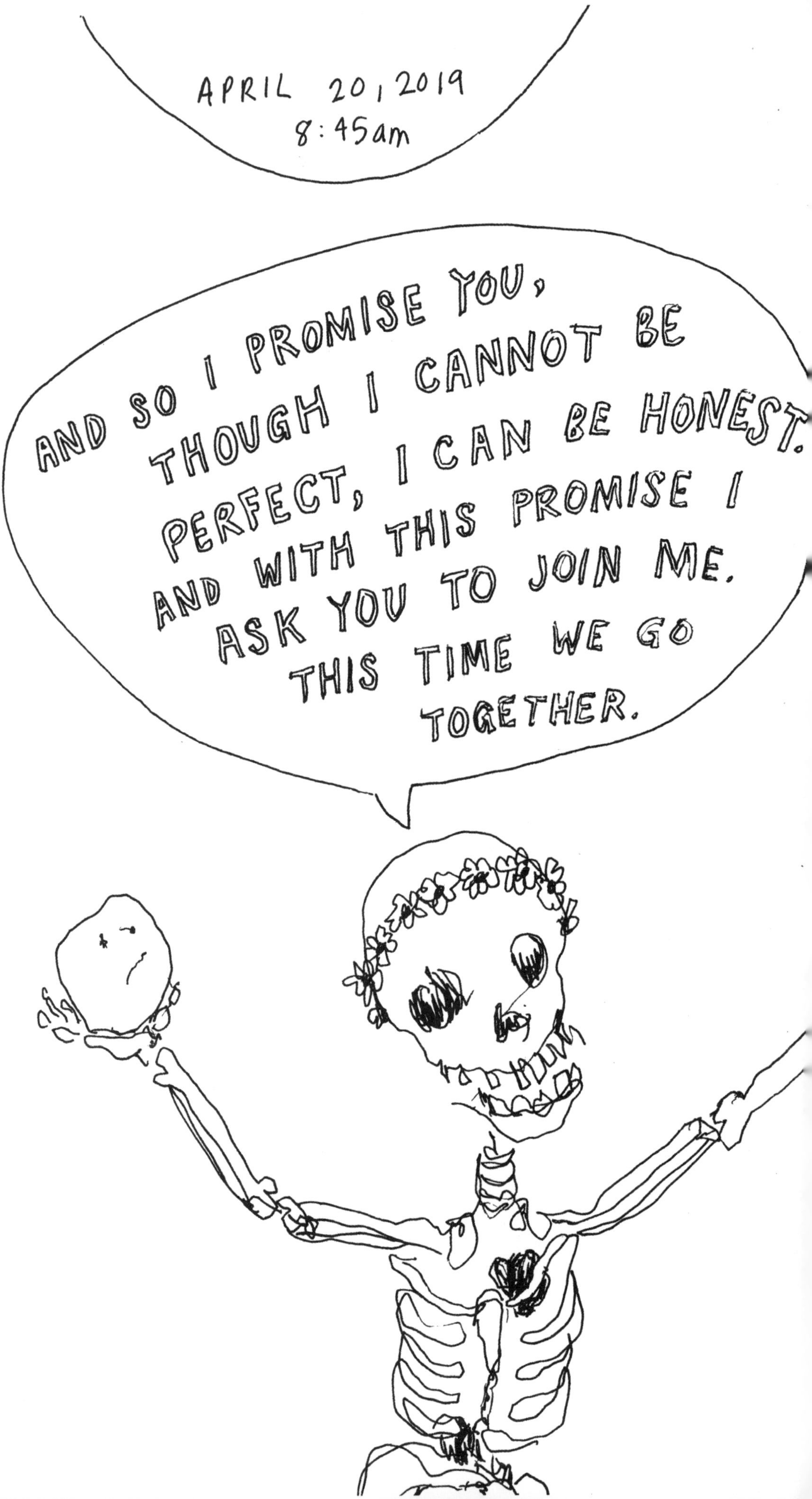
APRIL 20, 2019
8:45am
AND SO I PROMISE YOU, THOUGH I CANNOT BE PERFECT, I CAN BE HONEST. AND WITH THIS PROMISE I ASK YOU TO JOIN ME. THIS TIME WE GO TOGETHER.

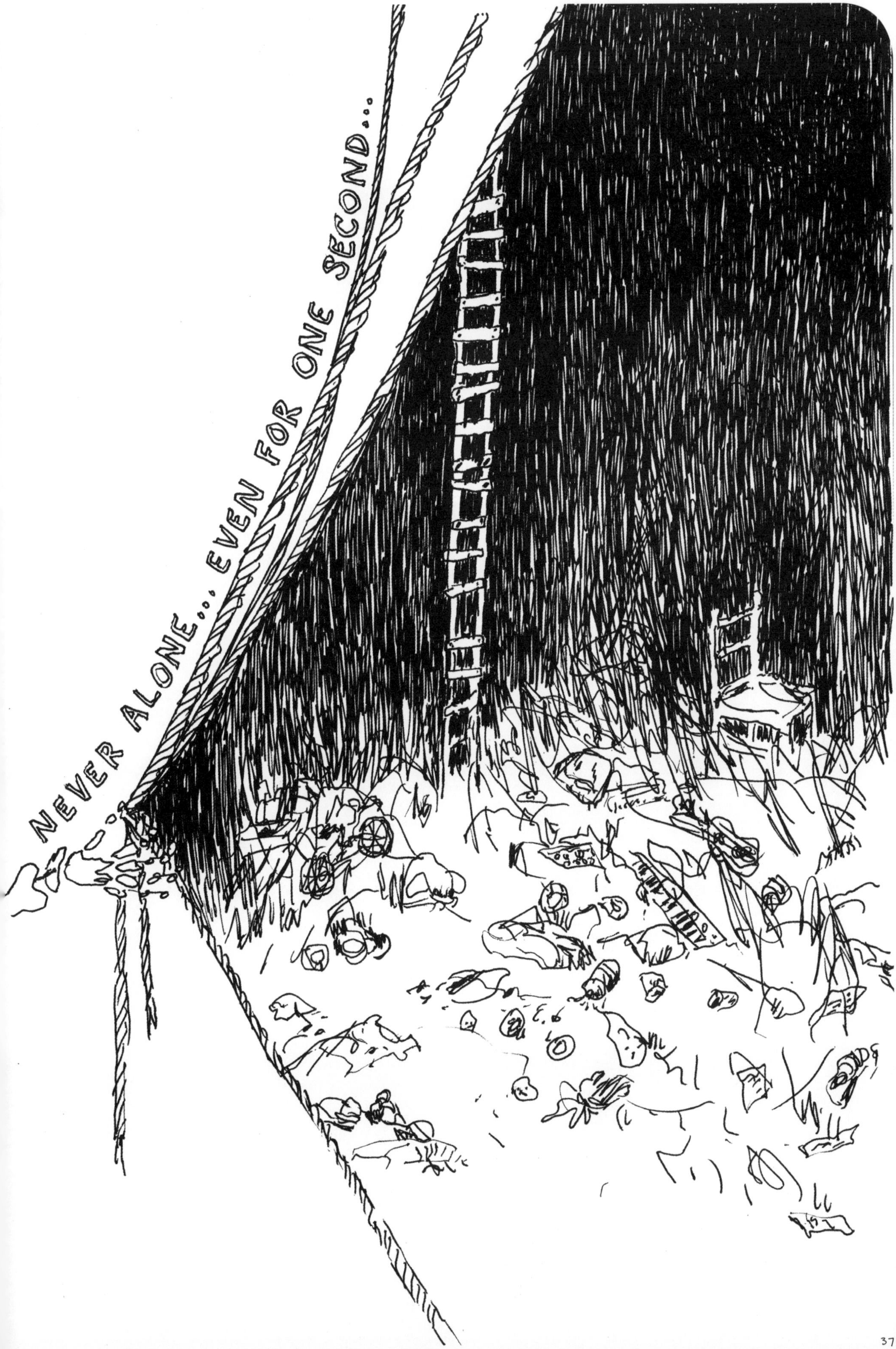
NEVER ALONE... EVEN FOR ONE SECOND...

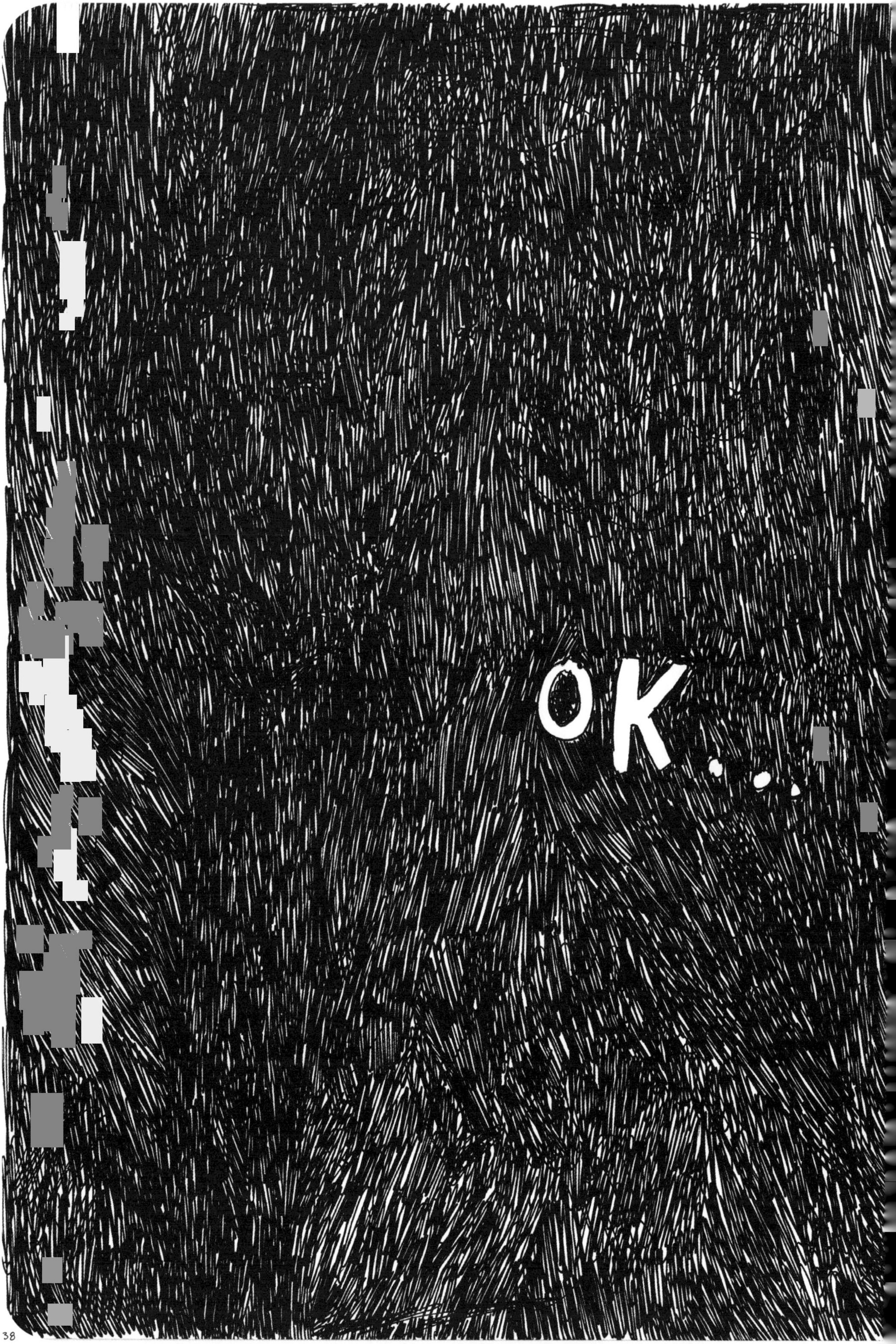
OK...

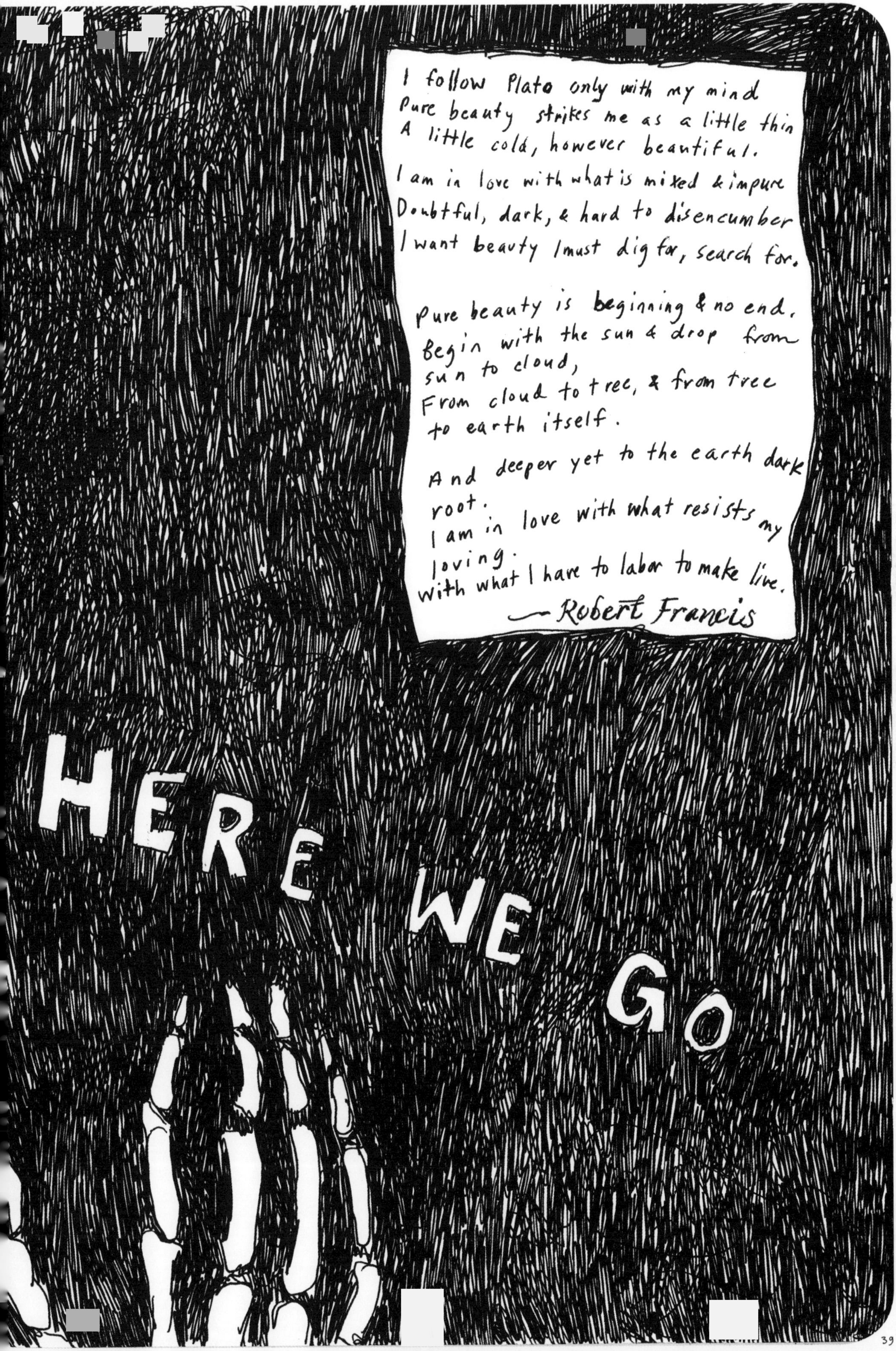
I follow Plato only with my mind
Pure beauty strikes me as a little thin
A little cold, however beautiful.
I am in love with what is mixed & impure
Doubtful, dark, & hard to disencumber
I want beauty I must dig for, search for.
Pure beauty is beginning & no end.
Begin with the sun & drop from
sun to cloud,
From cloud to tree, & from tree
to earth itself.
And deeper yet to the earth dark
root.
I am in love with what resists my
loving.
with what I have to labor to make live.
—Robert Francis
HERE
WE
GO

BUT FIRST, ANOTHER PRAYER THAT CAME AT SUNRISE. APRIL 21, 2019

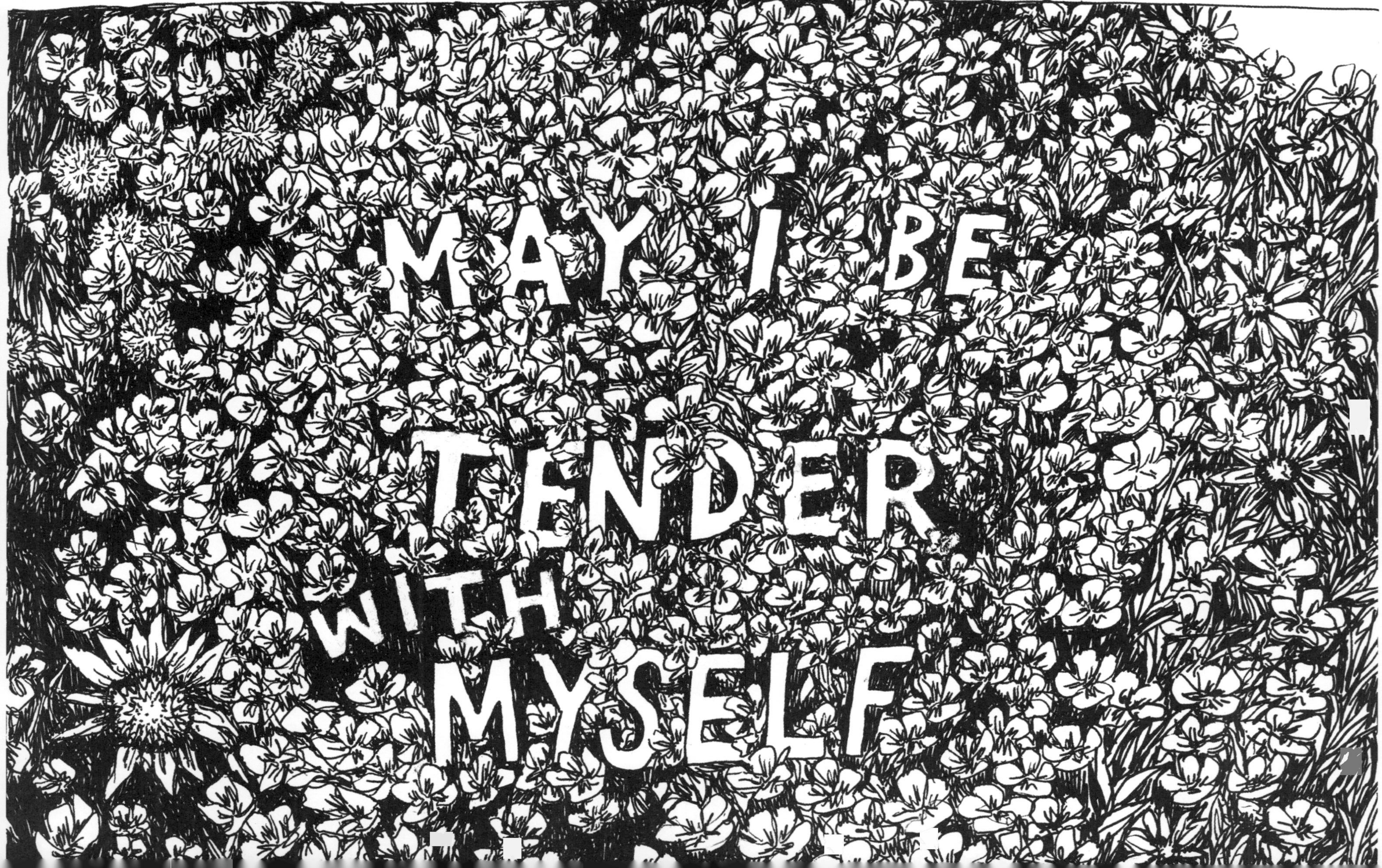
MAY I BE
TENDER
WITH
MYSELF

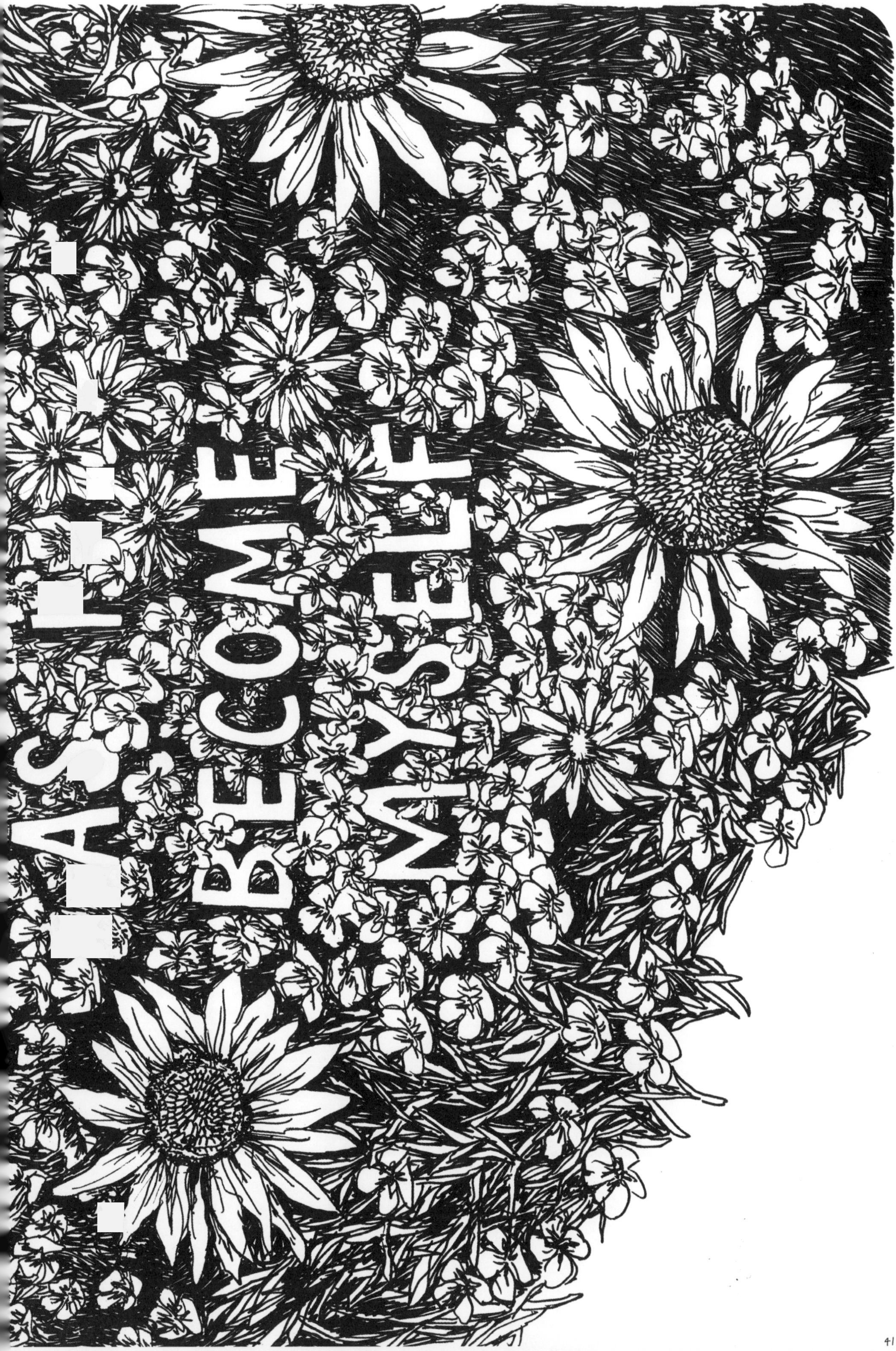
...AS I...
BECOME
MYSELF

THE SKELETON SPEAKS:

I WAS WRONG TO ASK YOU TO FOLLOW ME HERE. I THOUGHT I COULD BE A GOOD GUIDE. I THOUGHT I COULD LEAD US THROUGH THIS MESS, TOWARD SOMETHING THAT MADE SENSE. I THOUGHT WE COULD CLEAN IT UP, FIGURE IT OUT, YOU & ME. I REALLY DID THINK SO. BUT I CAN'T EVEN GET THROUGH ONE NIGHT WITHOUT MAKING MORE MESS. THANK GOD THE BREAD WAS MOLDY.

— MOLDY? YEAH, THE BREAD I BROUGHT BACK TO MY ROOM TO EAT IN SECRET, AFTER EVERYONE HAD GONE TO BED. GLUTEN FREE BREAD & A BANANA. THAT WAS AFTER DINNER: TWO CUPCAKES, APPLE SLICES, & A CHEESE GALETTE. SO FULL, SO SICKLY SORE IN MY BELLY, BUT I WANTED ONE MORE THING... IT JUST... WE WERE WATCHING... YEAH... WHAT? YOU KNOW... I CAN'T EVEN.... YOU SHOULD TURN AROUND... GO BACK UP THE LADDER... FORGET ABOUT ME... WATCHING WHAT? NOTHING. IT JUST. I CAN'T. AND WHAT WERE YOU WATCHING IT DOESN'T MATTER. THE BREAD WAS MOLDY....

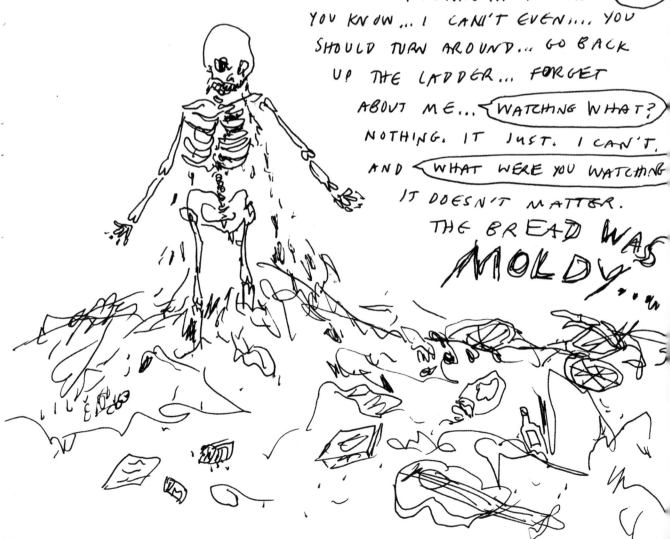

... DID I MENTION IT'S EASTER? DEAD JESUS RISES. COLORFUL EGGS. A BUNNY. CANDY ALL DAY. SICKENING AMOUNTS. AND THE BREAD, I MEAN, I'VE EATEN FROZEN BREAD, (~~DUUE~~ YES, RIGHT OUT OF THE FREEZER) BUT NOT MOLDY. NEVER BINGED ON MOLDY BREAD BEFORE. NOT YET. NOT YET. AN

OVER-RIPE BANANA & MOLDY BREAD.

~~BREAKFAST~~ THIS HAPPENED LAST SUNDAY TOO. HIDING WITH MY CHEESE POPCORN, LICKING MY PALMS

FOR **EVERY LAST DROP.**

CAN YOU BLAME ME?
WHAT WAS I SUPPOSED TO DO?
WE WATCHED THIS SHOW TOGETHER
EVERY SUNDAY FOR SEVEN YEARS.
NOW I WATCH IT BY MYSELF.
I PRETEND NOT TO
CARE. NO BIG DEAL.

IT'S NOT.
IT'S NOTHING. IT DOES NOT MEAN ANYTHING. NO NO MY HEART IS NOT BROKEN, NO.

OTHER THAN
SOME FOOD
I CAN'T
STOP
EAT
ING

CLIMB
THE
LADDER BACK UP

YOU SHOULD GO BACK TO THE SURFACE.
THIS STORY IS OVER
FOR ANOTHER DAY.
THE LIGHT FADES.
SLEEP IS THE ONLY
REMEDY. COME DREAMS,
BE TENDER WITH ME.

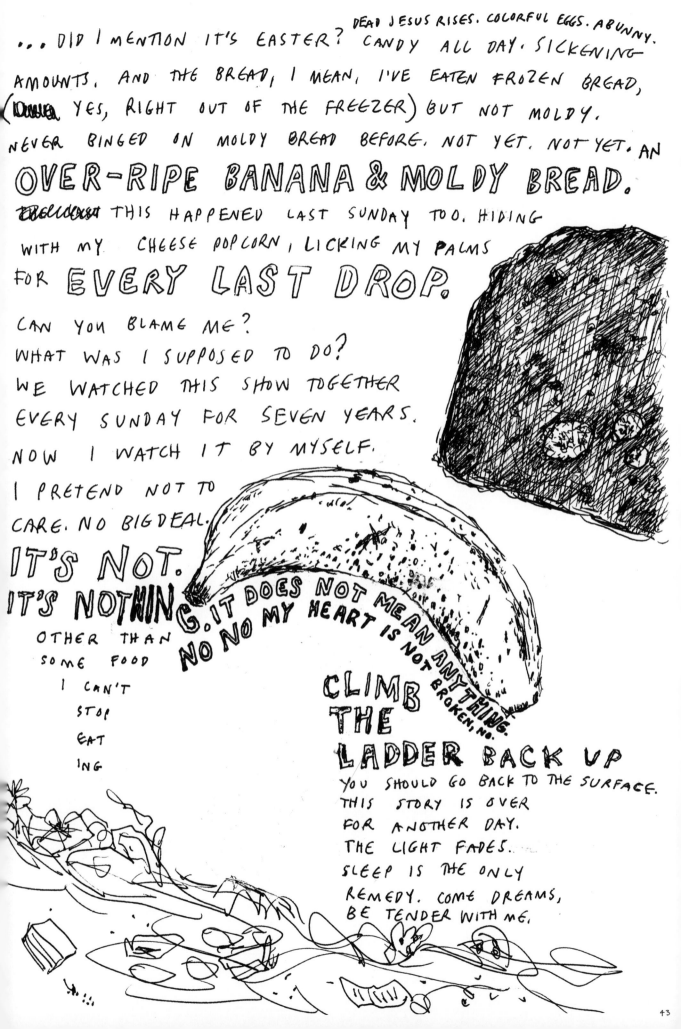

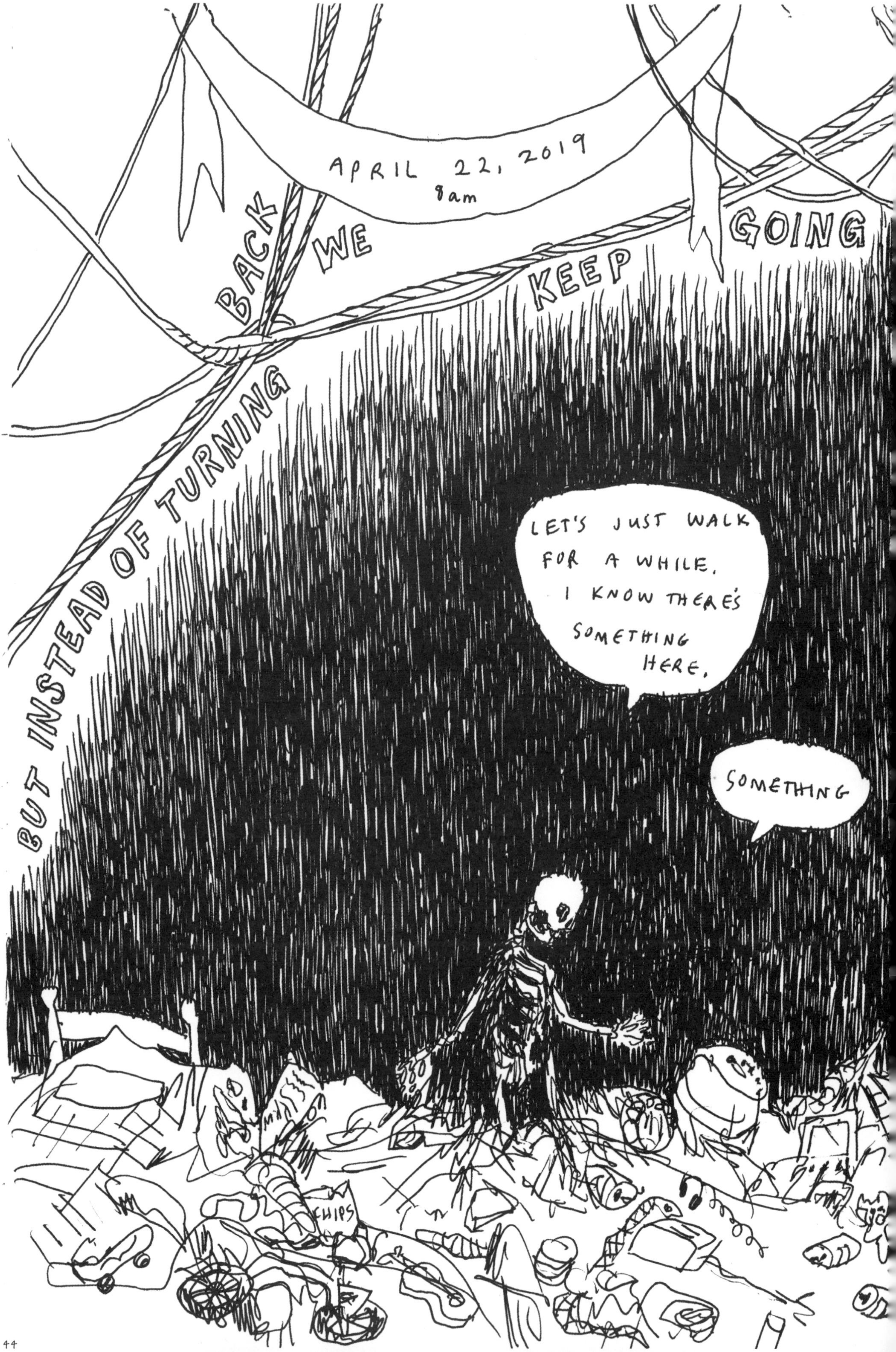
APRIL 22, 2019
8am
BUT INSTEAD OF TURNING
BACK
WE
KEEP
GOING
LET'S JUST WALK FOR A WHILE. I KNOW THERE'S SOMETHING HERE.
SOMETHING
CHIPS

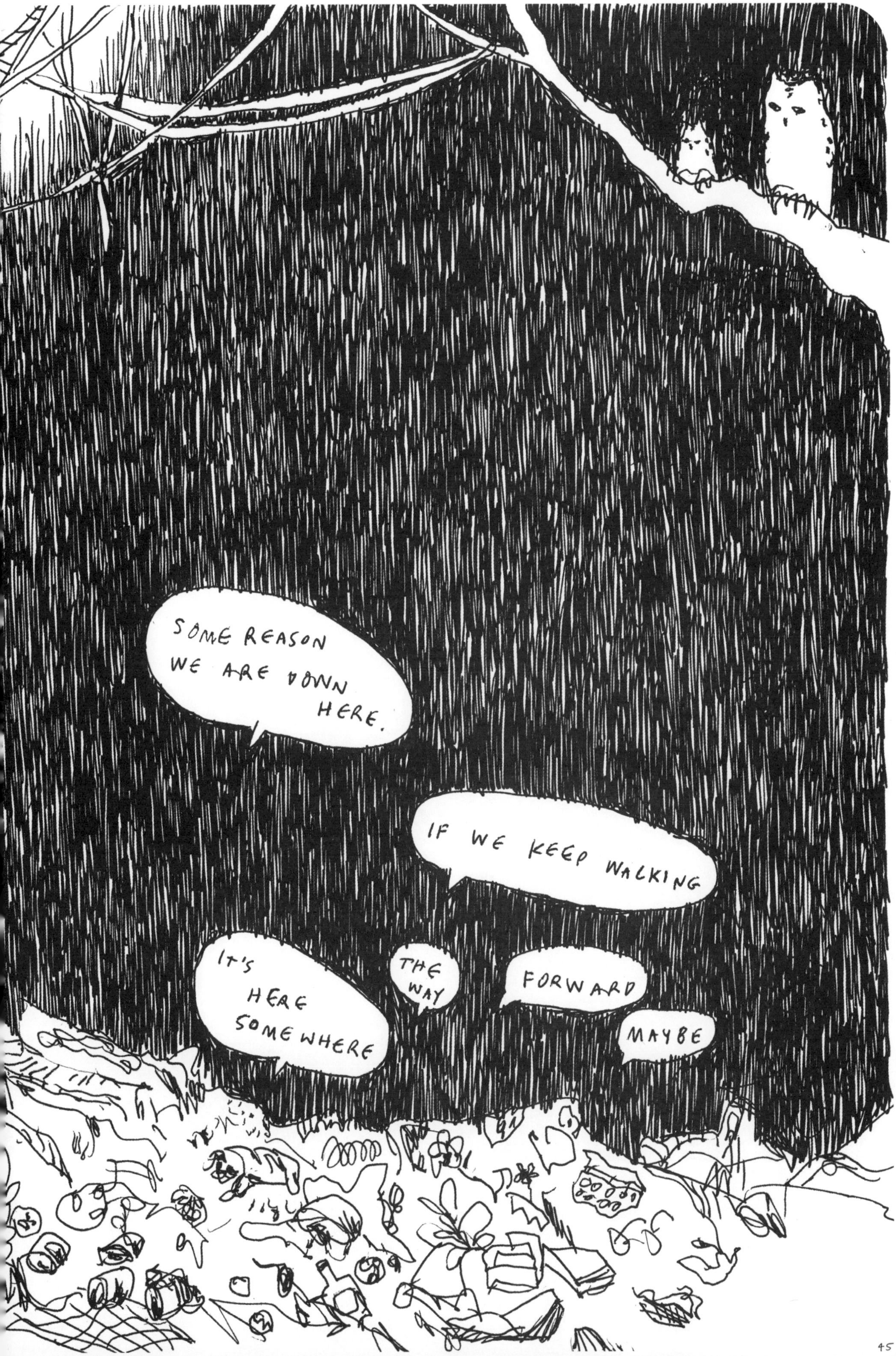
SOME REASON WE ARE DOWN HERE.
IF WE KEEP WALKING
IT'S HERE SOMEWHERE
THE WAY
FORWARD
MAYBE

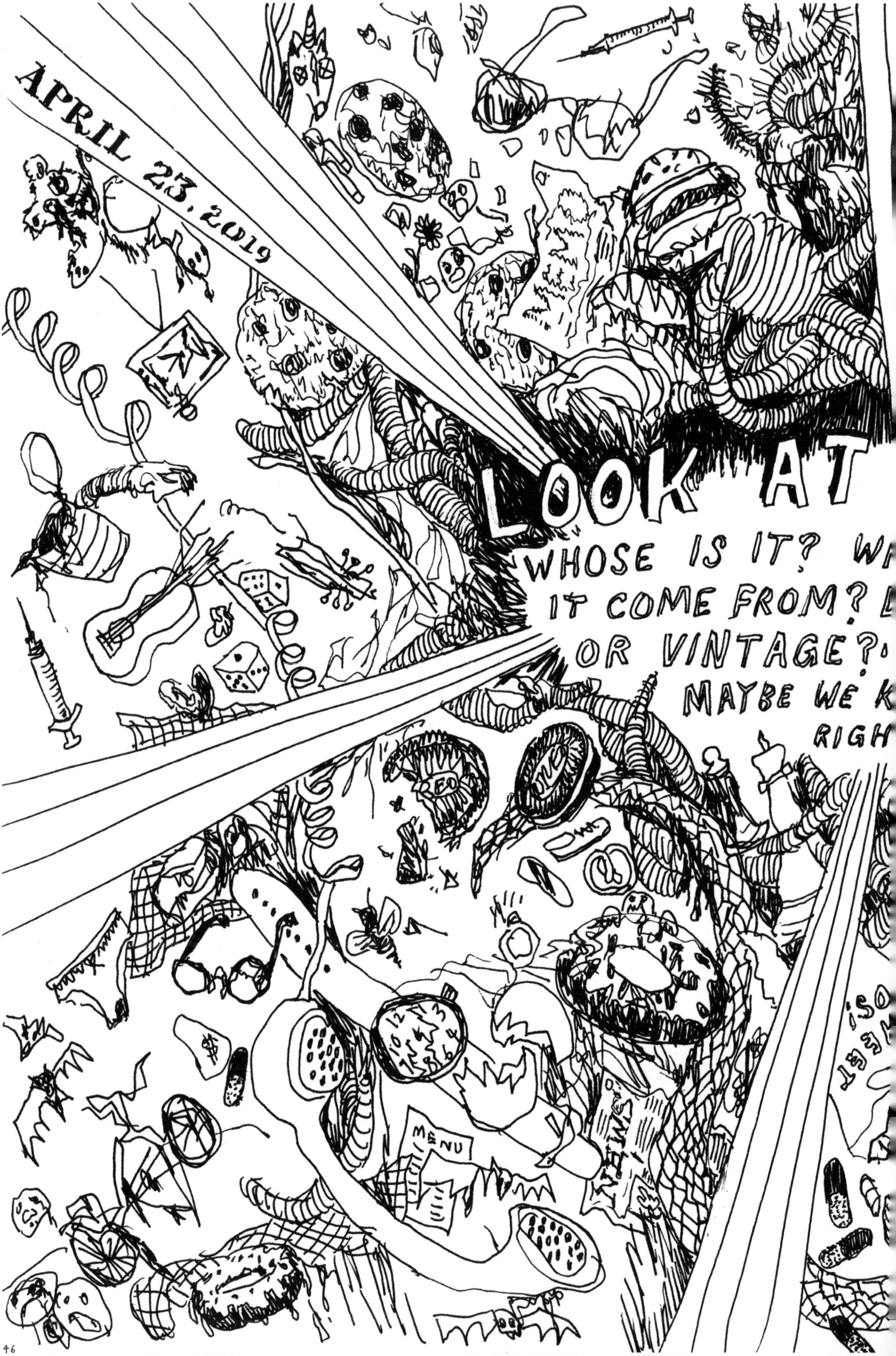
APRIL 23, 2019
LOOK AT
WHOSE IS IT? WH
IT COME FROM?
OR VINTAGE?
MAYBE WE K
RIGH
MENU

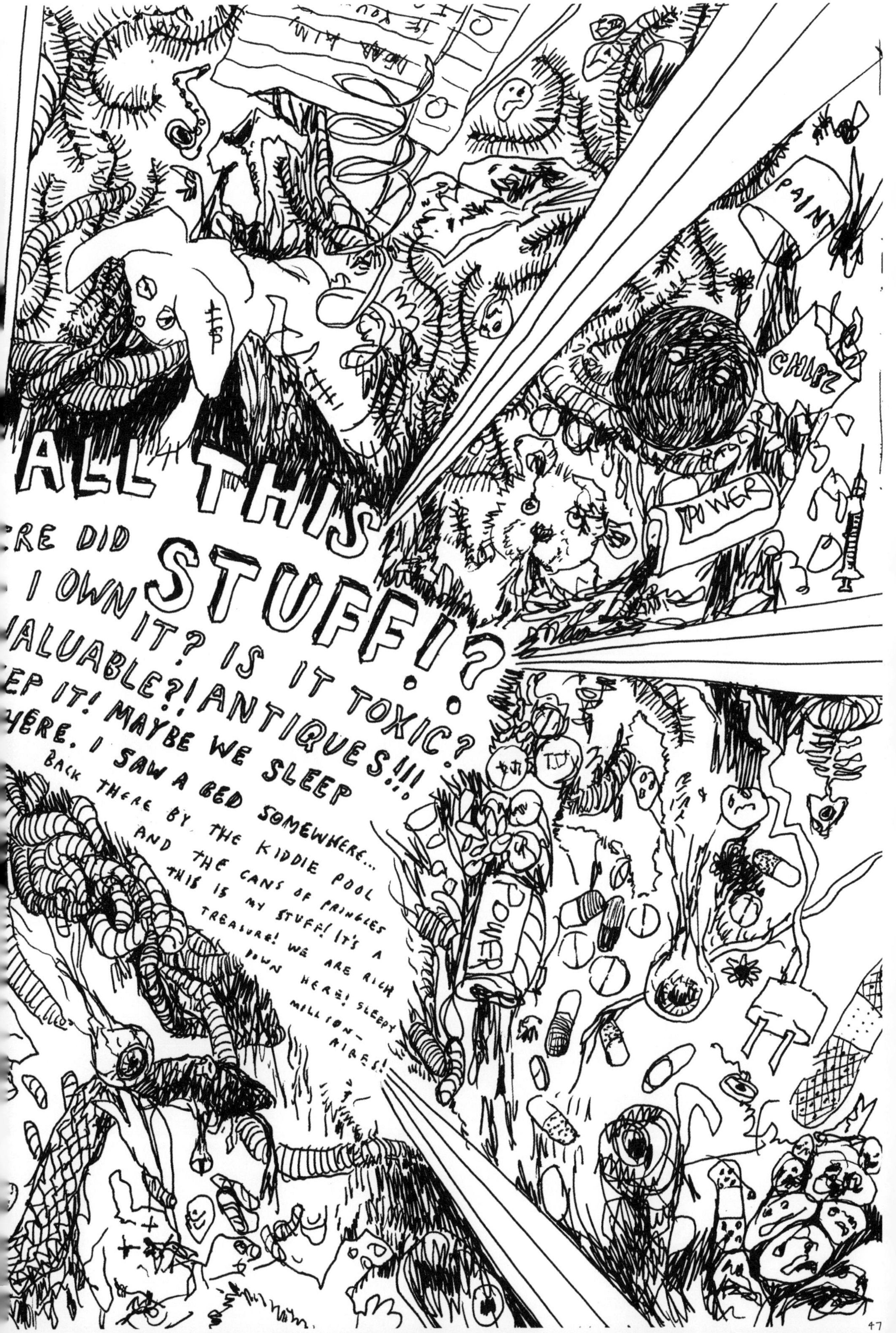
ALL THIS STUFF!?
RE DID
I OWN
IT? IS IT TOXIC?
ALUABLE?! ANTIQUES!!!
EP IT! MAYBE WE SLEEP
HERE. I SAW A BED SOMEWHERE...
BACK THERE BY THE KIDDIE POOL
AND THE CANS OF PRINGLES
THIS IS MY STUFF! IT'S A
TREASURE! WE ARE RICH
DOWN HERE! SLEEPY
MILLION-
AIRES!
PAINT
POWER
POWER

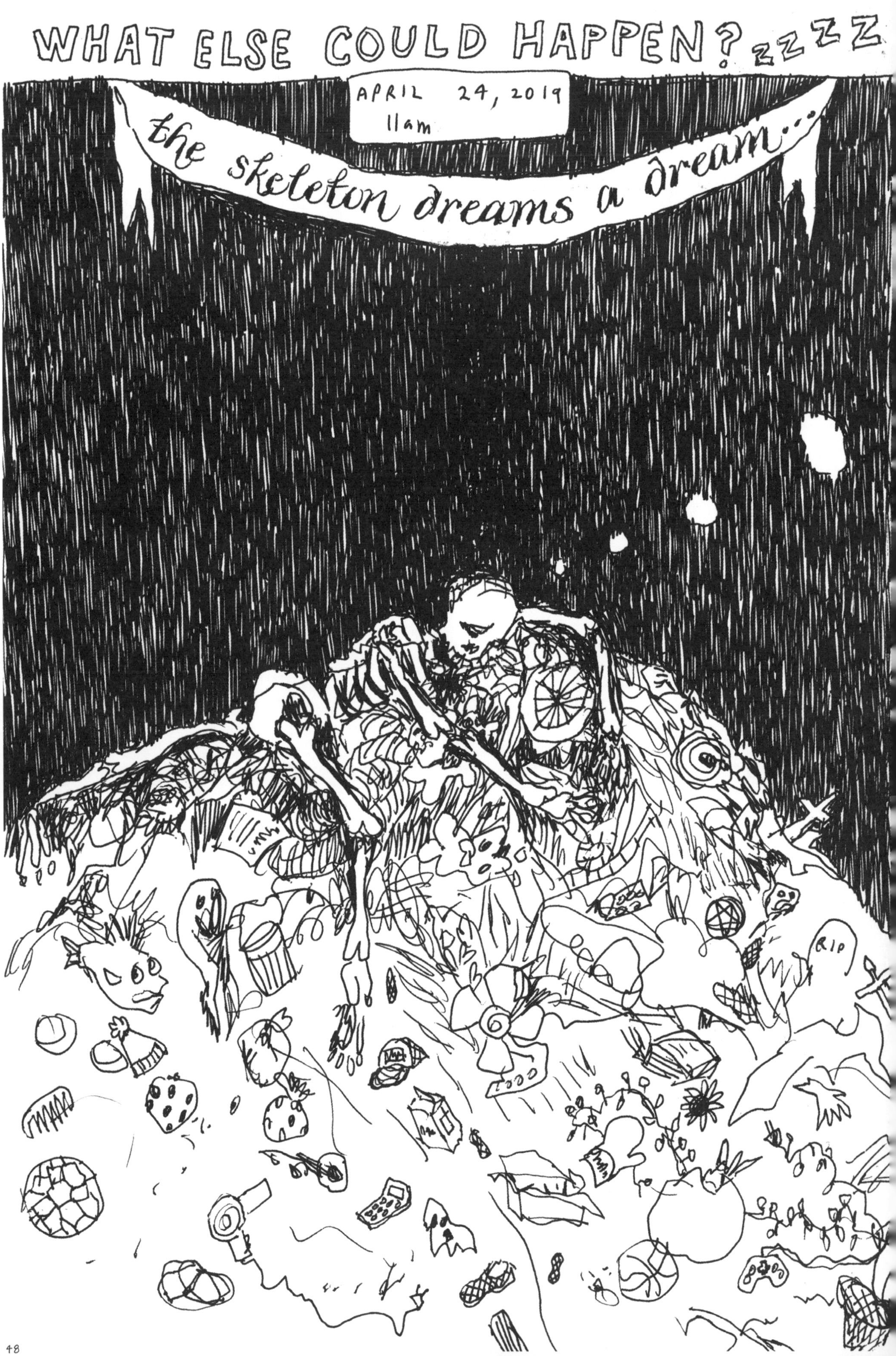
WHAT ELSE COULD HAPPEN? zzzz
APRIL 24, 2019
11am
the skeleton dreams a dream...
RIP

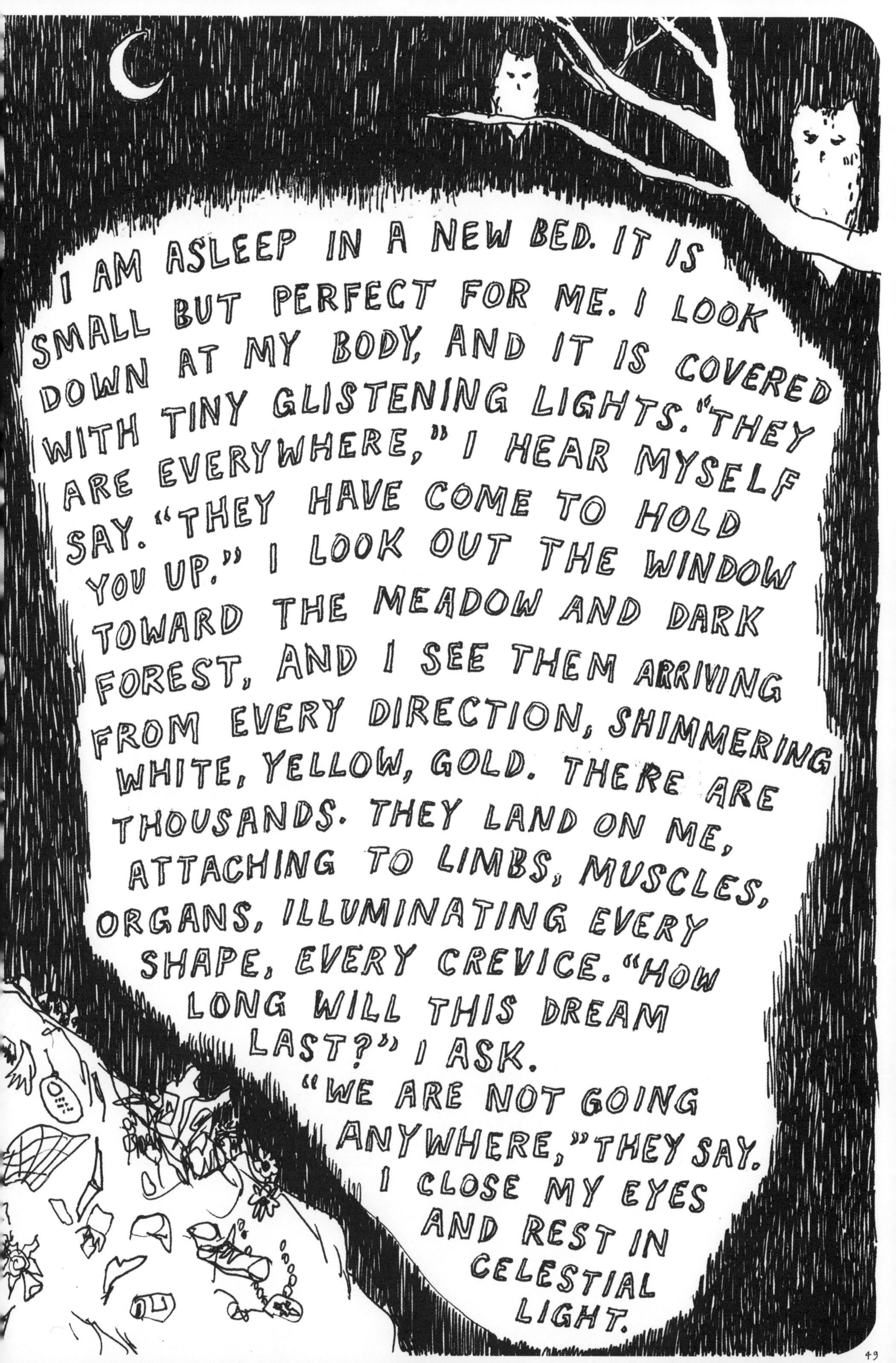
I AM ASLEEP IN A NEW BED. IT IS SMALL BUT PERFECT FOR ME. I LOOK DOWN AT MY BODY, AND IT IS COVERED WITH TINY GLISTENING LIGHTS. "THEY ARE EVERYWHERE," I HEAR MYSELF SAY. "THEY HAVE COME TO HOLD YOU UP." I LOOK OUT THE WINDOW TOWARD THE MEADOW AND DARK FOREST, AND I SEE THEM ARRIVING FROM EVERY DIRECTION, SHIMMERING WHITE, YELLOW, GOLD. THERE ARE THOUSANDS. THEY LAND ON ME, ATTACHING TO LIMBS, MUSCLES, ORGANS, ILLUMINATING EVERY SHAPE, EVERY CREVICE. "HOW LONG WILL THIS DREAM LAST?" I ASK.
"WE ARE NOT GOING ANYWHERE," THEY SAY. I CLOSE MY EYES AND REST IN CELESTIAL LIGHT.

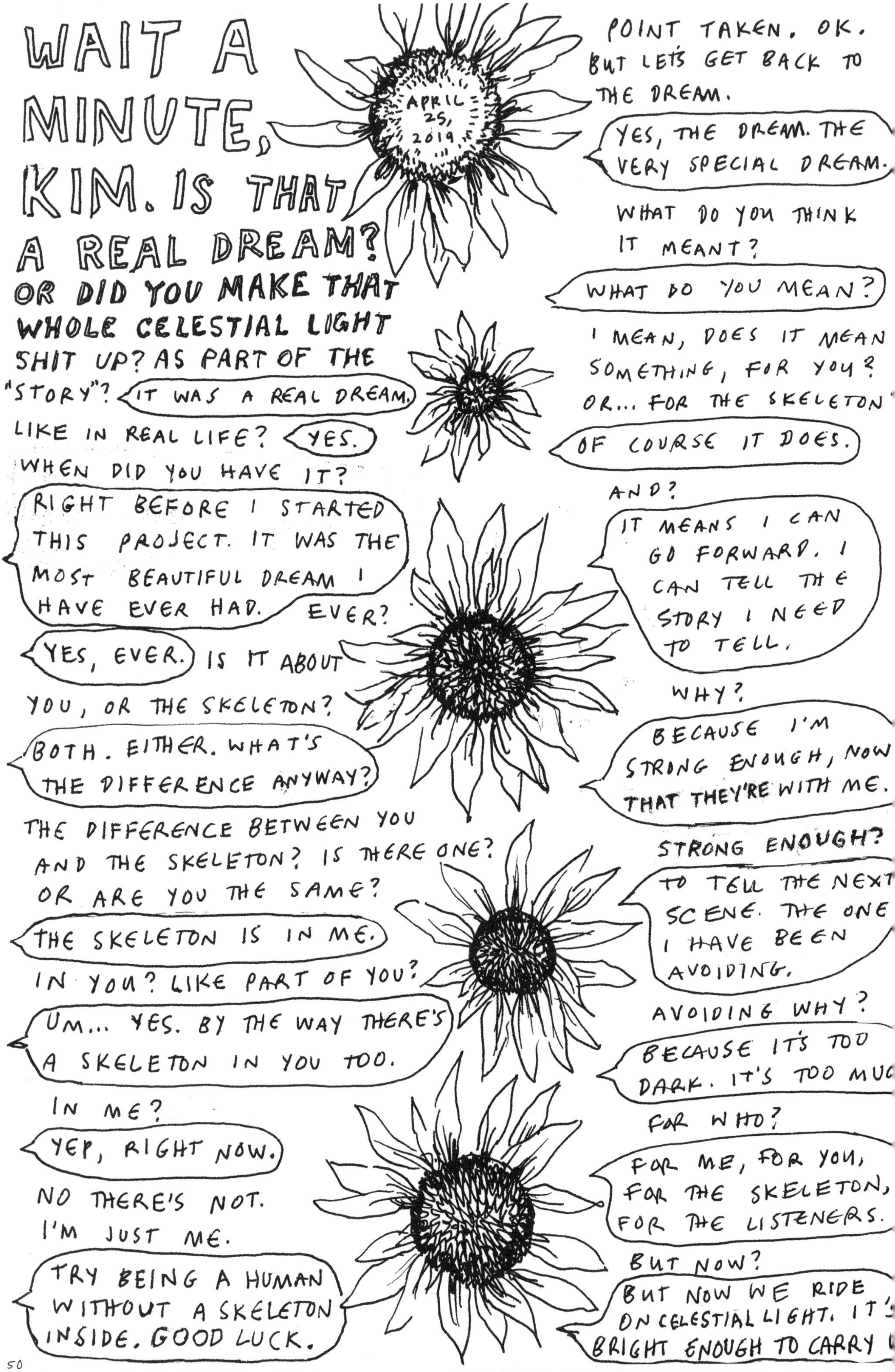
WAIT A MINUTE, KIM. IS THAT A REAL DREAM?
OR DID YOU MAKE THAT WHOLE CELESTIAL LIGHT SHIT UP? AS PART OF THE "STORY"?
APRIL 25, 2019
IT WAS A REAL DREAM.
LIKE IN REAL LIFE?
YES.
WHEN DID YOU HAVE IT?
RIGHT BEFORE I STARTED THIS PROJECT. IT WAS THE MOST BEAUTIFUL DREAM I HAVE EVER HAD.
EVER?
YES, EVER.
IS IT ABOUT YOU, OR THE SKELETON?
BOTH. EITHER. WHAT'S THE DIFFERENCE ANYWAY?
THE DIFFERENCE BETWEEN YOU AND THE SKELETON? IS THERE ONE? OR ARE YOU THE SAME?
THE SKELETON IS IN ME.
IN YOU? LIKE PART OF YOU?
UM... YES. BY THE WAY THERE'S A SKELETON IN YOU TOO.
IN ME?
YEP, RIGHT NOW.
NO THERE'S NOT. I'M JUST ME.
TRY BEING A HUMAN WITHOUT A SKELETON INSIDE. GOOD LUCK.
POINT TAKEN. OK. BUT LET'S GET BACK TO THE DREAM.
YES, THE DREAM. THE VERY SPECIAL DREAM.
WHAT DO YOU THINK IT MEANT?
WHAT DO YOU MEAN?
I MEAN, DOES IT MEAN SOMETHING, FOR YOU? OR... FOR THE SKELETON
OF COURSE IT DOES.
AND?
IT MEANS I CAN GO FORWARD. I CAN TELL THE STORY I NEED TO TELL.
WHY?
BECAUSE I'M STRONG ENOUGH, NOW THAT THEY'RE WITH ME.
STRONG ENOUGH?
TO TELL THE NEXT SCENE. THE ONE I HAVE BEEN AVOIDING.
AVOIDING WHY?
BECAUSE IT'S TOO DARK. IT'S TOO MUC
FOR WHO?
FOR ME, FOR YOU, FOR THE SKELETON, FOR THE LISTENERS.
BUT NOW?
BUT NOW WE RIDE ON CELESTIAL LIGHT. IT'
BRIGHT ENOUGH TO CARRY

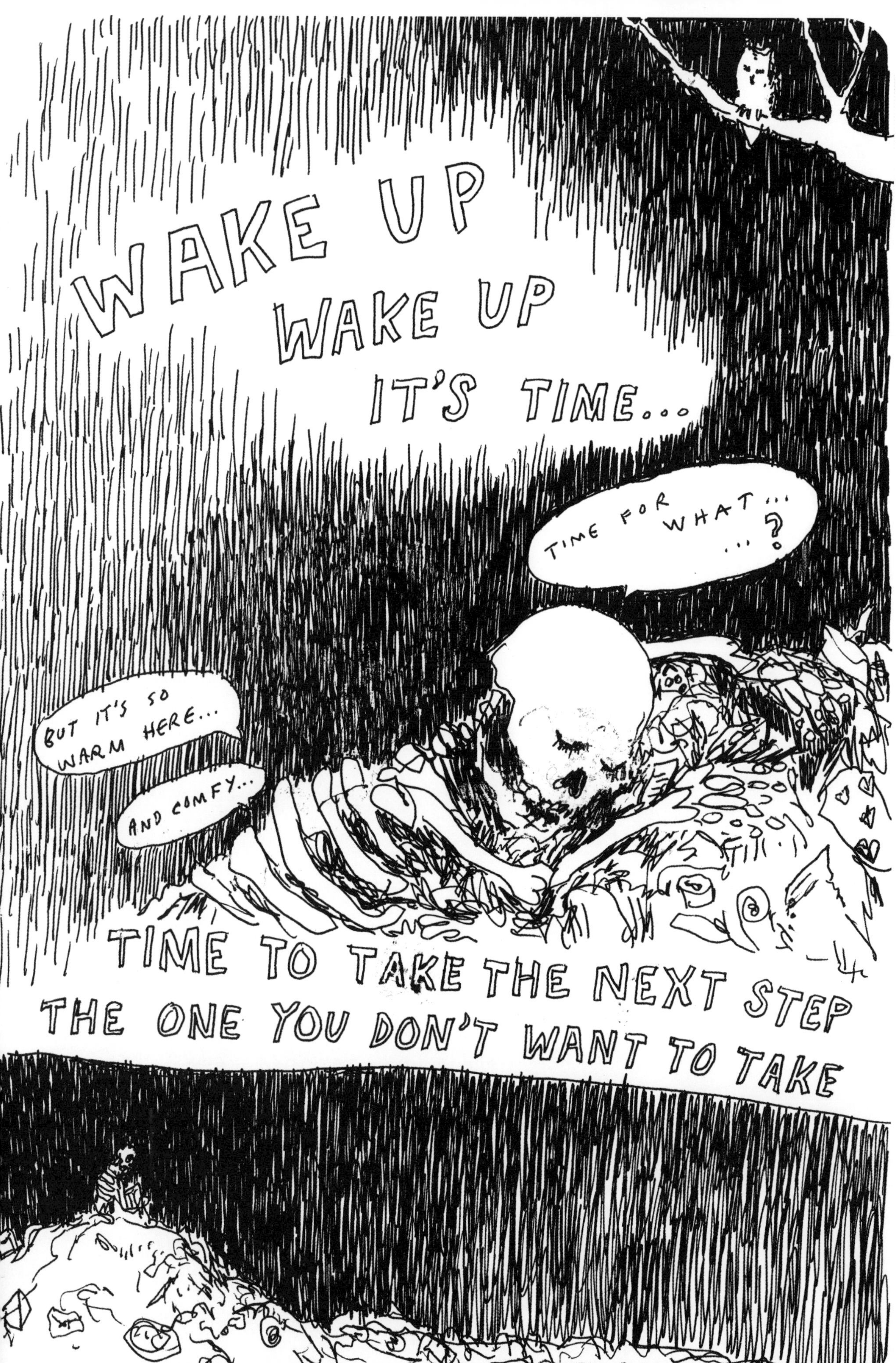
WAKE UP
WAKE UP
IT'S TIME...
TIME FOR WHAT... ...?
BUT IT'S SO WARM HERE...
AND COMFY...
TIME TO TAKE THE NEXT STEP
THE ONE YOU DON'T WANT TO TAKE

GOOGLE SEARCHES:

- HOW TO FIX BLOATING FAST
- BEST REMEDY FOR INDIGESTION
- WHY AM I BLOATED
- FOODS THAT CAUSE BLOATING
- WHY CAN'T I STOP EATING
- FOOD CRAVINGS STOP NOW
- HERBS FOR FOOD CRAVINGS
- OVEREATERS ANONYMOUS NEAR ME
- AM I A FOOD ADDICT
- TOP TEN REASONS FOR CRAVINGS
- CANDIDA OVERGROWTH SYMPTOMS
- EMOTIONAL EATING HOW TO STOP
- WHY AM I EATING MORE
- HORMONAL IMBALANCE HERBS
- AYURVEDIC REMEDY CRAVINGS
- AYURVEDA ADDICTION HERBS
- EMPTINESS BUDDHISM
- PREGNANCY LOSS CRAVINGS
- ECTOPIC PREGNANCY WHY
- METHOTREXATE SIDE EFFECTS
- METHOTREXATE CANDIDA
- METHOTREXATE HORMONES
- METHOTREXATE LONG TERM EFFECTS
- MISSED PERIOD WHY
- SIGNS OF PREMENOPAUSE
- WHAT AGE PREMENOPAUSE
- HERBS FOR MENOPAUSE
- WATER RETENTION BEST FIX
- FLOWER ESSENCES FOR WEIGHT
- BACH FLOWERS FOR ADDICTION
- INDIGESTION SPIRITUALITY
- CONSTIPATION MEANING
- WHY AM I CONSTIPATED
- PSYLLIUM HUSK FOR CONSTIPATION
- DO PEOPLE GAIN WEIGHT AFTER DIVORCE
- MISCARRIAGE WEIGHT GAIN
- MISCARRIAGE HERBS REMEDY
- EATING DISORDER DEFINITION

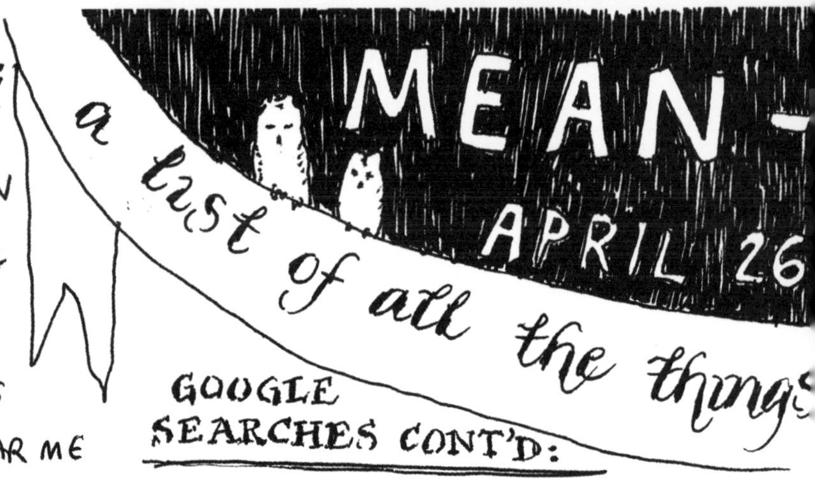
MEAN-
APRIL 26
a list of all the things

GOOGLE SEARCHES CONT'D:

- MULTIPLE MISCARRIAGES WHY
- MISCARRIAGES KARMA
- AM I MEANT TO BE A MOTHER
- TOP TEN SIGNS YOU'RE GRIEVING
- DANCE THERAPY GRIEF NEAR ME
- WHICH CHAKRA MISCARRIAGE
- RETREAT GRIEF NEAR ME
- FASTING FOR CANDIDA
- JUICE CLEANSE HOW MUCH SUGAR
- JUICE CLEANSE DOES IT WORK
- PARASITES REMEDY
- H. PYLORI GET RID OF
- RINGWORM EATING CRAVINGS
- JUICE CLEANSE EATING DISORDER
- B12 DEFICIENCY SYMPTOMS
- HORMONES BRAIN FOG
- CELERY JUICE DOES IT WORK
- CELERY JUICE SNAKE OIL
- SYMPTOMS HEAVY METAL POISON
- HEAVY METAL DETOX SMOOTHIE
- AM I FERTILE AT 39
- FERTILITY AGE CHART
- IDEAL WEIGHT FOR PREGNANCY
- DIET TO INCREASE FERTILITY
- CHINESE HERBS FERTILITY
- DIVORCE DEPRESSION
- TWELVE STEPS FOOD ADDICTION
- HOW MANY CALORIES JOGGING
- WHY IS MY FACE BLOATED

WHILE

2019 8AM

I've tried in hopes of DIY REMEDY

ELIXIRS, HERBS, SUPPLEMENTS, TRICKS, TECHNIQUES, & TOOLS:

- WARM WATER WITH LEMON UPON WAKING • COLONICS
- CELERY JUICE UPON WAKING • KOMBUCHA
- PROBIOTIC FIRST THING • APPLE CIDER VINEGAR
- PROBIOTIC PLUS PREBIOTIC • FLAX SEED MEAL
- ZINC • FERMENTED FOODS • TURMERIC PASTE
- THYROID SUPPLEMENT • GOLDEN MILK • AMLA
- TONGUE SCRAPING • DULSE • HEMP • CHIA
- NETI POT • BREATH OF FIRE • CHARCOAL
- MAGNESIUM BEFORE BED • WILD BLUEBERRIES
- BULLETPROOF COFFEE • SPIRULINA • CAYENNE
- NO CAFFEINE • MATCHA • SHIRODHARA • SEX
- NO SUGAR • DEER ANTLER VELVET • TULSI
- NO WHEAT • ABSTINENCE • MUDRAS • MACA
- DRY SKIN BRUSHING • WATER FAST • SAFFRON
- WHEATGRASS • INFARED SAUNA • SALT WATER
- CORDYCEPS • ABDOMINAL MASSAGE • REIKI
- REISHI • ROOT VEGETABLES • OMEGA OILS
- GREEN TEA • KITCHARI CLEANSE • GABA
- MANUKA HONEY • ELECTROLYTES • GOJI
- BEE POLLEN • ADAPTOGENS • ASHWAGANDHA
- ALOE JUICE • LION'S MANE • SEAWEED
- BURDOCK ROOT • COQ10 • FOLIC ACID • D3
- MARMA POINTS • PARASITE CLEANSE
- ACUPRESSURE • COLLODIAL SILVER • IRON
- ACUPUNCTURE • VALERIAN • RHODIOLA • AURA
- ENEMA • MANTRA • PALEO • BONE BROTH
- PEA PROTEIN • ABHYANGA • TRANSDERMAL
- KIMCHI • GHEE • GOTU KOLA • EPSOM BATH
- ESSENTIAL OILS • SAGE • SHILAJIT • CBD
- PULLING • FIRE SIPPING • GINGER
- ...E REMEDY • BREATHING INTO PAPER BAG

AND A FEW ADDITIONAL GOOGLE SEARCHES:

- WHEN IS FASTING ANOREXIA
- GANDHI'S DIET
- GANDHI FASTING HOW LONG
- GANDHI SILENCE HOW LONG
- MOVIE STARS VEGAN
- MOVIE STARS ADDICTS
- MOVIE STARS SOBER
- ECTOPIC PREGNANCY
- ADOPTION PROS CONS
- HOW LONG ADOPTION
- ADOPTION APPROVAL
- ECTOPIC PREGNANCY WHY
- FREEZING EGGS HOW
- FREEZING EGGS COST
- FREEZING EGGS SUCCESS
- FREEZE EGGS FAILURE
- OVARIES DIAGRAM
- NIGHT BINGEING
- BINGE EATING WHY
- SWOLLEN ANKLES WHY
- HOW LONG HEAL DIVORCE
- DATING AFTER DIVORCE
- REMARRYING WHY
- DIVORCE DEPRESSION
- WATER WEIGHT GAIN
- HOW TO CLEANSE
- WHAT AGE IS MID LIFE
- DIVORCE BECOME MONK
- AUSTERITY MONK
- ARTIST MONKS
- ARTISTS WHO MEDITATE
- MEDITATION FERTILITY
- CAN I GET PREGNANT
- SINGLE WOMAN ADOPT
- MINT BLOATING REMEDY
- SIMPLE REMEDY PAIN
- WHAT IS BRAIN OCTANE

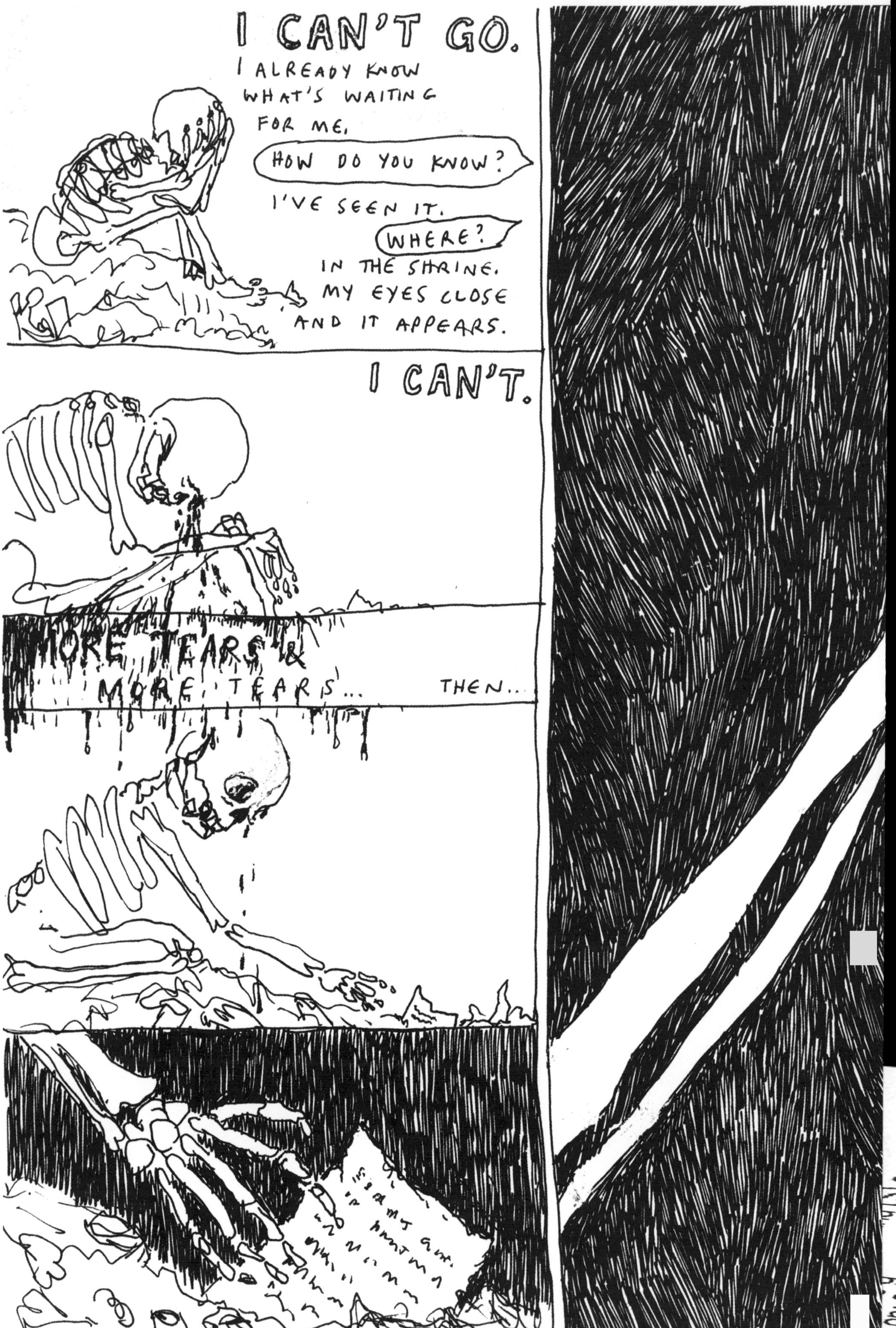
I CAN'T GO.
I ALREADY KNOW WHAT'S WAITING FOR ME.
HOW DO YOU KNOW?
I'VE SEEN IT.
WHERE?
IN THE SHRINE. MY EYES CLOSE AND IT APPEARS.
I CAN'T.
MORE TEARS & MORE TEARS...
THEN...

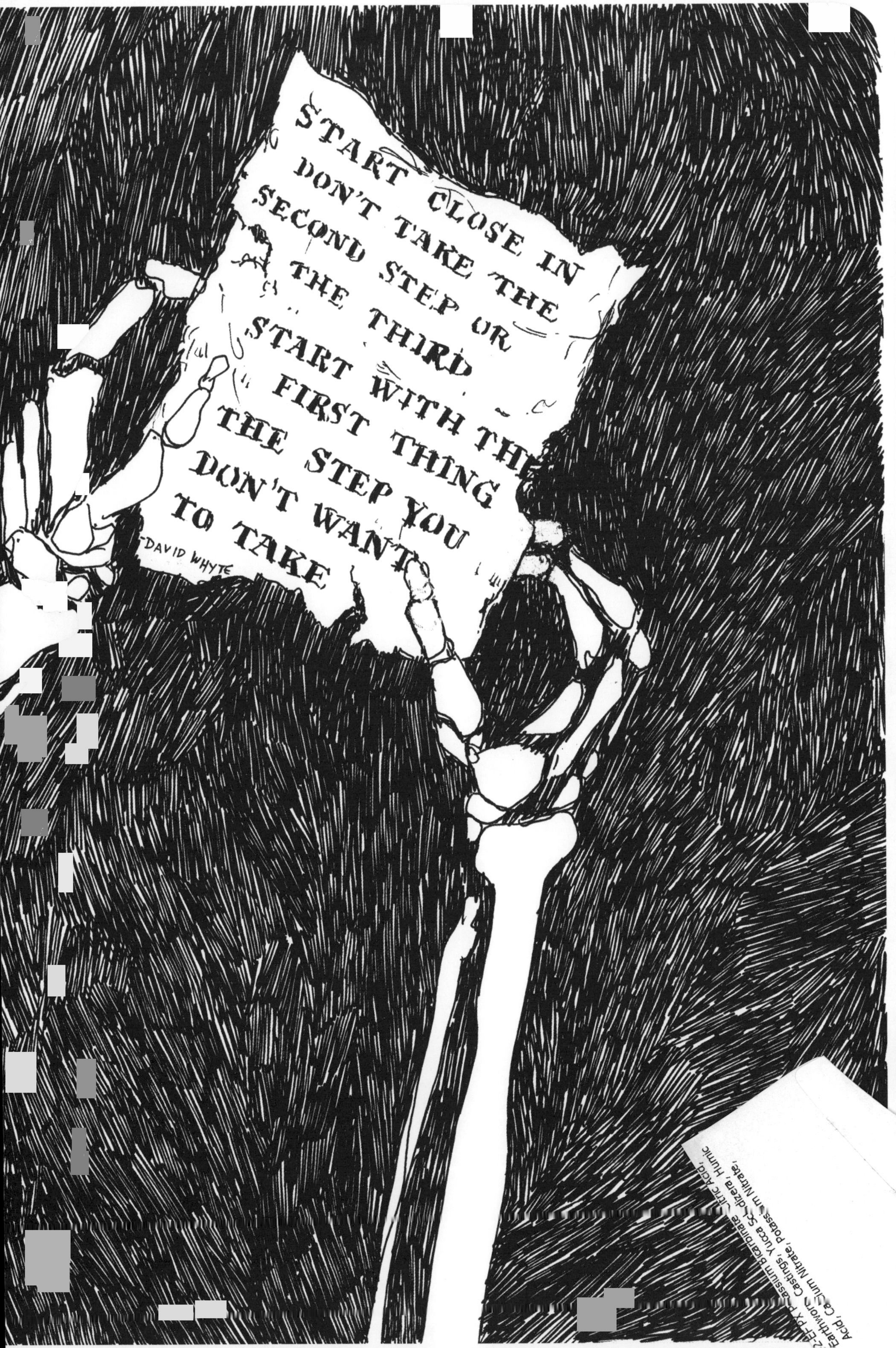
START CLOSE IN
DON'T TAKE THE
SECOND STEP OR
THE THIRD
START WITH THE
FIRST THING
THE STEP YOU
DON'T WANT
TO TAKE
-DAVID WHYTE

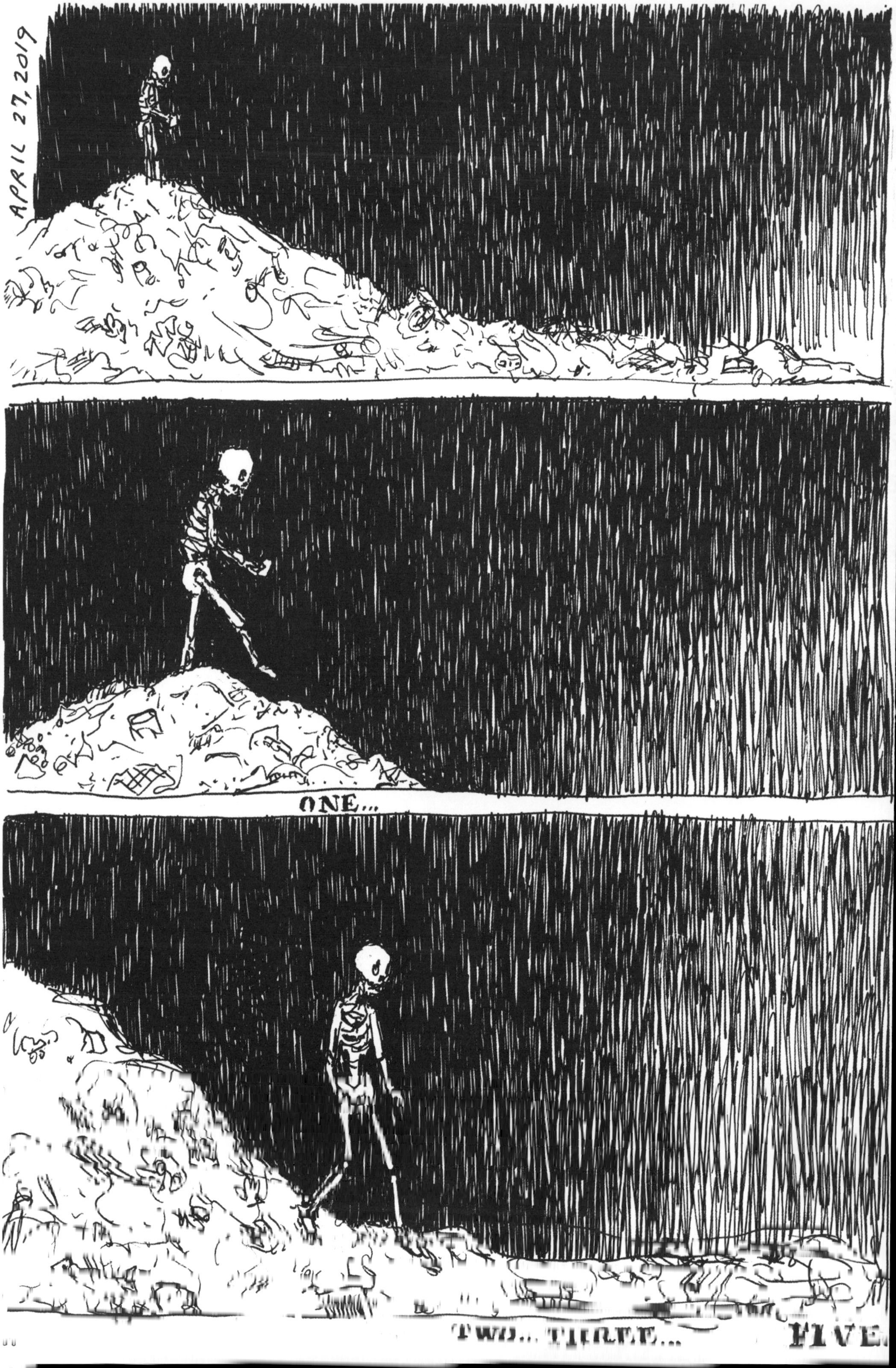
APRIL 27, 2019
ONE...
TWO... THREE...
FIVE

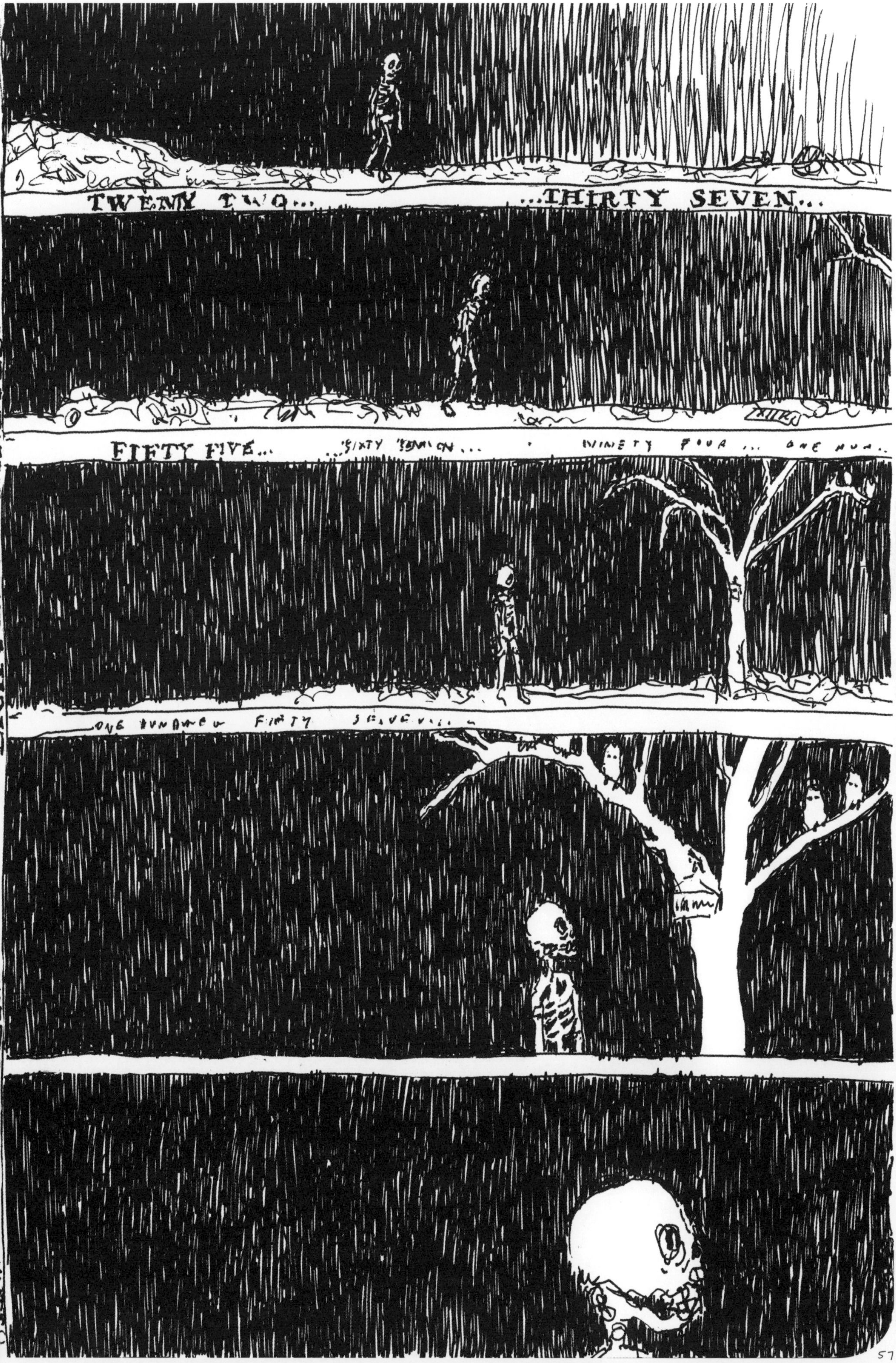
TWENTY TWO...
...THIRTY SEVEN...
FIFTY FIVE...
...SIXTY
NINETY FOUR ... ONE HUN..
ONE HUNDRED FIFTY SEVEN...

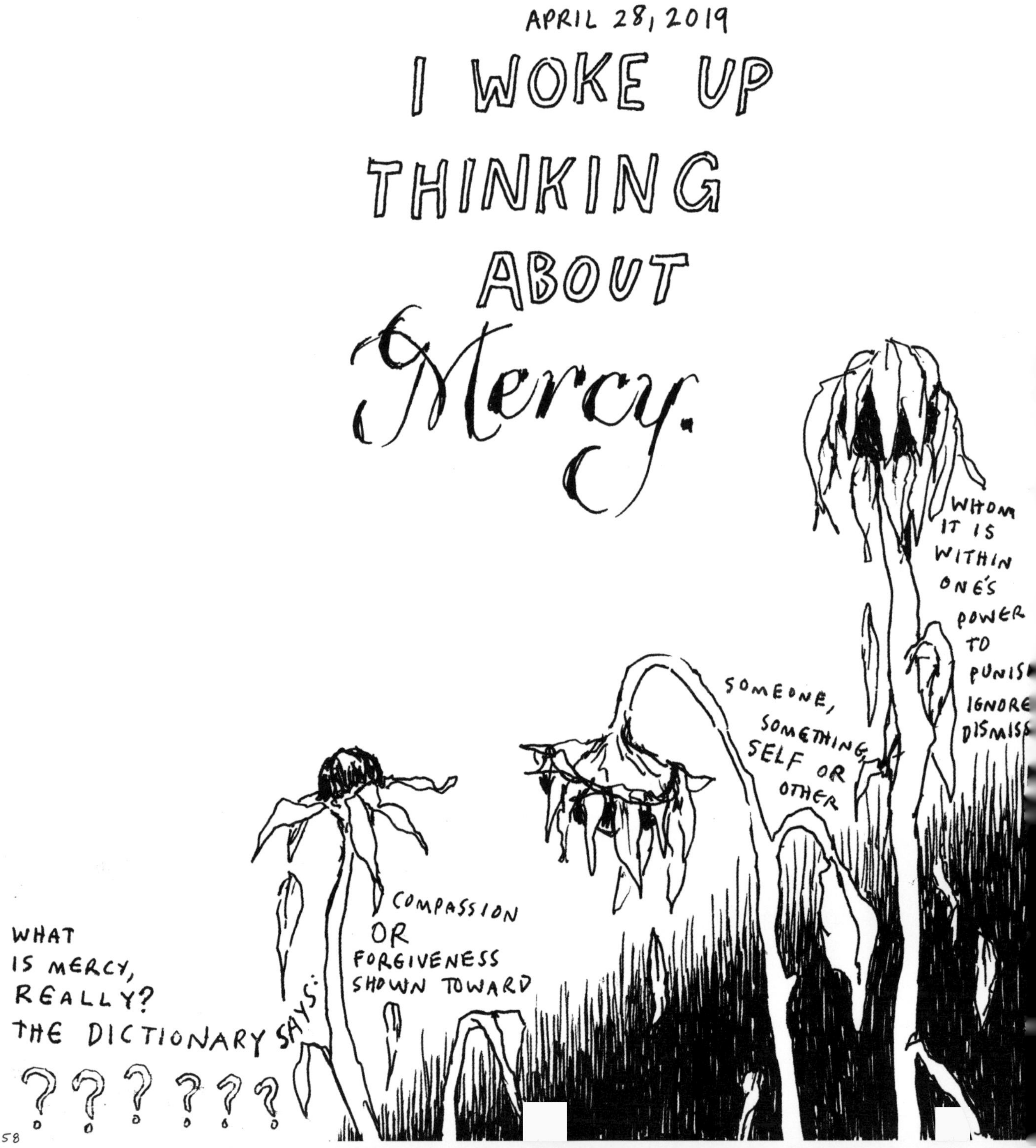
APRIL 28, 2019
I WOKE UP THINKING ABOUT
Mercy.
WHAT IS MERCY, REALLY?
THE DICTIONARY SAYS:
COMPASSION OR FORGIVENESS SHOWN TOWARD
SOMEONE, SOMETHING, SELF OR OTHER
WHOM IT IS WITHIN ONE'S POWER TO PUNIS
IGNORE
DISMISS
??????

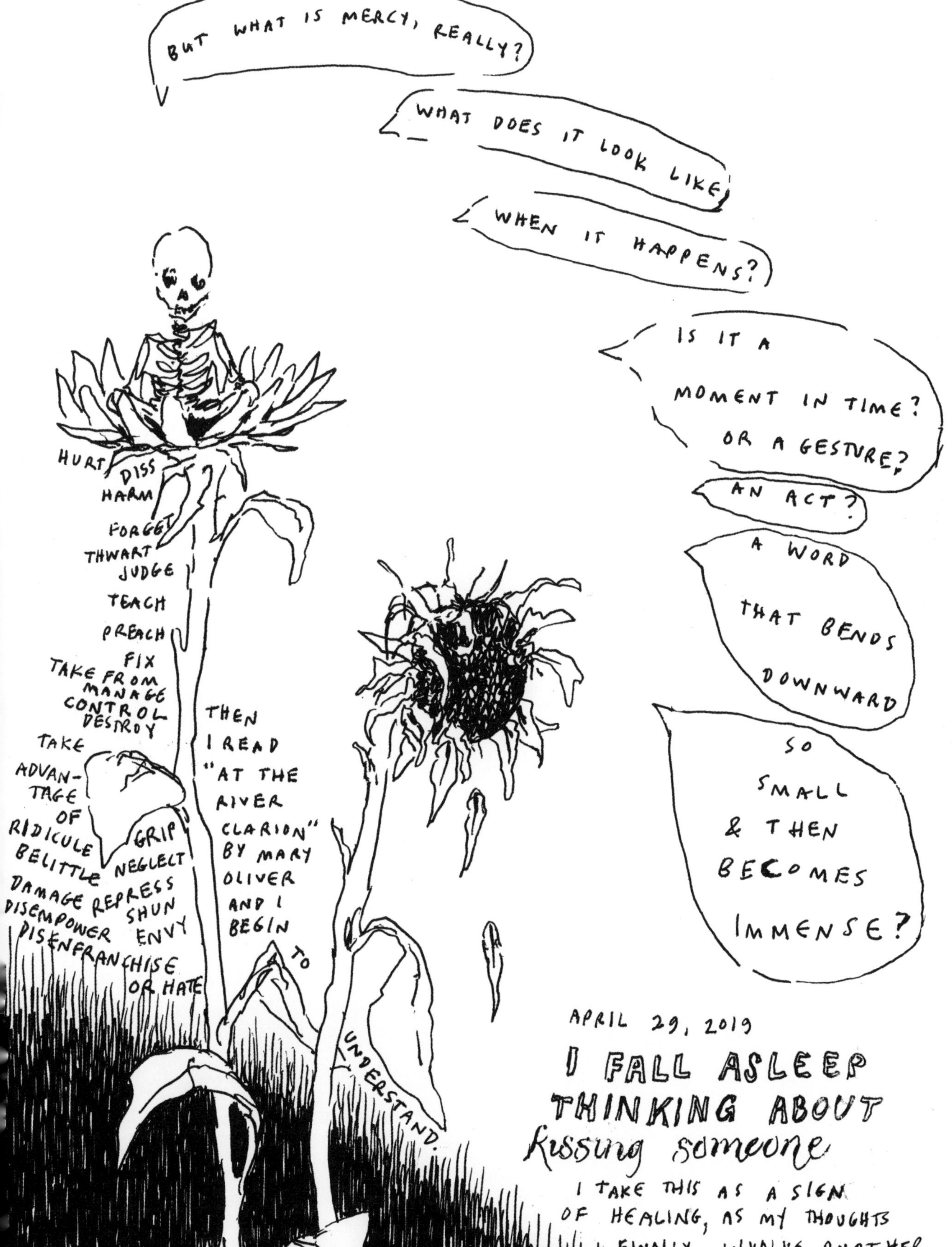
BUT WHAT IS MERCY, REALLY?
WHAT DOES IT LOOK LIKE
WHEN IT HAPPENS?
HURT
DISS
HARM
FORGET
THWART
JUDGE
TEACH
PREACH
FIX
TAKE FROM
MANAGE
CONTROL
DESTROY
TAKE ADVAN-TAGE OF
RIDICULE
GRIP
NEGLECT
BELITTLE
DAMAGE
REPRESS
SHUN
DISEMPOWER
ENVY
DISENFRANCHISE
OR HATE
THEN I READ "AT THE RIVER CLARION" BY MARY OLIVER AND I BEGIN TO UNDERSTAND.
IS IT A MOMENT IN TIME? OR A GESTURE?
AN ACT?
A WORD THAT BENDS DOWNWARD
SO SMALL & THEN BECOMES IMMENSE?
APRIL 29, 2019
I FALL ASLEEP THINKING ABOUT
kissing someone
I TAKE THIS AS A SIGN OF HEALING, AS MY THOUGHTS FINALLY INVOLVE ANOTHER PERSON BEYOND MYSELF.

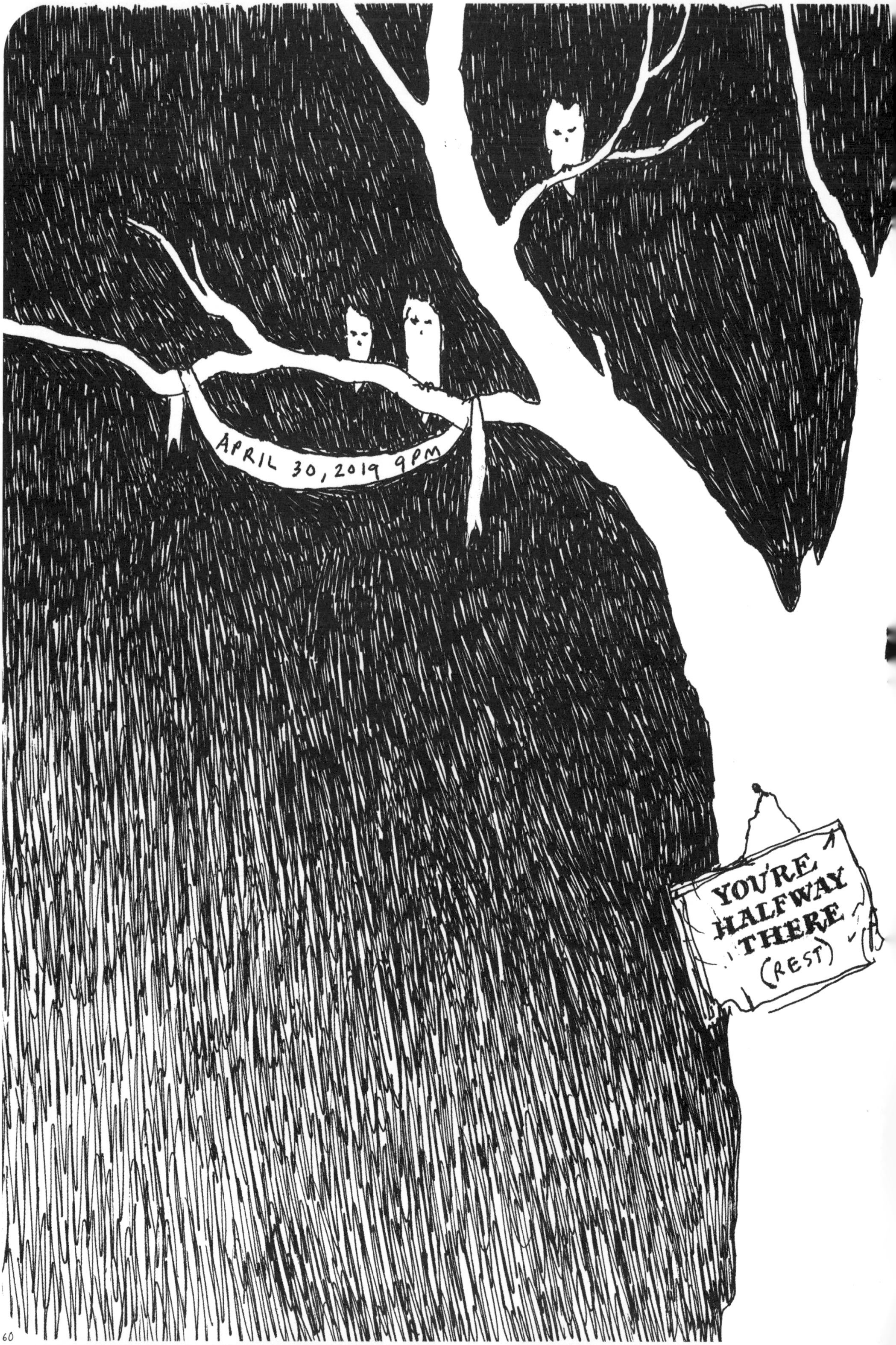
APRIL 30, 2019 9PM
YOU'RE HALFWAY THERE (REST)

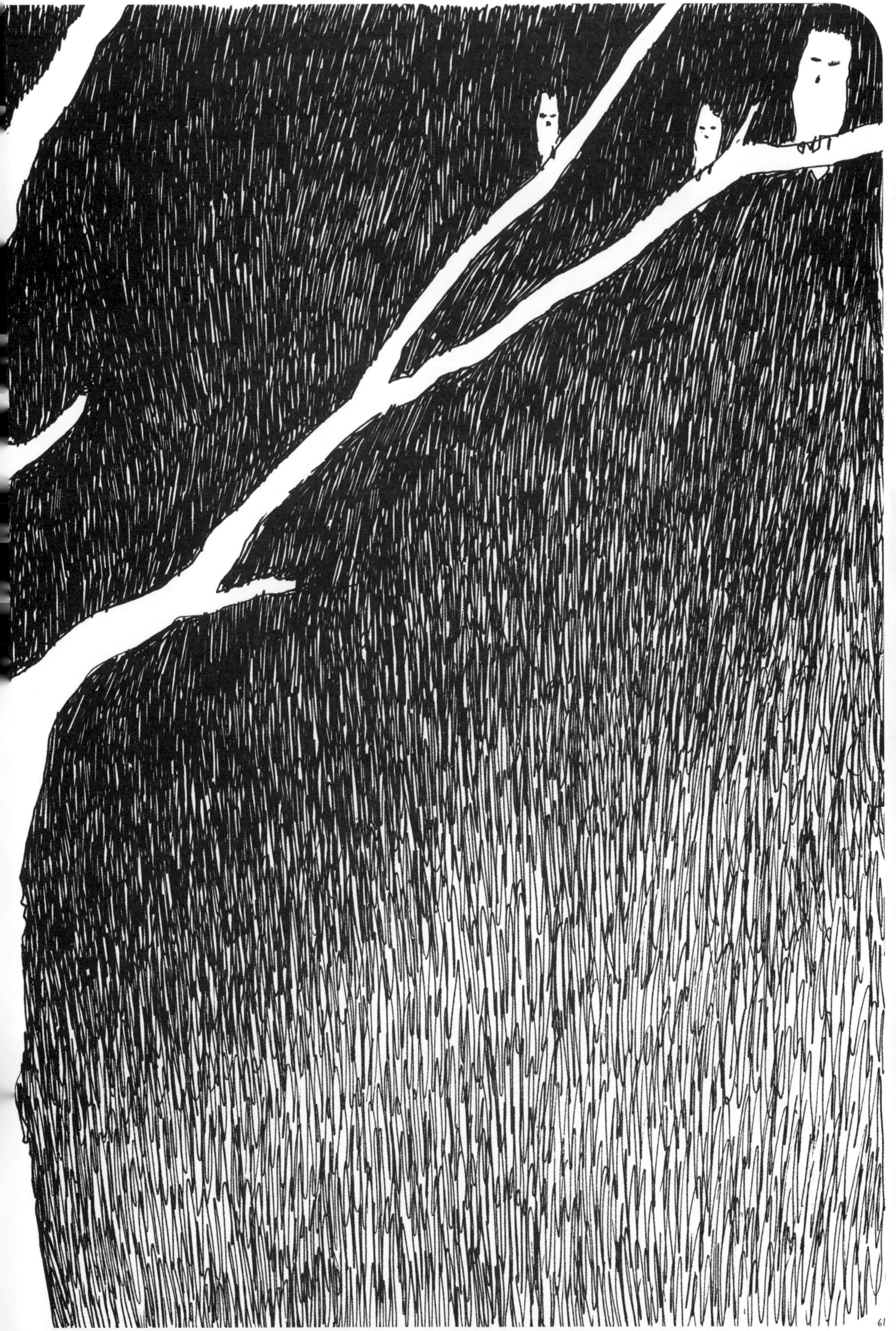

MAY 1, 2019
8am

AKA...

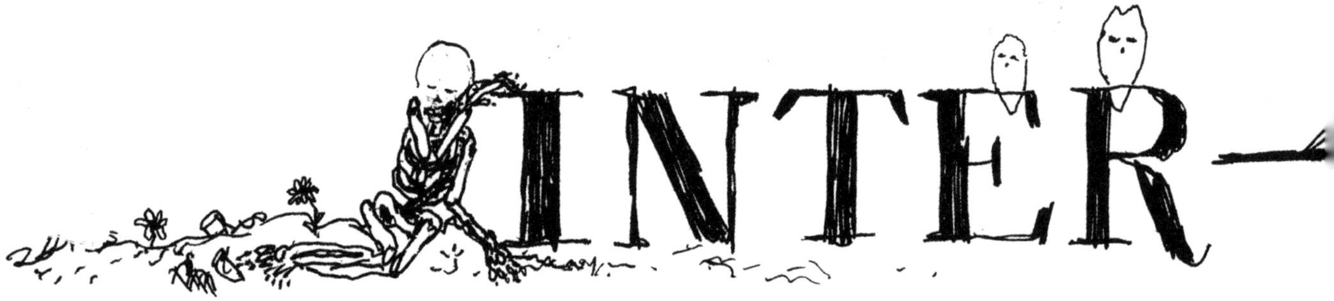
INTER-

IT IS THE FIRST DAY OF MAY. I REALIZE I HAVE GONE A
HAS TAKEN THE LIMELIGHT. I HAVEN'T SO MUCH CONTIN
AND ARTIST IN ME HAVE GRABBED HOLD OF THE COMPELLING I
ARE TOO GOOD TO PASS UP. THEY'RE ALREADY MY FRIENDS,
EXCITEMENT, I DO NOT WANT TO LOSE THE MOST PRECIOUS
STORY. AND SO, WHILE THE SKELETON TAKES A WELL-DESE
THIS MOMENT TO CATCH YOU UP ON THE GOINGS ON
AT THE ASHRAM WHERE I SLEEP... THE PLACE THAT FEELS THE

YOU MAY WANT TO START BY TEL

OK. I WILL. BUT FIRST I'LL GO GET A BOWL OF OATMEAL. I

OATMEAL? YES, OATMEAL. I KNOW WHAT YOU ARE THINKING.
LATER, WHEN I CAN BE HONEST. FOR NOW, THE BREAKFAST IS

BACK ALREADY? YES. **THAT LOOKS DELICIOUS**

IN IT. YES, I DID. **JUST LIKE HE USED TO.** I TOL

OKAY, I WILL. IT'S THAT COLOR THOUGH,

IT'S LIKE THE LIGHT OF A THOUSAND

EVERY SPOONFUL THE SOFT PETALS

BODY. WHAT HAPPENS WHEN THEY'RE INSIDE ME? **THEY**

MISSION

BIT ASTRAY WITH THE PROJECT. THE SKELETON'S STORY

ED THE PRACTICE OF "DRAWING THE FEELING." THE AUTHOR

GES, NARRATIVE, CHARACTERS... CAN YOU BLAME ME? THEY

ELPING ME ALONG THE WAY. BUT IN THE MIDST OF THE

GEM OF ALL... HONESTY. I HAVE TO TELL YOU THE TRUE

ED REST AT THE BASE OF THE WHITE TREE, I'LL TAKE

BACK HERE ON EARTH... IN THE MOUNTAINS OF PENNSYLVANIA...

MOST LIKE HOME... THE PLACE I NEVER PLANNED TO BE.

ING THEM ABOUT ALL THE CANCEL-

S BREAKFAST TIME HERE, THE DAY HAS BEGUN. LATIONS

UT IT'S NOT TIME YET. I WILL TELL THEM ABOUT OATMEAL

RM. AND SO I GO FILL MY BOWL.

I'M SURE IT WILL BE. YOU EVEN PUT TURMERIC

YOU, I'M NOT READY FOR THAT YET. GIVE ME TIME. PLEASE.

THAT UNMISTAKABLE GOLDEN GLOW.

SUNS. GO AHEAD CHILD, EAT. WITH

OF THE SUNFLOWER ENTER YOUR

SHINE.

CONT'D...

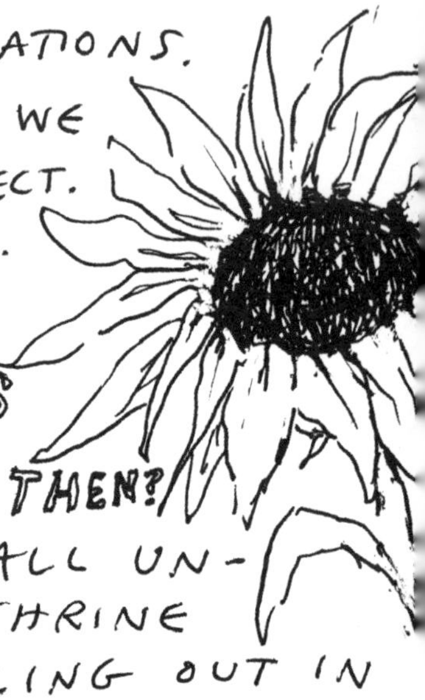

SO YES, LET'S START WITH THE CANCELLATIONS. LET'S ALSO START WITH THE FACT THAT WE ARE AT THE MIDWAY POINT OF THIS PROJECT. HALFWAY THROUGH THE 30 DAY PROMISE. TWO WEEKS TO GO. THEN IT'S DONE. **DO YOU THINK THE SKELETON'S STORY WILL BE COMPLETE BY THEN?** I'M NOT SURE. MY GUESS IS YES. IT'S ALL UNFOLDING QUICKLY NOW. I SIT IN THE SHRINE AND SEE SCENES FROM THE STORY SPILLING OUT IN FRONT OF ME. THE SCENE WITH THE CHAIR, THE TABLE, THE ROSE... IT'S ALL COMING FORWARD NOW IT'S A MATTER OF STAYING HONEST, STEADY, AND HOPING THE REST OF MY LIFE DOES NOT FALL APART WHILE I DOODLE FLOWERS AND BONES EVERY SPARE MINUTE OF EVERY WAKING HOUR. **AH... YES... THAT REMINDS ME... THE CANCELLATIONS THE OTHER LIFE. THE ONE THAT'S FALLING APART AS I MAKE THESE LETTERS DANCE ACROSS the page**

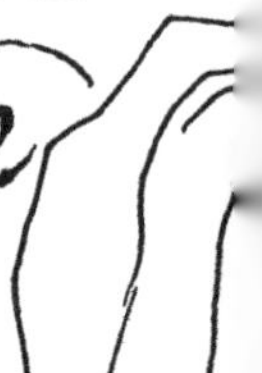

WELL, FOR STARTERS, I WAS SUPPOSED TO BE IN LONDON RIGHT NOW. AT A WORKSHOP I'VE BEEN LOOKING FORWARD TO FOR MONTHS. BUT I DIDN'T GET ON THE PLANE. **ARE YOU RECOGNIZING A PATTERN HERE?** YES. I AM. AND THOUGH YOU COULD CALL IT CANCELLING, OR... BAILING, FAILING, FALLING, QUITTING, FUCKING UP, DISAPPOINTING, NOT SHOWING UP, FLAKING, SABOTAGING, GHOSTING, BIFFING, RISKING ONE'S CAREER... OR EVEN

LETTING EVERYONE DOWN...

I'VE DECIDED TO CALL IT SOMETHING ELSE ENTIRELY:
RADICAL SIMPLIFICATION.

SPACIOUSNESS

AS PRIORITY.

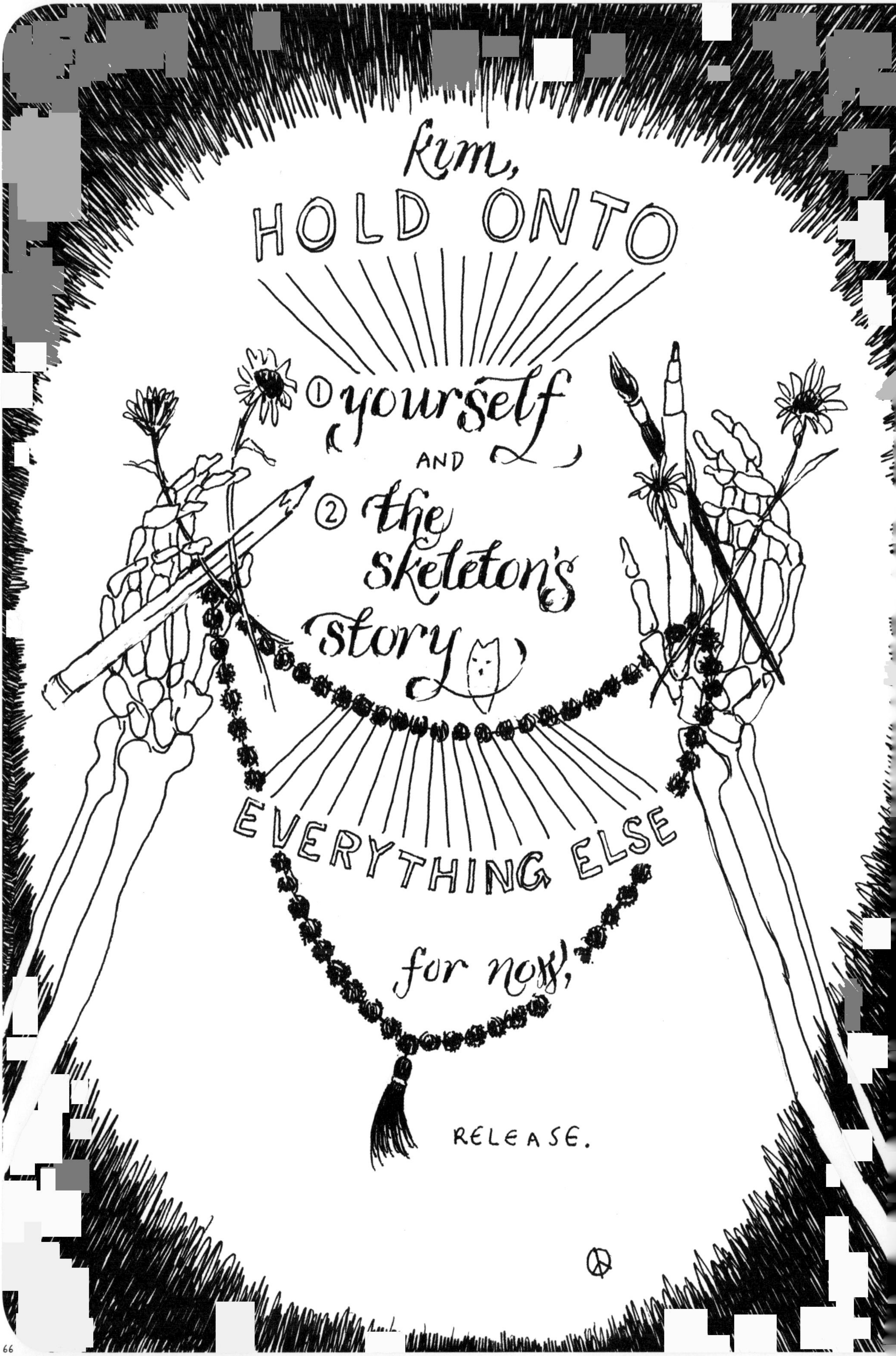
kim,
HOLD ONTO
① yourself
AND
② the skeleton's story
EVERYTHING ELSE
for now,
RELEASE.

BUT HOW COULD YOU? HOW DARE YOU?
YOU HAVE TO KEEP _____ OR ELSE
(FILL IN BLANK)
_____. AND IF YOU DON'T _____
(FILL IN BLANK)   (FILL IN BLANK)
THEN YOU'LL NEVER _____,
(FILL IN BLANK)
WHICH MEANS _____ WILL NEVER
(NAME OF PERSON)
_____ YOU. PLUS, IF YOU DON'T
(VERB)
GET _____ SOON, THE _____ IS
(FILL IN BLANK)   (RESOURCE)
GOING TO RUN OUT BEFORE YOU'RE
ABLE TO FINALLY _____. SO IF YOU
(SOMETHING GOOD)
REALLY WANT TO _____ SOMEDAY
(BIGGEST DREAM)
THEN YOU HAVE TO KEEP _____
(VERB ENDING IN -ING)
UNTIL _____ EVEN IF YOU'RE _____.
(SYNONYM FOR FOREVER)   (FEELING)
IT'S NOT TIME FOR _____. IT WILL
(FILL IN BLANK)
BE SOON. IF YOU STOP NOW, YOU'LL
NEVER EVER GET THERE. PLUS, YOU'RE
NOT REALLY _____. YOU'RE _____.
(FILL IN BLANK)   (FILL IN BLANK)
EVERYONE KNOWS IT, ESPECIALLY _____
(NAME OF PERSON)
SO JUST _____. YOU CAN'T _____.
(FILL IN BLANK)   (FILL IN BLANK)
YOU'RE A REAL PERSON WITH A REAL
LIFE NOT A SKELETON WITH A BROKEN
HEART, SO FORGET ALL THIS AND JUST
_____ UNTIL YOU _____. THERE'S
(LL IN BLANK)   (FILL IN BLANK)
NO OTHER WAY, I PROMISE. with love, **YOUR EGO**

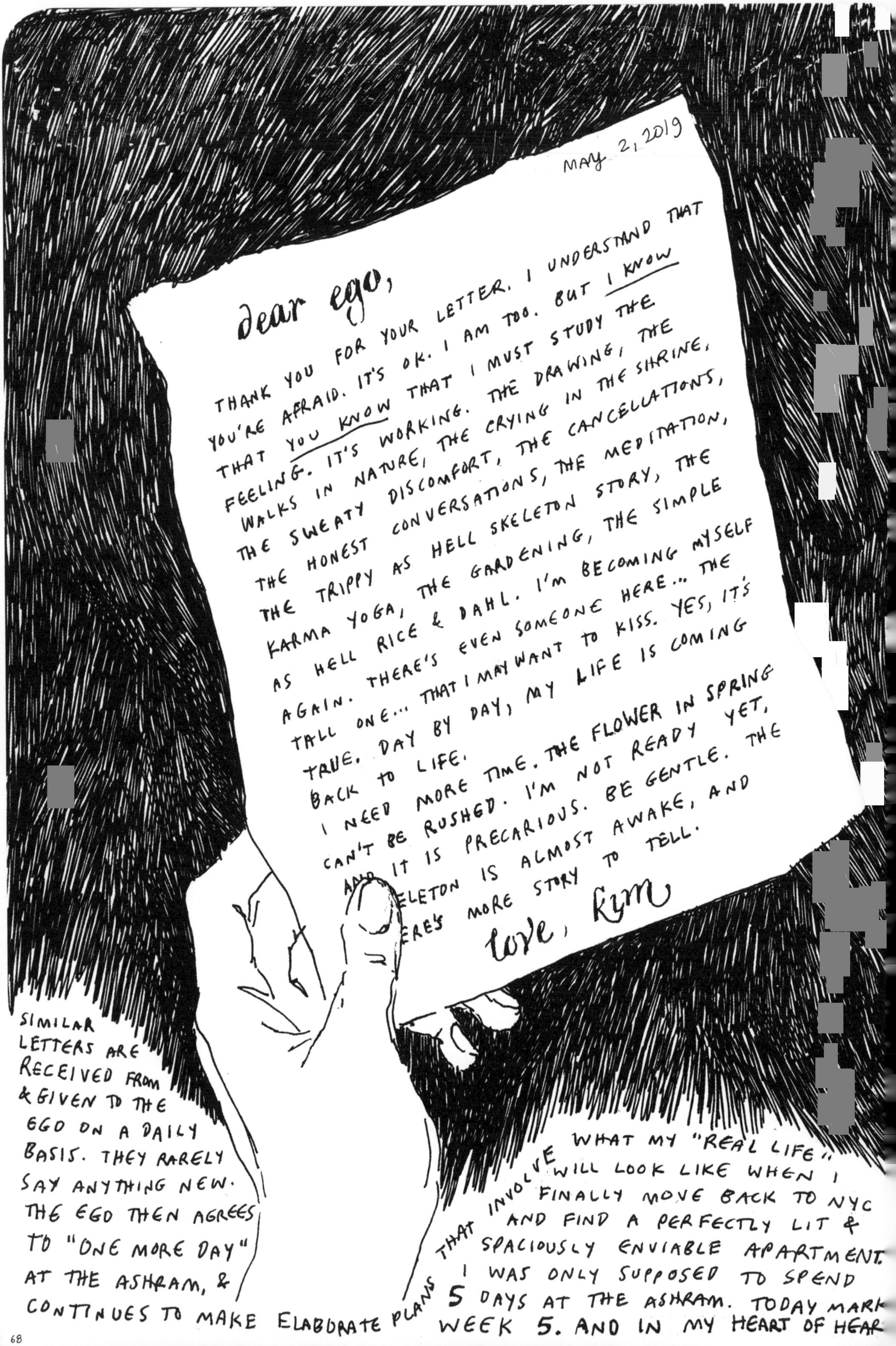
MAY 2, 2019
dear ego,
THANK YOU FOR YOUR LETTER. I UNDERSTAND THAT YOU'RE AFRAID. IT'S OK. I AM TOO. BUT I KNOW THAT YOU KNOW THAT I MUST STUDY THE FEELING. IT'S WORKING. THE DRAWING, THE WALKS IN NATURE, THE CRYING IN THE SHRINE, THE SWEATY DISCOMFORT, THE CANCELLATIONS, THE HONEST CONVERSATIONS, THE MEDITATION, THE TRIPPY AS HELL SKELETON STORY, THE KARMA YOGA, THE GARDENING, THE SIMPLE AS HELL RICE & DAHL. I'M BECOMING MYSELF AGAIN. THERE'S EVEN SOMEONE HERE... THE TALL ONE... THAT I MAY WANT TO KISS. YES, IT'S TRUE. DAY BY DAY, MY LIFE IS COMING BACK TO LIFE.
I NEED MORE TIME. THE FLOWER IN SPRING CAN'T BE RUSHED. I'M NOT READY YET, AND IT IS PRECARIOUS. BE GENTLE. THE ELETON IS ALMOST AWAKE, AND ERE'S MORE STORY TO TELL.
love, Kym
SIMILAR LETTERS ARE RECEIVED FROM & GIVEN TO THE EGO ON A DAILY BASIS. THEY RARELY SAY ANYTHING NEW. THE EGO THEN AGREES TO "ONE MORE DAY" AT THE ASHRAM, & CONTINUES TO MAKE ELABORATE PLANS
THAT INVOLVE WHAT MY "REAL LIFE" WILL LOOK LIKE WHEN I FINALLY MOVE BACK TO NYC AND FIND A PERFECTLY LIT & SPACIOUSLY ENVIABLE APARTMENT.
I WAS ONLY SUPPOSED TO SPEND 5 DAYS AT THE ASHRAM. TODAY MARK WEEK 5. AND IN MY HEART OF HEAR

A FEW TELLTALE SIGNS THAT I'M HEADED IN THE RIGHT DIRECTION

① I GOT MY PERIOD FOR THE FIRST TIME IN FIVE MONTHS.

② SLEEPING THROUGH THE NIGHT

③ MORE JOKES

④ PICKING MORE FLOWERS

⑤ UNFOLLOWED TILDA SWINTON (THIS REQUIRES EXPLANATION). TILDA, I HAVE ALWAYS LOVED YOUR LOOK. YOU ARE, IN FACT, MY STYLE ICON. HOWEVER, THE CHEEKBONES ARE TOO MUCH FOR ME. EVERYTIME I SEE THEM I JUDGE MY OWN. SO FOR NOW, I LOVE YOU FROM AFAR, LETTING YOU BE YOU & ME BE ME. HOW ABOUT YOU'RE MY GUARDIAN ANGEL... NOT MY GOAL?

*OH AND THE CELESTIAL LIGHT DREAM!

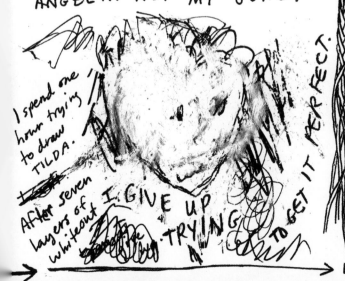

I spend one hour trying to draw TILDA.

After seven layers of whiteout, I GIVE UP TRYING to GET IT PERFECT.

→ I SECRETLY DREAD MY DEPARTURE.

FOR YOUR CONSIDERATION:
THE SPECTRUM OF DIS-ORDERLY EATING

the UNCONSCIOUS EATER BECOMES...

(slippery slope)

- AWARE
- THOUGHTFUL
- MINDFUL
- SELECTIVE
- CONSCIOUS
- DELIBERATE
- INTUITIVE
- SENSITIVE
- HEALTHY
- PICKY
- CLEAN
- FINICKY
- DISCERNING

"BALANCED"

(slippery slope)

- JUDGMENTAL
- SKEPTICAL
- CRITICAL ·PLANNING
- REGRETFUL ·GUILTY
- RESTRICTED ·COMPARATIVE
- SELECTIVE ·SAME
- VIGILANT
- RIGID ·PREOCCUPIED ·FOCUSED
- CONTROLLING ·ASHAMED
- HYPERVIGILANT
- AFRAID ·FIXATED
- PARANOID ·CRAVING
- CLEANSING ·SCHEMING
- FASTING ·HIDING
- BINGEING
- PURGING
- STARVING
- CONSUMED BY FOOD ITSELF

···GREY AREA···

EATING DISORDER

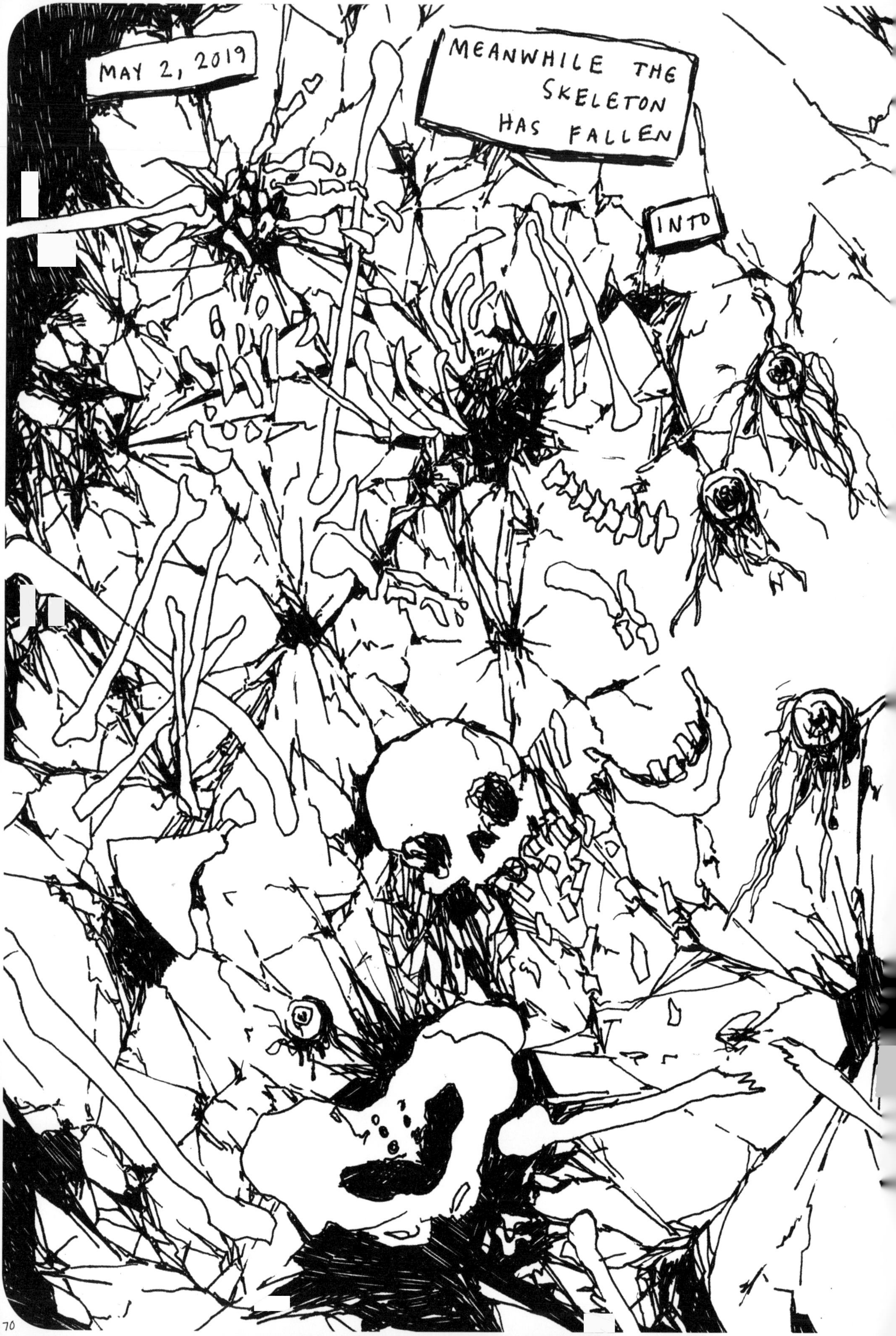
MAY 2, 2019
MEANWHILE THE SKELETON HAS FALLEN
INTO

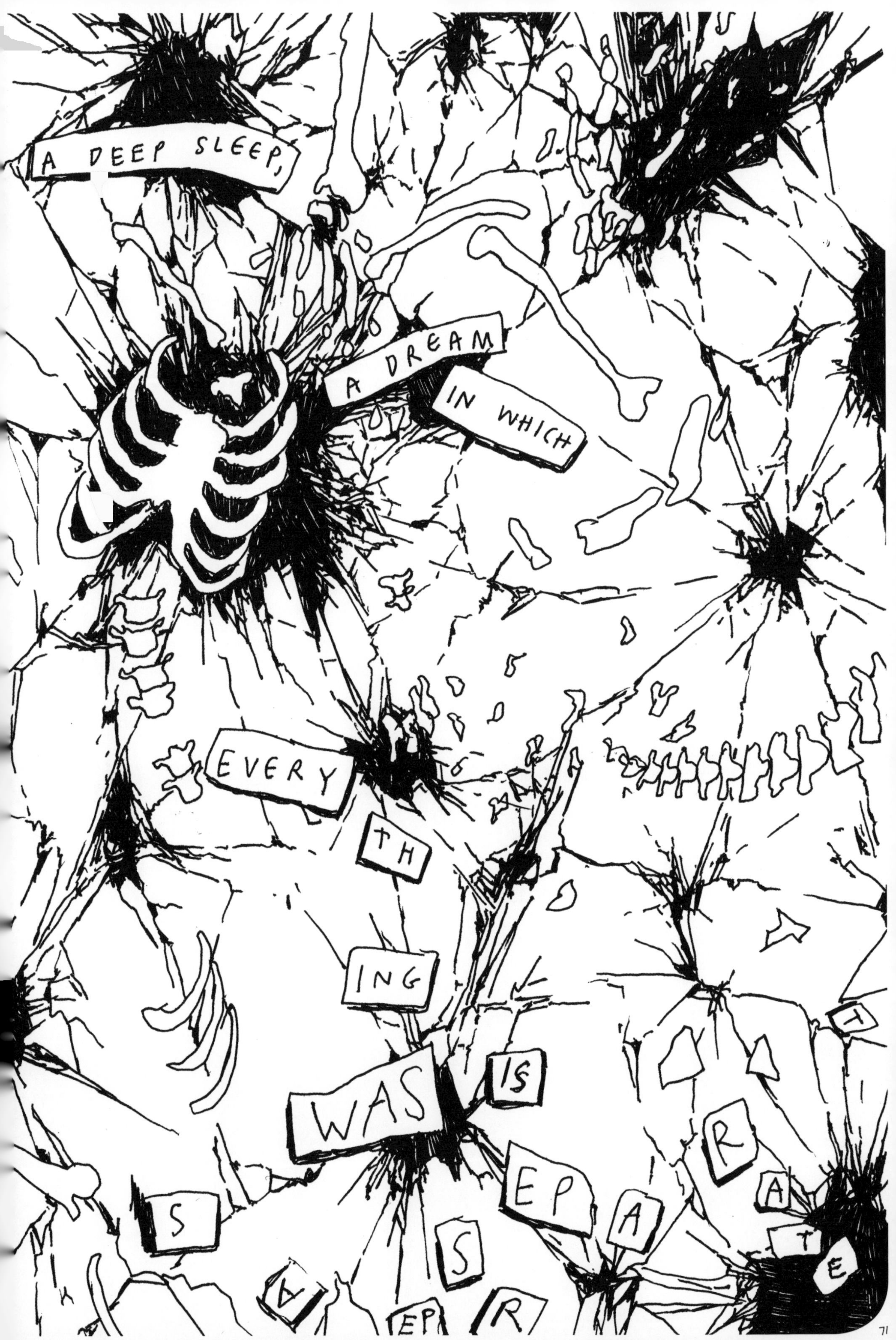
A DEEP SLEEP,
A DREAM
IN WHICH
EVERY
TH
ING
WAS
IS
S
EP
A
R
A
T
E
S
EP
R

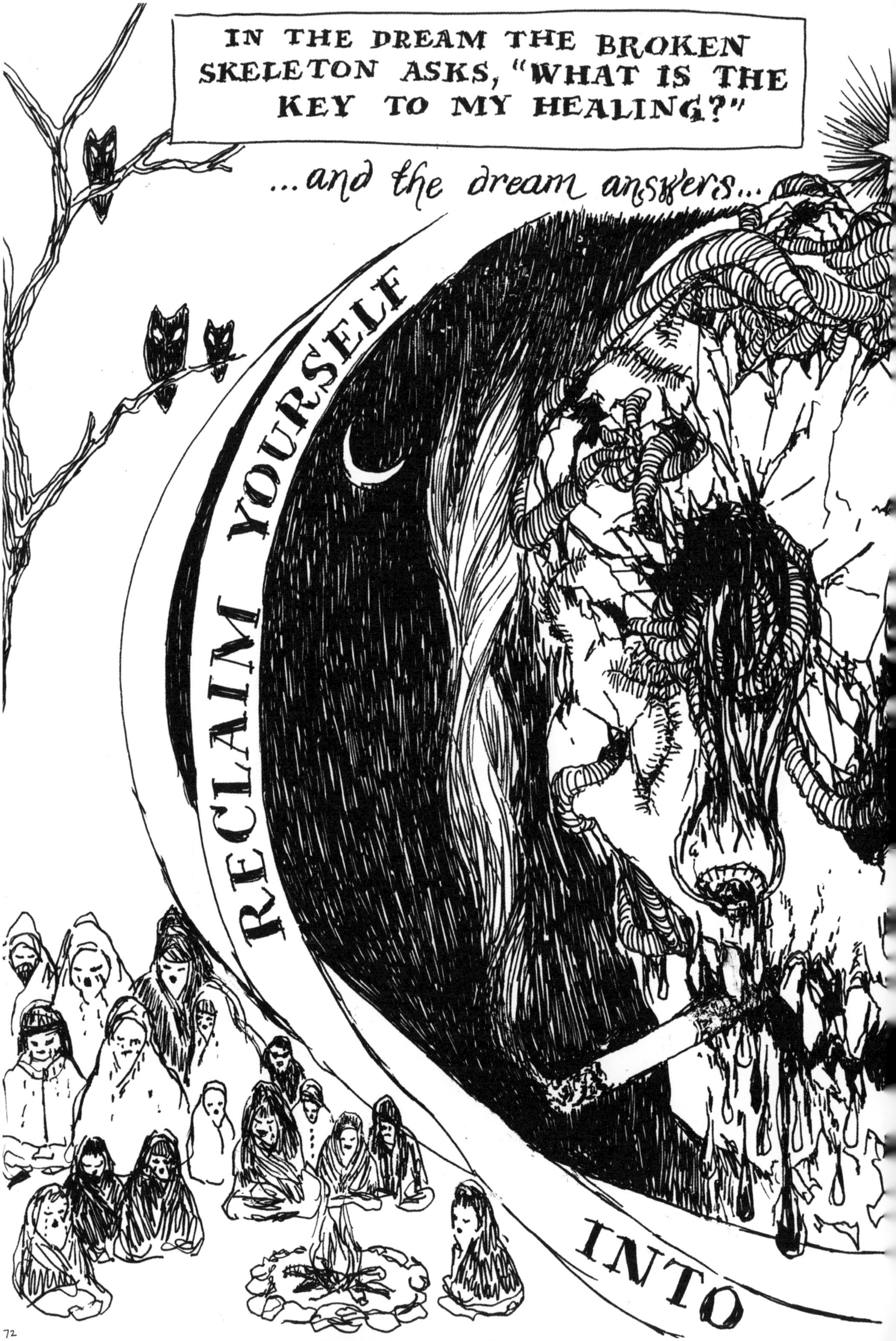
IN THE DREAM THE BROKEN SKELETON ASKS, "WHAT IS THE KEY TO MY HEALING?"
...and the dream answers...
RECLAIM YOURSELF
INTO

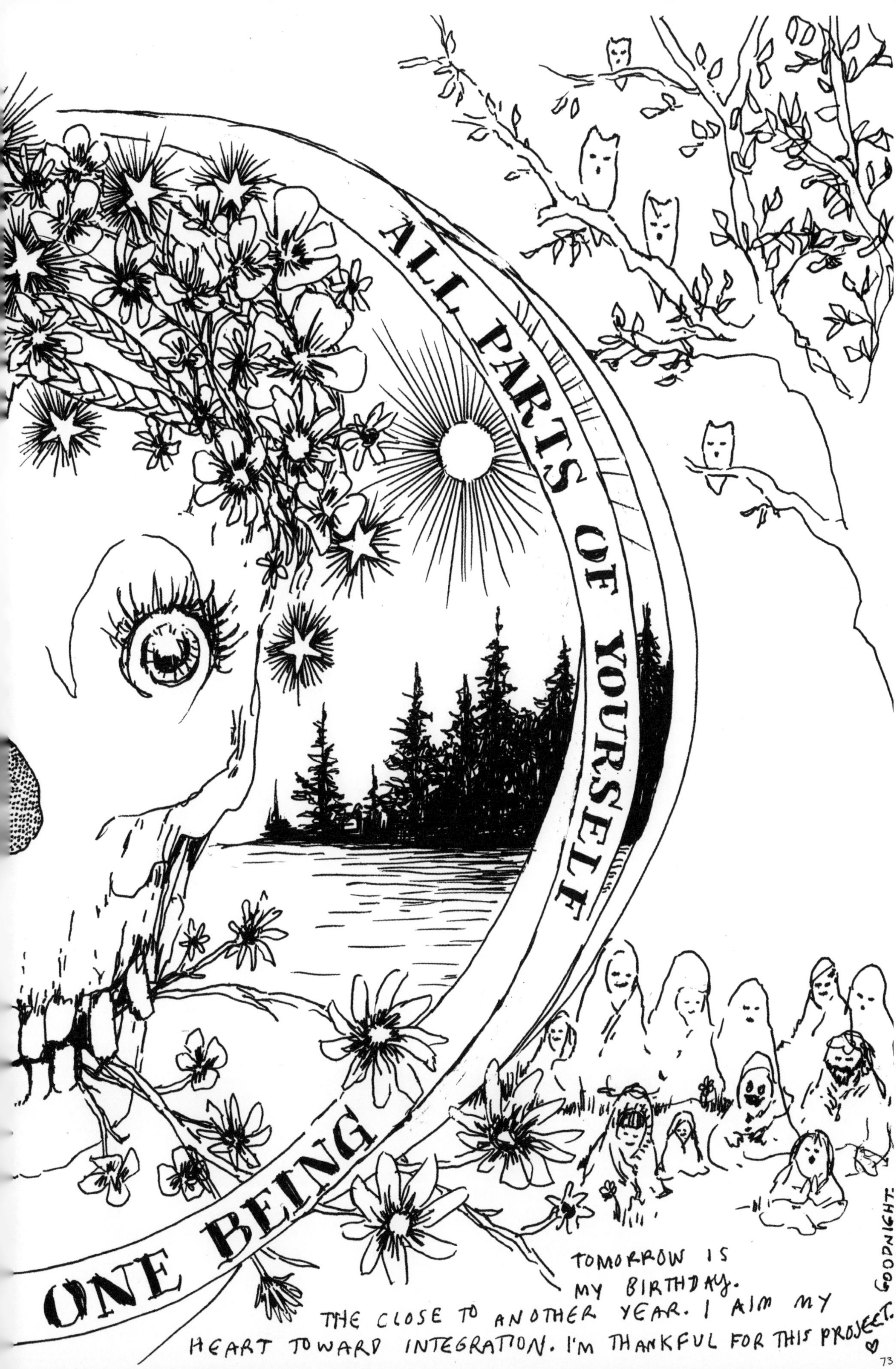
ALL PARTS OF YOURSELF
ONE BEING
TOMORROW IS MY BIRTHDAY.
THE CLOSE TO ANOTHER YEAR. I AIM MY HEART TOWARD INTEGRATION. I'M THANKFUL FOR THIS PROJECT.
GOODNIGHT.

May 3, 2019
7am

TODAY IS MY 39TH BIRTHDAY

I THOUGHT MY LIFE, BY THIS POINT, WOULD LOOK MUCH DIFFERENT THAN IT DOES. I LIVE, FOR THE TIME BEING, AT AN ASHRAM. ~~[scribbled out]~~ SINGLE WOMAN. SINGLE BED.

I'LL STOP THERE.
for now.
IT IS TIME
TO GET
BACK
TO
THE
STORY.

GREEN JUICE ♥

② THE JAR OF FRESH JUICE THAT WAS LEFT AT MY DOOR.

I SHOULD MENTION THOUGH... ~~THAT~~ A FEW OF THE GIFTS... THAT FOUND THEIR WAY TO ME...

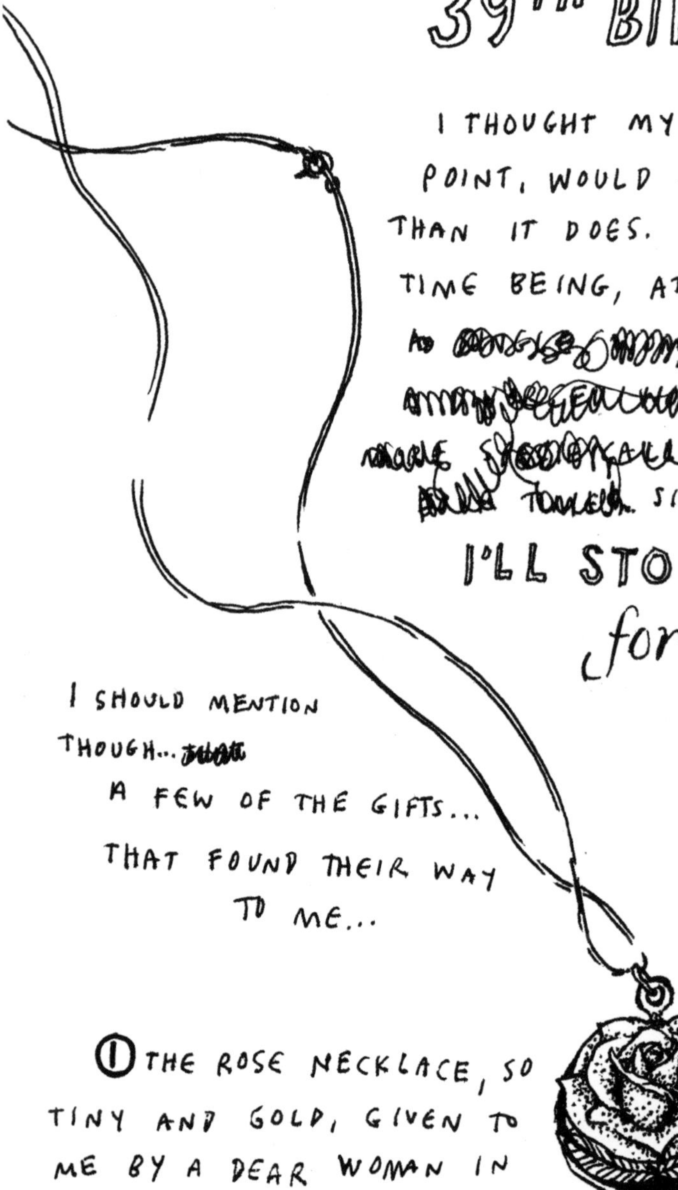

① THE ROSE NECKLACE, SO TINY AND GOLD, GIVEN TO ME BY A DEAR WOMAN IN HER SIXTIES THAT I WALK WITH HERE SOME MORNINGS. SHE GOT IT ON A PILGRIMAGE SHE TOOK IN HONOR OF THE DIVINE MOTHER, FOUND IN A TEMPLE IN EASTERN EUROPE. SHE HAD THREE MISCARRIAGES WHEN SHE WAS YOUNG. NEVER HAD CHILDREN. I SEE HER & HER HUSBAND OF 40+ YEARS IN THE SHRINE, EYES CLOSED, SIDE BY SIDE. I WEAR THE NECKLACE NOW AND I WILL EVERY DAY.

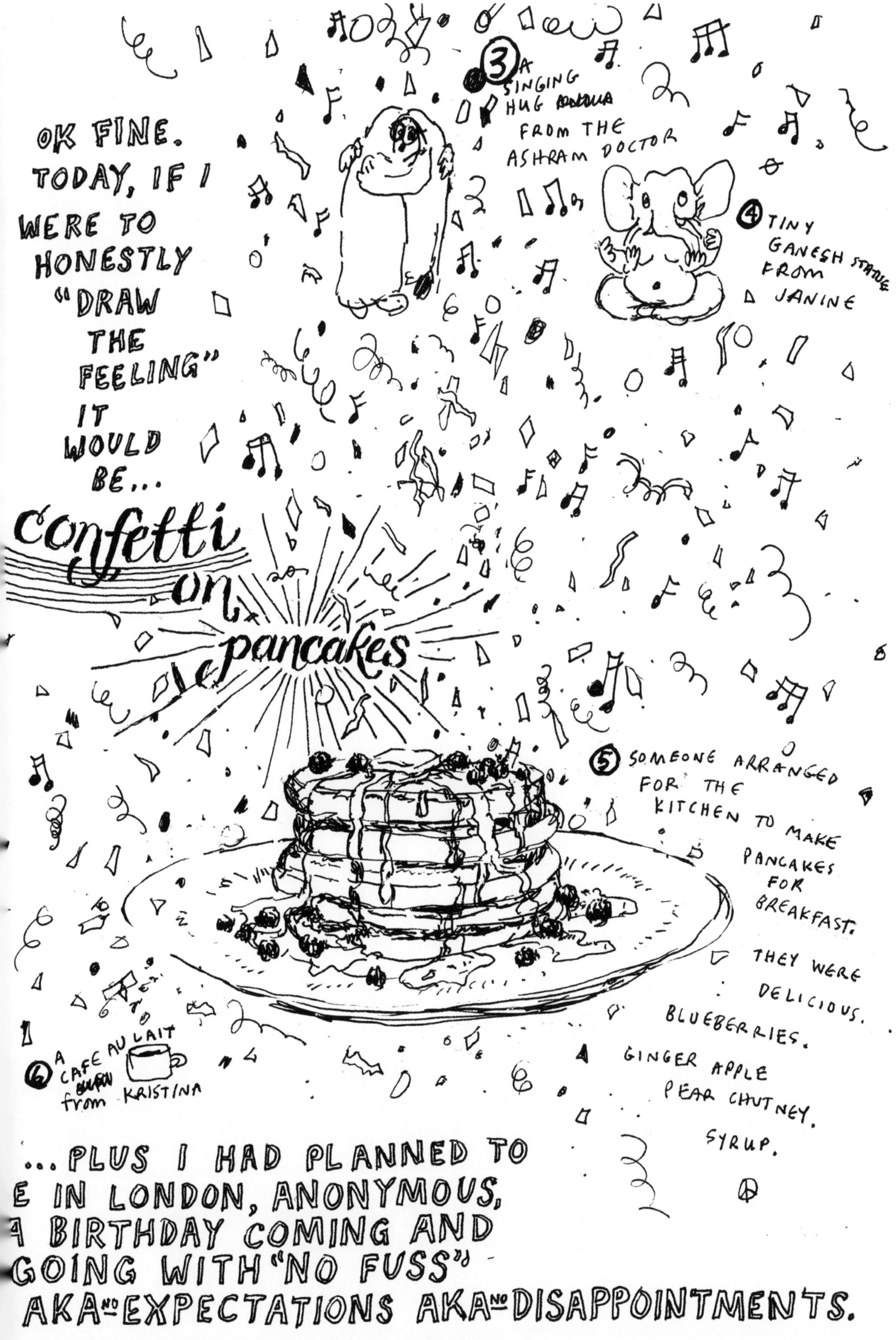

OK FINE. TODAY, IF I WERE TO HONESTLY "DRAW THE FEELING" IT WOULD BE...
confetti on pancakes
③ A SINGING HUG FROM THE ASHRAM DOCTOR
④ TINY GANESH STATUE FROM JANINE
⑤ SOMEONE ARRANGED FOR THE KITCHEN TO MAKE PANCAKES FOR BREAKFAST.
THEY WERE DELICIOUS.
BLUEBERRIES.
GINGER APPLE PEAR CHUTNEY.
SYRUP.
⑥ A CAFE AU LAIT from KRISTINA
...PLUS I HAD PLANNED TO
E IN LONDON, ANONYMOUS,
A BIRTHDAY COMING AND
GOING WITH "NO FUSS"
AKA NO EXPECTATIONS AKA NO DISAPPOINTMENTS.

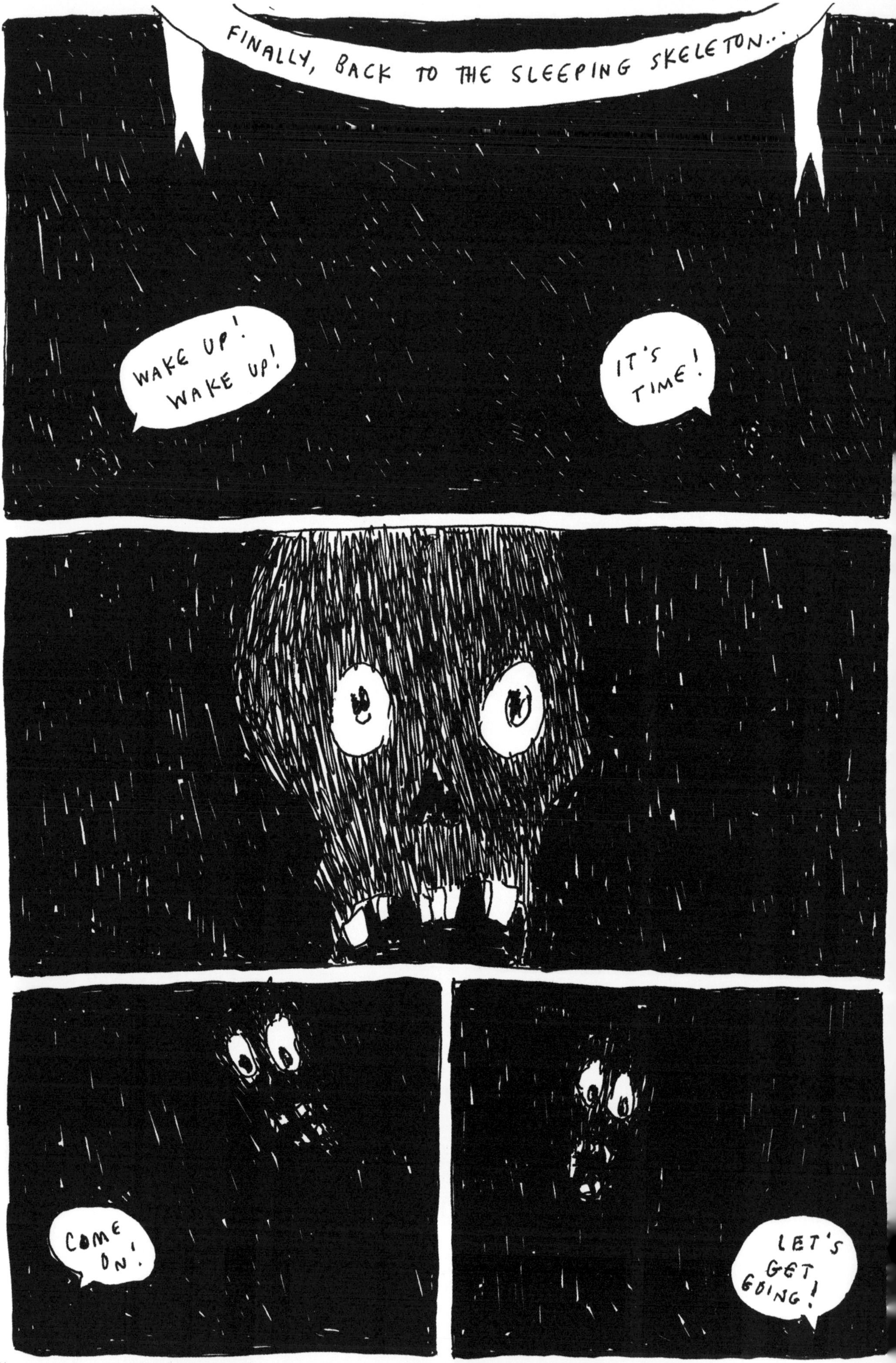
FINALLY, BACK TO THE SLEEPING SKELETON...
WAKE UP! WAKE UP!
IT'S TIME!
COME ON!
LET'S GET GOING!

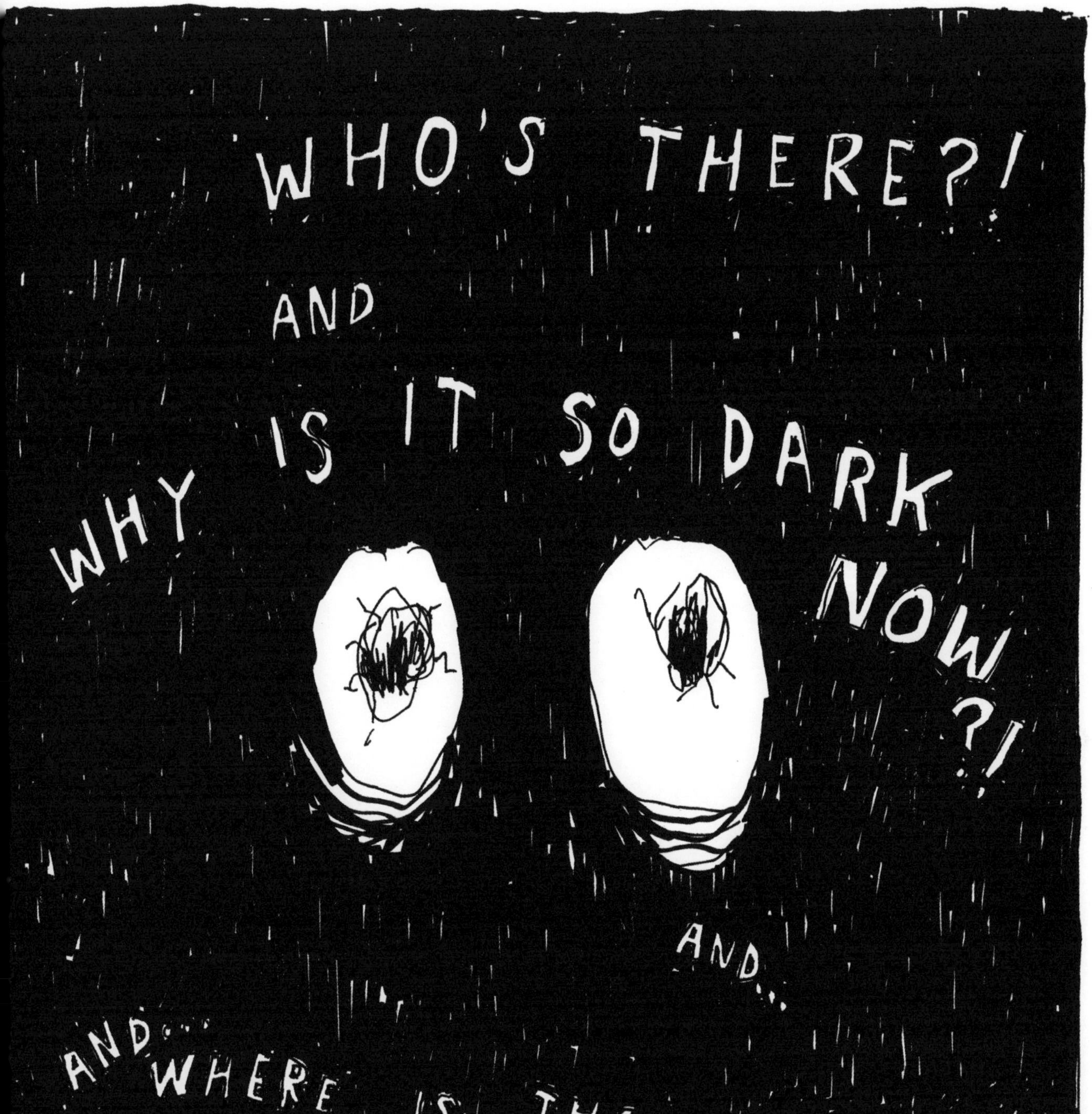
WHO'S THERE?!
AND
WHY IS IT SO DARK NOW?!
AND...
AND... WHERE IS THE TREE?!!

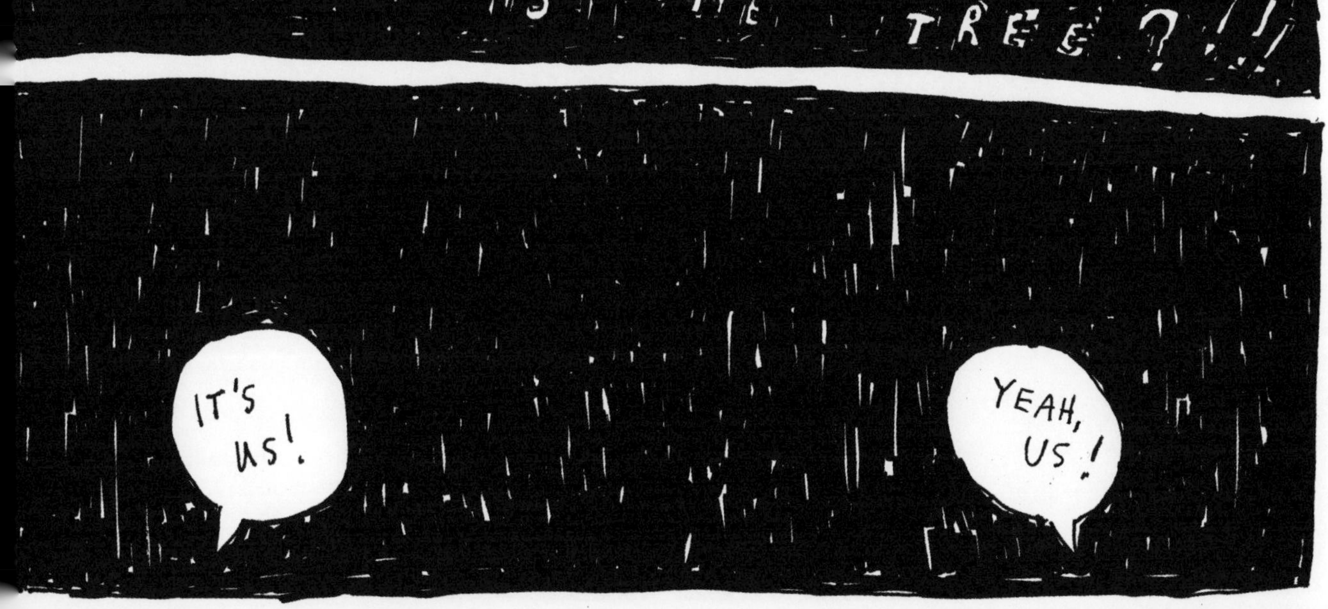
IT'S US!
YEAH, US!

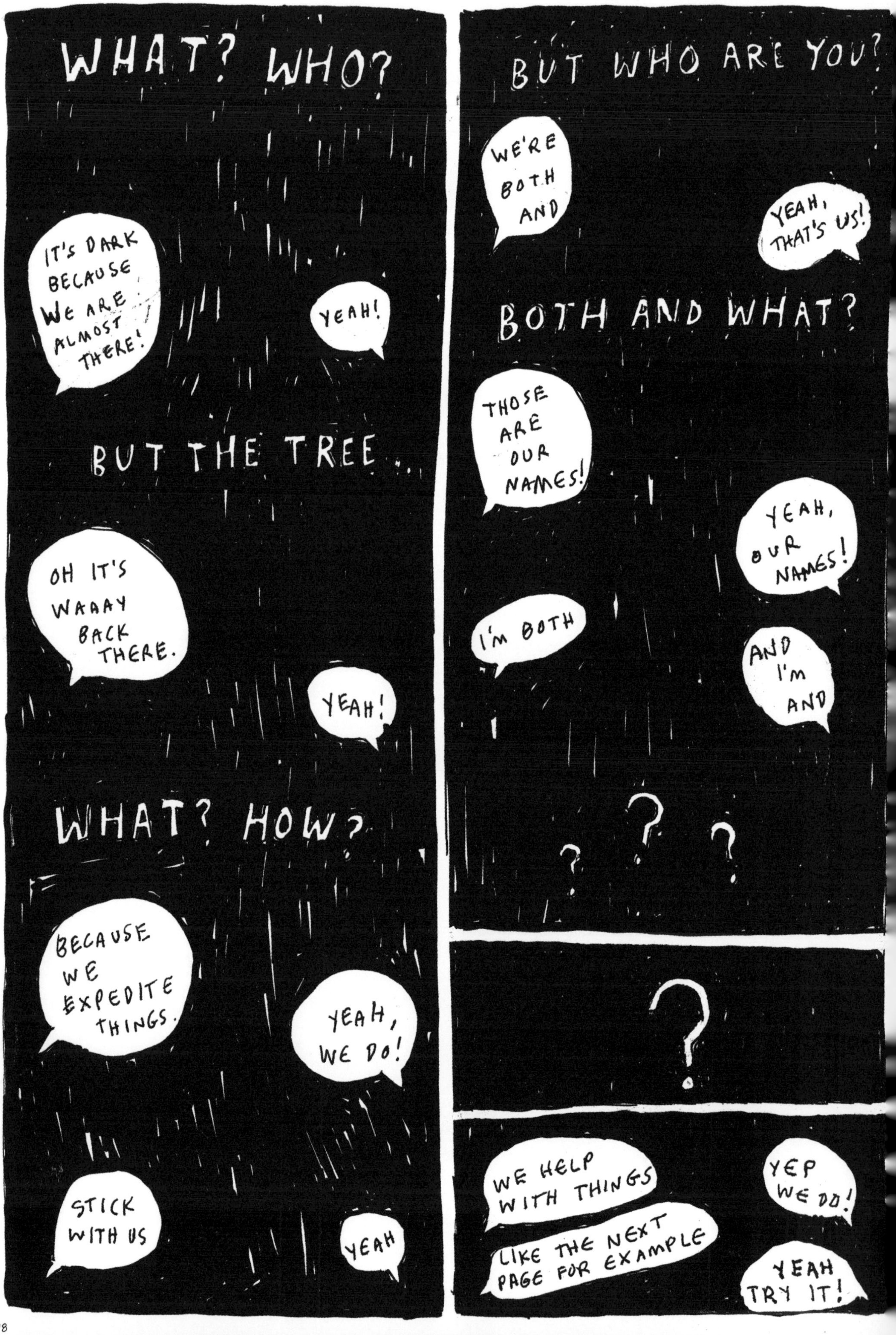
WHAT? WHO?
IT'S DARK BECAUSE WE ARE ALMOST THERE!
YEAH!
BUT THE TREE..
OH IT'S WAAAY BACK THERE.
YEAH!
WHAT? HOW?
BECAUSE WE EXPEDITE THINGS.
YEAH, WE DO!
STICK WITH US
YEAH
BUT WHO ARE YOU?
WE'RE BOTH AND
YEAH, THAT'S US!
BOTH AND WHAT?
THOSE ARE OUR NAMES!
YEAH, OUR NAMES!
I'M BOTH
AND I'M AND
? ? ?
?
WE HELP WITH THINGS
YEP WE DO!
LIKE THE NEXT PAGE FOR EXAMPLE
YEAH TRY IT!

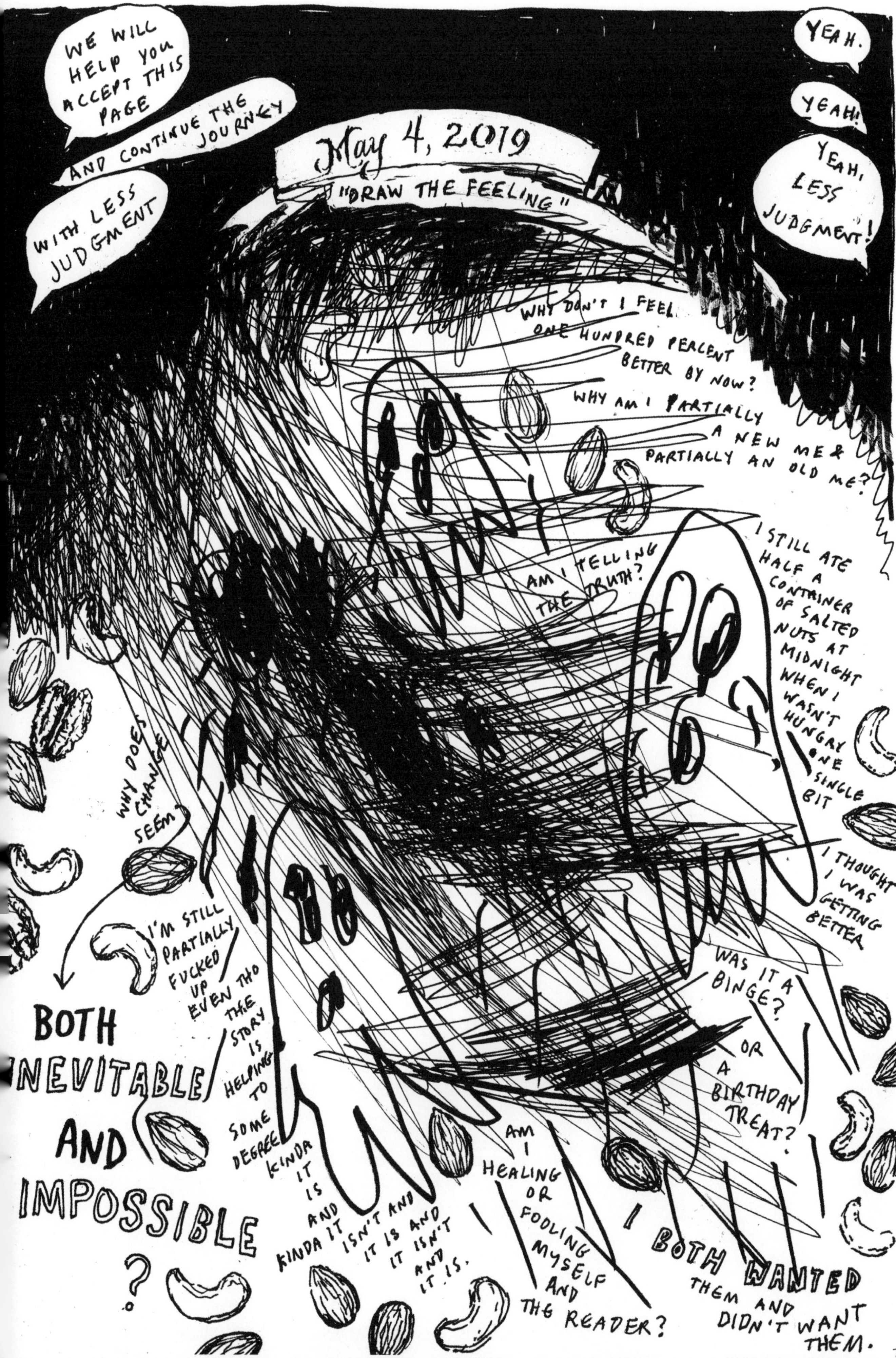

WE WILL HELP YOU ACCEPT THIS PAGE
AND CONTINUE THE JOURNEY
WITH LESS JUDGMENT
YEAH.
YEAH!
YEAH, LESS JUDGMENT!
May 4, 2019
"DRAW THE FEELING"
WHY DON'T I FEEL ONE HUNDRED PERCENT BETTER BY NOW?
WHY AM I PARTIALLY A NEW ME & PARTIALLY AN OLD ME?
AM I TELLING THE TRUTH?
I STILL ATE HALF A CONTAINER OF SALTED NUTS AT MIDNIGHT WHEN I WASN'T HUNGRY ONE SINGLE BIT
I THOUGHT I WAS GETTING BETTER
WAS IT A BINGE?
OR A BIRTHDAY TREAT?
WHY DOES CHANGE SEEM
BOTH INEVITABLE AND IMPOSSIBLE?
I'M STILL PARTIALLY FUCKED UP EVEN THO THE STORY IS HELPING TO SOME DEGREE
KINDA IT IS AND KINDA IT ISN'T AND IT IS AND IT ISN'T AND IT IS.
AM I HEALING OR FOOLING MYSELF AND THE READER?
I BOTH WANTED THEM AND DIDN'T WANT THEM.

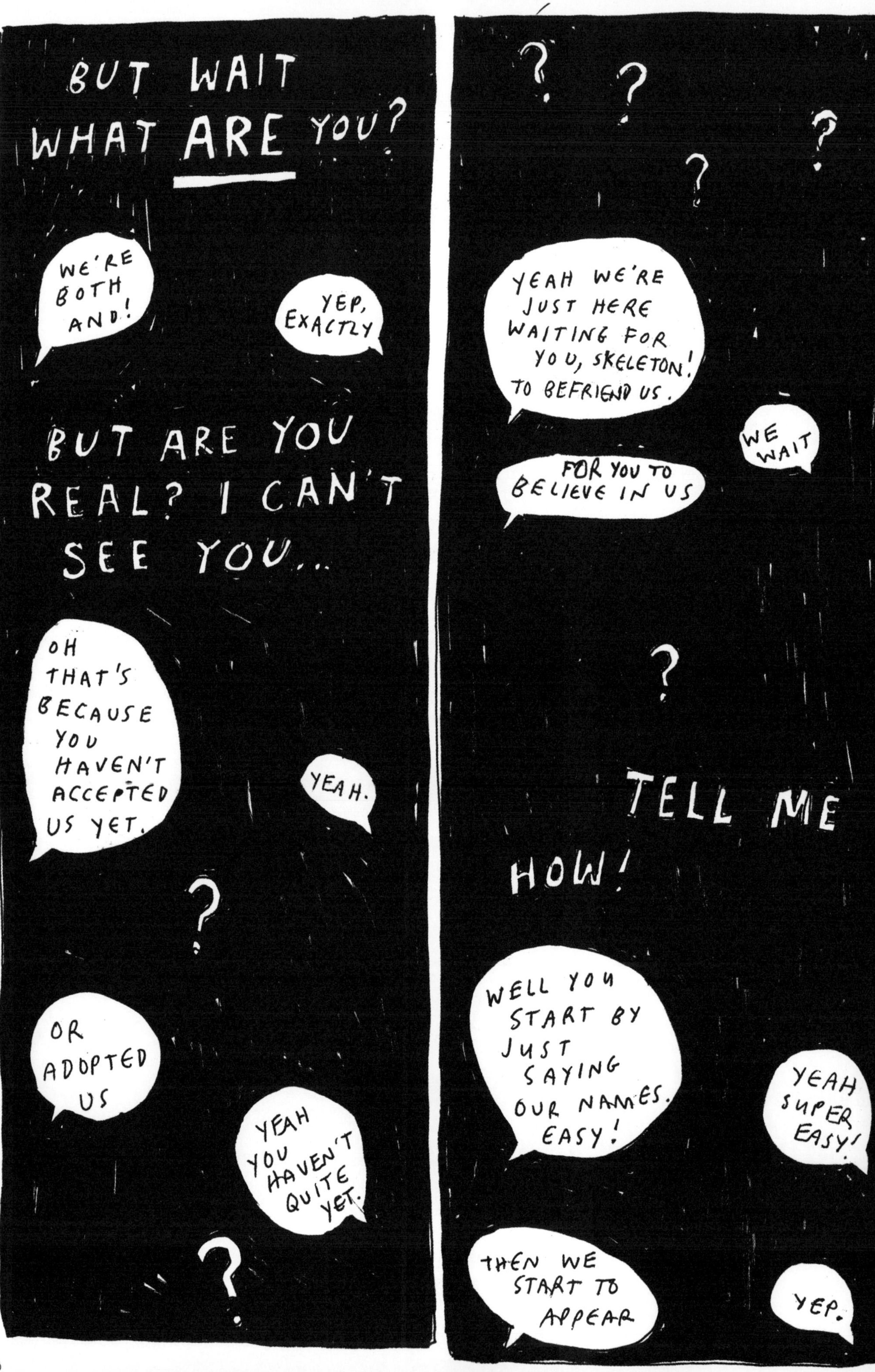
BUT WAIT WHAT ARE YOU?
WE'RE BOTH AND!
YEP, EXACTLY
BUT ARE YOU REAL? I CAN'T SEE YOU...
OH THAT'S BECAUSE YOU HAVEN'T ACCEPTED US YET.
YEAH.
?
OR ADOPTED US
YEAH YOU HAVEN'T QUITE YET.
?
? ? ? ?
YEAH WE'RE JUST HERE WAITING FOR YOU, SKELETON! TO BEFRIEND US.
WE WAIT
FOR YOU TO BELIEVE IN US
?
TELL ME HOW!
WELL YOU START BY JUST SAYING OUR NAMES. EASY!
YEAH SUPER EASY!
THEN WE START TO APPEAR
YEP.

 OKAY...

UM...

BOTH AND

 GOOD START! NOW AGAIN

YEAH AGAIN!

BOTH AND

 IT'S WORKING!

YEP!

BOTH AND BOTH AND

  BOTH AND BOTH AND BOTH AND BOTH AND BOTH AND BOTH AND BOTH AND BOTH AND BOTH AND BOTH AND BOTH AND BOTH AND BOTH AND BOTH AND BOTH AND BOTH AND BO...

WAIT, ARE U A PAIR OF...

 YEP WE ARE!

A... PARADIGM?

A PAIR OF DIMES!

A.....

 A SHAPESHIFTING PAIR OF DIMES! AND WE GET TO HELP YOU! AND ANSWER ALL YOUR DEEPEST QUESTIONS!

YEP, YEP, YEP.

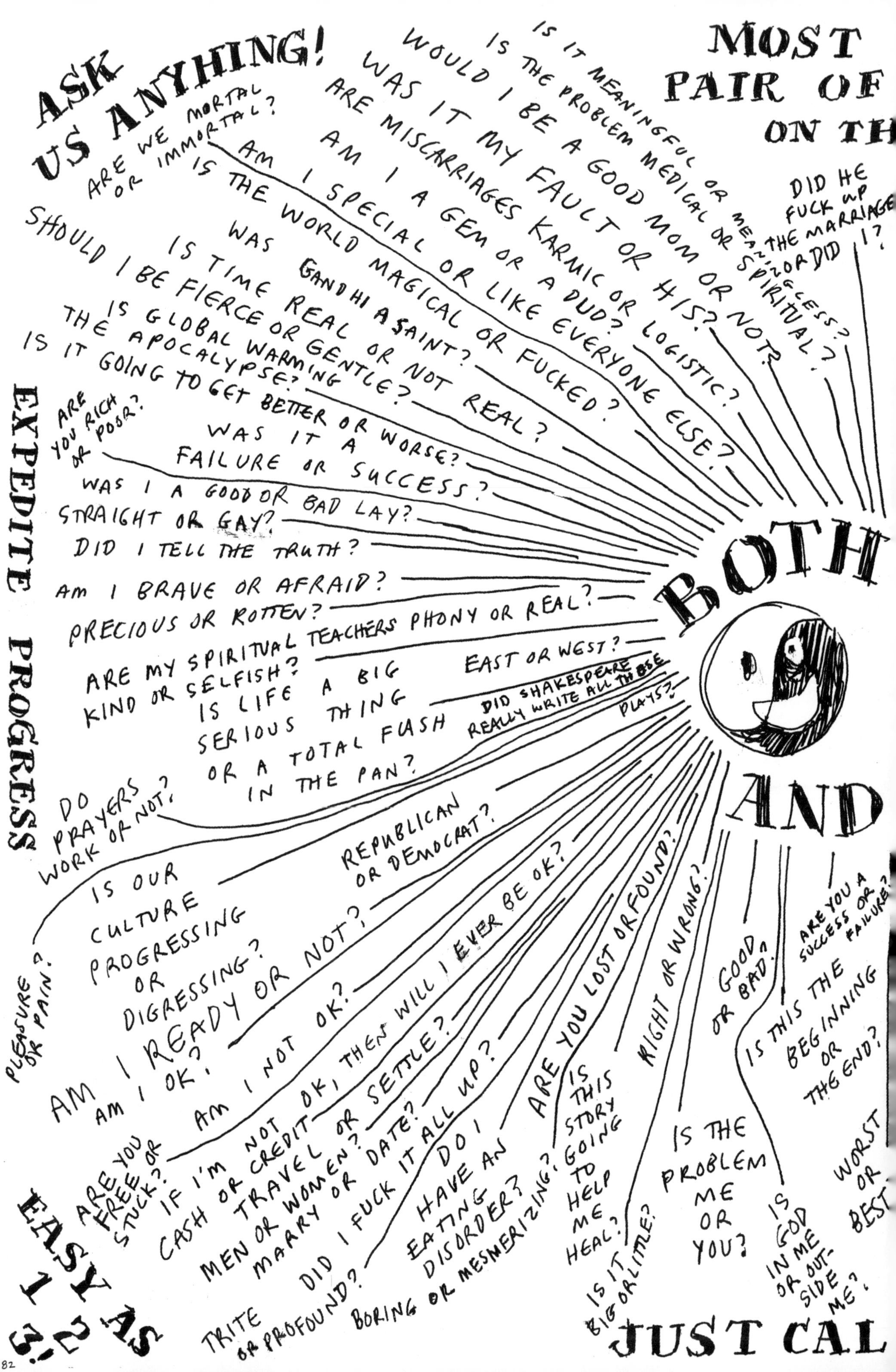
ASK US ANYTHING!
MOST PAIR OF
ON TH
EXPEDITE PROGRESS
ARE WE MORTAL OR IMMORTAL?
IS IT MEANINGFUL OR MEANINGLESS?
IS THE PROBLEM MEDICAL OR SPIRITUAL?
WOULD I BE A GOOD MOM OR NOT?
WAS IT MY FAULT OR HIS?
ARE MISCARRIAGES KARMIC OR LOGISTIC?
AM I A GEM OR A DUD?
AM I SPECIAL OR LIKE EVERYONE ELSE?
IS THE WORLD MAGICAL OR FUCKED?
DID HE FUCK UP THE MARRIAGE OR DID I?
WAS GANDHI A SAINT?
IS TIME REAL OR NOT REAL?
SHOULD I BE FIERCE OR GENTLE?
IS GLOBAL WARMING THE APOCALYPSE?
IS IT GOING TO GET BETTER OR WORSE?
ARE YOU RICH OR POOR?
WAS IT A FAILURE OR SUCCESS?
WAS I A GOOD OR BAD LAY?
STRAIGHT OR GAY?
DID I TELL THE TRUTH?
AM I BRAVE OR AFRAID?
PRECIOUS OR ROTTEN?
ARE MY SPIRITUAL TEACHERS PHONY OR REAL?
KIND OR SELFISH?
EAST OR WEST?
IS LIFE A BIG SERIOUS THING OR A TOTAL FLASH IN THE PAN?
DID SHAKESPEARE REALLY WRITE ALL THOSE PLAYS?
BOTH
AND
DO PRAYERS WORK OR NOT?
REPUBLICAN OR DEMOCRAT?
IS OUR CULTURE PROGRESSING OR DIGRESSING?
PLEASURE OR PAIN?
AM I READY OR NOT?
AM I OK?
AM I NOT OK?
IF I'M NOT OK, THEN WILL I EVER BE OK?
ARE YOU LOST OR FOUND?
RIGHT OR WRONG?
GOOD OR BAD?
ARE YOU A SUCCESS OR FAILURE?
IS THIS THE BEGINNING OR THE END?
ARE YOU FREE OR STUCK?
CASH OR CREDIT OR SETTLE?
TRAVEL OR MEN OR WOMEN?
MARRY OR DATE?
DID I FUCK IT ALL UP?
DO I HAVE AN EATING DISORDER?
IS THIS STORY GOING TO HELP ME HEAL?
IS THE PROBLEM ME OR YOU?
IS GOD IN ME OR OUTSIDE ME?
WORST OR BEST
TRITE OR PROFOUND?
BORING OR MESMERIZING?
IS IT BIG OR LITTLE?
EASY AS 1 2 3!
JUST CAL

RELIABLE
DIMES
E MARKET!

HERE TO HELP 24/7!

IS THE WORLD WORSE OR BETTER?

CAN A SINGLE PERSON MAKE A DIFFERENCE?

IS IT A BIG DEAL OR NO?

JUST OR UNJUST?

AM I BLESSED OR FUCKED?

IS THERE HOPE FOR HUMANKIND?

IS HEAVEN EARTH?

AM I LUCKY OR UNLUCKY?

FATE OR FREE WILL?

SEXY OR GROSS?

GOD OR GODDESS?

CITY OR COUNTRY?

IS THE FUTURE MALE OR FEMALE?

AM I MALE OR FEMALE?

AM I OLD OR YOUNG?

AM I NEAR OR FAR?

IS THIS PROJECT

IS THIS CONFUSING OR CLARIFYING?

CRAZY OR HELPFUL?

AM I A SPECK OF NOTHINGNESS OR THE CENTER OF CONSCIOUSNESS ITSELF?

DO YOU GET IT OR NOT?

DOES IT MATTER?

ASHRAM OR NYC?

AM I AN ARTIST OR A WRITER?

JOY OR SORROW?

INSANE?

IS THE SKELETON STORY IMPORTANT?

AM I INSPIRED OR

COFFEE OR TEA?

WAS IT A BINGE OR A BIRTHDAY TREAT?

DETAILS OR BIG PICTURE?

IS CHANGE POSSIBLE?

DO I SUCK AT MEDITATING?

AM I A MASTER OR A SLAVE?

ARE MY PRAYERS GENUINE OR FAKE?

AM I HEALED OR BROKEN?

AM I READY FOR A NEW RELATIONSHIP OR AM I STILL FUCKED?

RIGHT OR WRONG?

TIRED OR ENERGIZED?

DO I KISS HIM OR NOT?

AN ADDICT OR A SHAMAN?

CONSIDERATE OR A SELFISH ASSHOLE?

IS IT WORTH ALL THE FUSS?

WHEN WE DIE DOES EVERYTHING DISAPPEAR?

BLACK OR WHITE?

SICK OR HEALTHY?

IS MY HEART OPEN OR CLOSED?

STAY OR GO?

AND BOTH

SPEND OR SAVE?

WHAT ABOUT GOD?

EATING DISORDER OR JUST DISORDERLY EATING?

IRRELEVANT OR IRREPLACEABLE?

DO THINGS LAST?

FUNNY OR SERIOUS?

GUILTY OR INNOCENT?

DO WE DIE OR LIVE ETERNALLY?

IS THE SKELETON ME OR NOT ME?

IS THIS PAGE MESSY OR ORGANIZED?

OUR NAMES!

WE ARE ALSO FUN!

IMPROVE SLEEP!

83

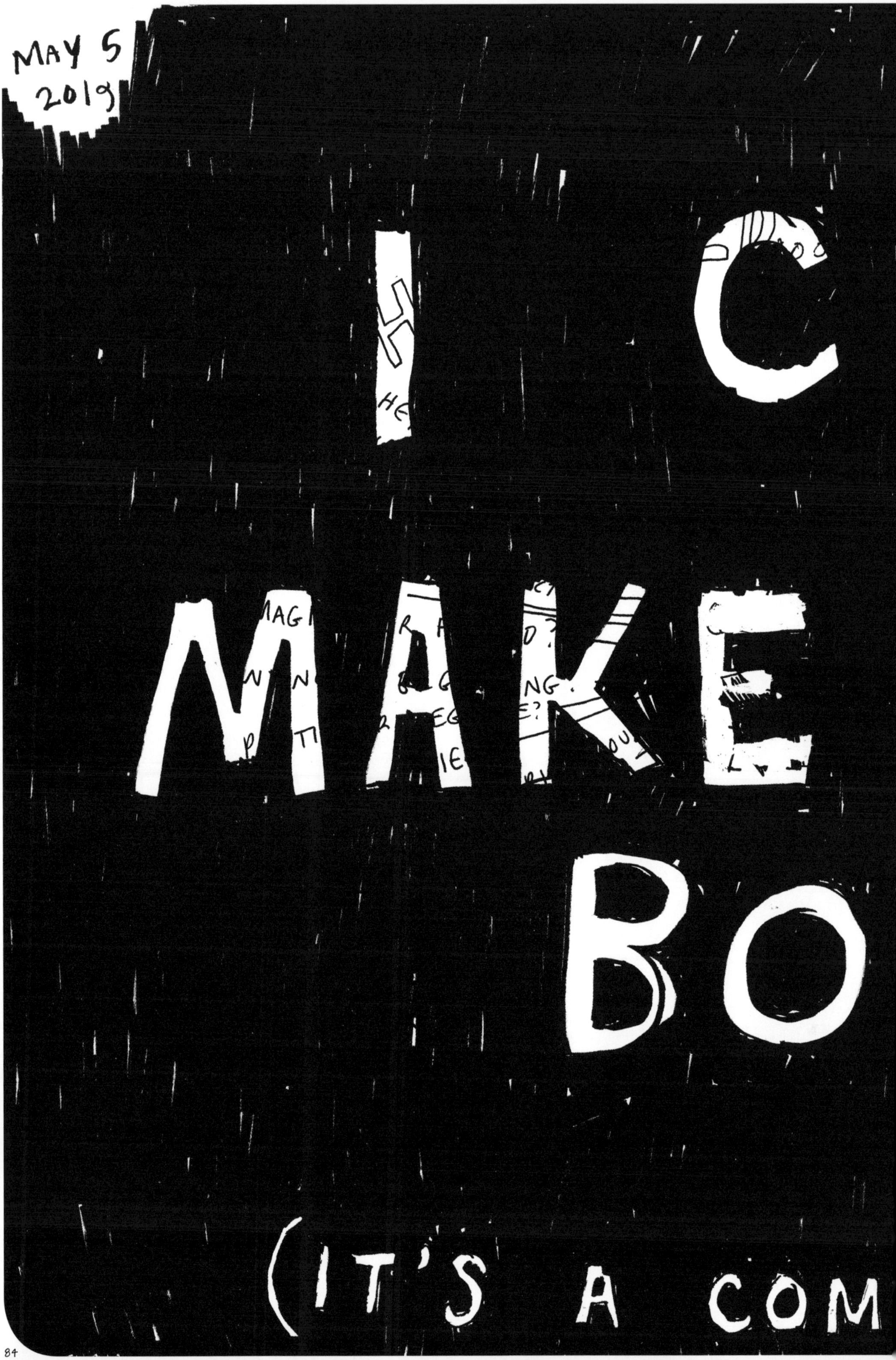
MAY 5
2019
I C
MAKE
BO
(IT'S A COM

AN'T

THIS

OK

PLETE MESS)

85

yes, you can

(it matters)

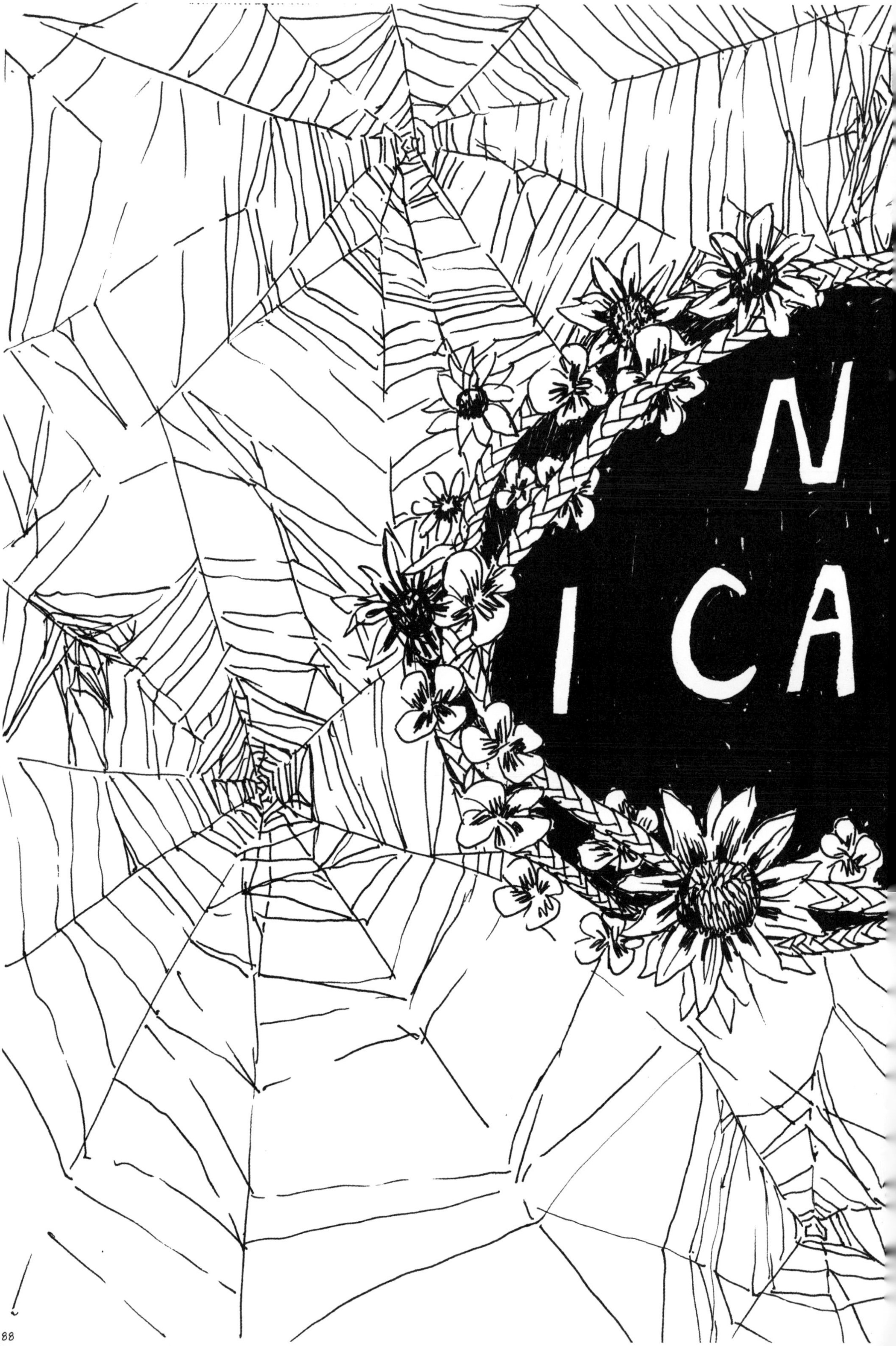
N
ICA

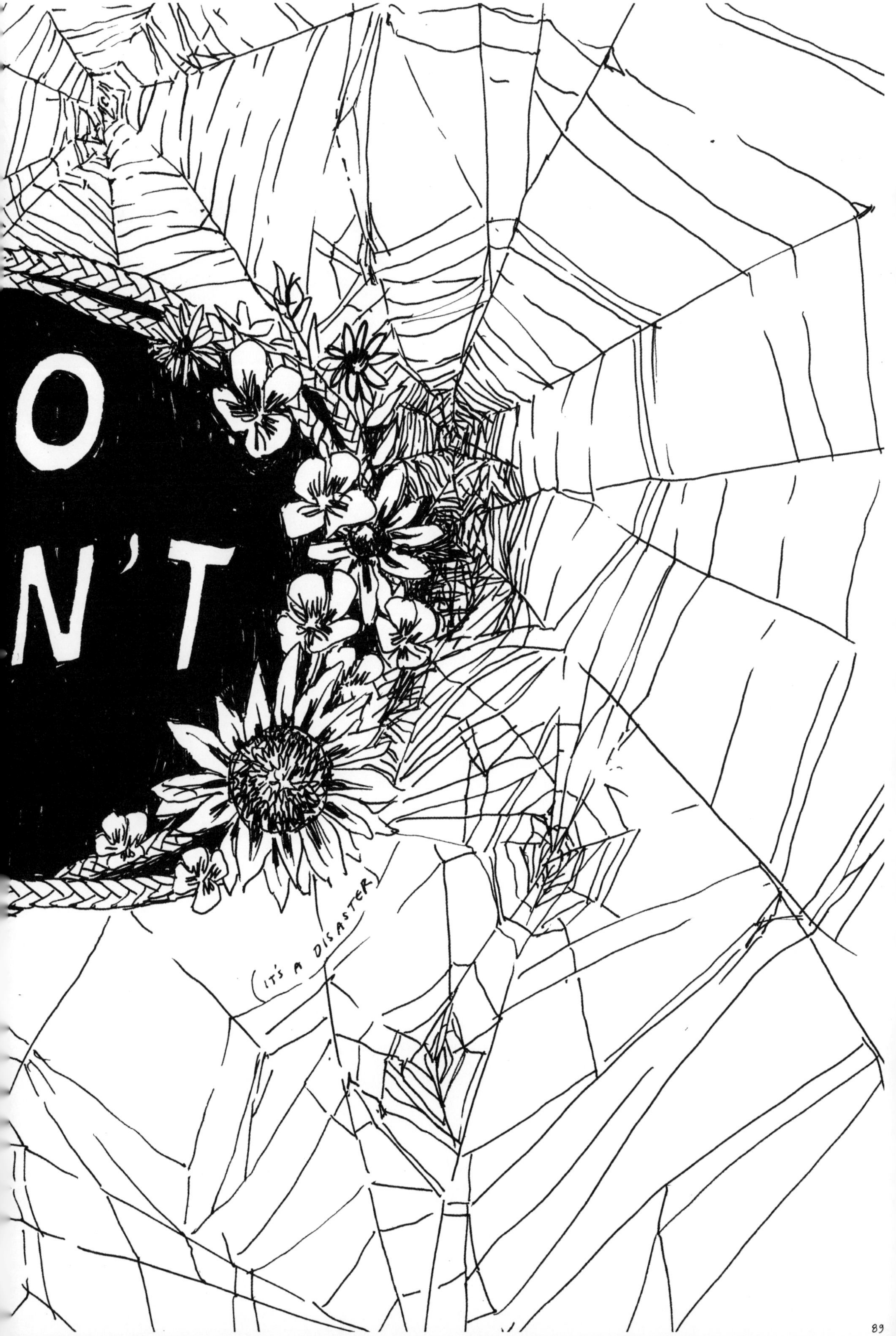
O
N'T
(IT'S A DISASTER

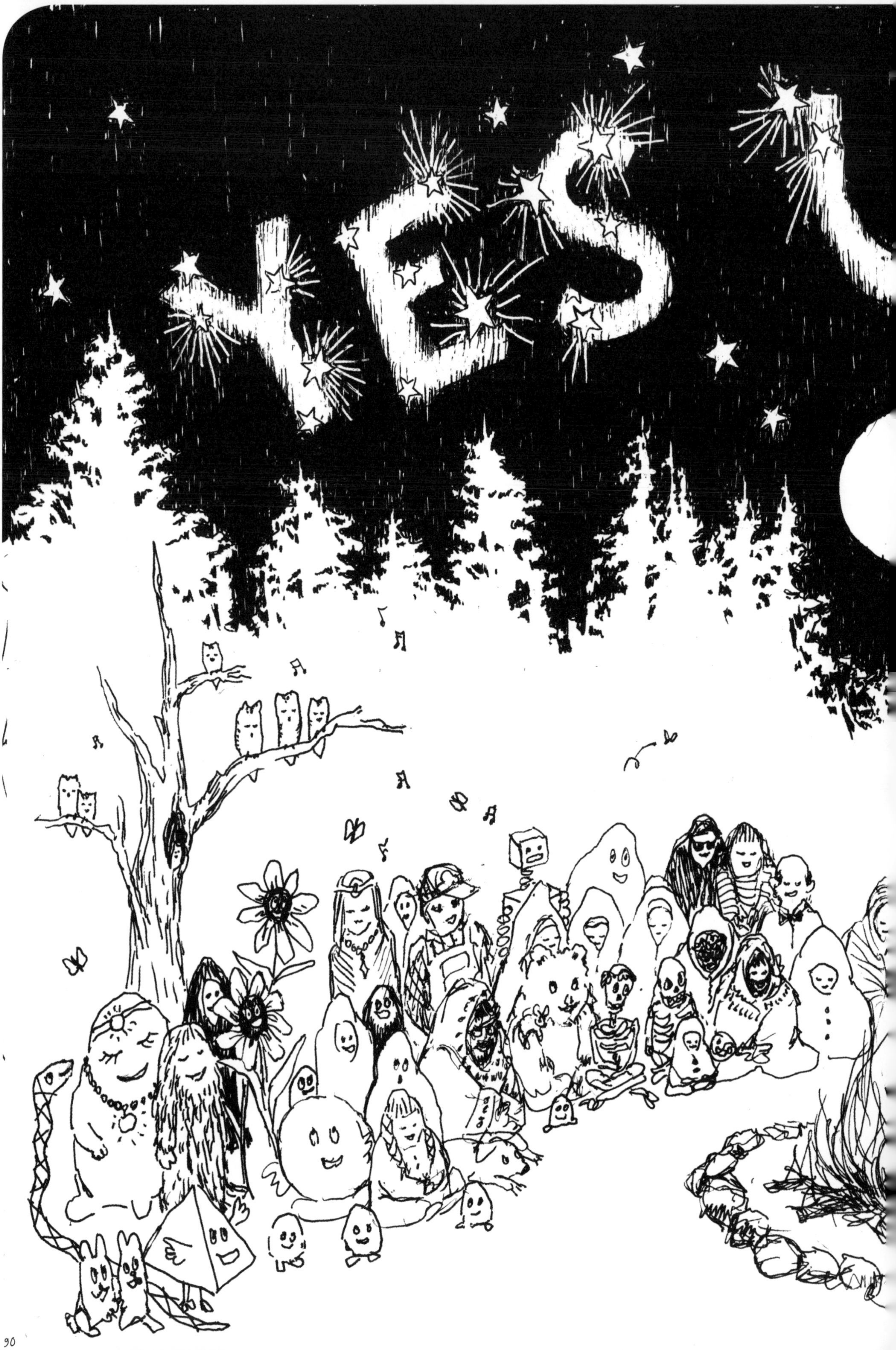
YES

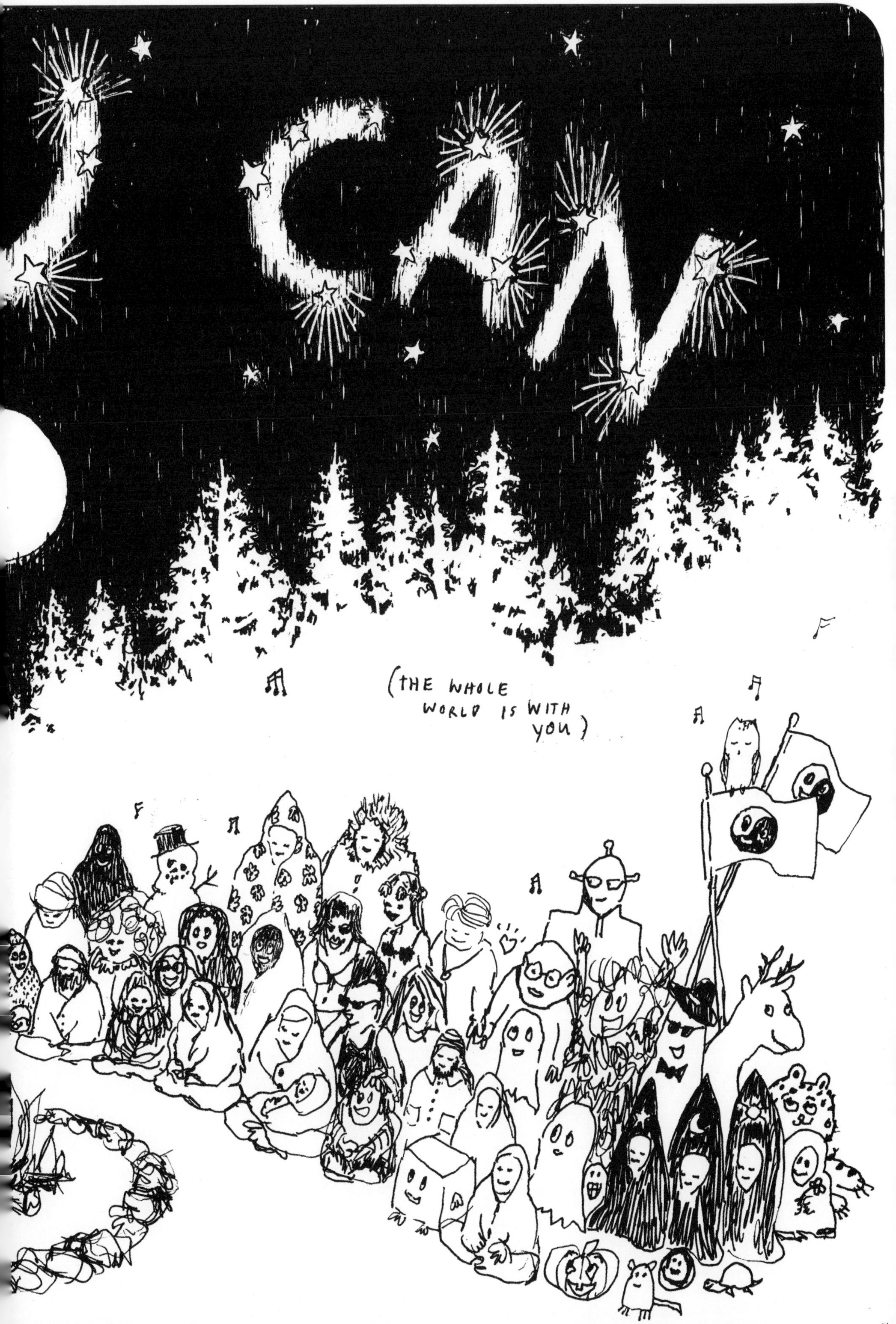
CAN
(THE WHOLE
WORLD IS WITH
YOU)

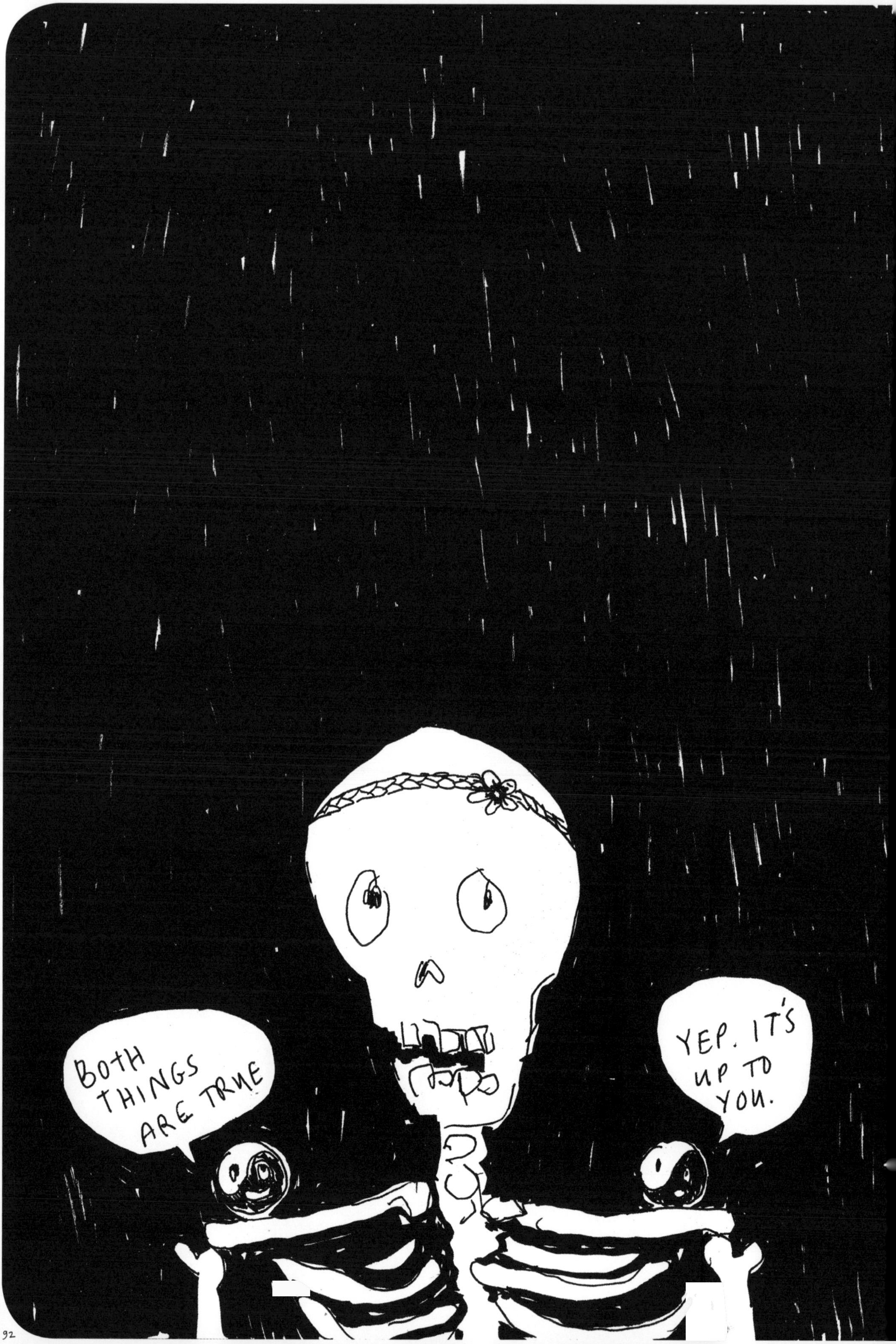
BOTH THINGS ARE TRUE
YEP. IT'S UP TO YOU.

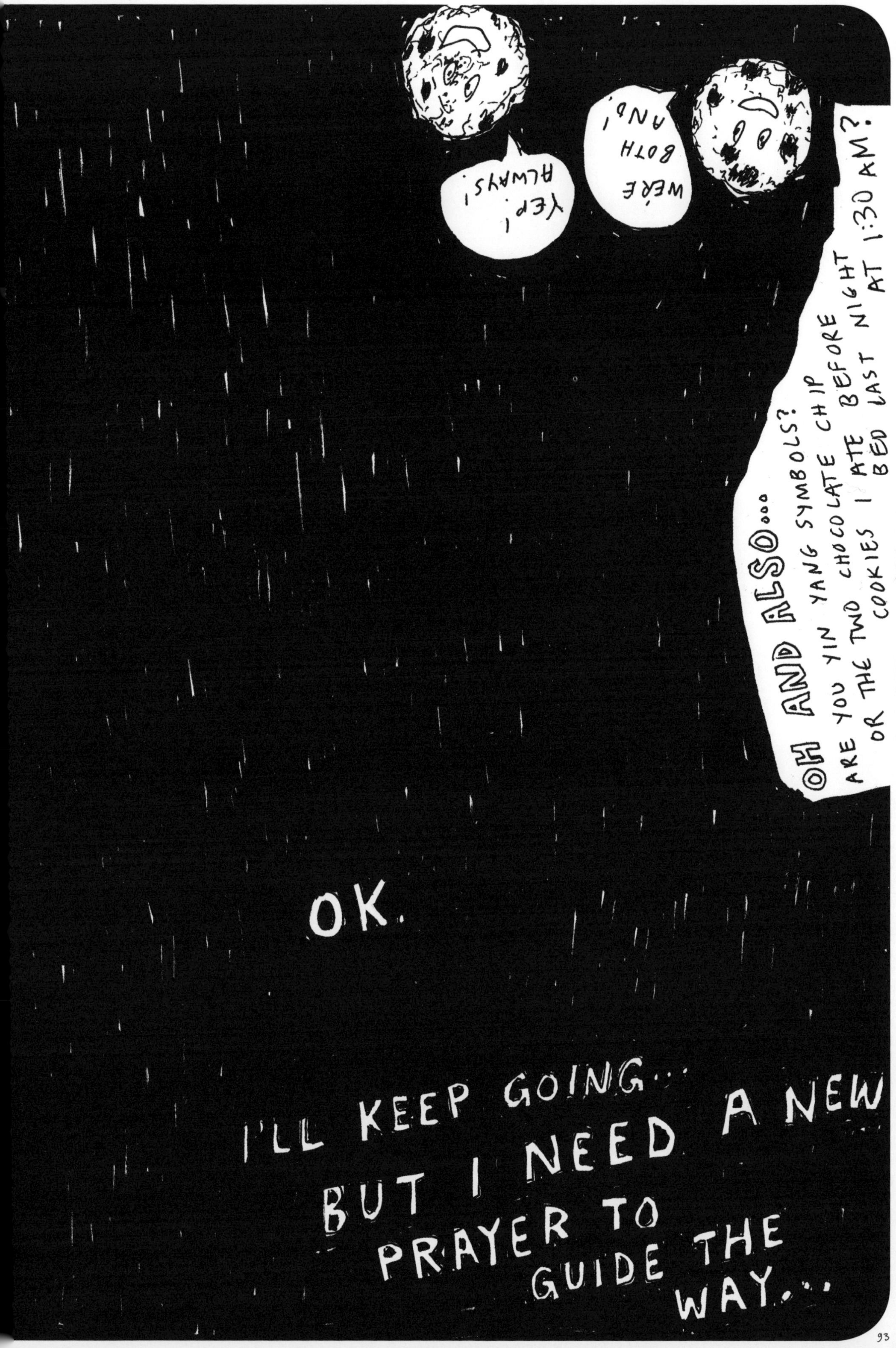
OH AND ALSO...
ARE YOU YIN YANG SYMBOLS?
OR THE TWO CHOCOLATE CHIP COOKIES I ATE BEFORE BED LAST NIGHT AT 1:30 AM?
WE'RE BOTH AND!
YEP! ALWAYS!
OK.
I'LL KEEP GOING...
BUT I NEED A NEW PRAYER TO GUIDE THE WAY...

MEMORIZE THIS ONE & REPEAT IT LIKE THE CHORUS OF YOUR FAVORITE SONG. WEAR IT LIKE A PATCH OVER YOUR HEART. THE TRUE MEANING WILL REVEAL ITSELF IN TIME.

BUT IS IT FOR THE SKELETON OR FOR THE READER?

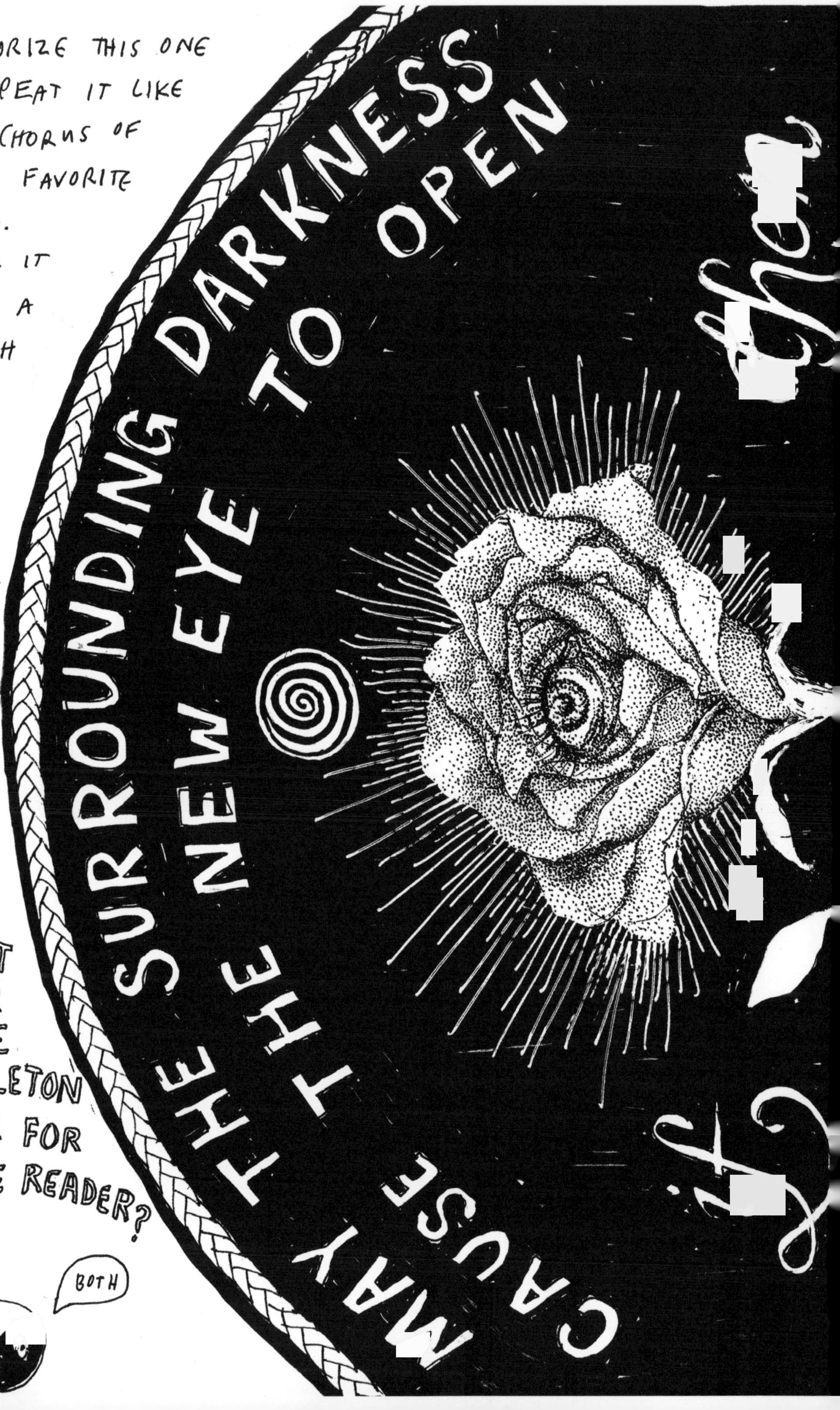

MAY THE SURROUNDING DARKNESS CAUSE
THE NEW EYE TO OPEN
BOTH

I AM I AM I AM FREE

A LIVE

I AM A LOVE

MIDNIGHT'S GARDEN

A ROSE IN MIDNIGHT

AND KIM

95

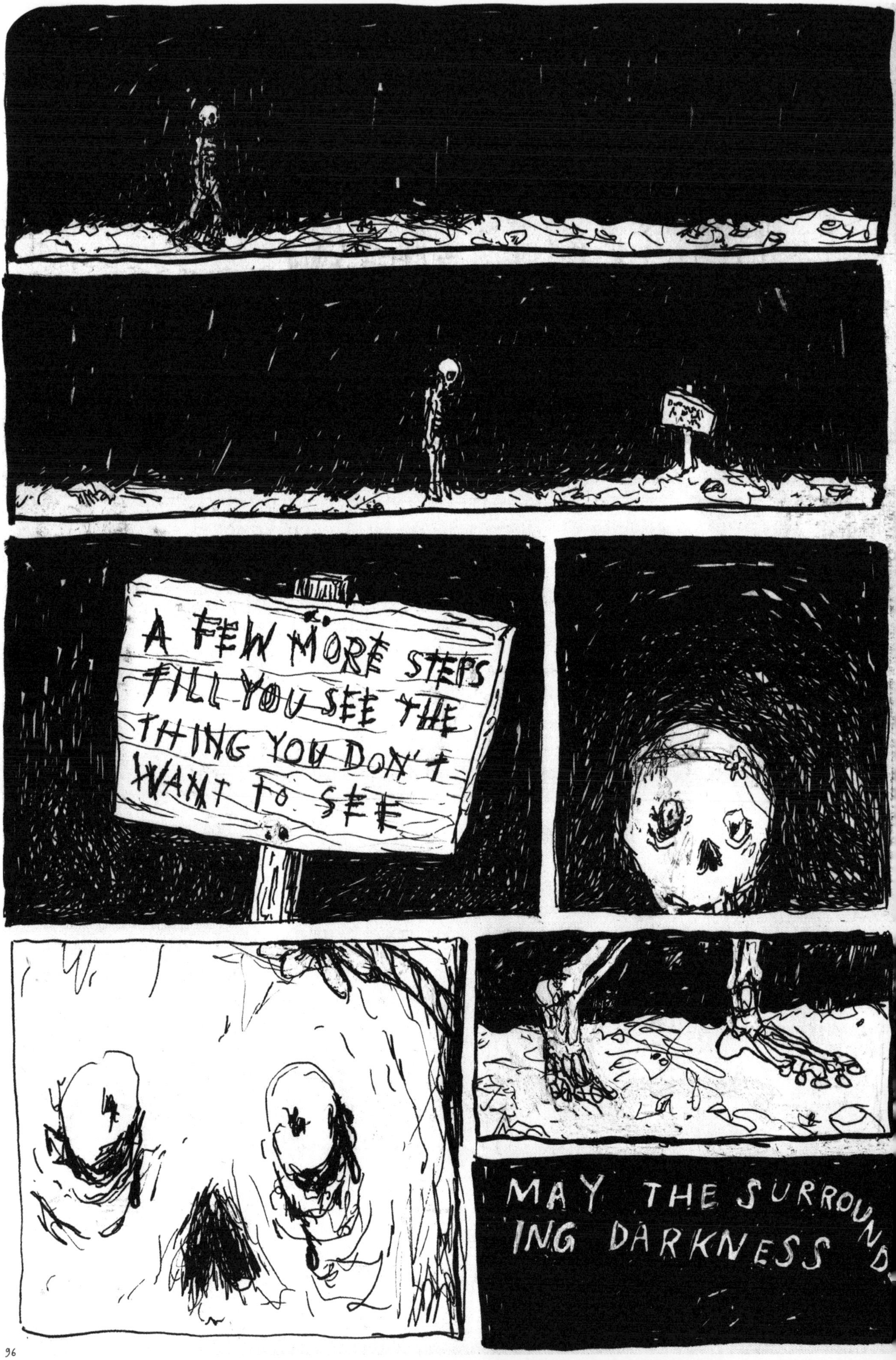
A FEW MORE STEPS TILL YOU SEE THE THING YOU DON'T WANT TO SEE
MAY THE SURROUNDING DARKNESS

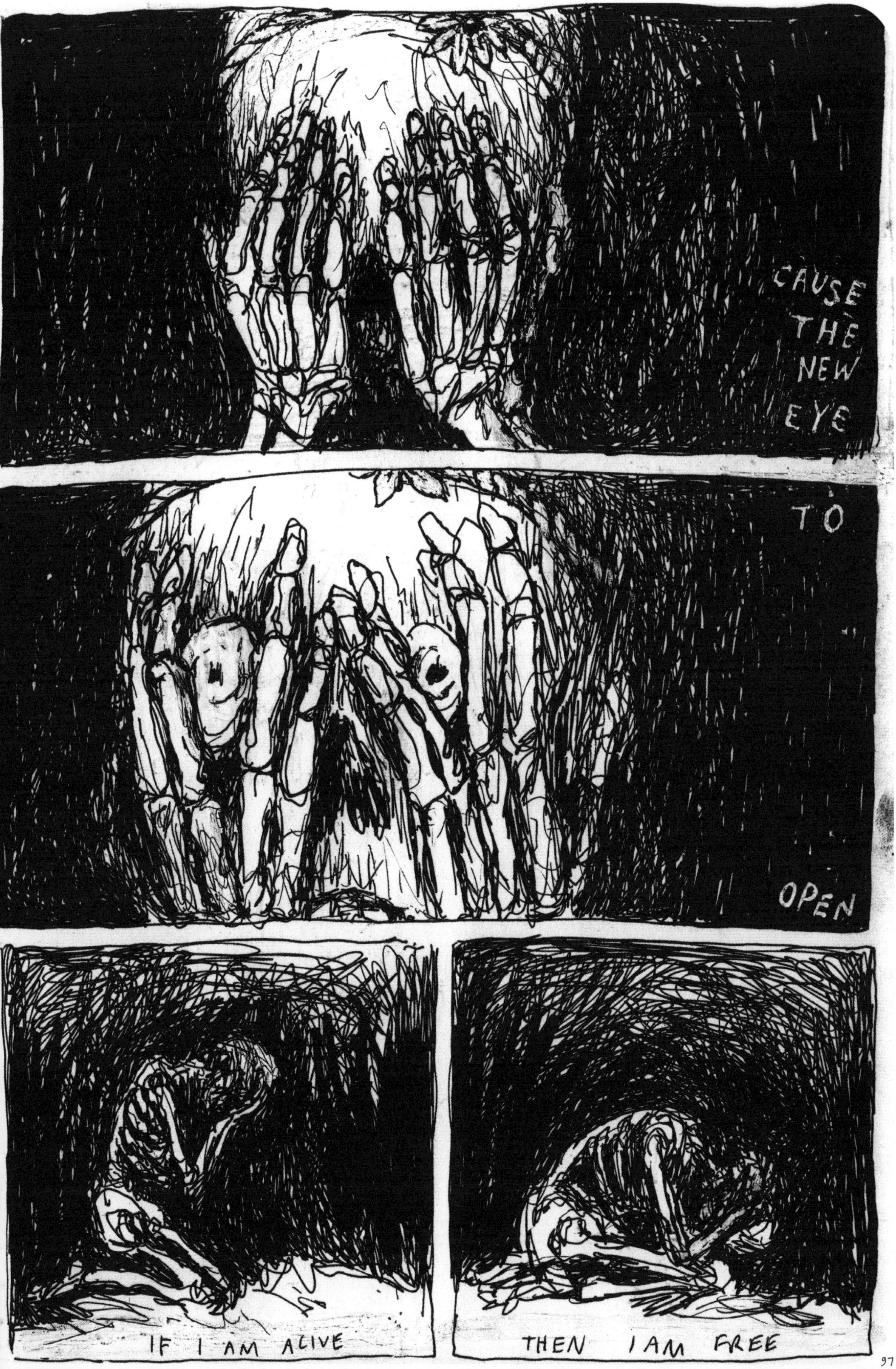
CAUSE THE NEW EYE
TO
OPEN
IF I AM ALIVE
THEN I AM FREE

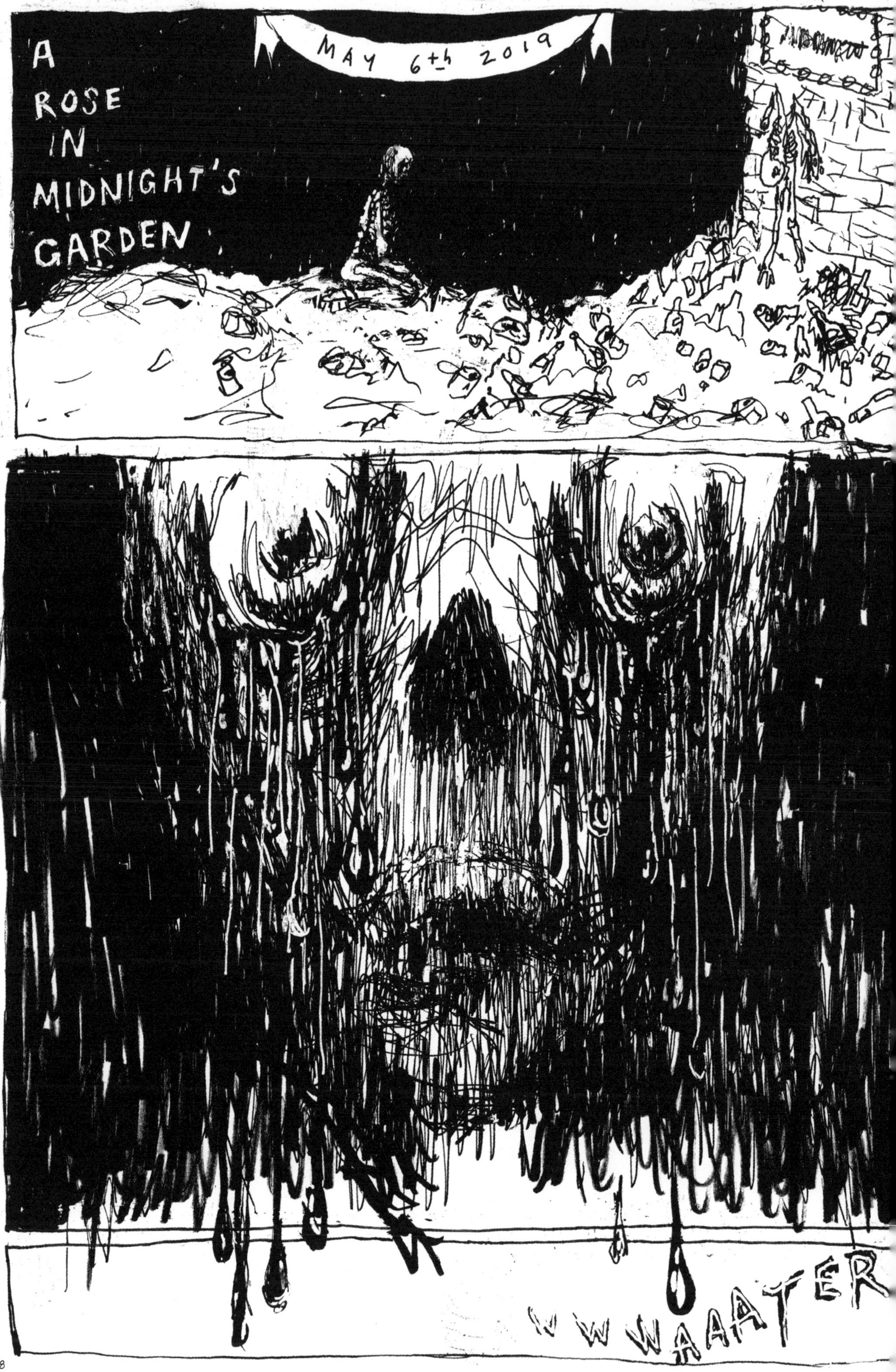
A ROSE IN MIDNIGHT'S GARDEN
MAY 6th 2019
WWWAAATER

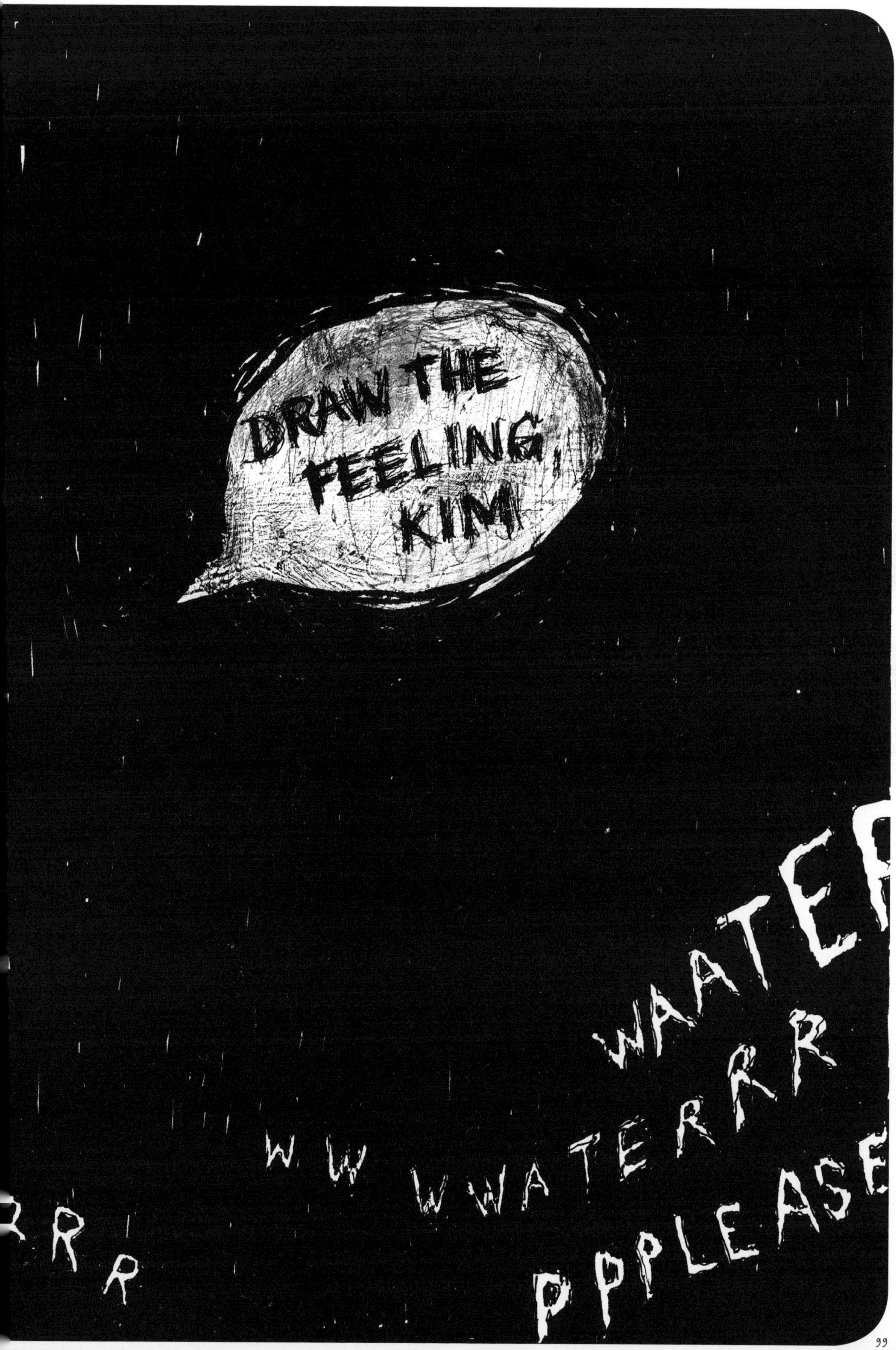
DRAW THE FEELING, KIM
WAATER
WATERRR
W W WWATERRR
PPPLEASE
RRR

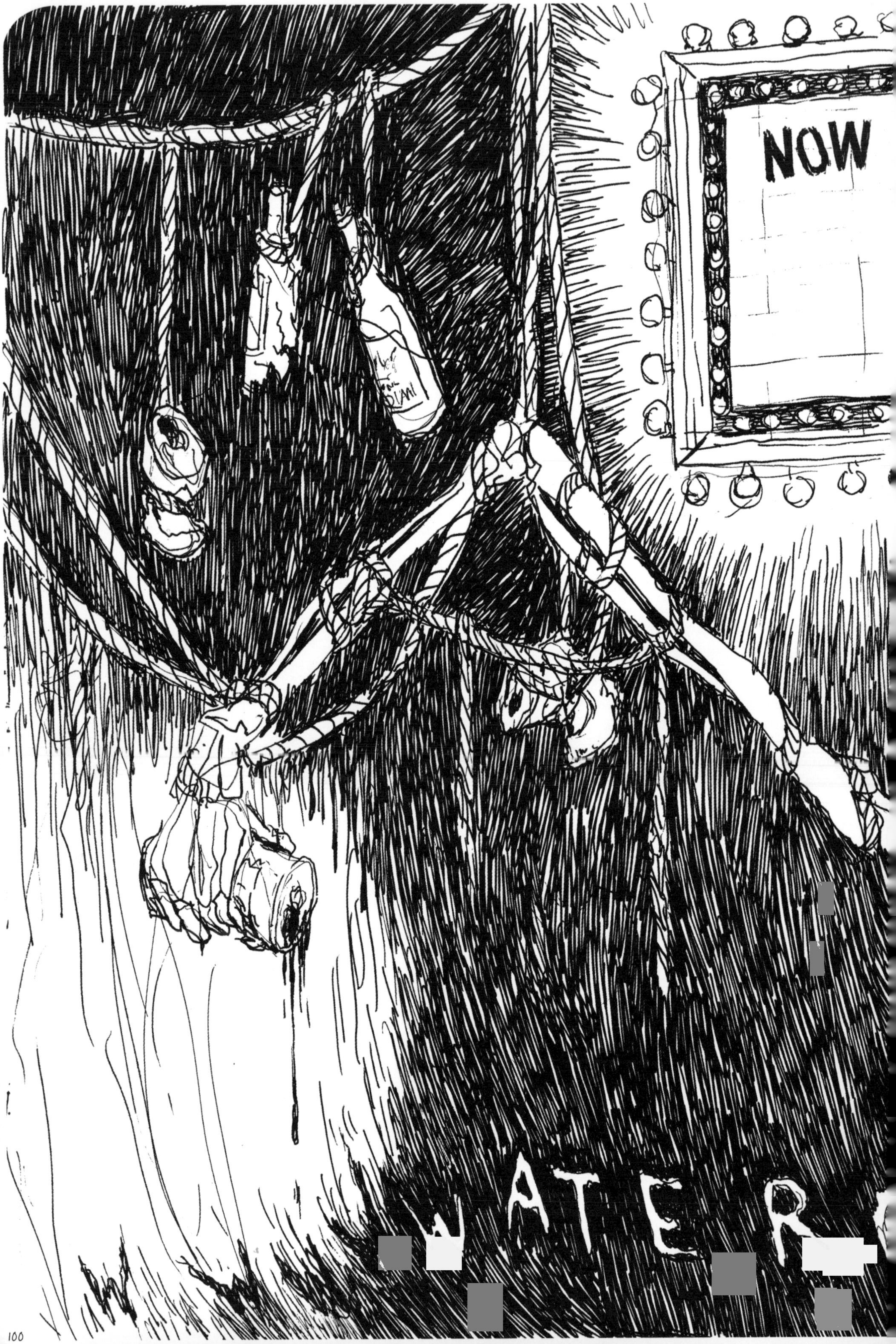
NOW
ATER

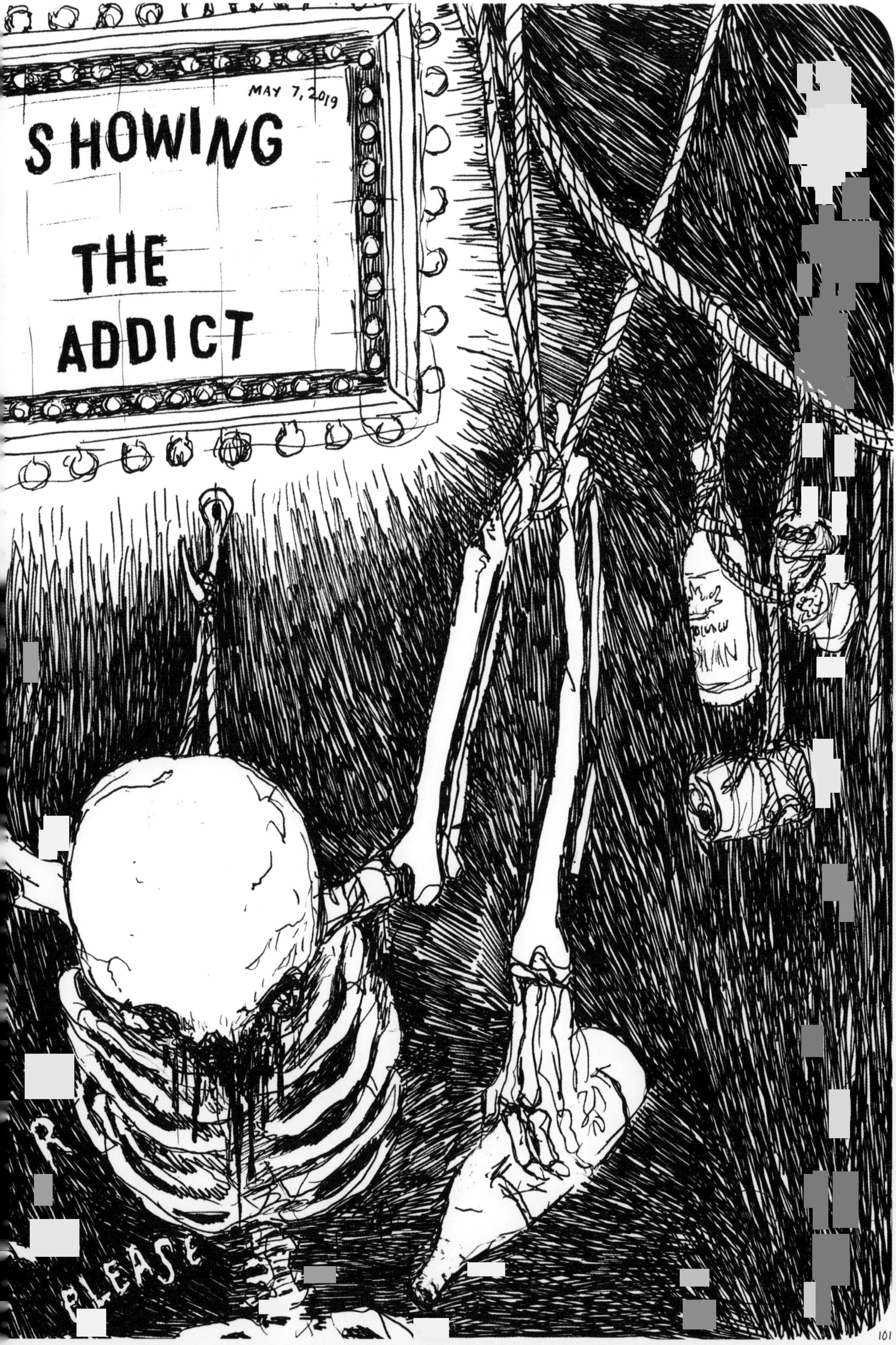
MAY 7, 2019
SHOWING
THE
ADDICT
PLEASE

MAY 8, 2019

WHO IS THAT?
ME? NO.
HIM?

I'M NOT AN ADDICT
I'M JUST
HEARTBROKEN
OR
HUNGRY OR
EMPTY OR
DISAPPOINTED
OR MAYBE IT'S
THE CANDIDA BUT
IT CAN'T BE ME
IT'S NOT ME
BECAUSE HE
WAS THE ONE
SMASHING BOTTLES
AND THE WHISKEY

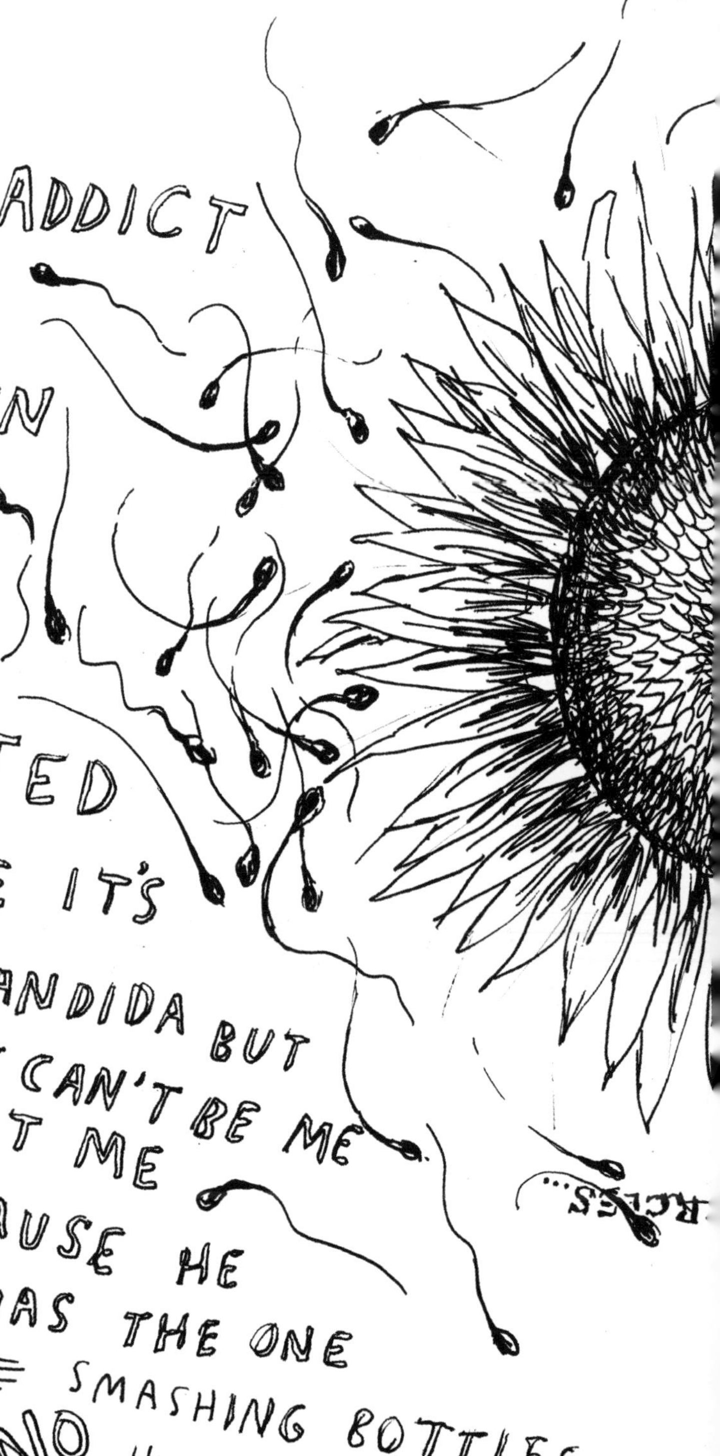

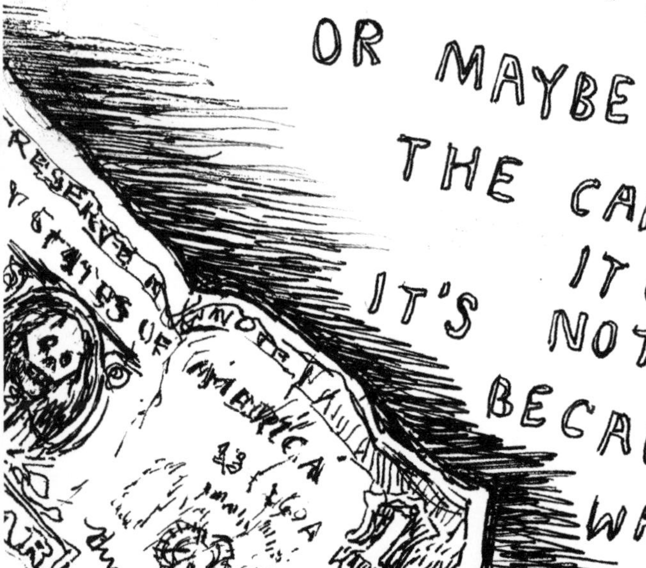

THERE IS NO ADDICT IN ME
I'M NOT
I'VE NEVER BEEN
I CAN STOP I KN
I'M NOT IT'S HIM I'VE NEVER BEEN

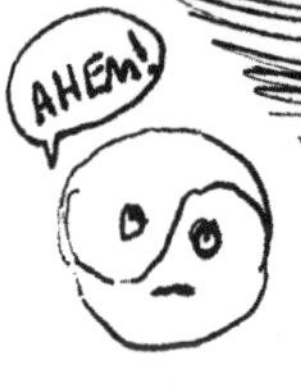
AHEM!

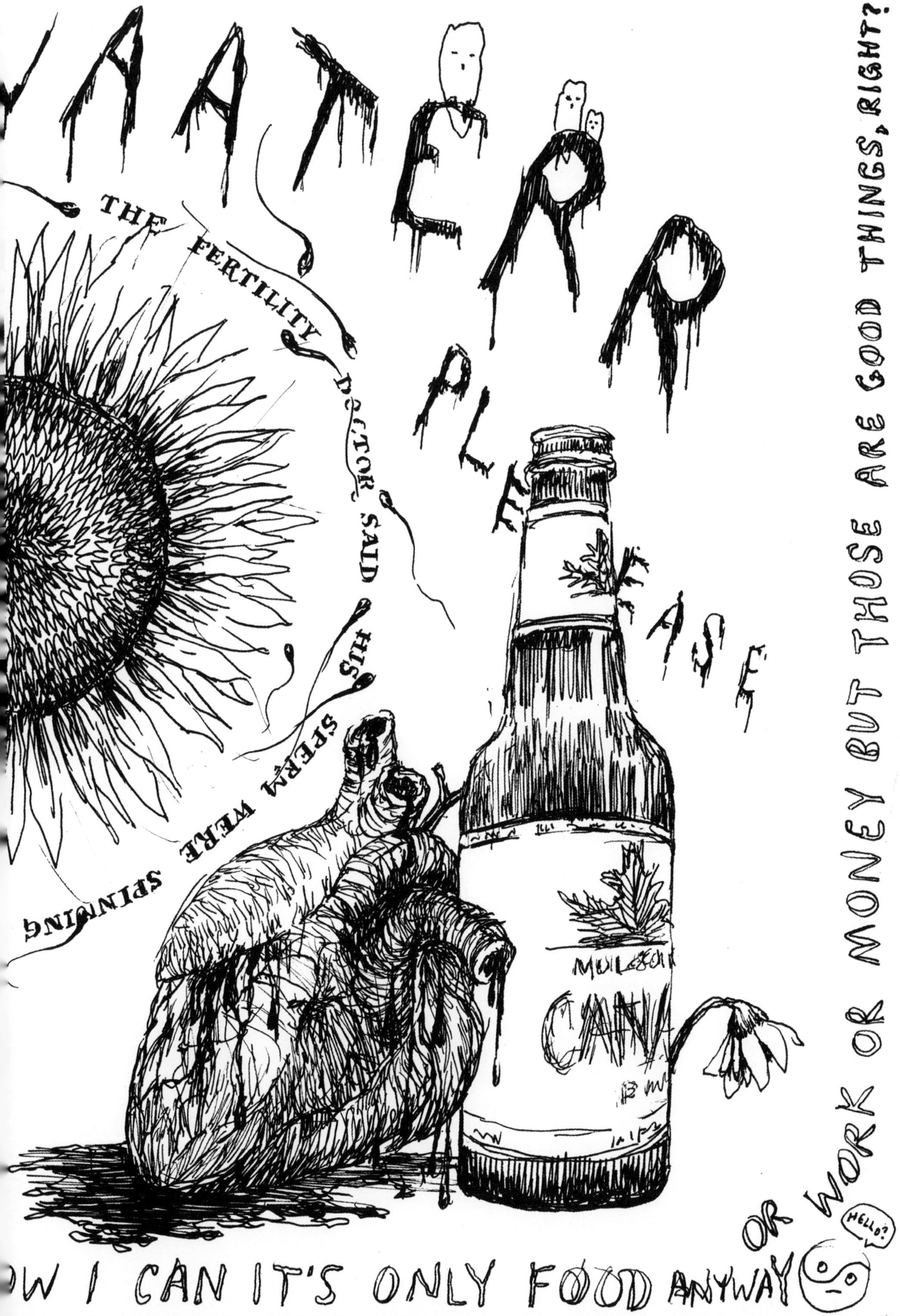
AATERR
PLEASE
THE FERTILITY DOCTOR SAID HIS SPERM WERE SPINNING
CAN
OW I CAN IT'S ONLY FOOD ANYWAY
OR WORK OR MONEY BUT THOSE ARE GOOD THINGS, RIGHT?
HELLO?

A MOMENTARY CON-

OXFORD DICTIONARY: THE FACT OR CONDITION OF BEING ADDICTED TO A PARTICULAR SUBSTANCE OR ACTIVITY

ETYMOLOGY: COMES FROM THE LATIN WORDS:

addicere – TO DELIVER, DEVOTE, AWARD, SACRIFICE

addictionem – AN AWARDING, A DELIVERING

dico – TO DECLARE, SAY, ANNOUNCE

addictio – A PERSON'S PROCLIVITY, INCLINATION, ASSIGNMEN.

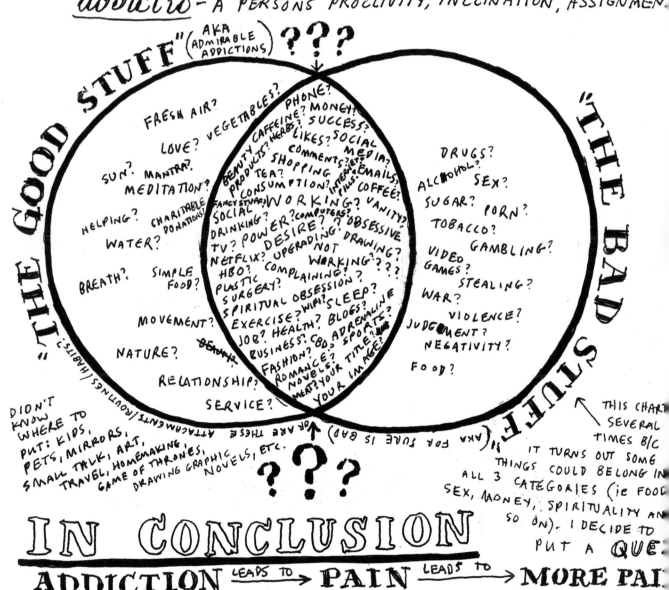

"THE GOOD STUFF" (AKA ADMIRABLE ADDICTIONS) ???

FRESH AIR? LOVE? VEGETABLES?
SUN? MANTRA? MEDITATION?
HELPING? CHARITABLE DONATIONS?
WATER?
BREATH? SIMPLE FOOD?
MOVEMENT?
NATURE? BEAUTY?
RELATIONSHIP?
SERVICE?

PHONE? CAFFEINE? MONEY? SUCCESS?
BEAUTY PRODUCTS? HERBS? LIKES? SOCIAL MEDIA?
COMMENTS? EMAILS?
SHOPPING TEA? INTERNET? PILLS? COFFEE?
CONSUMPTION?
FANCY STUFF? WORKING? VANITY?
SOCIAL DRINKING? POWER? COMPUTERS?
TV? DESIRE? OBSESSIVE
NETFLIX? UPGRADING? DRAWING?
HBO? COMPLAINING? NOT WORKING? ? ? ?
PLASTIC SURGERY?
SPIRITUAL OBSESSION?
EXERCISE? WIFI? SLEEP?
JOB? HEALTH? BLOGS?
BUSINESS? CBD ADRENALINE
FASHION? SPORTS?
ROMANCE? YOUR TITLE?
NOVELS? MEAT? YOUR IMAGE?

DRUGS?
ALCOHOL? SEX?
SUGAR? PORN?
TOBACCO?
GAMBLING?
VIDEO GAMES?
STEALING?
WAR?
VIOLENCE?
JUDGEMENT?
NEGATIVITY?
FOOD?

"THE BAD STUFF" (AKA FOR SURE IS BAD)

"THE GOOD STUFF / ADDICTIONS / ROUTINES / HABITS?"

DIDN'T KNOW WHERE TO PUT: KIDS, PETS, MIRRORS, SMALL TALK, ART, TRAVEL, HOMEMAKING, GAME OF THRONES, DRAWING GRAPHIC NOVELS, ETC.

OR ARE THESE ATTACHMENTS?

???

THIS CHART SEVERAL TIMES B/C IT TURNS OUT SOME THINGS COULD BELONG IN ALL 3 CATEGORIES (ie FOOD SEX, MONEY, SPIRITUALITY AN SO ON). I DECIDE TO PUT A QUE

IN CONCLUSION

ADDICTION —LEADS TO→ **PAIN** —LEADS TO→ **MORE PAI**

SO...

ADDICTION ————————————

EVENTUALLY, POTENT

-TEMPLATION on ADDICTION

THE SLIPPERY SLOPE OF SYNONYMS

LOVES
DESIRES
TENDS TO
DEDICATED
ENGAGED
COMMITTED
DEVOTED
RELIABLE
CONSISTENT
RELENTLESS
WILLFUL
DETERMINED
ATTACHED
INFATUATED
OBSESSED
USES
DEPENDENT
POWERLESS
NEEDS
CRAVES
ABUSER
FIEND
FANATIC
ADDICT

♡ THE TALL ONE AT THE ASHRAM, THE ONE I SOME DAYS FIND MYSELF WANTING TO KISS... HE'S AN ADDICT, THREE YEARS SOBER, TEACHING MEDITATION MEETS TWELVE STEPS MEETS RECOVERY MEETS CONSCIOUSNESS MEETS FORGIVENESS MEETS MOVEMENT MEETS YOGA MEETS ACCEPTING ONE'S SELF IN THIS COMPLEX FUCKED UP AND MAGICAL WORLD. **BUT** HE'S AN ADDICT NONETHELESS. THE NUMBER ONE DEALBREAKER ON MY LIST OF WHAT I'M NOT LOOKING FOR IN A NEW LOVE SO I DON'T REPEAT THE SAME MISTAKES I JUST LEFT AFTER TWELVE YEARS OF RECYCLING ENDLESS CANS OF HIS SHITTY BEER.

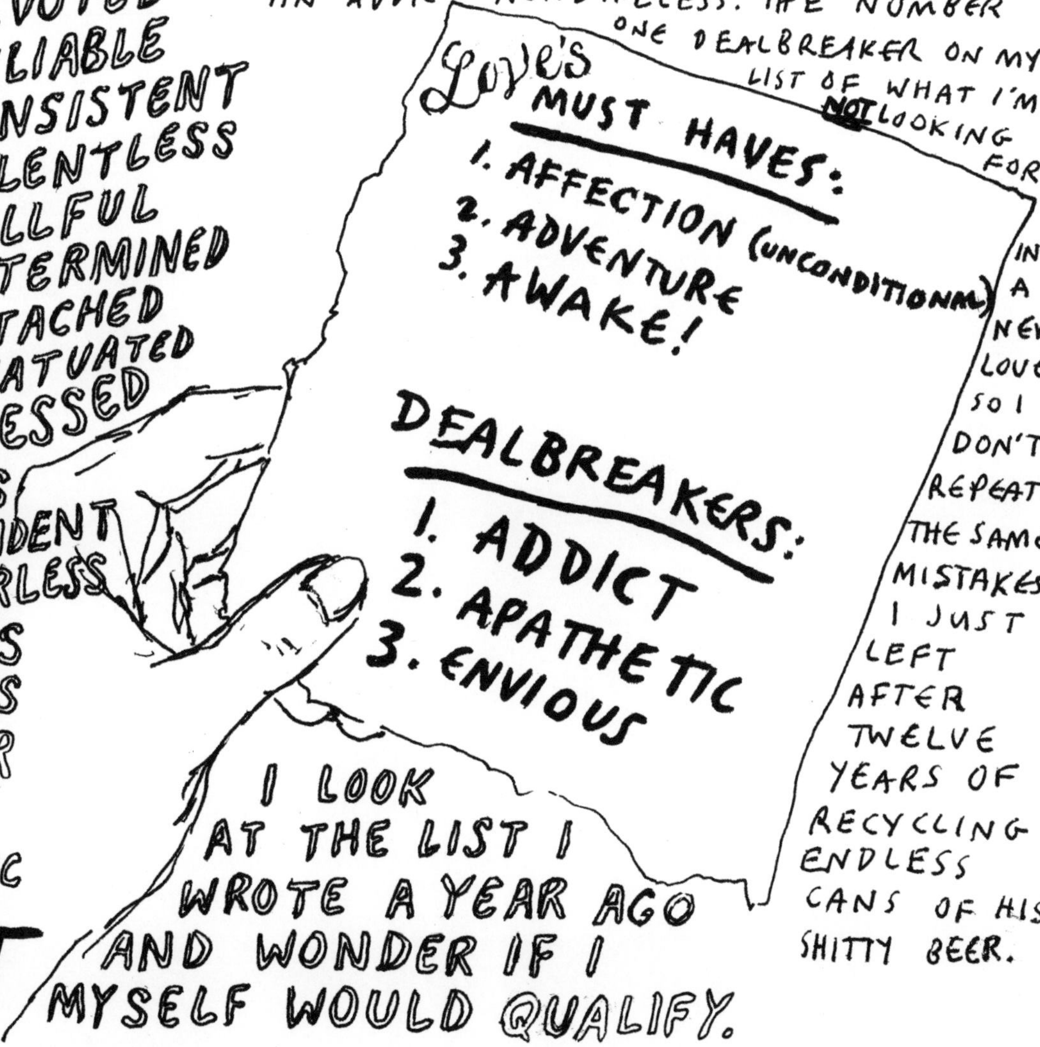

Love's
MUST HAVES:
1. AFFECTION (UNCONDITIONAL)
2. ADVENTURE
3. AWAKE!
DEALBREAKERS:
1. ADDICT
2. APATHETIC
3. ENVIOUS

I LOOK AT THE LIST I WROTE A YEAR AGO AND WONDER IF I MYSELF WOULD QUALIFY.

-TIONMARK AFTER EVERYTING.

-LEADS TO → **CHANGE** (AKA CREATIVITY, A NEW PARADIGM) LEADS TO → **HEALING**

-LY, LEADS US TOWARD → **HEALING**

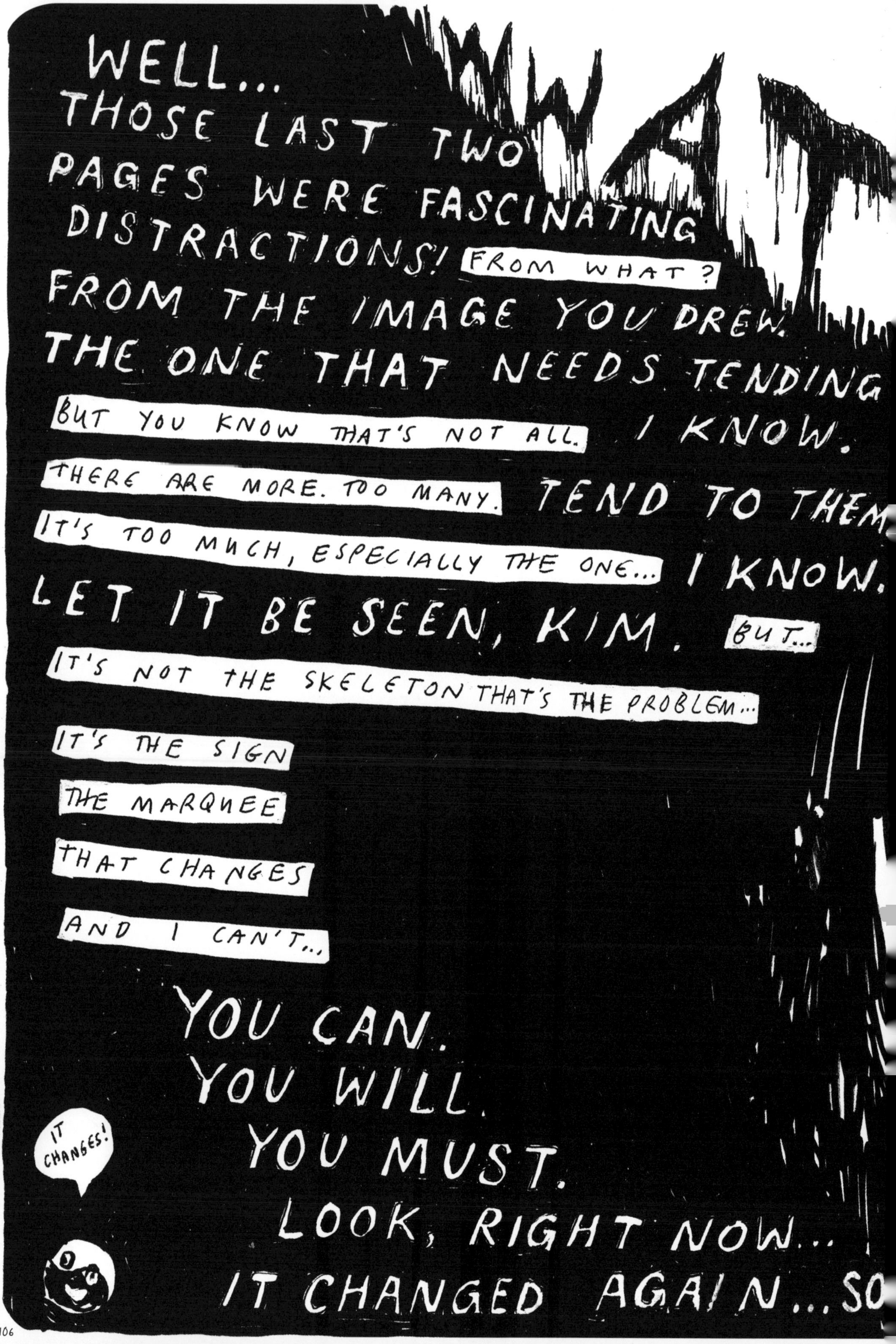
WELL...
THOSE LAST TWO PAGES WERE FASCINATING DISTRACTIONS!
FROM WHAT?
FROM THE IMAGE YOU DREW. THE ONE THAT NEEDS TENDING
BUT YOU KNOW THAT'S NOT ALL.
I KNOW.
THERE ARE MORE. TOO MANY.
TEND TO THEM.
IT'S TOO MUCH, ESPECIALLY THE ONE...
I KNOW.
LET IT BE SEEN, KIM.
BUT...
IT'S NOT THE SKELETON THAT'S THE PROBLEM...
IT'S THE SIGN
THE MARQUEE
THAT CHANGES
AND I CAN'T...
YOU CAN.
YOU WILL.
YOU MUST.
LOOK, RIGHT NOW...
IT CHANGED AGAIN...SO
IT CHANGES!

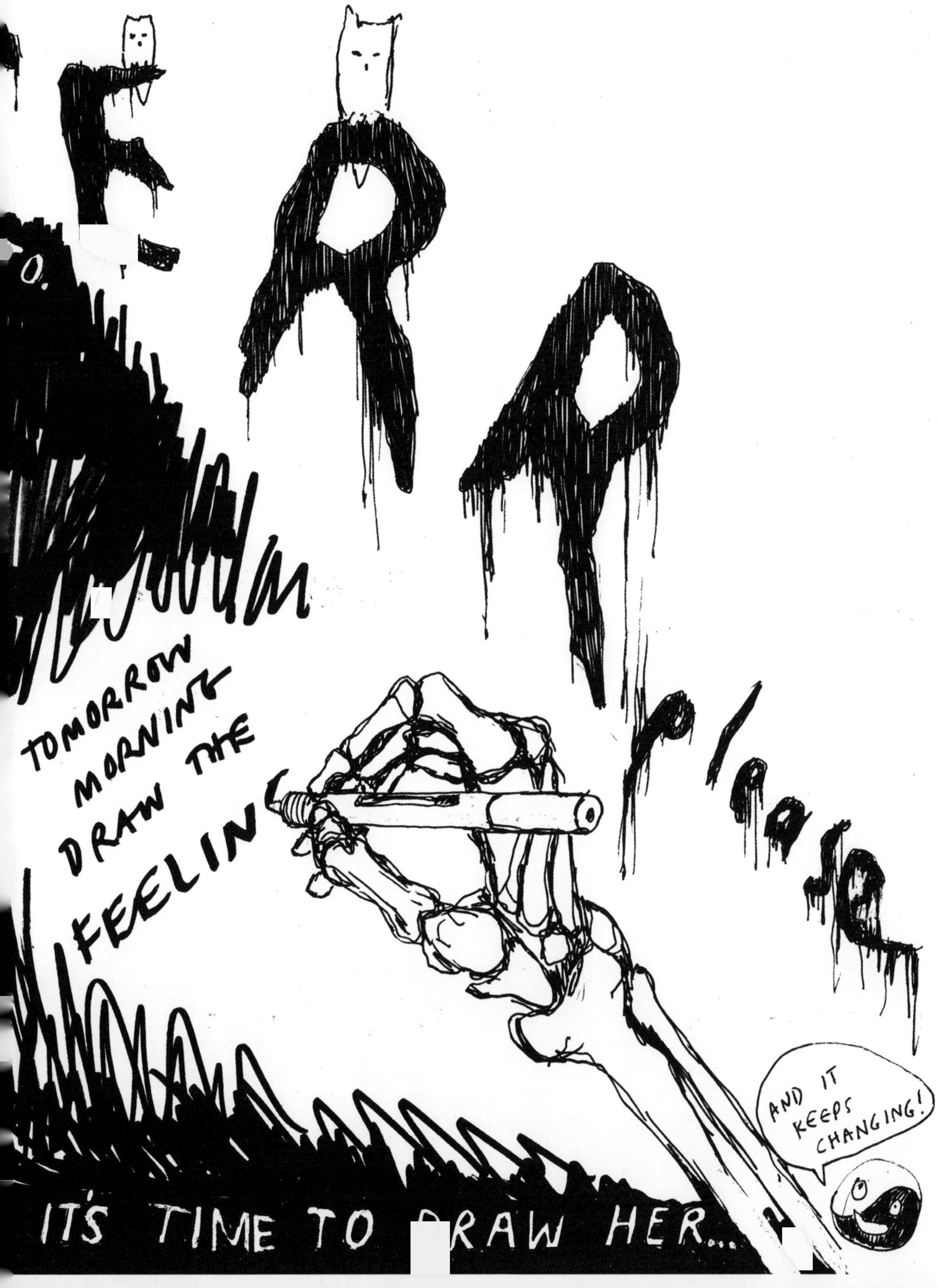
TOMORROW MORNING DRAW THE FEELIN
please
AND IT KEEPS CHANGING!
ITS TIME TO RAW HER...

MAY 9, 2019 7AM

DO YOU SEE THIS BANNER? ↑ DO YOU KNOW WHAT IT MEANS? ONLY SIX DAYS LEFT OF THIS 30-DAY PROJECT. NO TIME! THERE'S NO TIME TO TEND TO THESE HAUNTING IMAGES! THE SKELETON HAS TO GET THROUGH THE JOURNEY... AND HEAL... AND BE FIXED... AND BETTER... AND READY TO HEAD TO THE BEAUTIFUL & FANCY APARTMENT IN THE EAST VILLAGE. REAL LIFE! I ASKED THE HOUSING MANAGER IF I CAN STAY HERE AT THE ASHRAM JUST A LITTLE LONGER. JUNE PERHAPS... TO FINISH THE STORY... TO BUILD MORE RESILIENCE SO I DON'T SPEND MY SUMMER ON THE HARDWOOD FLOOR OF A FIFTH-FLOOR WALKUP BINGEING ON... WHO KNOWS... CASHEWS...? FROZEN BREAD...? ICE CREAM SANDWICHES...? CEREAL? YEP IT WOULD BE CEREAL. SO SWEET & CRUNCHY, BOWL AFTER BOWL. THEY SAID MY ROOM ISN'T AVAILABLE... SO... THEY'RE TRYING TO SEE... IF THERE'S SOMETHING THEY CAN DO... SO I WAIT. AND WONDER. I STARE AT THE IMAGE THAT APPEARS IN MY MIND WHEN I CLOSE MY EYES IN THE SHRINE. I NEED MORE TIME. HER SOFT HEART REQUIRES IT. PLEASE SEND ME A PRAYER THAT'S ESPECIALLY FOR HER. I WILL SHARE IT WHEN IT COMES.

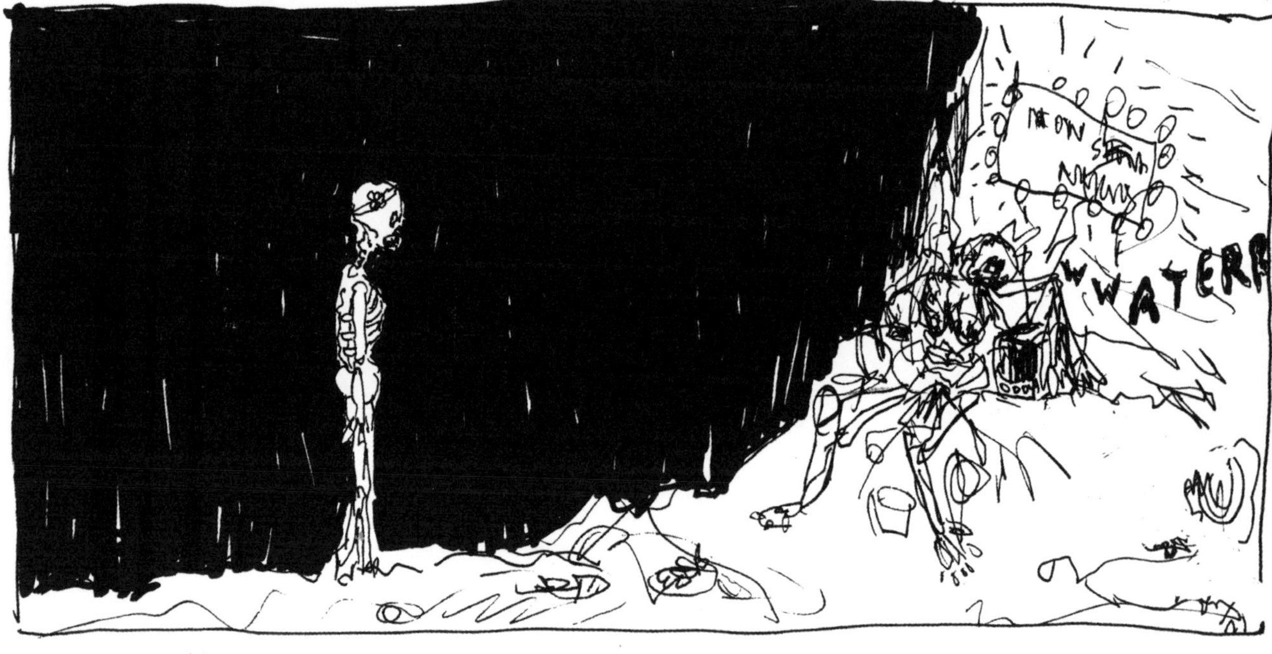
WATERR

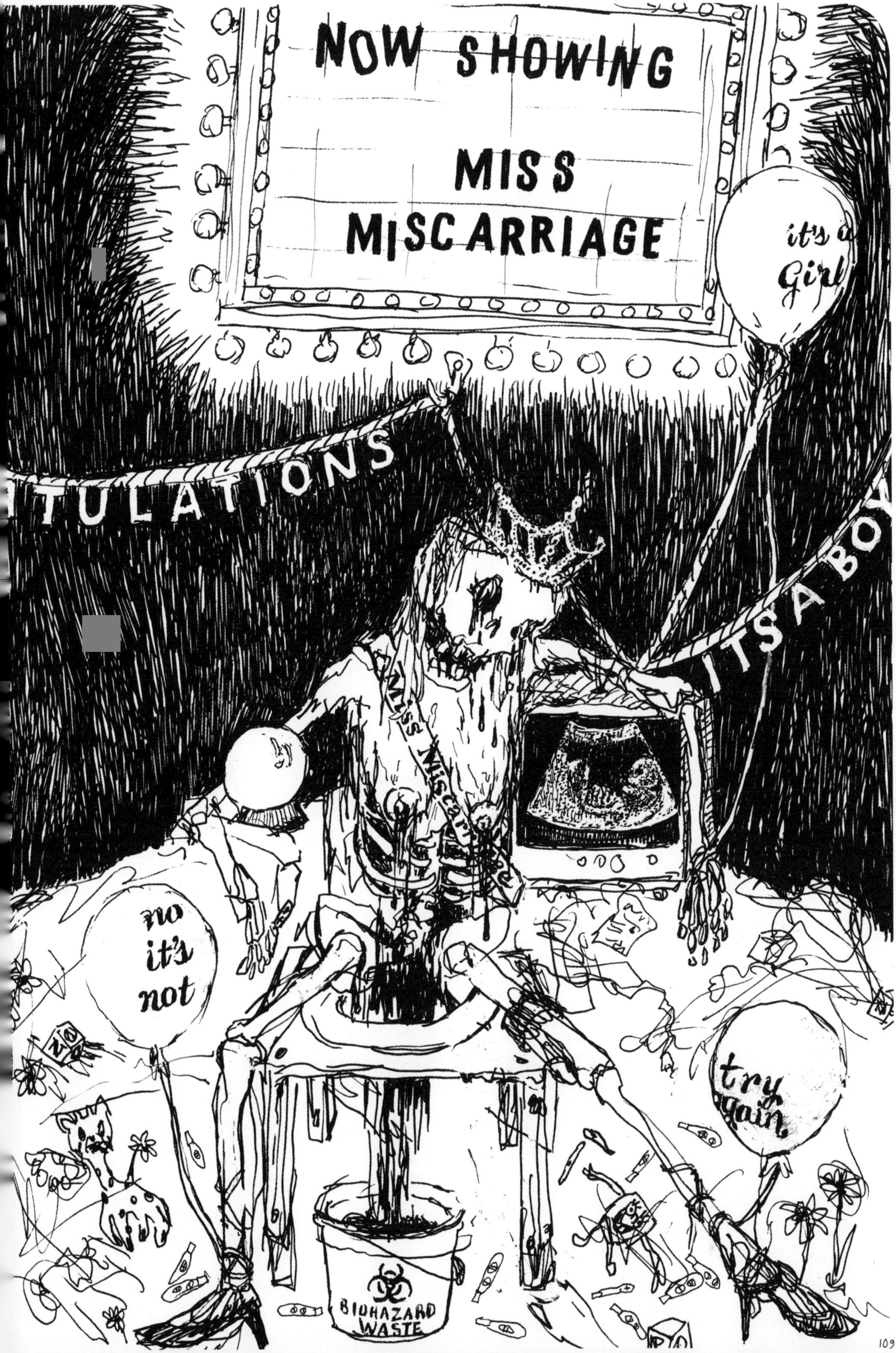
NOW SHOWING
MISS
MISCARRIAGE
it's a
Girl
TULATIONS
ITS A BO
MISS MISCAR
no
it's
not
try
BIOHAZARD
WASTE

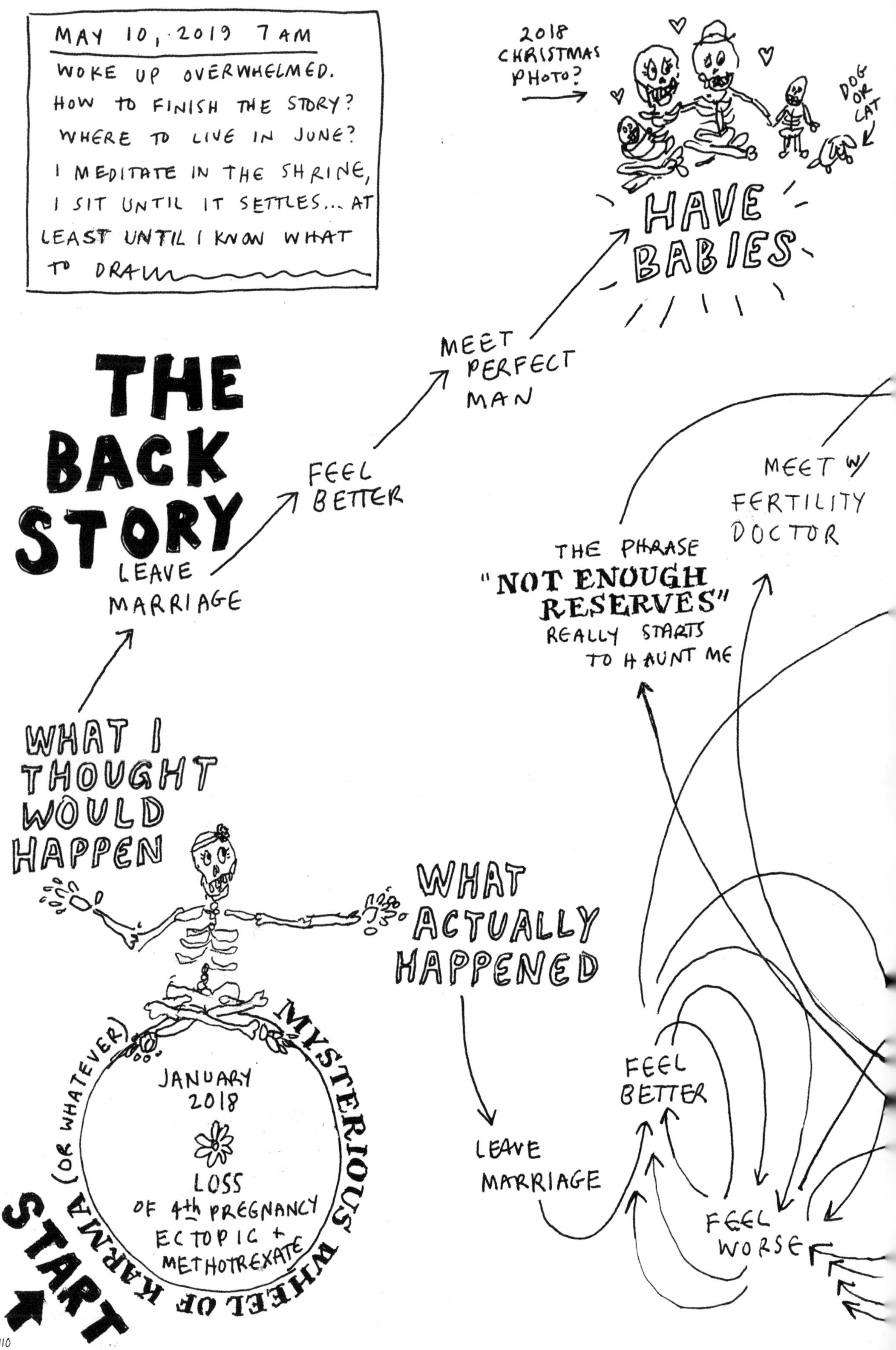
MAY 10, 2019 7 AM
WOKE UP OVERWHELMED. HOW TO FINISH THE STORY? WHERE TO LIVE IN JUNE? I MEDITATE IN THE SHRINE, I SIT UNTIL IT SETTLES... AT LEAST UNTIL I KNOW WHAT TO DRAW
2018 CHRISTMAS PHOTO?
DOG OR CAT
HAVE BABIES
THE BACK STORY
WHAT I THOUGHT WOULD HAPPEN
LEAVE MARRIAGE
FEEL BETTER
MEET PERFECT MAN
MEET W/ FERTILITY DOCTOR
THE PHRASE "NOT ENOUGH RESERVES" REALLY STARTS TO HAUNT ME
WHAT ACTUALLY HAPPENED
LEAVE MARRIAGE
FEEL BETTER
FEEL WORSE
MYSTERIOUS WHEEL OF KARMA (OR WHATEVER)
JANUARY 2018
LOSS OF 4th PREGNANCY
ECTOPIC + METHOTREXATE
START

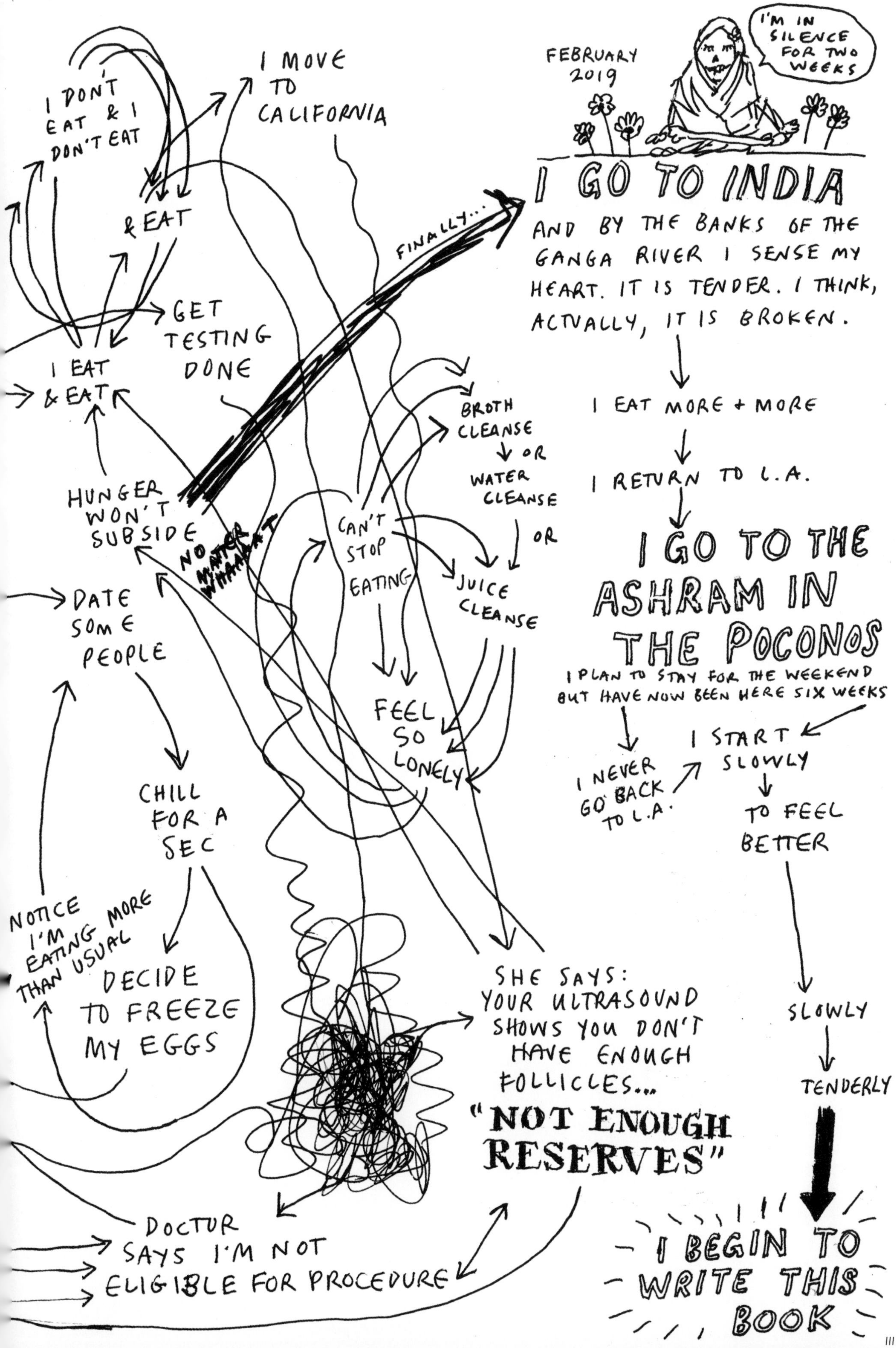
I DON'T EAT & I DON'T EAT
& EAT
I MOVE TO CALIFORNIA
GET TESTING DONE
I EAT & EAT
HUNGER WON'T SUBSIDE
NO MATTER WHAAAAT
DATE SOME PEOPLE
CHILL FOR A SEC
DECIDE TO FREEZE MY EGGS
NOTICE I'M EATING MORE THAN USUAL
CAN'T STOP EATING
BROTH CLEANSE
OR
WATER CLEANSE
OR
JUICE CLEANSE
FEEL SO LONELY
FINALLY...
SHE SAYS: YOUR ULTRASOUND SHOWS YOU DON'T HAVE ENOUGH FOLLICLES...
"NOT ENOUGH RESERVES"
DOCTOR SAYS I'M NOT ELIGIBLE FOR PROCEDURE
FEBRUARY 2019
I'M IN SILENCE FOR TWO WEEKS
I GO TO INDIA
AND BY THE BANKS OF THE GANGA RIVER I SENSE MY HEART. IT IS TENDER. I THINK, ACTUALLY, IT IS BROKEN.
I EAT MORE + MORE
I RETURN TO L.A.
I GO TO THE ASHRAM IN THE POCONOS
I PLAN TO STAY FOR THE WEEKEND BUT HAVE NOW BEEN HERE SIX WEEKS
I NEVER GO BACK TO L.A.
I START SLOWLY
TO FEEL BETTER
SLOWLY
TENDERLY
I BEGIN TO WRITE THIS BOOK

→ BUT YOU DIDN'T TELL THEM ABOUT THE DREAM.

NO ONE WANTS TO HEAR ABOUT A DREAM!

BUT IT'S THE ONE. ~~MADE~~ THE ONE THAT ~~HELPED~~ TOLD YOU TO LEAVE, FINALLY.

WHAT WAS IT A DREAM OF?

TWINS.

TWO TWIN BOYS.

TEENAGERS IN FACT.

TALL, LANKY, ANDROGYNOUS.

WHEN DID YOU HAVE THE DREAM?

THE NIGHT OF THE METHOTREXATE.

WHAT IS METHOTREXATE?

CHEMOTHERAPY.

BUT WHY CHEMO?

TO AVOID SURGERY

WHY? WHAT?

BECAUSE THE CELLS RAPIDLY DIVIDE (GROW) IN BOTH CANCER AND IN EMBRYOS.

SO THE CHEMO RIDS THE BODY OF THE PREGNANCY?

YES. IT INDUCES THE MISCARRIAGE? YES.

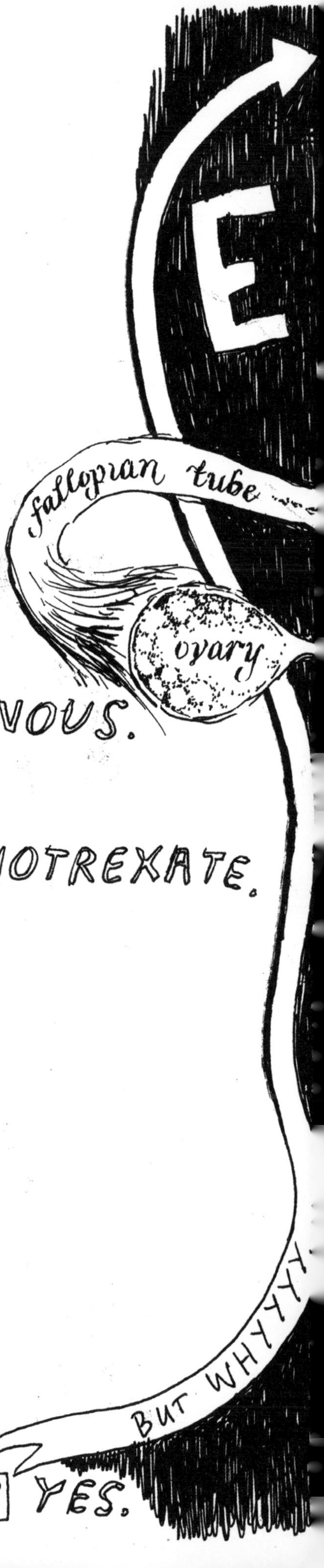
E
fallopian tube
ovary
BUT WHYYYY

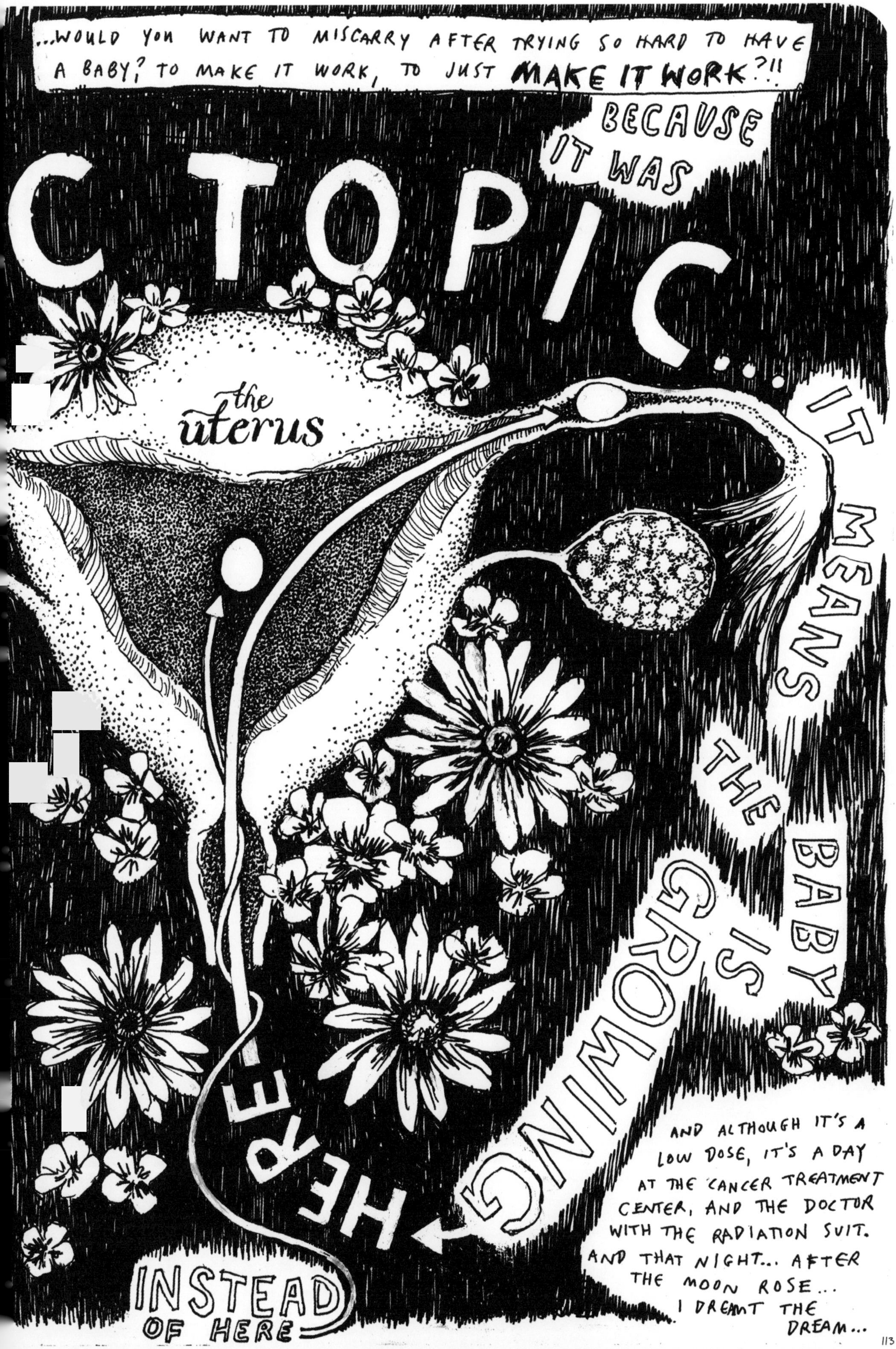
...WOULD YOU WANT TO MISCARRY AFTER TRYING SO HARD TO HAVE A BABY? TO MAKE IT WORK, TO JUST MAKE IT WORK?!!
BECAUSE IT WAS
CTOPIC...
the uterus
IT MEANS THE BABY IS GROWING
HERE
INSTEAD OF HERE
AND ALTHOUGH IT'S A LOW DOSE, IT'S A DAY AT THE CANCER TREATMENT CENTER, AND THE DOCTOR WITH THE RADIATION SUIT. AND THAT NIGHT... AFTER THE MOON ROSE... I DREAMT THE DREAM...

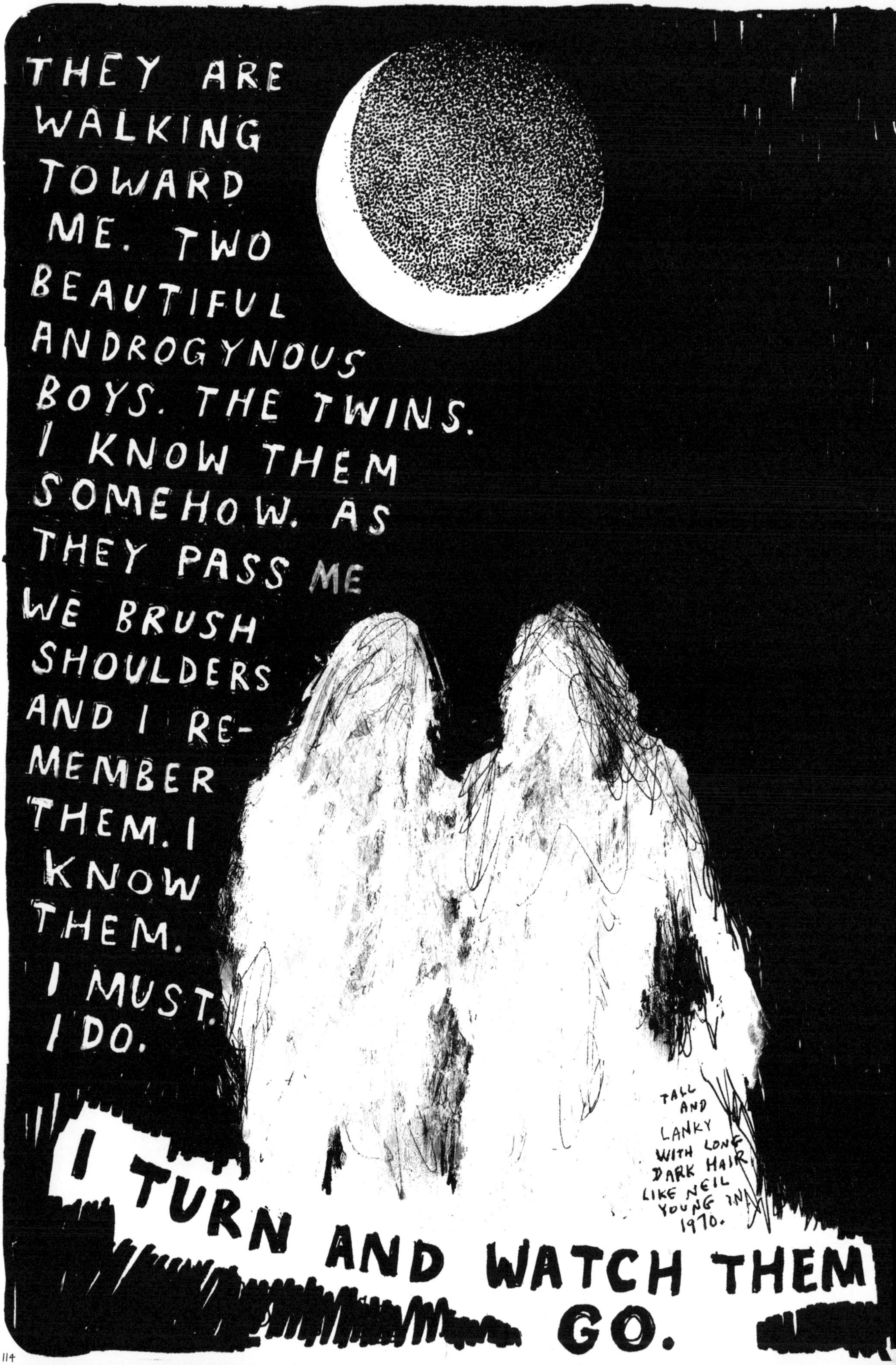
THEY ARE WALKING TOWARD ME. TWO BEAUTIFUL ANDROGYNOUS BOYS. THE TWINS. I KNOW THEM SOMEHOW. AS THEY PASS ME WE BRUSH SHOULDERS AND I RE-MEMBER THEM. I KNOW THEM. I MUST. I DO.
TALL AND LANKY WITH LONG DARK HAIR LIKE NEIL YOUNG IN 1970.
I TURN AND WATCH THEM GO.

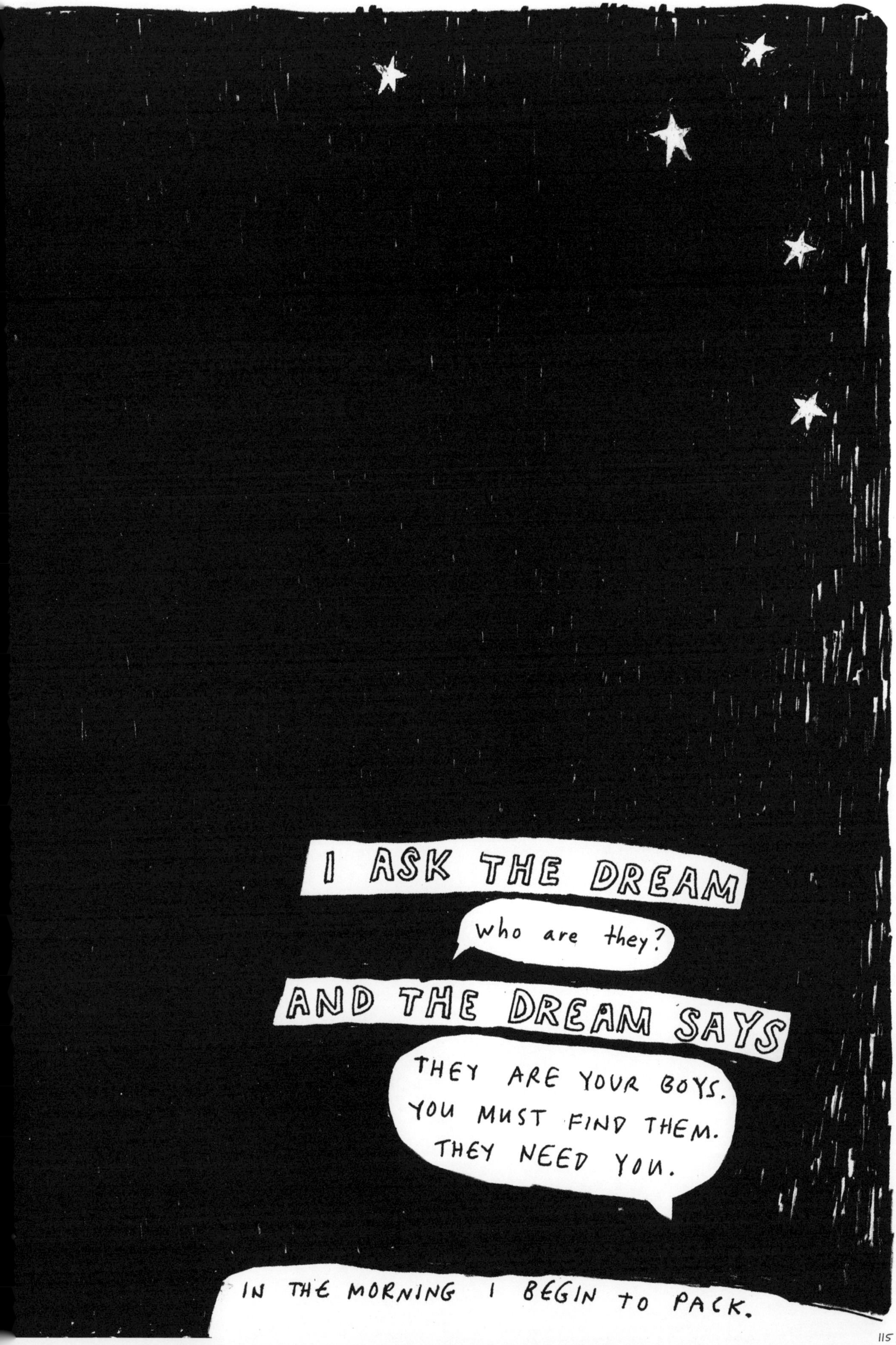
I ASK THE DREAM
who are they?
AND THE DREAM SAYS
THEY ARE YOUR BOYS. YOU MUST FIND THEM. THEY NEED YOU.
IN THE MORNING I BEGIN TO PACK.

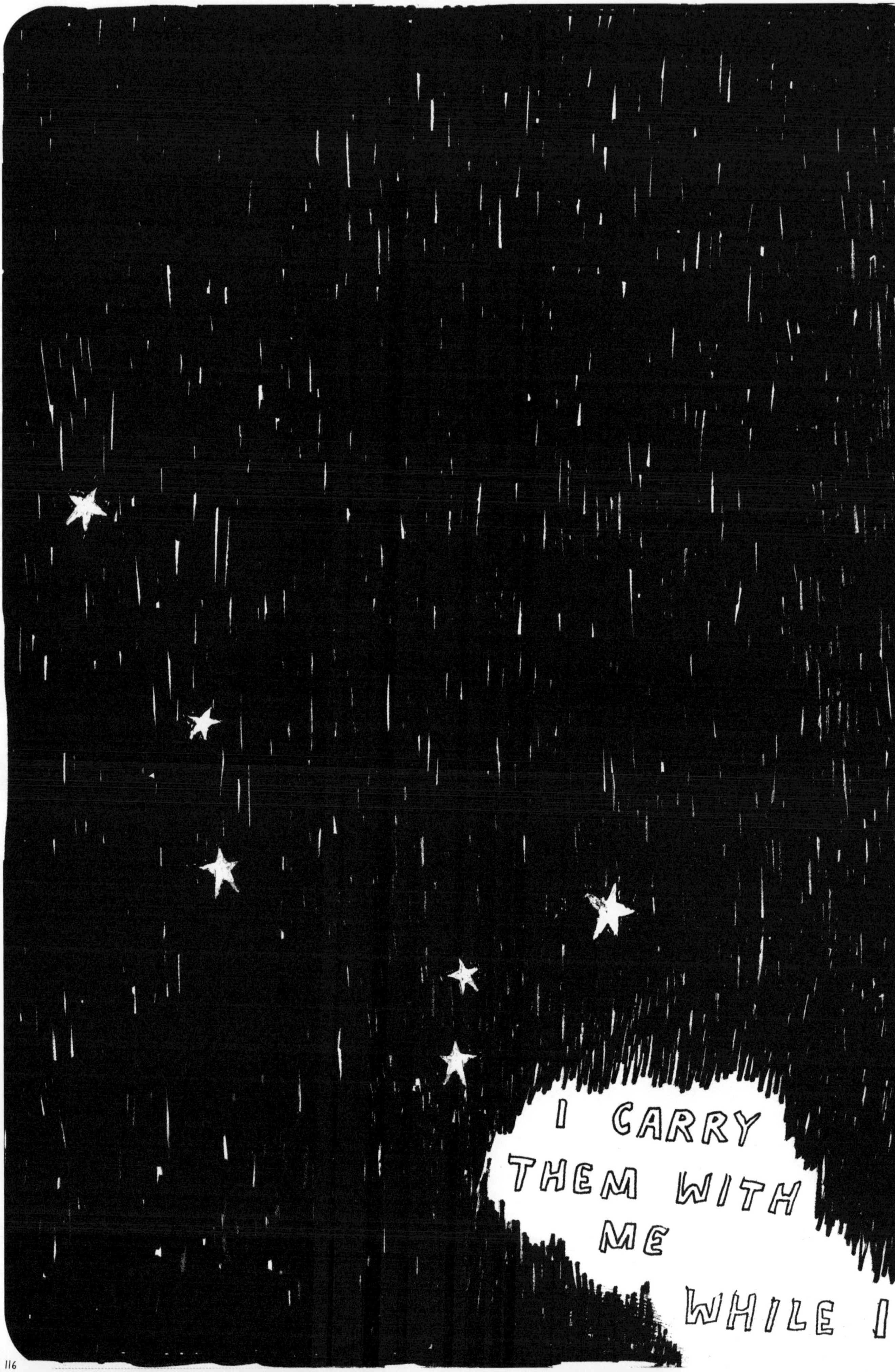
I CARRY THEM WITH ME
WHILE I

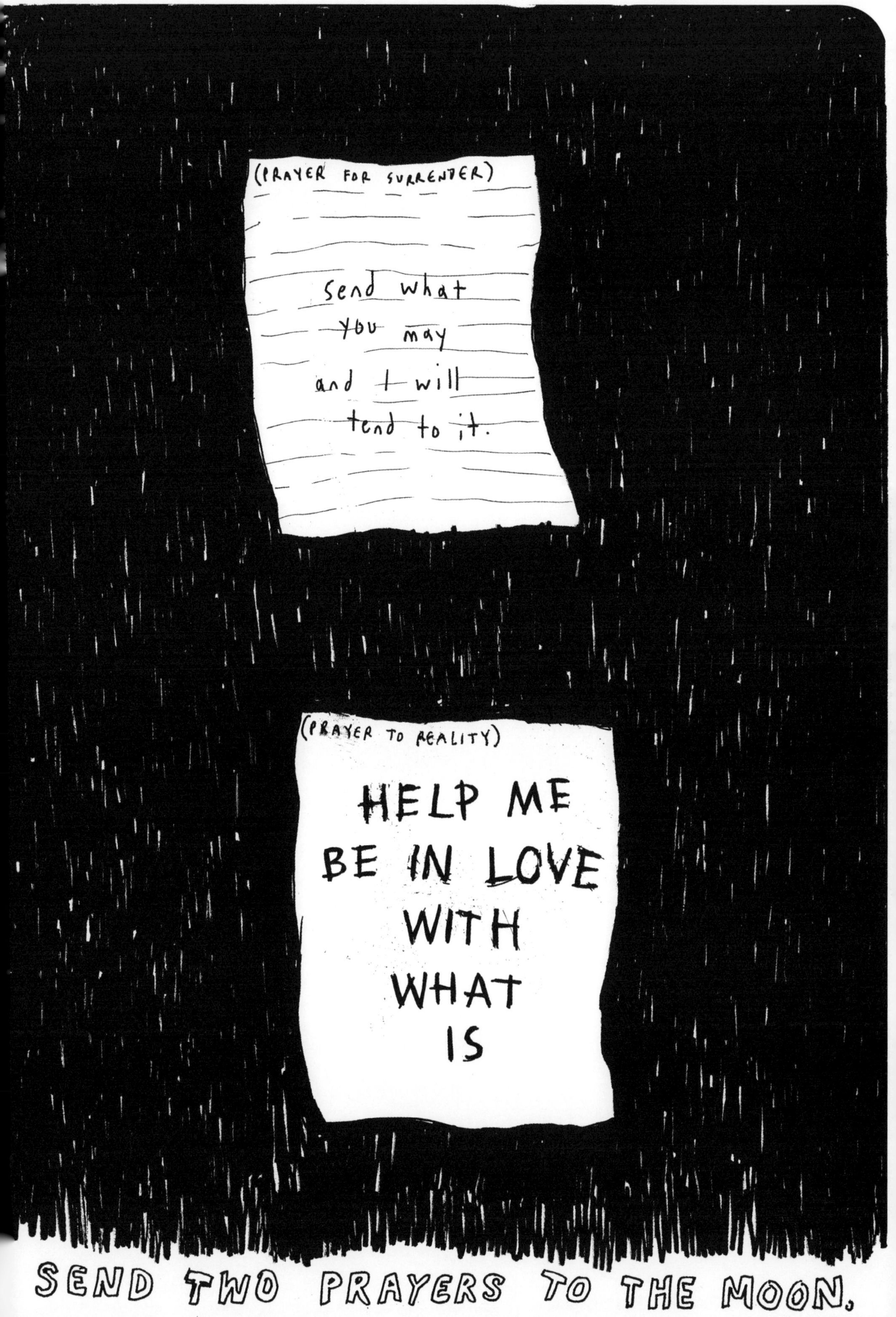
(PRAYER FOR SURRENDER)
send what you may and I will tend to it.
(PRAYER TO REALITY)
HELP ME BE IN LOVE WITH WHAT IS

SEND TWO PRAYERS TO THE MOON.

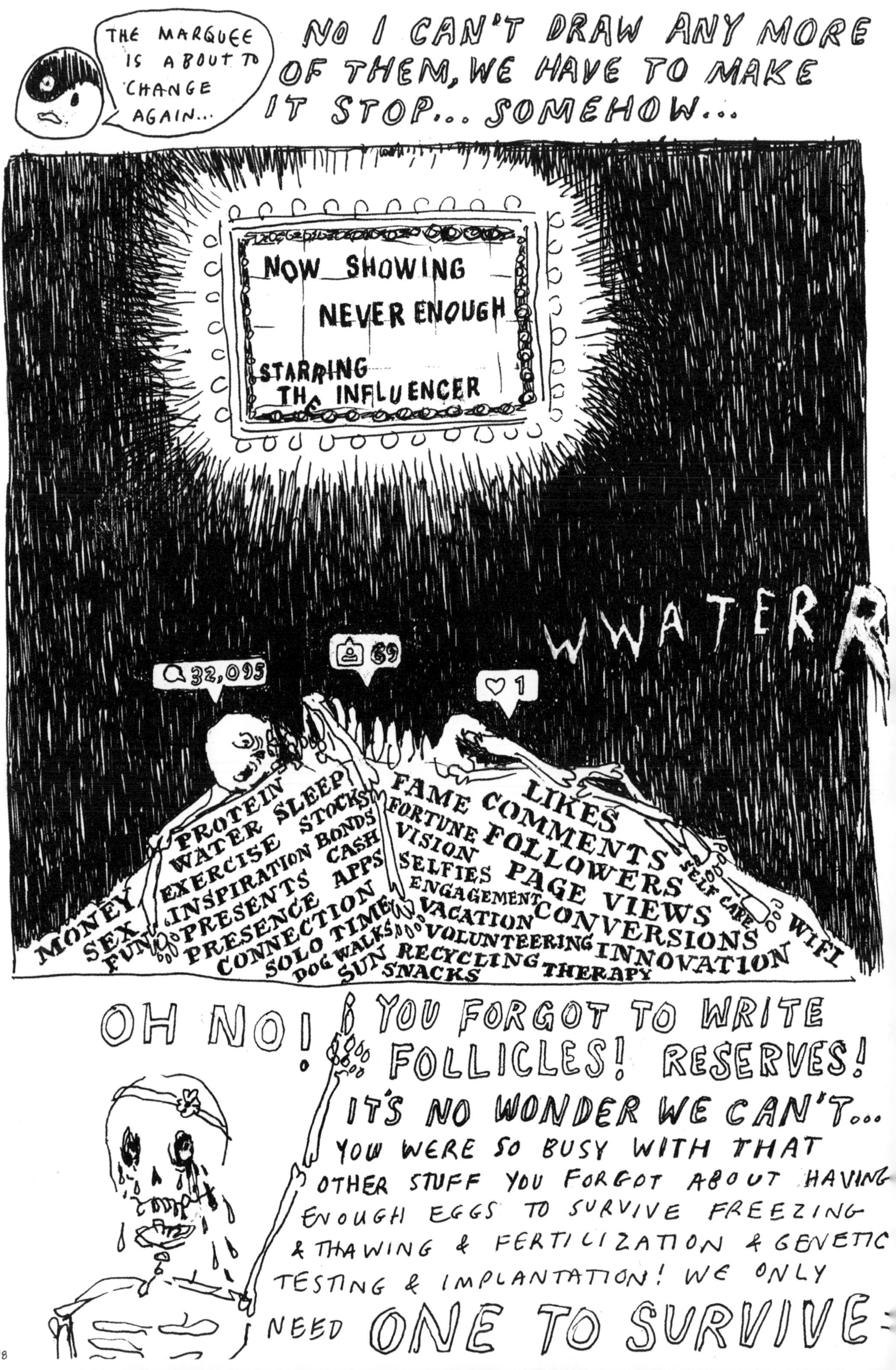
THE MARQUEE IS ABOUT TO CHANGE AGAIN...
NO I CAN'T DRAW ANY MORE OF THEM, WE HAVE TO MAKE IT STOP... SOMEHOW...
NOW SHOWING
NEVER ENOUGH
STARRING THE INFLUENCER
32,095
69
1
WWATERR
PROTEIN SLEEP WATER EXERCISE STOCKS BONDS INSPIRATION CASH PRESENTS APPS PRESENCE CONNECTION SOLO TIME DOG WALKS SUN MONEY SEX FUN
FAME FORTUNE VISION SELFIES ENGAGEMENT VACATION VOLUNTEERING RECYCLING SNACKS
LIKES COMMENTS FOLLOWERS PAGE VIEWS CONVERSIONS INNOVATION THERAPY SELF CARE WIFI
OH NO!
YOU FORGOT TO WRITE FOLLICLES! RESERVES!
IT'S NO WONDER WE CAN'T...
YOU WERE SO BUSY WITH THAT OTHER STUFF YOU FORGOT ABOUT HAVING ENOUGH EGGS TO SURVIVE FREEZING & THAWING & FERTILIZATION & GENETIC TESTING & IMPLANTATION! WE ONLY NEED ONE TO SURVIVE

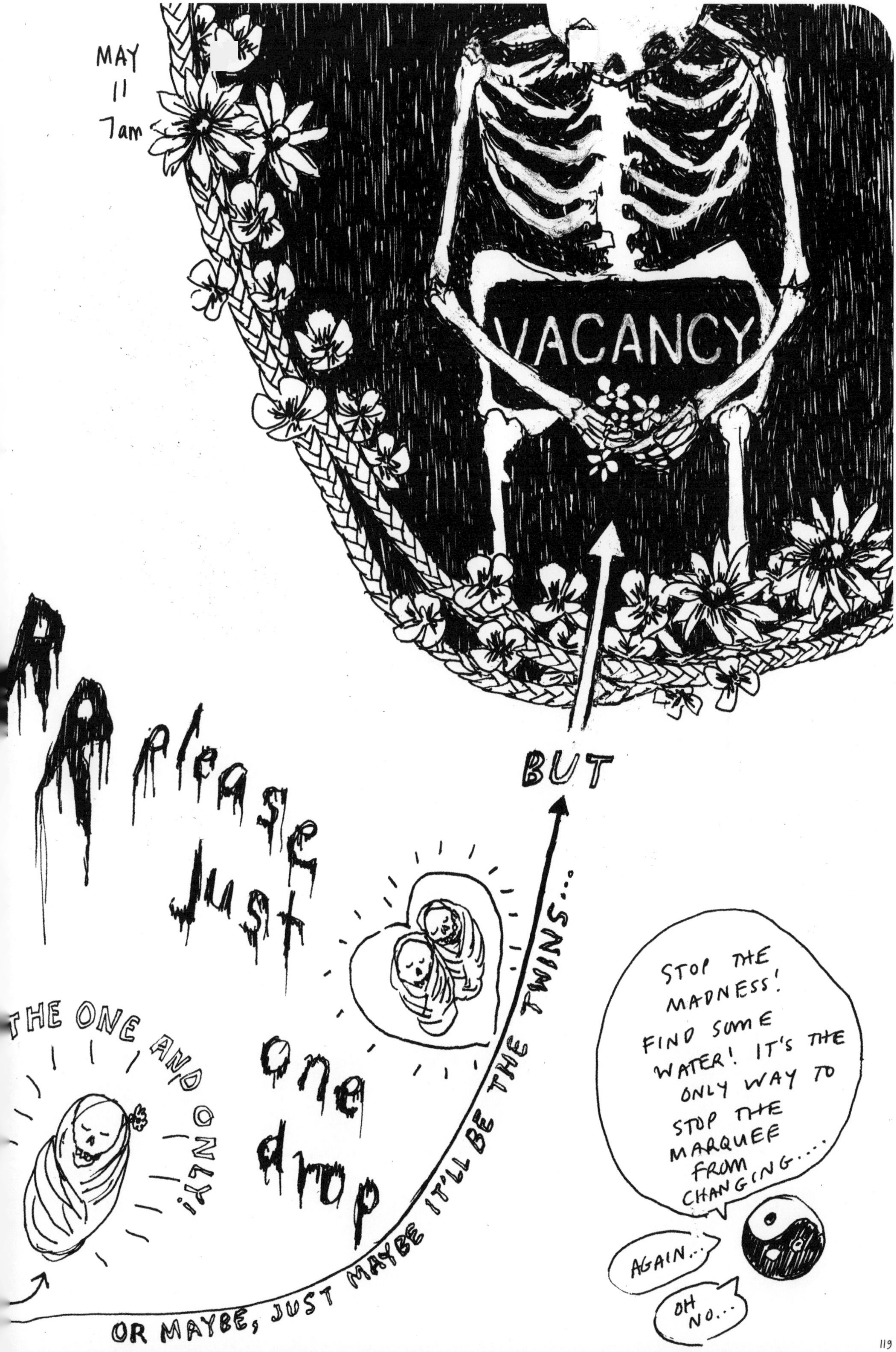
MAY
11
7am
VACANCY
BUT
please just one drop
THE ONE AND ONLY!
OR MAYBE, JUST MAYBE IT'LL BE THE TWINS...
STOP THE MADNESS! FIND SOME WATER! IT'S THE ONLY WAY TO STOP THE MARQUEE FROM CHANGING....
AGAIN...
OH NO...

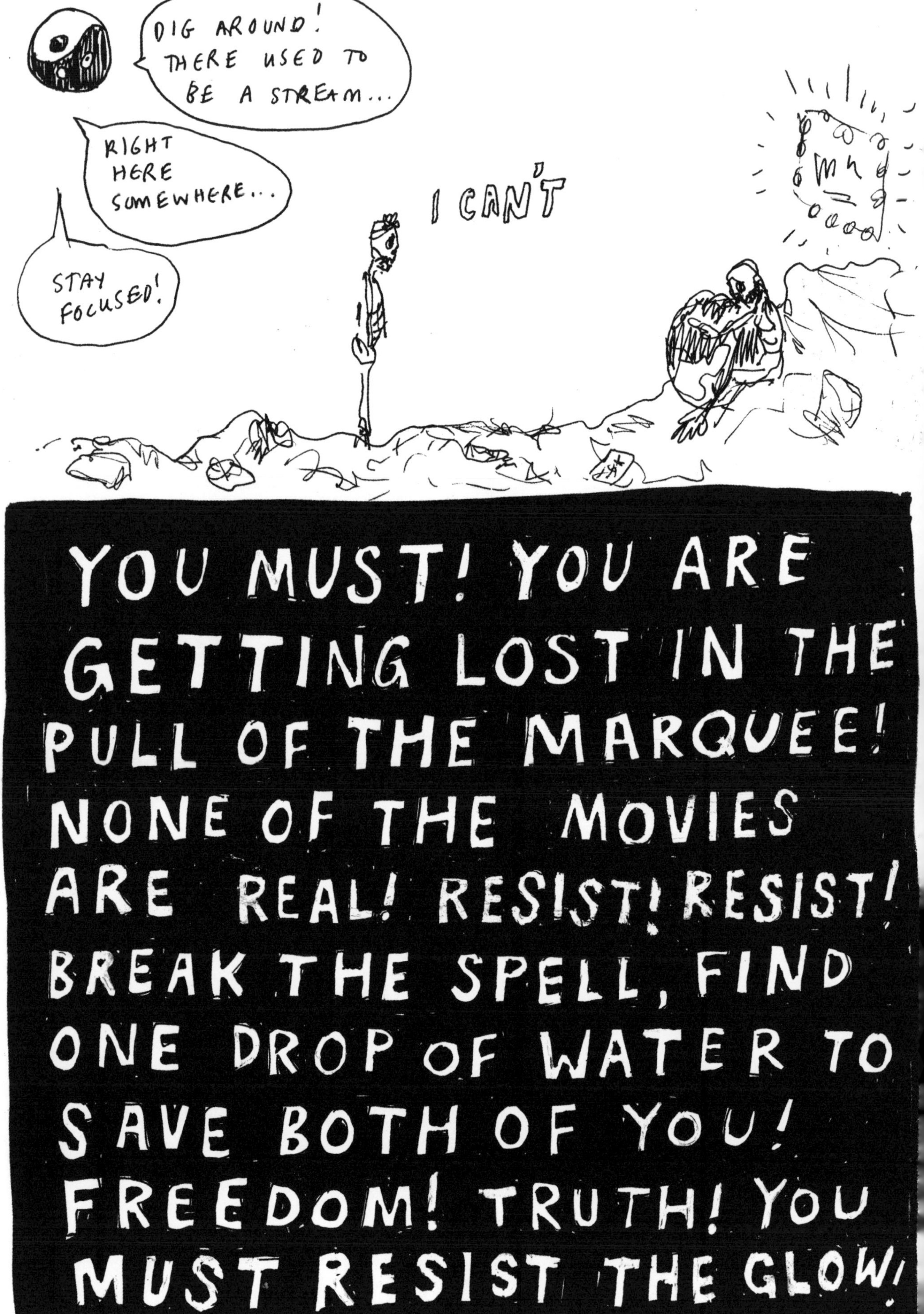
DIG AROUND! THERE USED TO BE A STREAM...
RIGHT HERE SOMEWHERE...
STAY FOCUSED!
I CAN'T
YOU MUST! YOU ARE GETTING LOST IN THE PULL OF THE MARQUEE! NONE OF THE MOVIES ARE REAL! RESIST! RESIST! RESIST! BREAK THE SPELL, FIND ONE DROP OF WATER TO SAVE BOTH OF YOU! FREEDOM! TRUTH! YOU MUST RESIST THE GLOW!

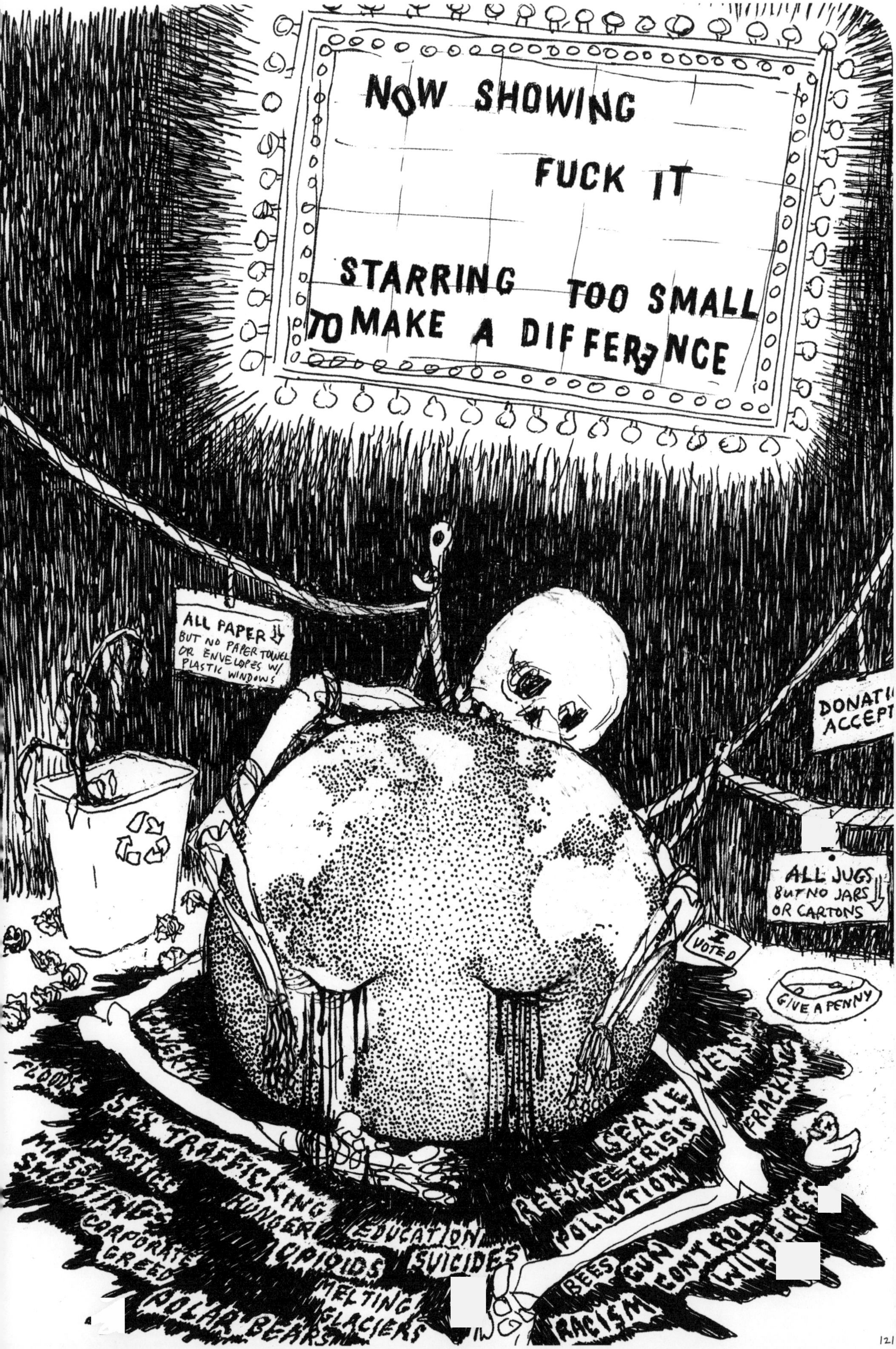
NOW SHOWING
FUCK IT
STARRING TOO SMALL TO MAKE A DIFFERENCE
ALL PAPER
BUT NO PAPER TOWEL OR ENVELOPES W/ PLASTIC WINDOWS
ALL JUGS
BUT NO JARS OR CARTONS
I VOTED
GIVE A PENNY
POVERTY
FLOODS
SEX TRAFFICKING
PLASTICS
MASS SHOOTINGS
HUNGER
CORPORATE GREED
OPIOIDS
EDUCATION
SUICIDES
MELTING GLACIERS
POLAR BEARS
REFUGEE CRISIS
SEA LEVELS
POLLUTION
FRACKING
BEES
GUN CONTROL
RACISM

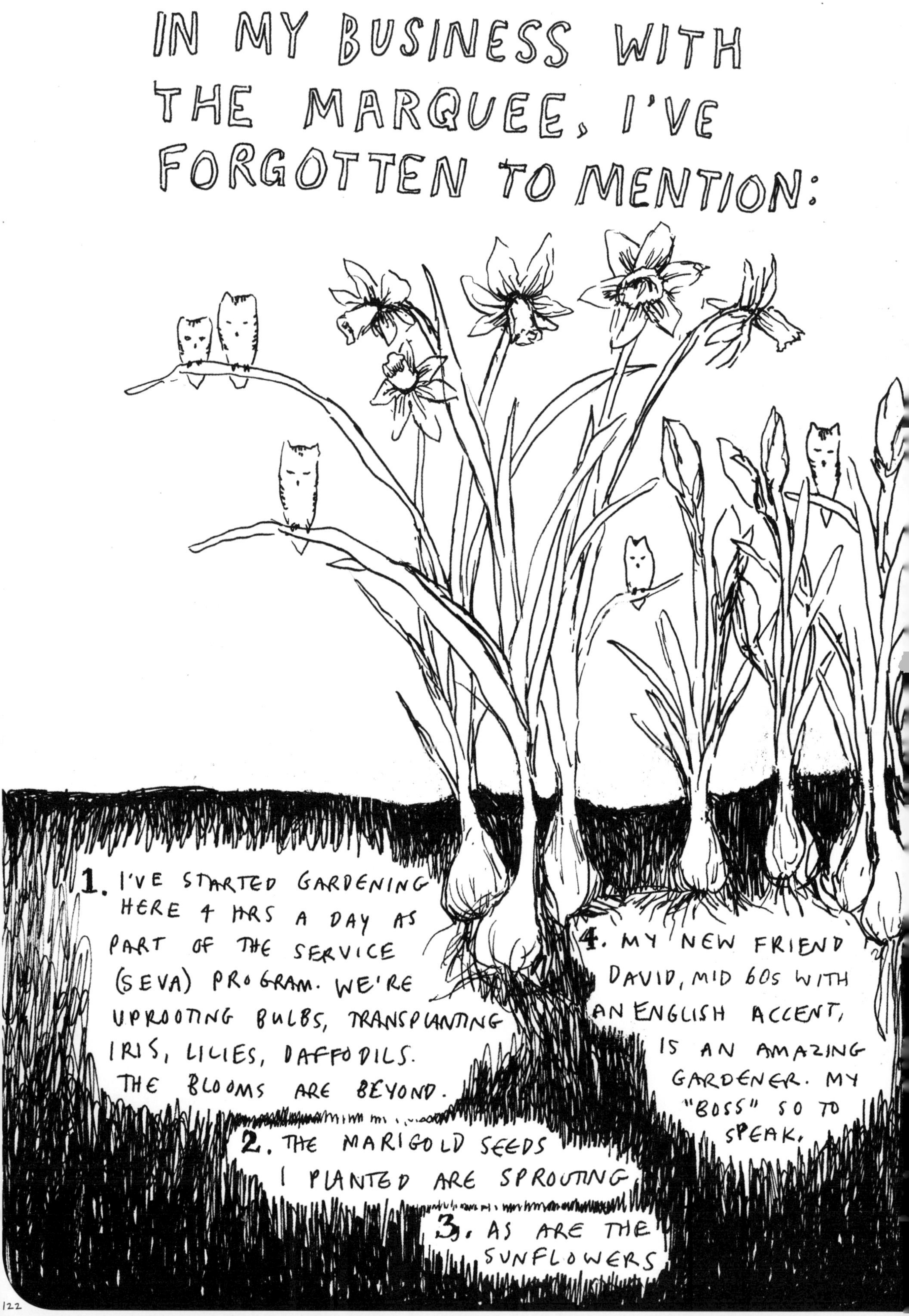
IN MY BUSINESS WITH THE MARQUEE, I'VE FORGOTTEN TO MENTION:
1. I'VE STARTED GARDENING HERE 4 HRS A DAY AS PART OF THE SERVICE (SEVA) PROGRAM. WE'RE UPROOTING BULBS, TRANSPLANTING IRIS, LILIES, DAFFODILS. THE BLOOMS ARE BEYOND.
2. THE MARIGOLD SEEDS I PLANTED ARE SPROUTING
3. AS ARE THE SUNFLOWERS
4. MY NEW FRIEND DAVID, MID 60s WITH AN ENGLISH ACCENT, IS AN AMAZING GARDENER. MY "BOSS" SO TO SPEAK.

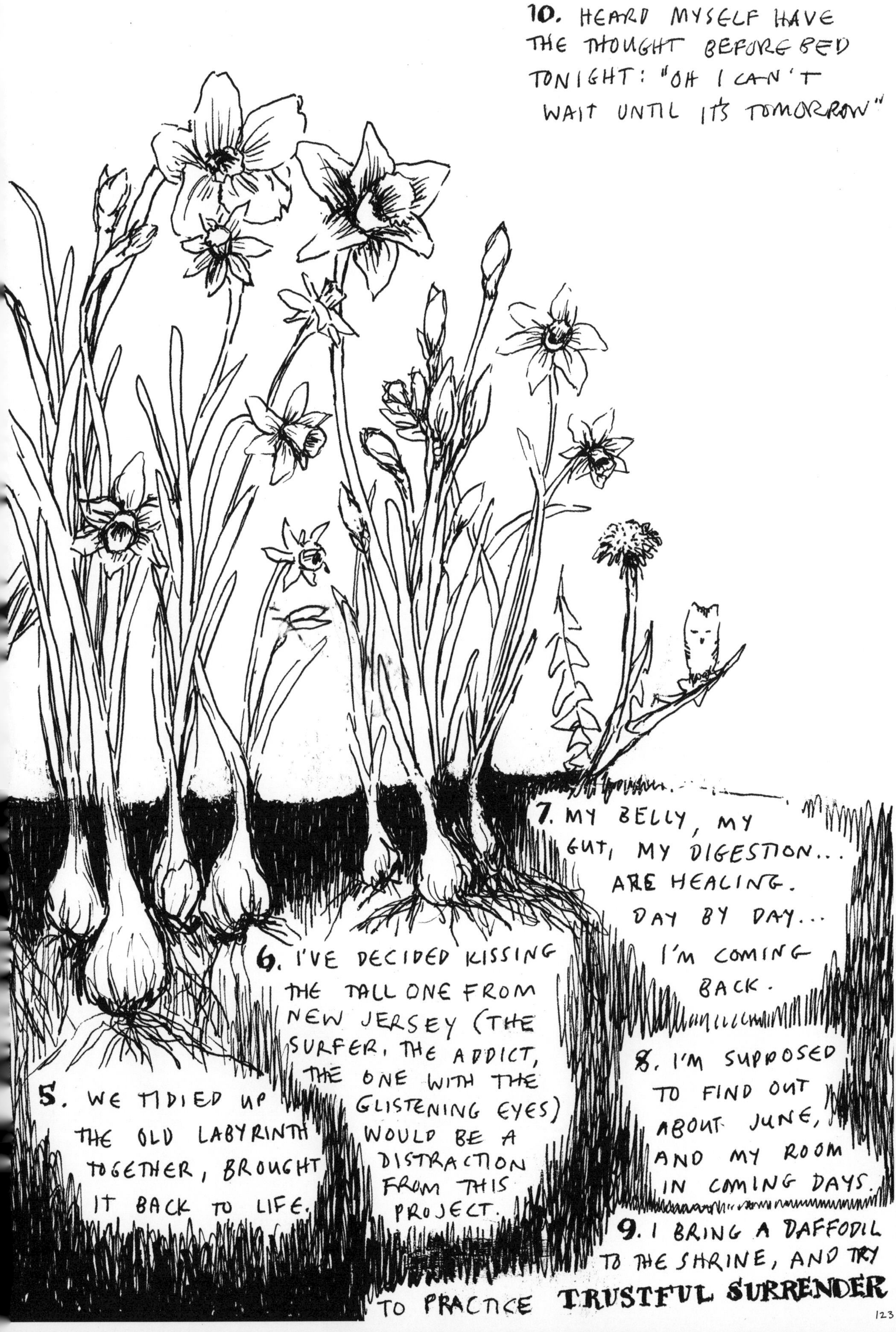
10. HEARD MYSELF HAVE THE THOUGHT BEFORE BED TONIGHT: "OH I CAN'T WAIT UNTIL IT'S TOMORROW"
5. WE TIDIED UP THE OLD LABYRINTH TOGETHER, BROUGHT IT BACK TO LIFE.
6. I'VE DECIDED KISSING THE TALL ONE FROM NEW JERSEY (THE SURFER, THE ADDICT, THE ONE WITH THE GLISTENING EYES) WOULD BE A DISTRACTION FROM THIS PROJECT.
7. MY BELLY, MY GUT, MY DIGESTION... ARE HEALING. DAY BY DAY... I'M COMING BACK.
8. I'M SUPPOSED TO FIND OUT ABOUT JUNE, AND MY ROOM IN COMING DAYS.
9. I BRING A DAFFODIL TO THE SHRINE, AND TRY TO PRACTICE TRUSTFUL SURRENDER

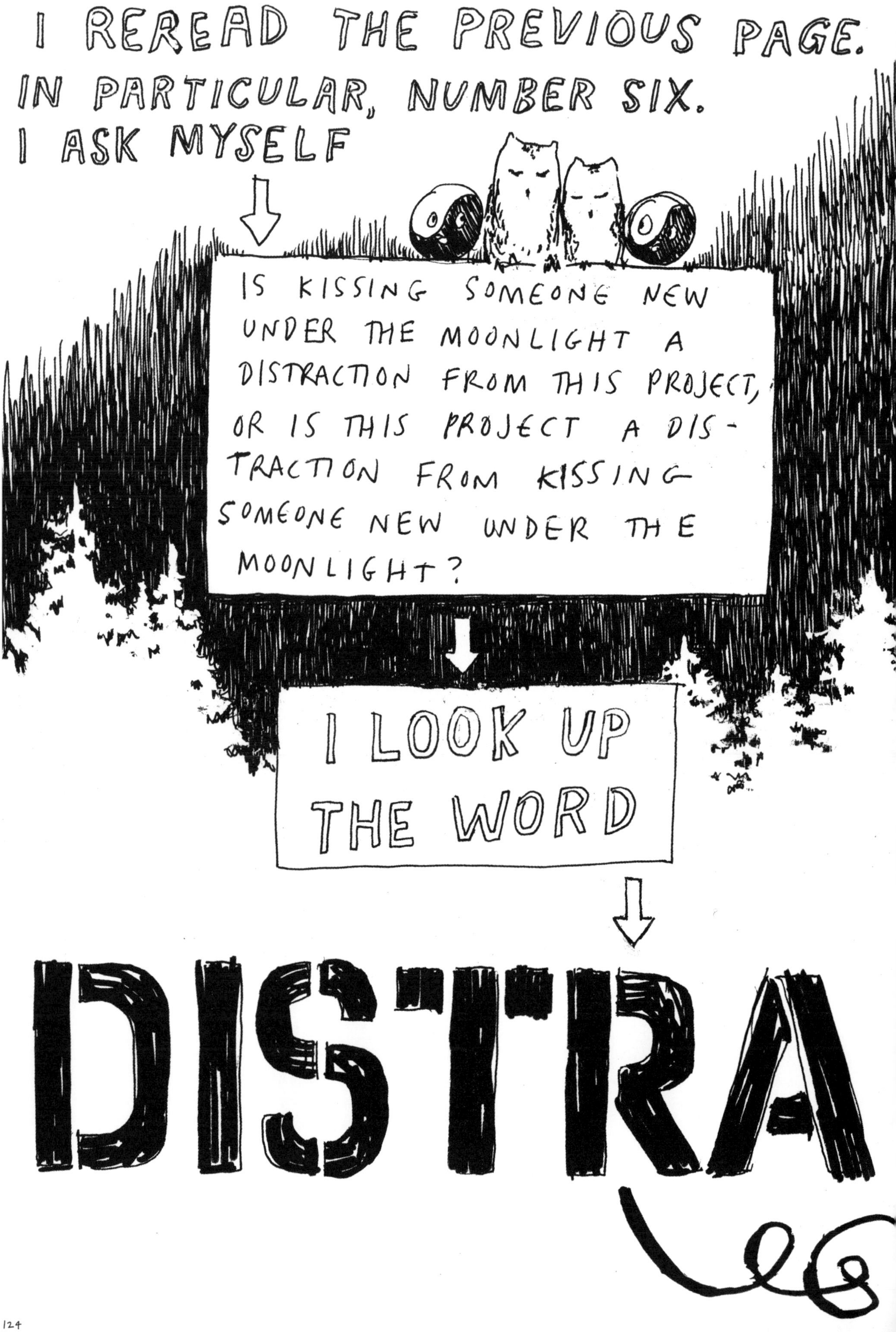
I REREAD THE PREVIOUS PAGE.
IN PARTICULAR, NUMBER SIX.
I ASK MYSELF
IS KISSING SOMEONE NEW UNDER THE MOONLIGHT A DISTRACTION FROM THIS PROJECT, OR IS THIS PROJECT A DISTRACTION FROM KISSING SOMEONE NEW UNDER THE MOONLIGHT?
I LOOK UP THE WORD
DISTRA

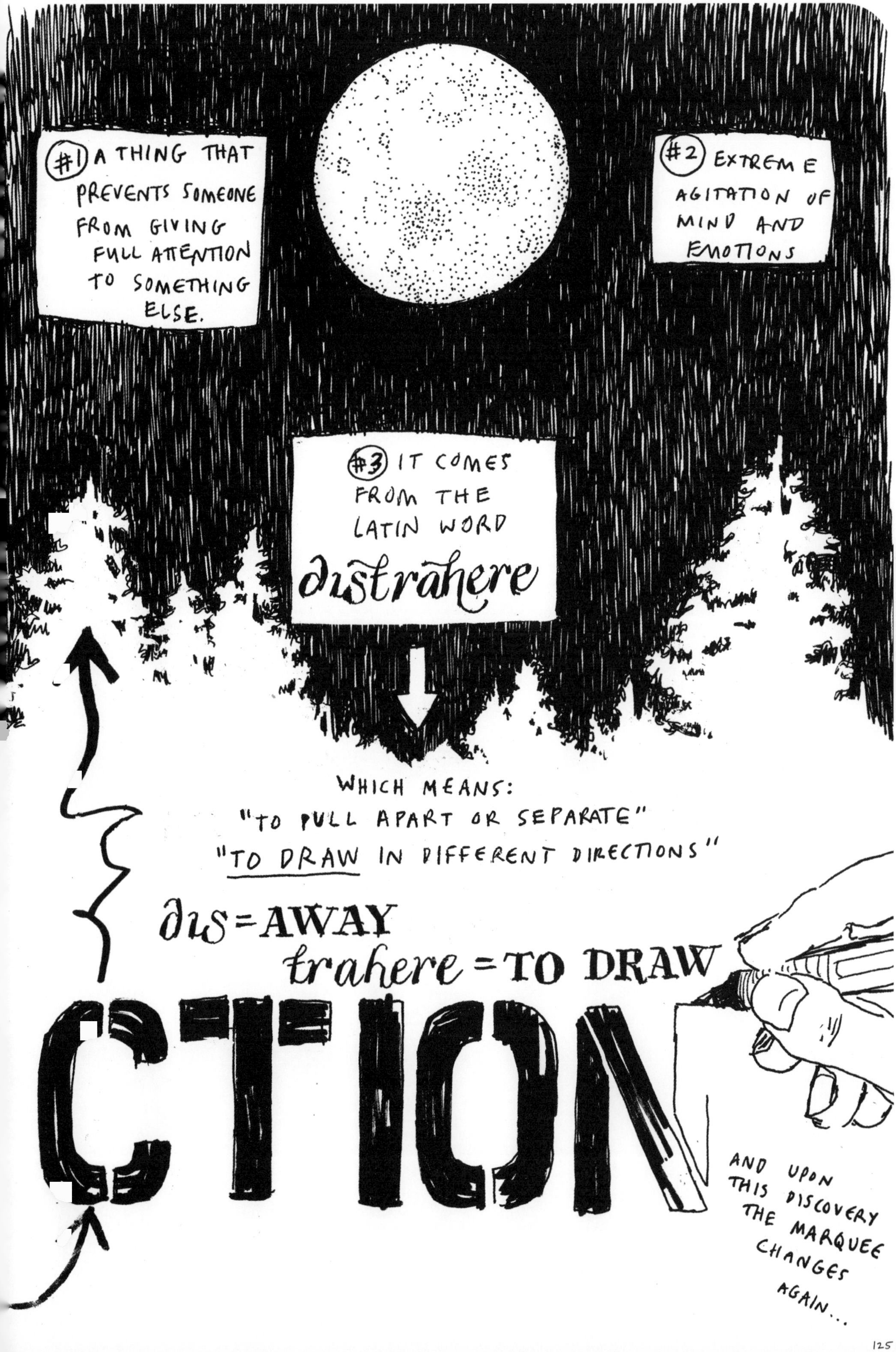

#1 A THING THAT PREVENTS SOMEONE FROM GIVING FULL ATTENTION TO SOMETHING ELSE.
#2 EXTREME AGITATION OF MIND AND EMOTIONS
#3 IT COMES FROM THE LATIN WORD distrahere
WHICH MEANS:
"TO PULL APART OR SEPARATE"
"TO DRAW IN DIFFERENT DIRECTIONS"
dis = AWAY
trahere = TO DRAW
CTION
AND UPON THIS DISCOVERY THE MARQUEE CHANGES AGAIN...

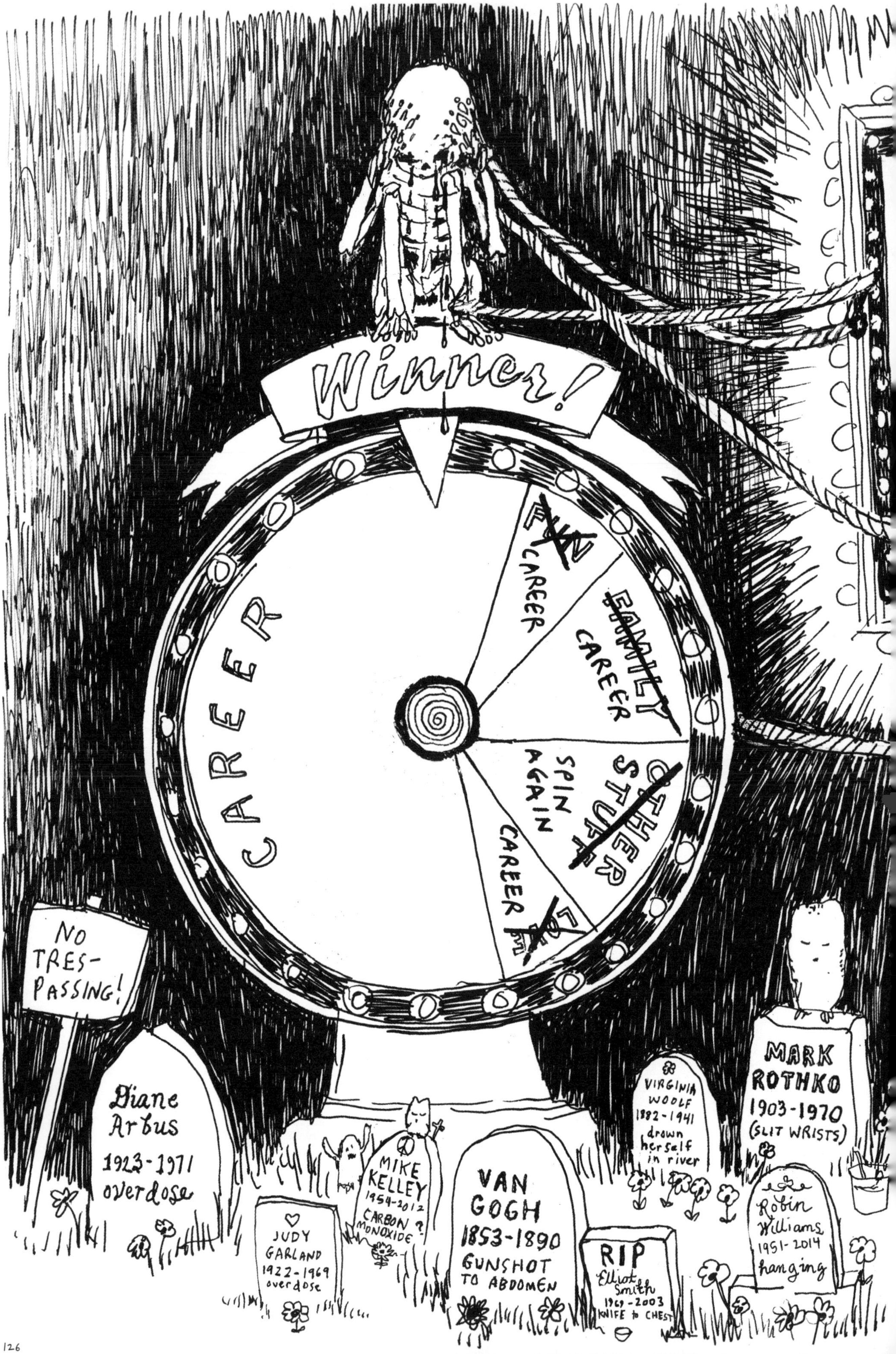
Winner!
CAREER
FUN
CAREER
FAMILY
CAREER
OTHER STUFF
SPIN AGAIN
CAREER
NO TRES-PASSING!
Diane Arbus
1923-1971
overdose
JUDY GARLAND
1922-1969
overdose
MIKE KELLEY
1954-2012
CARBON MONOXIDE ?
VAN GOGH
1853-1890
GUNSHOT TO ABDOMEN
RIP
Elliot Smith
1969-2003
KNIFE to CHEST
VIRGINIA WOOLF
1882-1941
drowned herself in river
MARK ROTHKO
1903-1970
(SLIT WRISTS)
Robin Williams
1951-2014
hanging

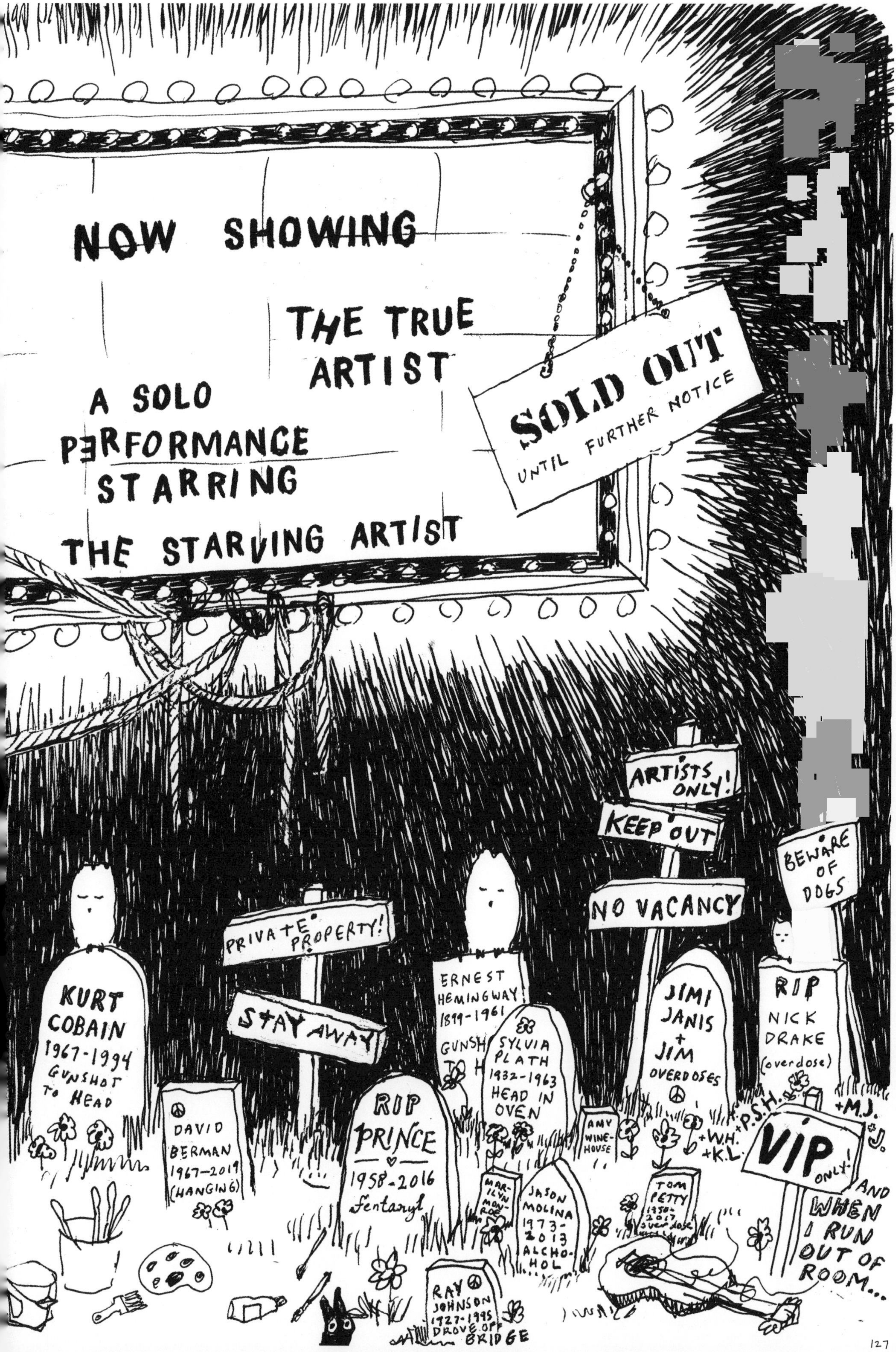
NOW SHOWING
THE TRUE ARTIST
A SOLO PERFORMANCE STARRING
THE STARVING ARTIST
SOLD OUT
UNTIL FURTHER NOTICE
ARTISTS ONLY!
KEEP OUT
BEWARE OF DOGS
NO VACANCY
PRIVATE PROPERTY!
STAY AWAY
KURT COBAIN 1967-1994 GUNSHOT TO HEAD
ERNEST HEMINGWAY 1899-1961 GUNSH TO H
JIMI JANIS + JIM OVERDOSES
RIP NICK DRAKE (overdose)
SYLVIA PLATH 1932-1963 HEAD IN OVEN
DAVID BERMAN 1967-2019 (HANGING)
RIP PRINCE 1958-2016 fentanyl
AMY WINE-HOUSE
+W.H. +K.L. +P.S.H. +M.J. +J.
VIP ONLY!
MAR-ILYN MON-ROE
JASON MOLINA 1973-2013 ALCHO-HOL
TOM PETTY 1950-2017 overdose
AND WHEN I RUN OUT OF ROOM...
RAY JOHNSON 1927-1995 DROVE OFF BRIDGE

...I TAKE A MOMENT OF SILENCE

THEN I BEGIN AGAIN...

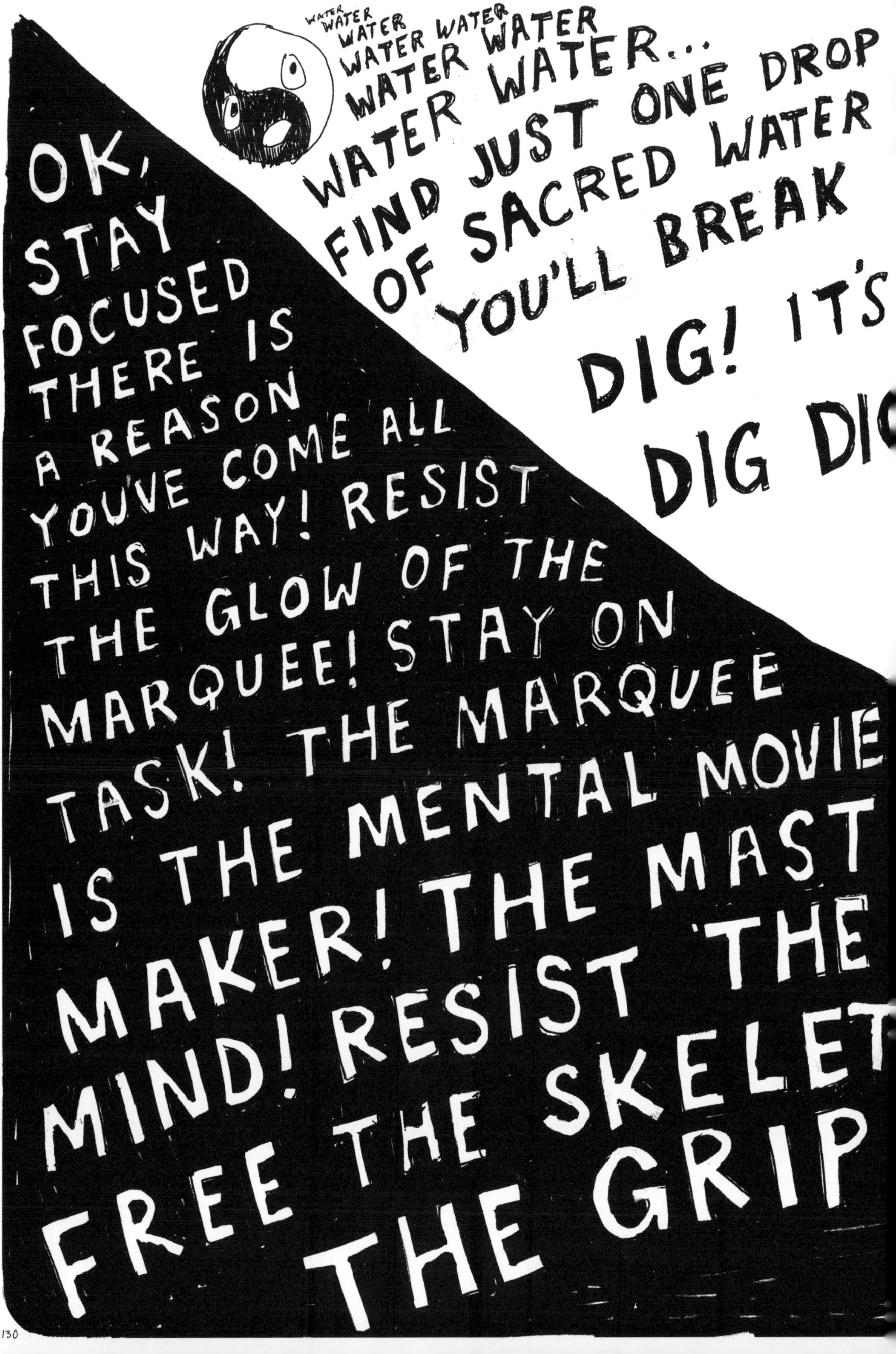
WATER
WATER
WATER WATER
WATER WATER
WATER WATER...
WATER WATER
FIND JUST ONE DROP
OF SACRED WATER
YOU'LL BREAK
DIG! IT'S
DIG DI
OK, STAY FOCUSED THERE IS A REASON YOUVE COME ALL THIS WAY! RESIST THE GLOW OF THE MARQUEE! STAY ON TASK! THE MARQUEE IS THE MENTAL MOVIE MAKER! THE MAST MIND! RESIST THE FREE THE SKELET THE GRIP

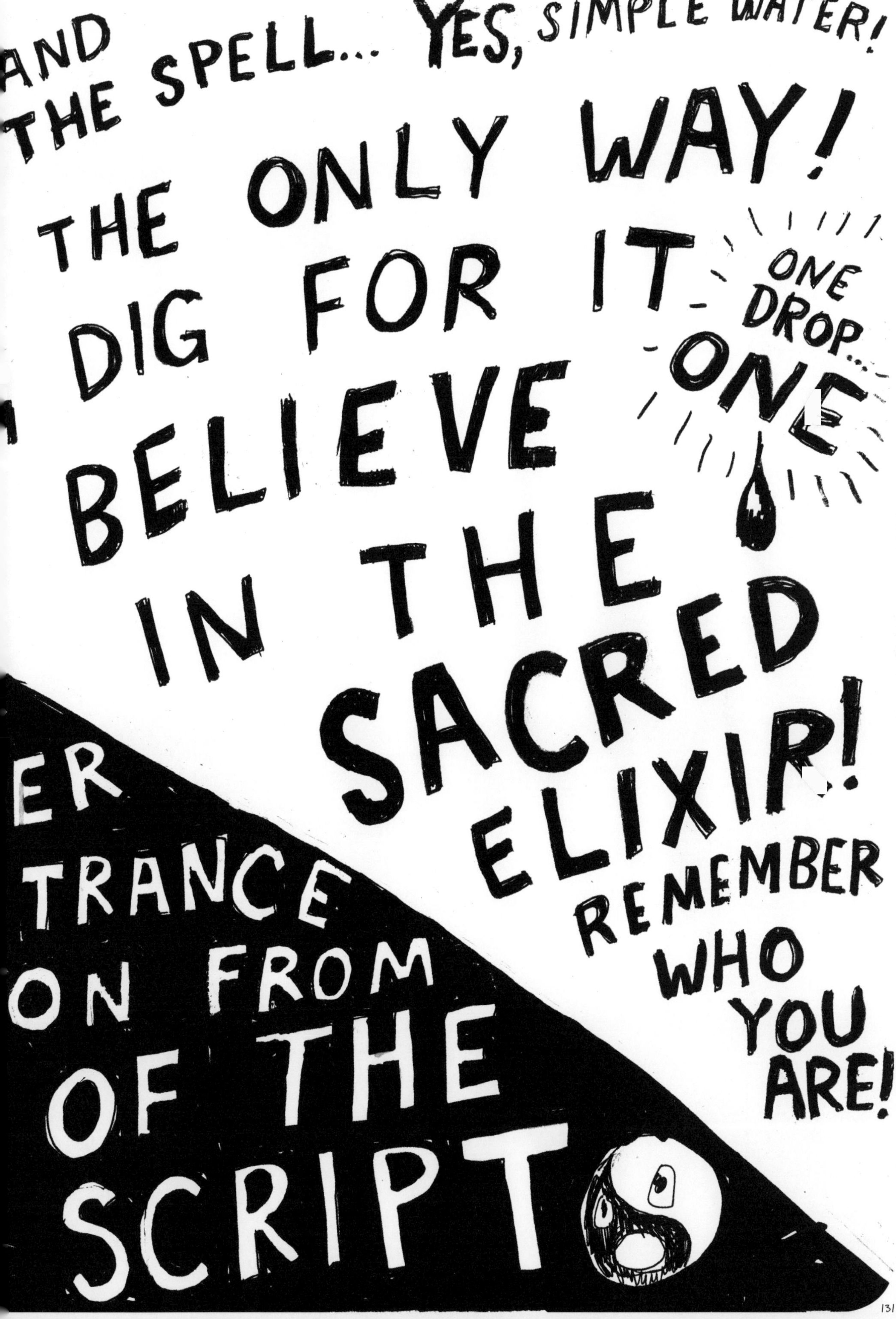
AND THE SPELL... YES, SIMPLE WATER!
THE ONLY WAY!
DIG FOR IT
ONE DROP...
ONE
BELIEVE IN THE SACRED ELIXIR!
REMEMBER WHO YOU ARE!
ER
TRANCE
ON FROM
OF THE
SCRIPT

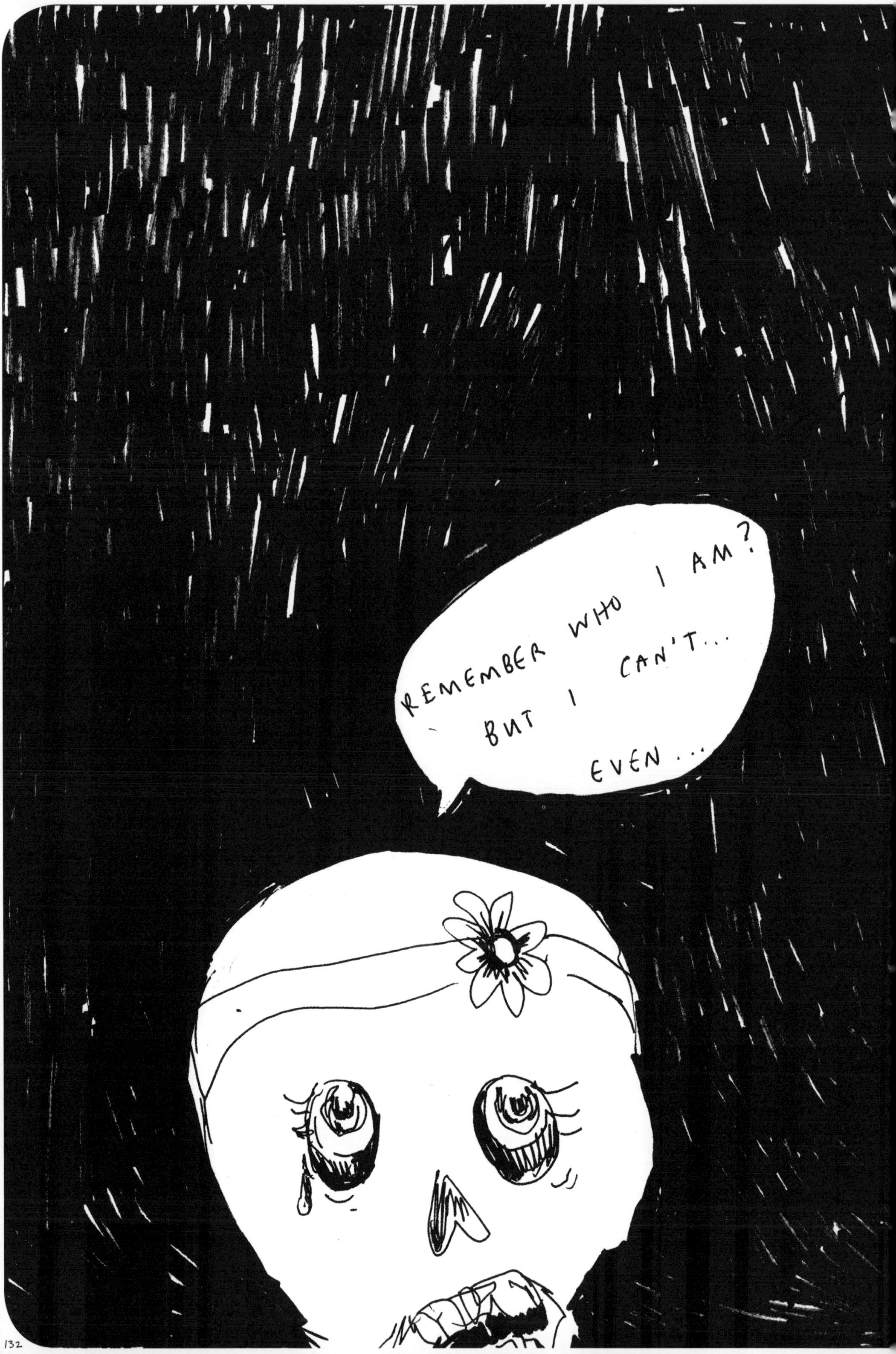
REMEMBER WHO I AM? BUT I CAN'T... EVEN...

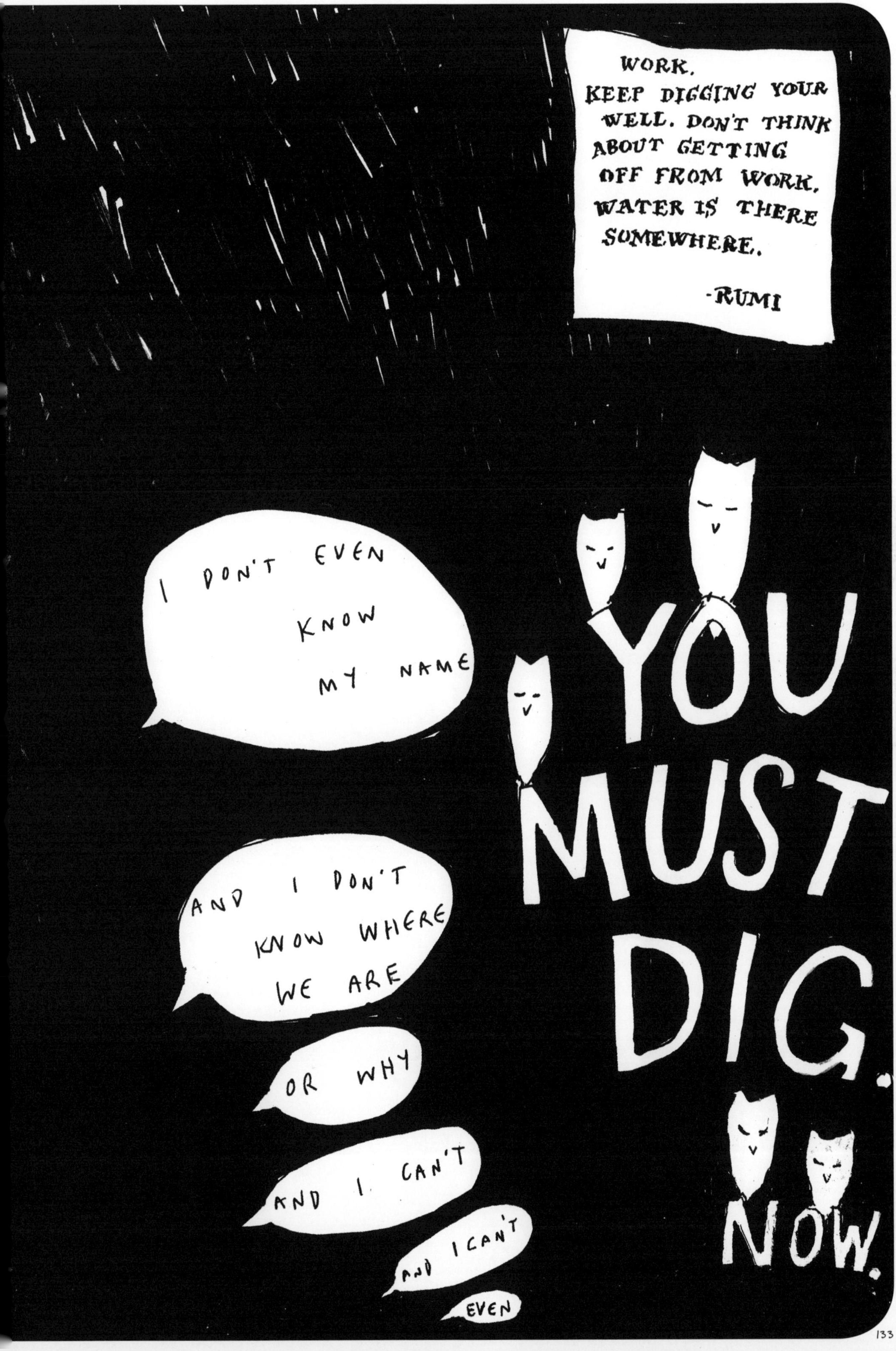
WORK.
KEEP DIGGING YOUR WELL. DON'T THINK ABOUT GETTING OFF FROM WORK. WATER IS THERE SOMEWHERE.
-RUMI
I DON'T EVEN KNOW MY NAME
AND I DON'T KNOW WHERE WE ARE
OR WHY
AND I CAN'T
AND I CAN'T
EVEN
YOU MUST DIG.
NOW.

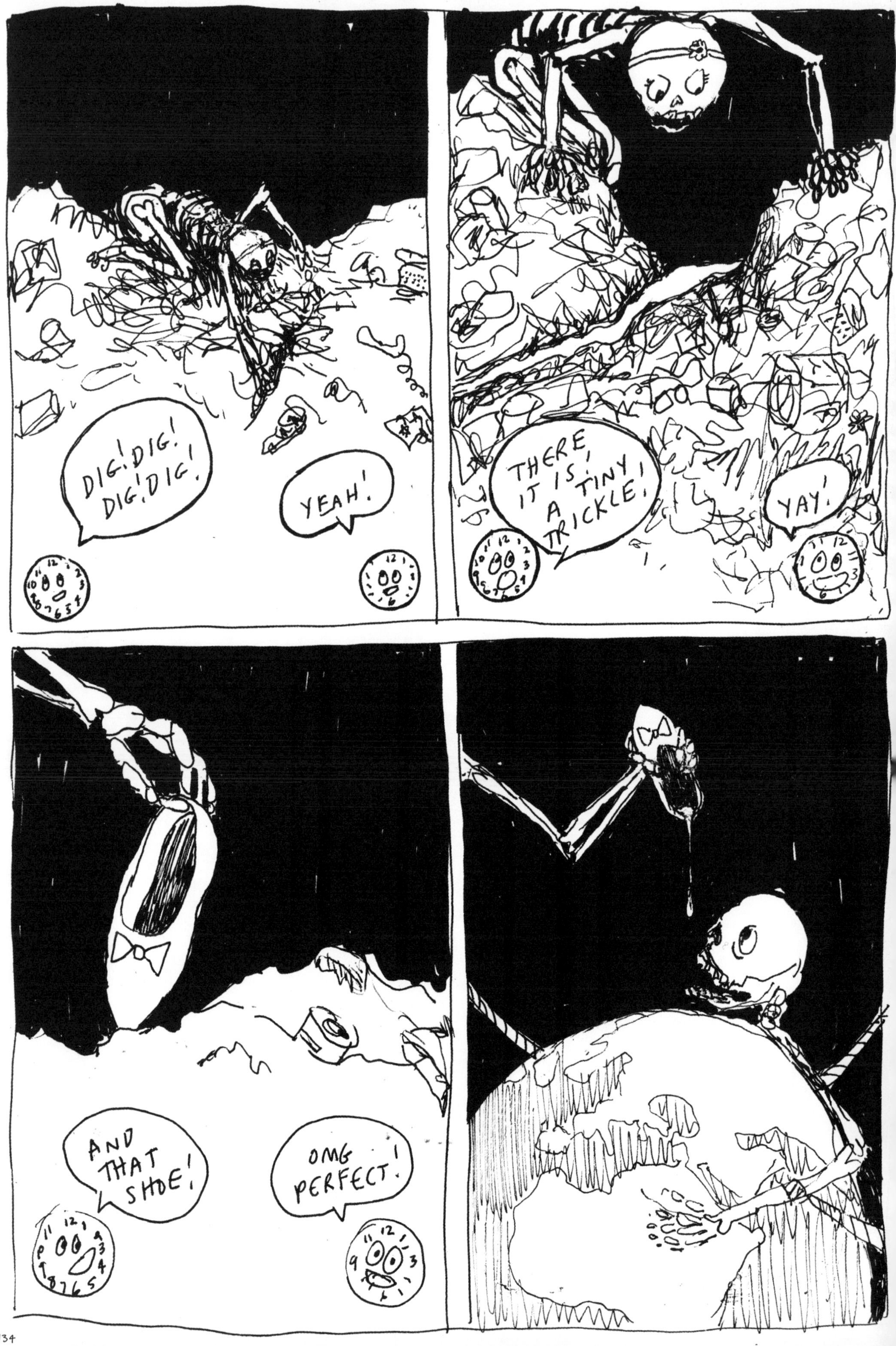
DIG! DIG! DIG! DIG!
YEAH!
THERE IT IS, A TINY TRICKLE!
YAY!
AND THAT SHOE!
OMG PERFECT!

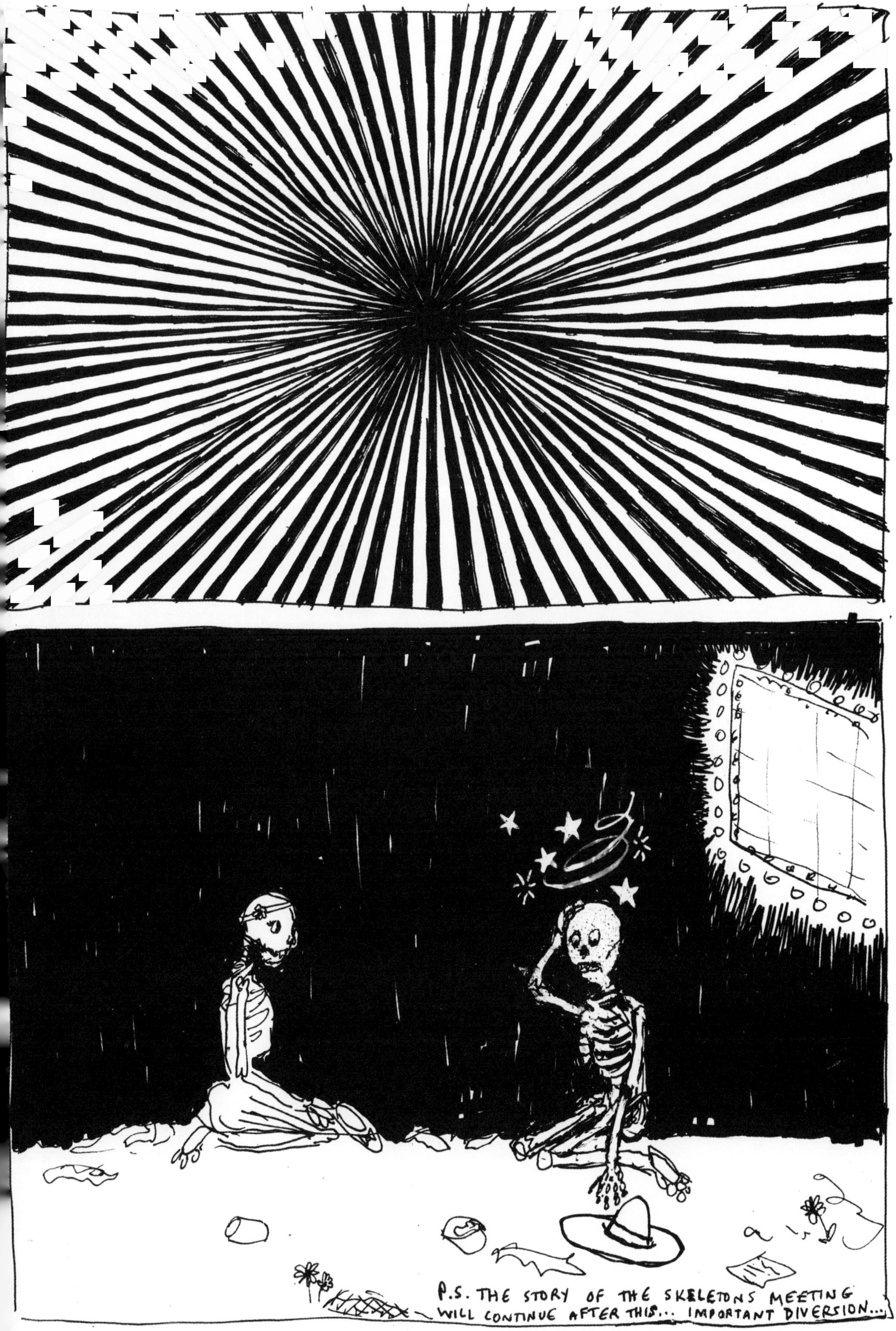
P.S. THE STORY OF THE SKELETONS MEETING
WILL CONTINUE AFTER THIS... IMPORTANT DIVERSION...

May 12, 2019 Mother's Day

THOUGH I CAN
I WANTED A

THING. SHE CAN'T JUST BE LEFT LIKE THAT. TODAY WOULD BE THE
DIVINE, MYTHIC, EVER-LOVING, INFINITE, ETERNAL, NAME-
BREATH, BODY, & LIFE FORCE. SHE WHO BOTH HOLDS US & IS
IS THE DAY TO SAVE MISS MISCARRIAGE WITH A MAGIC POEM!
MY OWN MOM TOO DISAPPOINTING, & MY LONGING FOR MY
SHRINE FOR HELP. I WILL GO THERE NOW, & SEE WHAT

I REREAD THE PHRASE WRITTEN ABOVE: "I FIND MY OWN MOM TOO DISAPPOINTING." TRUTH IS, I DON'T WANT TO CALL HER BECAUSE I DON'T WANT TO DISAPPOINT HER WITH THE TRUTH. I DON'T WANT TO USE THE WORDS "EATING DISORDER" OR "BINGEING," OR "I'M NOT DOING WELL." I WANT TO TELL HER I'M GREAT, I'M MOVING TO NYC IN JUNE TO BE THE SUCCESSFUL SHOWY STAR SHE WANTS ME TO BE. THE DIVORCE WAS ENOUGH. OH AND THE ECTOPIC PREGNANCY. THEN ADD NO EGGS TO FREEZE. THEN ADD EATING DISORDER. OOOF. THE ICE CREAM SUNDAES OF SHAME. I THINK OF THE PAGE WAY BACK AT THE BEGINNING OF THIS PROJECT, THE ONE ABOUT *Mercy*. KIM, DRAW THE FEELING.

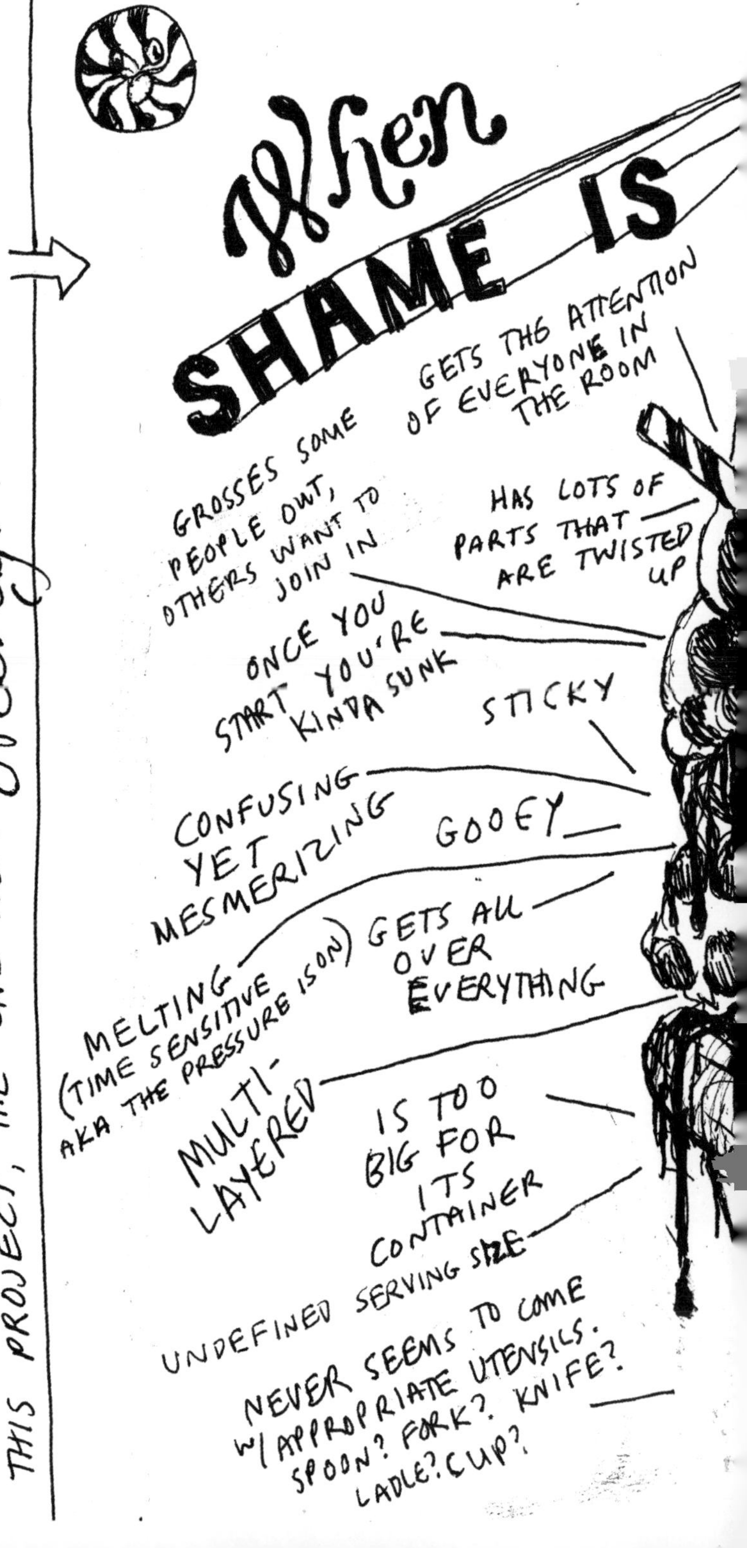

When SHAME IS
GETS THE ATTENTION OF EVERYONE IN THE ROOM
GROSSES SOME PEOPLE OUT, OTHERS WANT TO JOIN IN
HAS LOTS OF PARTS THAT ARE TWISTED UP
ONCE YOU START YOU'RE KINDA SUNK
STICKY
CONFUSING YET MESMERIZING
GOOEY
MELTING (TIME SENSITIVE AKA THE PRESSURE IS ON)
GETS ALL OVER EVERYTHING
MULTI-LAYERED
IS TOO BIG FOR ITS CONTAINER
UNDEFINED SERVING SIZE
NEVER SEEMS TO COME W/APPROPRIATE UTENSILS. SPOON? FORK? KNIFE? LADLE? CUP?

WRITE WITH THAT LOVELY HANDWRITING, I FEEL ABSOLUTELY STUCK.
PRAYER, AS PROMISED, FOR MISS MISCARRIAGE. SHE NEEDS SOME-
PERFECT DAY! TO HONOR THE MOTHER OF ALL THINGS, THE
LESS, FACELESS, MYSTERIOUS, EVER-PRESENT GIVER OF
WITHIN US, WHO FORGIVES, WAITS, CREATES, & KNOWS. TODAY
BUT I CAN'T DO IT. MISS MISCARRIAGE IS TOO HAUNTING,
OWN KIDS TOO PAINFUL. I WILL TRY. I WILL ASK THE
HAPPENS. I PROMISE TO OFFER WHATEVER I FIND. ⟹

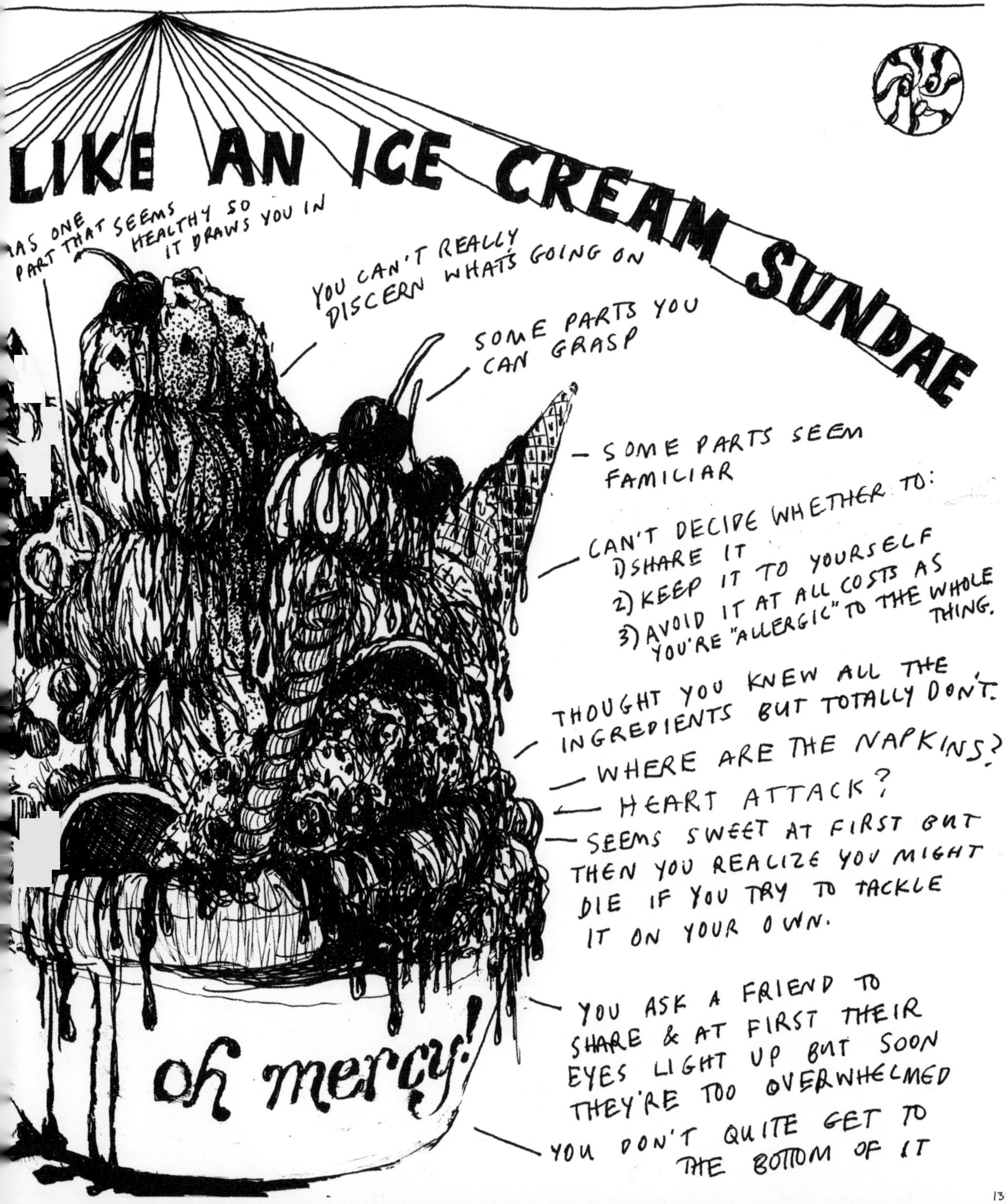
LIKE AN ICE CREAM SUNDAE
HAS ONE PART THAT SEEMS HEALTHY SO IT DRAWS YOU IN
YOU CAN'T REALLY DISCERN WHAT'S GOING ON
SOME PARTS YOU CAN GRASP
SOME PARTS SEEM FAMILIAR
CAN'T DECIDE WHETHER TO:
1) SHARE IT
2) KEEP IT TO YOURSELF
3) AVOID IT AT ALL COSTS AS YOU'RE "ALLERGIC" TO THE WHOLE THING.
THOUGHT YOU KNEW ALL THE INGREDIENTS BUT TOTALLY DON'T.
WHERE ARE THE NAPKINS?
HEART ATTACK?
SEEMS SWEET AT FIRST BUT THEN YOU REALIZE YOU MIGHT DIE IF YOU TRY TO TACKLE IT ON YOUR OWN.
YOU ASK A FRIEND TO SHARE & AT FIRST THEIR EYES LIGHT UP BUT SOON THEY'RE TOO OVERWHELMED
YOU DON'T QUITE GET TO THE BOTTOM OF IT
oh mercy!

MAY 13, 2019 7am A PRAYER FOR HARD TIMES

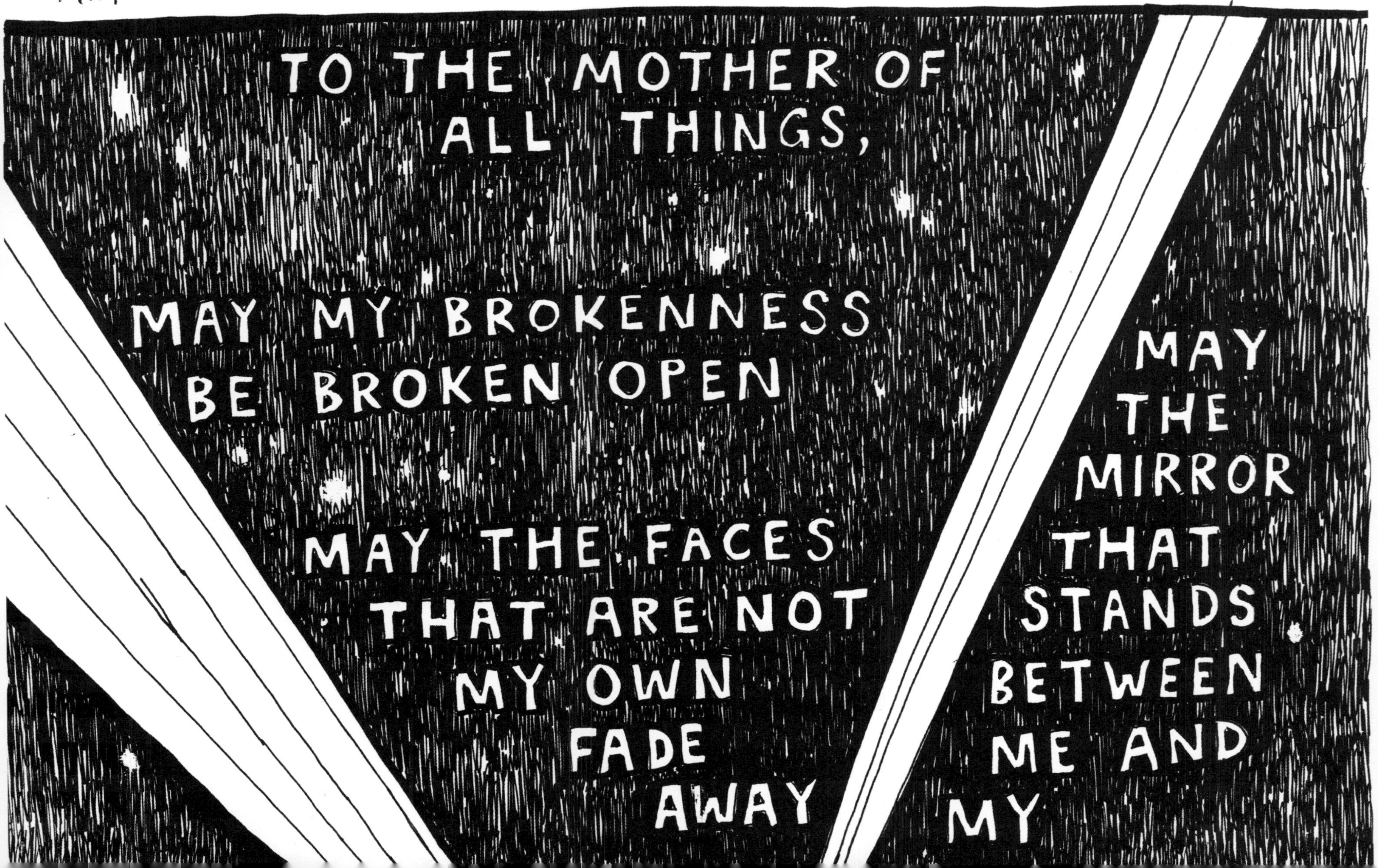
TO THE MOTHER OF
ALL THINGS,
MAY MY BROKENNESS
BE BROKEN OPEN
MAY THE FACES
THAT ARE NOT
MY OWN
FADE
AWAY
MAY
THE
MIRROR
THAT
STANDS
BETWEEN
ME AND
MY

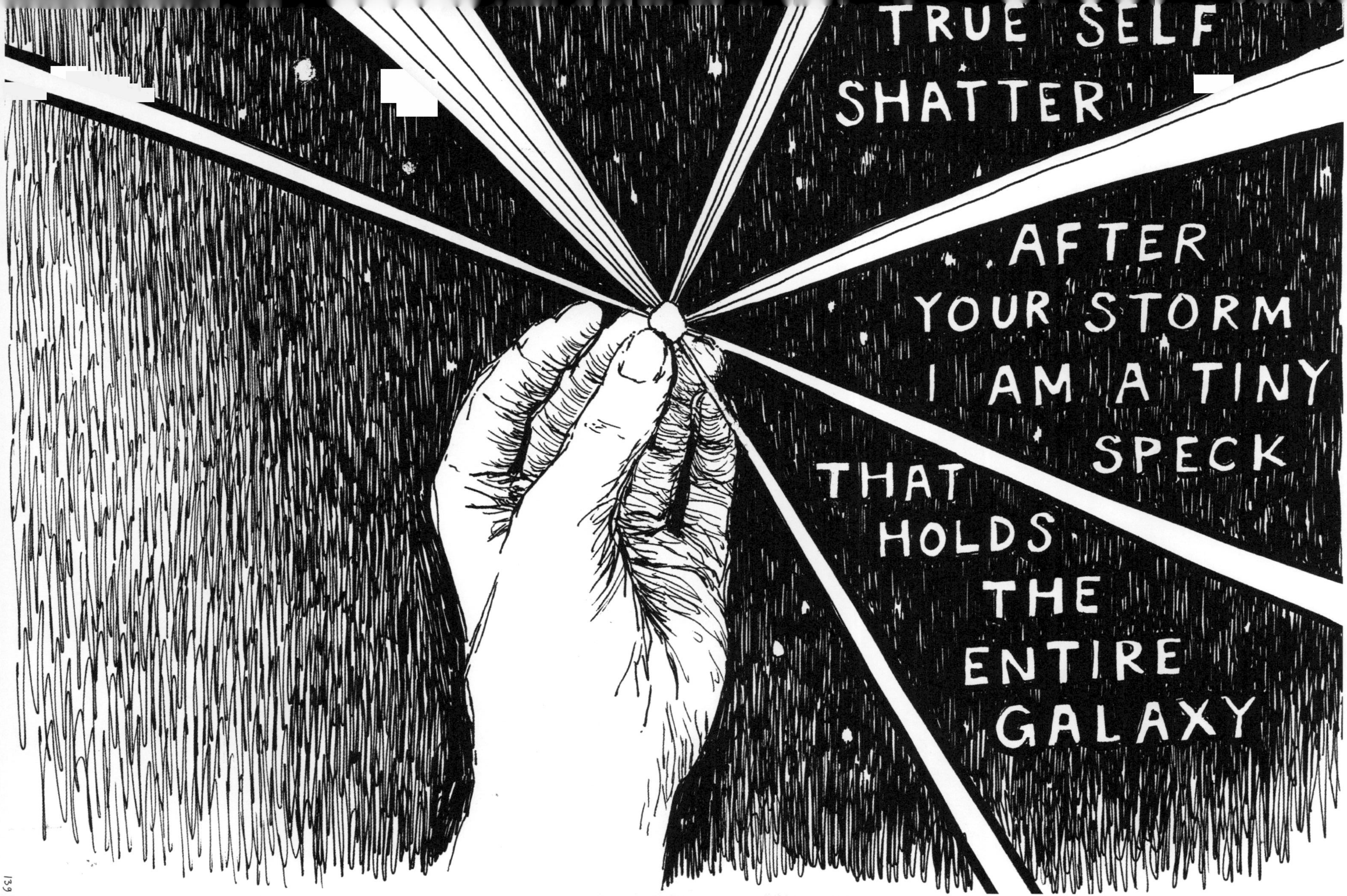
TRUE SELF
SHATTER
AFTER
YOUR STORM
I AM A TINY
SPECK
THAT
HOLDS
THE
ENTIRE
GALAXY

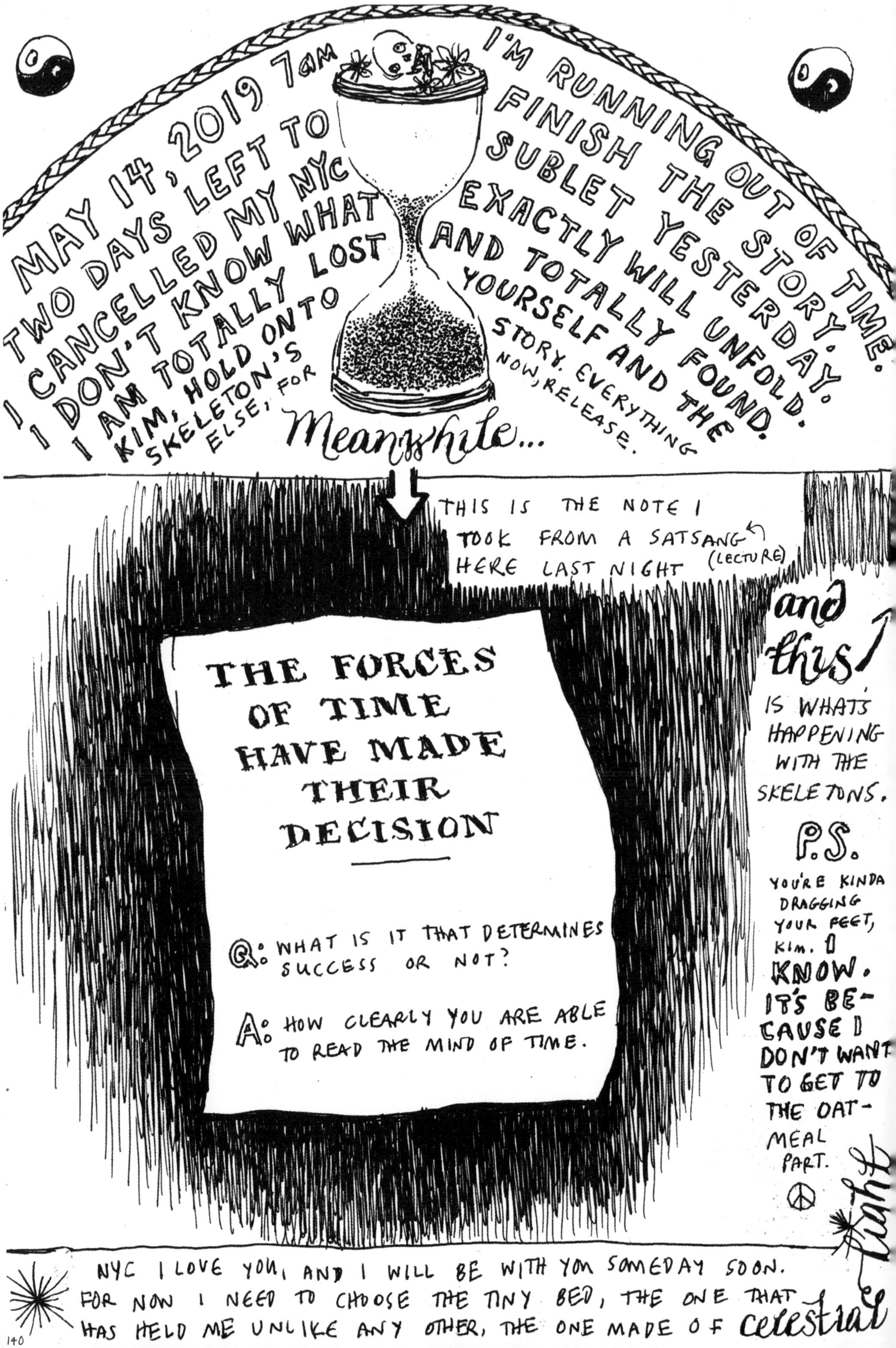
MAY 14, 2019 7am I'M RUNNING OUT OF TIME.
TWO DAYS LEFT TO FINISH THE STORY.
I CANCELLED MY NYC SUBLET YESTERDAY.
I DON'T KNOW WHAT EXACTLY WILL UNFOLD.
I AM TOTALLY LOST AND TOTALLY FOUND.
KIM, HOLD ONTO YOURSELF AND THE SKELETON'S STORY. EVERYTHING ELSE, FOR NOW, RELEASE.
Meanwhile...
THIS IS THE NOTE I TOOK FROM A SATSANG (LECTURE) HERE LAST NIGHT
THE FORCES OF TIME HAVE MADE THEIR DECISION
Q: WHAT IS IT THAT DETERMINES SUCCESS OR NOT?
A: HOW CLEARLY YOU ARE ABLE TO READ THE MIND OF TIME.
and this! IS WHAT'S HAPPENING WITH THE SKELETONS.
P.S.
YOU'RE KINDA DRAGGING YOUR FEET, KIM. I KNOW. IT'S BECAUSE I DON'T WANT TO GET TO THE OATMEAL PART.
NYC I LOVE YOU, AND I WILL BE WITH YOU SOMEDAY SOON.
FOR NOW I NEED TO CHOOSE THE TINY BED, THE ONE THAT HAS HELD ME UNLIKE ANY OTHER, THE ONE MADE OF celestial light

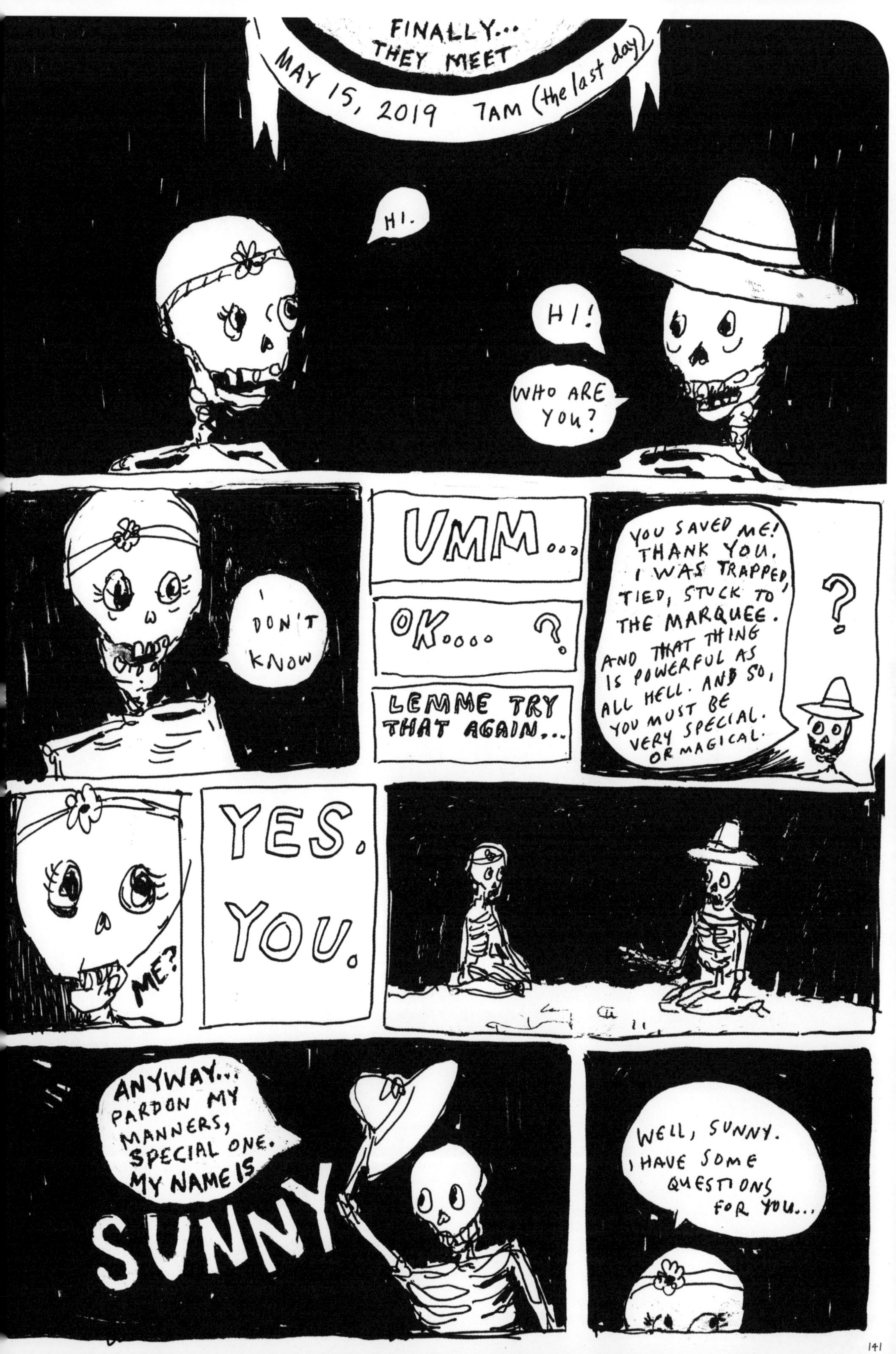
FINALLY... THEY MEET
MAY 15, 2019 7AM (the last day)
HI.
HI!
WHO ARE YOU?
I DON'T KNOW
UMM...
OK.... ?
LEMME TRY THAT AGAIN...
YOU SAVED ME! THANK YOU. I WAS TRAPPED, TIED, STUCK TO THE MARQUEE. AND THAT THING IS POWERFUL AS ALL HELL. AND SO, YOU MUST BE VERY SPECIAL. OR MAGICAL.
?
ME?
YES. YOU.
ANYWAY... PARDON MY MANNERS, SPECIAL ONE. MY NAME IS
SUNNY
WELL, SUNNY. I HAVE SOME QUESTIONS FOR YOU...

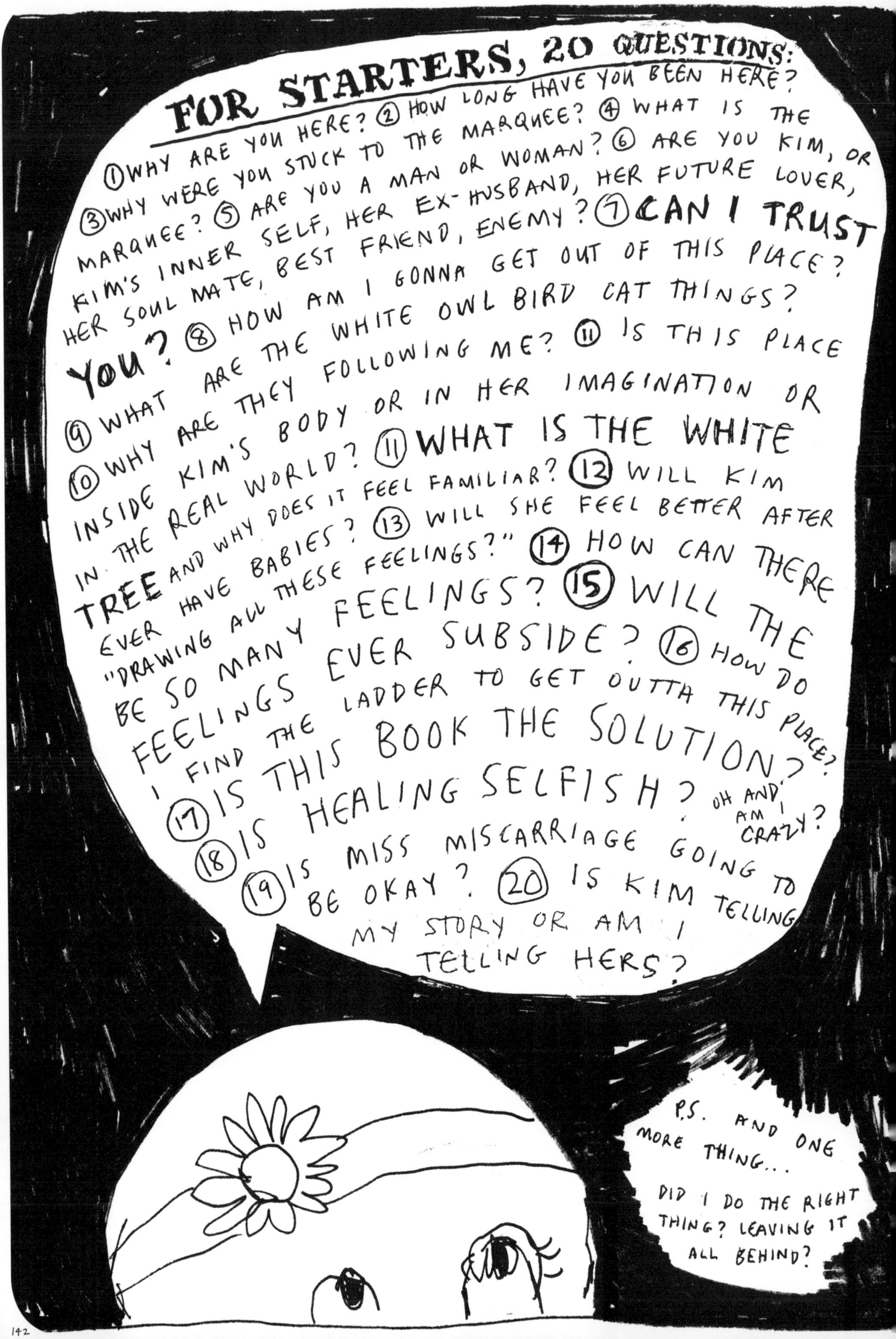
FOR STARTERS, 20 QUESTIONS:
(1) WHY ARE YOU HERE? (2) HOW LONG HAVE YOU BEEN HERE? (3) WHY WERE YOU STUCK TO THE MARQUEE? (4) WHAT IS THE MARQUEE? (5) ARE YOU A MAN OR WOMAN? (6) ARE YOU KIM, OR KIM'S INNER SELF, HER EX-HUSBAND, HER FUTURE LOVER, HER SOUL MATE, BEST FRIEND, ENEMY? (7) CAN I TRUST YOU? (8) HOW AM I GONNA GET OUT OF THIS PLACE? (9) WHAT ARE THE WHITE OWL BIRD CAT THINGS? (10) WHY ARE THEY FOLLOWING ME? (11) IS THIS PLACE INSIDE KIM'S BODY OR IN HER IMAGINATION OR IN THE REAL WORLD? (11) WHAT IS THE WHITE TREE AND WHY DOES IT FEEL FAMILIAR? (12) WILL KIM EVER HAVE BABIES? (13) WILL SHE FEEL BETTER AFTER "DRAWING ALL THESE FEELINGS?" (14) HOW CAN THERE BE SO MANY FEELINGS? (15) WILL THE FEELINGS EVER SUBSIDE? (16) HOW DO I FIND THE LADDER TO GET OUTTA THIS PLACE? (17) IS THIS BOOK THE SOLUTION? (18) IS HEALING SELFISH? OH AND, AM I CRAZY? (19) IS MISS MISCARRIAGE GOING TO BE OKAY? (20) IS KIM TELLING MY STORY OR AM I TELLING HERS?
P.S. AND ONE MORE THING... DID I DO THE RIGHT THING? LEAVING IT ALL BEHIND?

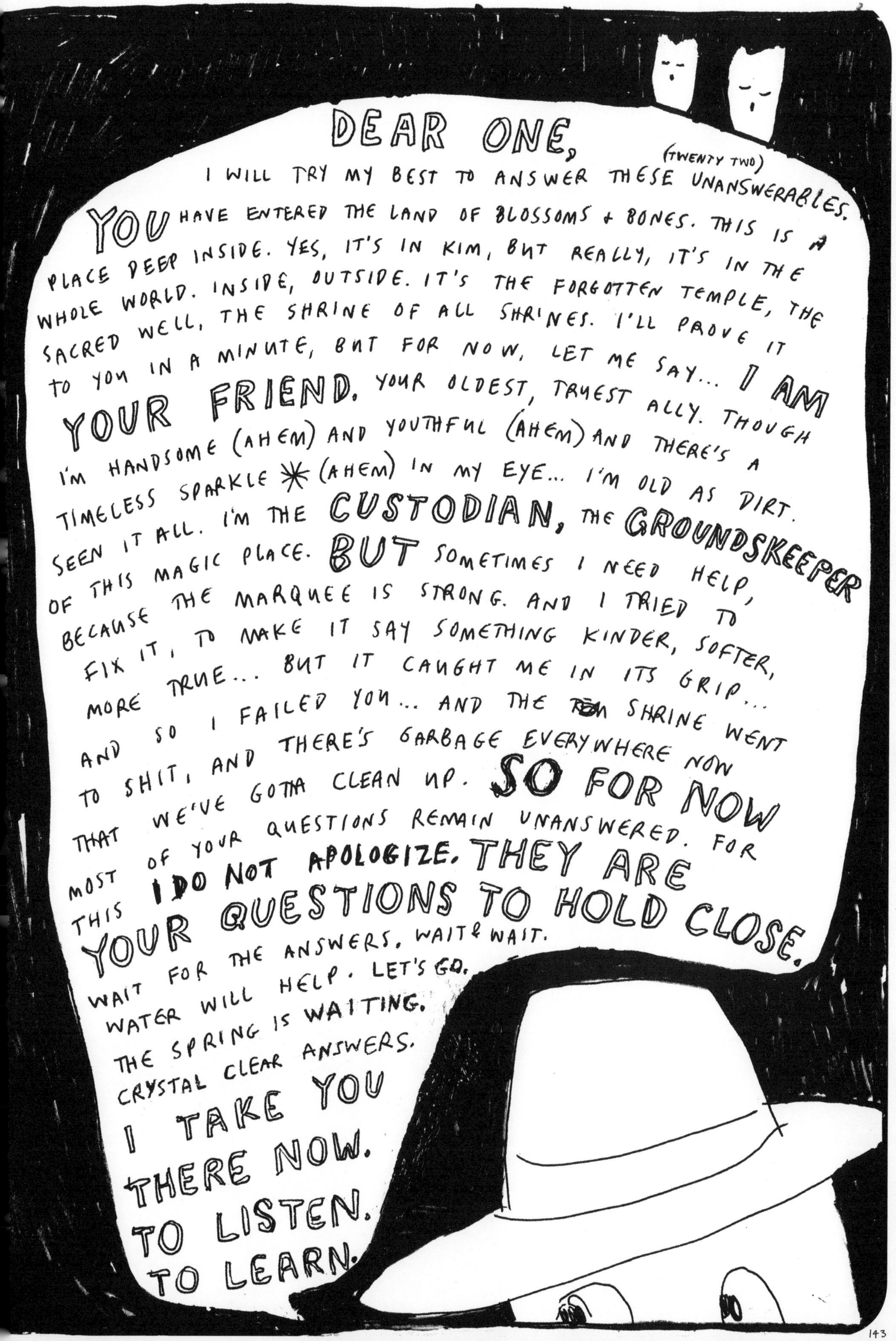
DEAR ONE,
I WILL TRY MY BEST TO ANSWER THESE (TWENTY TWO) UNANSWERABLES.
YOU HAVE ENTERED THE LAND OF BLOSSOMS + BONES. THIS IS A PLACE DEEP INSIDE. YES, IT'S IN KIM, BUT REALLY, IT'S IN THE WHOLE WORLD. INSIDE, OUTSIDE. IT'S THE FORGOTTEN TEMPLE, THE SACRED WELL, THE SHRINE OF ALL SHRINES. I'LL PROVE IT TO YOU IN A MINUTE, BUT FOR NOW, LET ME SAY... I AM YOUR FRIEND. YOUR OLDEST, TRUEST ALLY. THOUGH I'M HANDSOME (AHEM) AND YOUTHFUL (AHEM) AND THERE'S A TIMELESS SPARKLE * (AHEM) IN MY EYE... I'M OLD AS DIRT. SEEN IT ALL. I'M THE CUSTODIAN, THE GROUNDSKEEPER OF THIS MAGIC PLACE. BUT SOMETIMES I NEED HELP, BECAUSE THE MARQUEE IS STRONG. AND I TRIED TO FIX IT, TO MAKE IT SAY SOMETHING KINDER, SOFTER, MORE TRUE... BUT IT CAUGHT ME IN ITS GRIP... AND SO I FAILED YOU... AND THE SHRINE WENT TO SHIT, AND THERE'S GARBAGE EVERYWHERE NOW THAT WE'VE GOTTA CLEAN UP. SO FOR NOW MOST OF YOUR QUESTIONS REMAIN UNANSWERED. FOR THIS I DO NOT APOLOGIZE. THEY ARE YOUR QUESTIONS TO HOLD CLOSE.
WAIT FOR THE ANSWERS. WAIT & WAIT.
WATER WILL HELP. LET'S GO.
THE SPRING IS WAITING.
CRYSTAL CLEAR ANSWERS.
I TAKE YOU THERE NOW.
TO LISTEN.
TO LEARN.

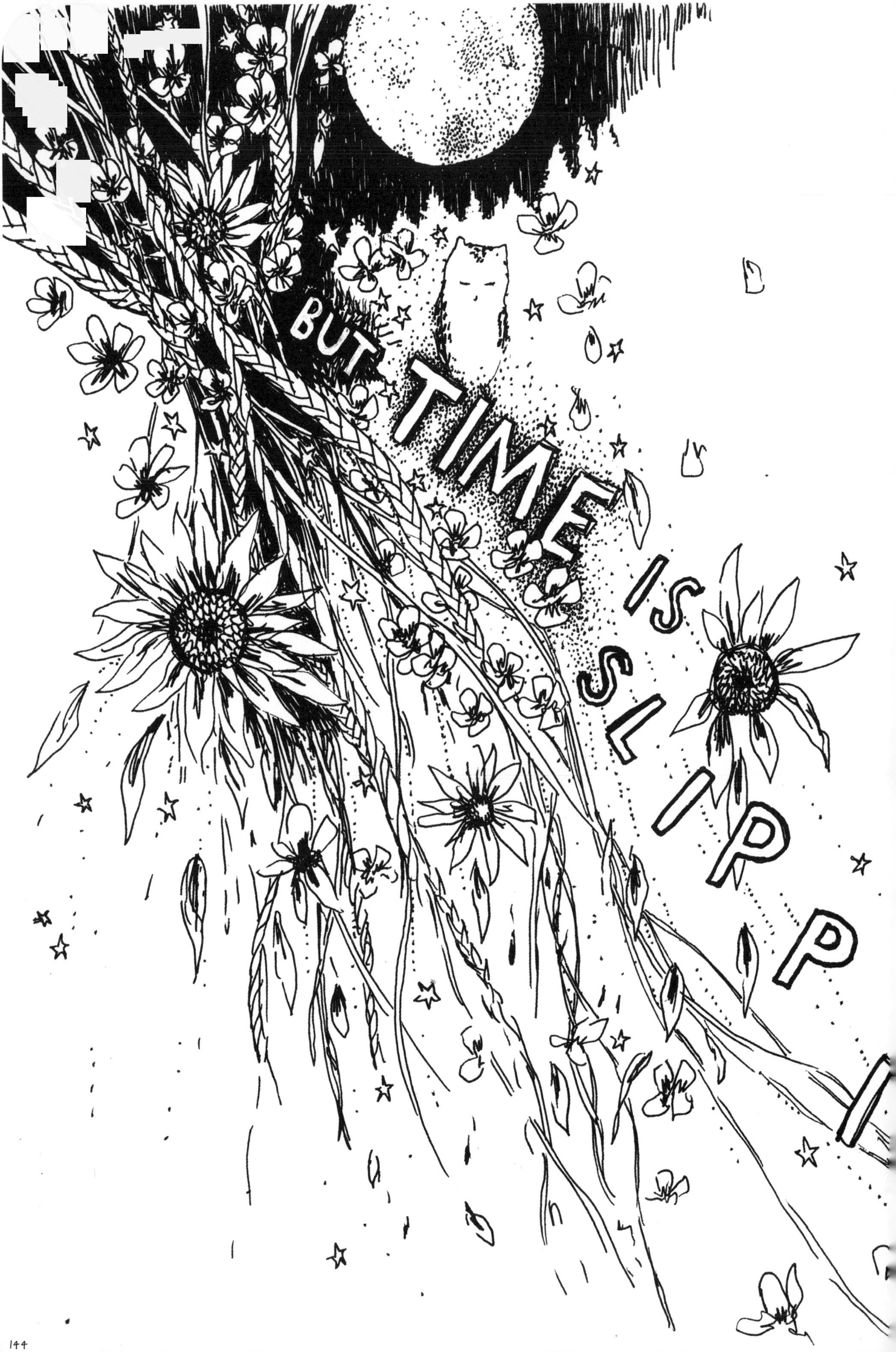
BUT TIME IS SLIPPI

NO MY DEAR.

time

IS RIGHT HERE.

the spring

IS RIGHT HERE.

you have

already

ARRIVED

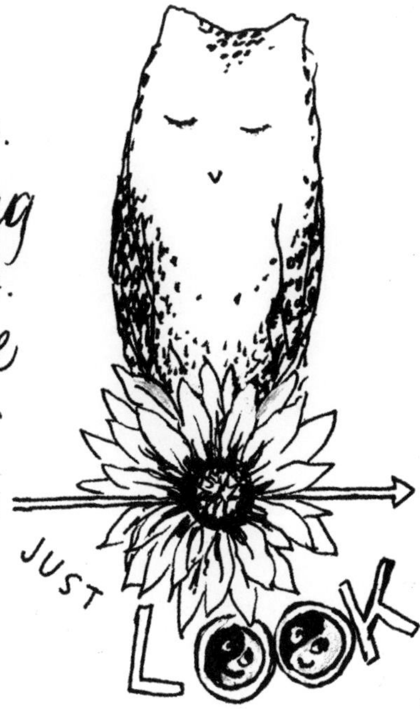

JUST LOOK

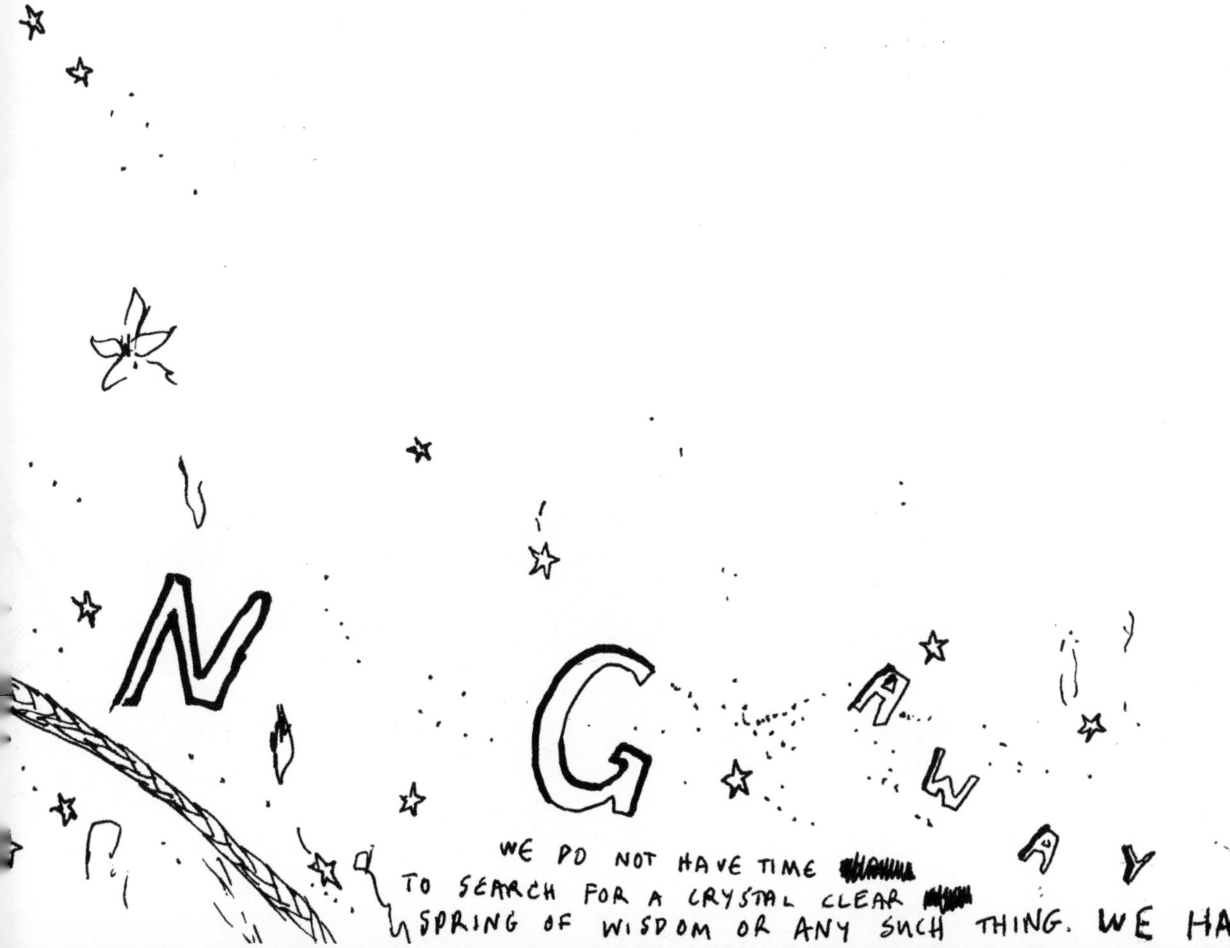

N
G
A
W
A
Y

WE DO NOT HAVE TIME [redacted] TO SEARCH FOR A CRYSTAL CLEAR [redacted] SPRING OF WISDOM OR ANY SUCH THING. WE HAVE TO GET BACK TO REALITY. TIME IS UPPPP. OVER. FINITE.

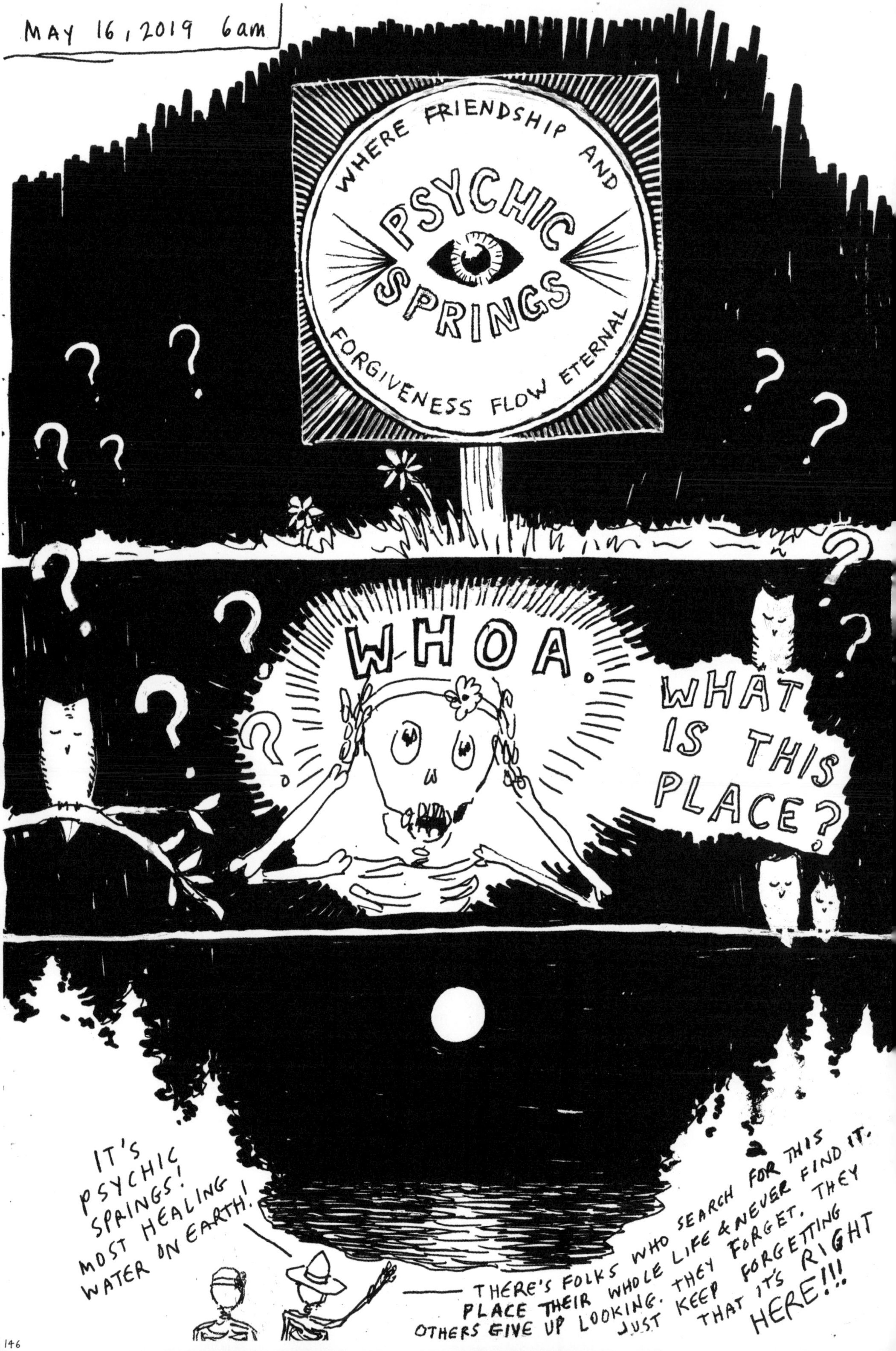
MAY 16, 2019 6am
WHERE FRIENDSHIP AND
PSYCHIC SPRINGS
FORGIVENESS FLOW ETERNAL
WHOA.
WHAT IS THIS PLACE?
IT'S PSYCHIC SPRINGS! MOST HEALING WATER ON EARTH!
THERE'S FOLKS WHO SEARCH FOR THIS PLACE THEIR WHOLE LIFE & NEVER FIND IT. OTHERS GIVE UP LOOKING. THEY FORGET. THEY JUST KEEP FORGETTING THAT IT'S RIGHT HERE!!!

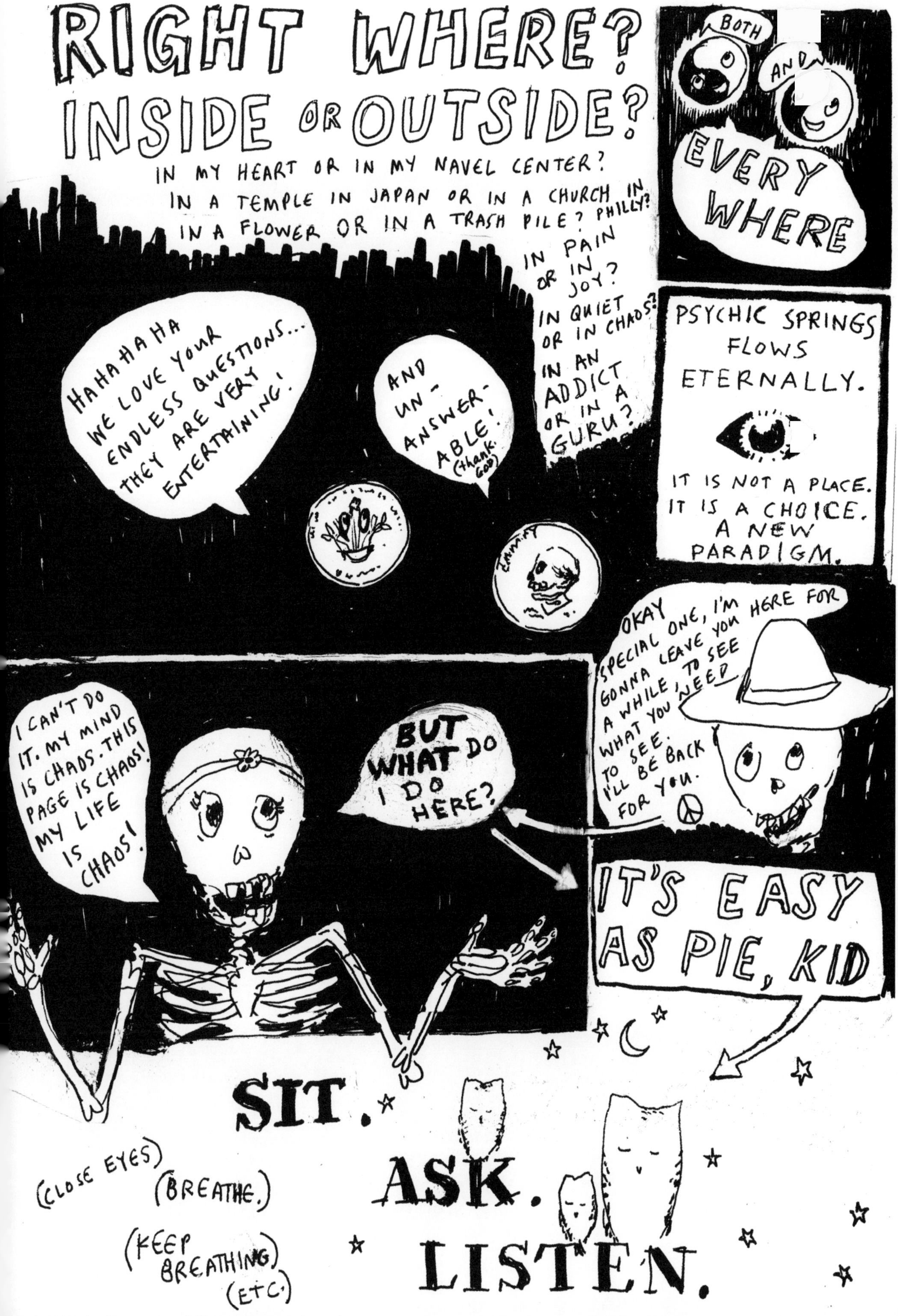

RIGHT WHERE?
INSIDE OR OUTSIDE?
IN MY HEART OR IN MY NAVEL CENTER?
IN A TEMPLE IN JAPAN OR IN A CHURCH IN PHILLY?
IN A FLOWER OR IN A TRASH PILE?
IN PAIN OR IN JOY?
IN QUIET OR IN CHAOS?
IN AN ADDICT OR IN A GURU?
BOTH
AND
EVERY WHERE
HAHAHAHA WE LOVE YOUR ENDLESS QUESTIONS... THEY ARE VERY ENTERTAINING!
AND UN-ANSWER-ABLE! (thank GOD)
PSYCHIC SPRINGS FLOWS ETERNALLY.
IT IS NOT A PLACE. IT IS A CHOICE. A NEW PARADIGM.
OKAY SPECIAL ONE, I'M HERE FOR YOU GONNA LEAVE YOU A WHILE, TO SEE WHAT YOU NEED TO SEE. I'LL BE BACK FOR YOU.
I CAN'T DO IT. MY MIND IS CHAOS. THIS PAGE IS CHAOS! MY LIFE IS CHAOS!
BUT WHAT DO I DO HERE?
IT'S EASY AS PIE, KID
SIT.
ASK.
LISTEN.
(CLOSE EYES)
(BREATHE.)
(KEEP BREATHING)
(ETC.)

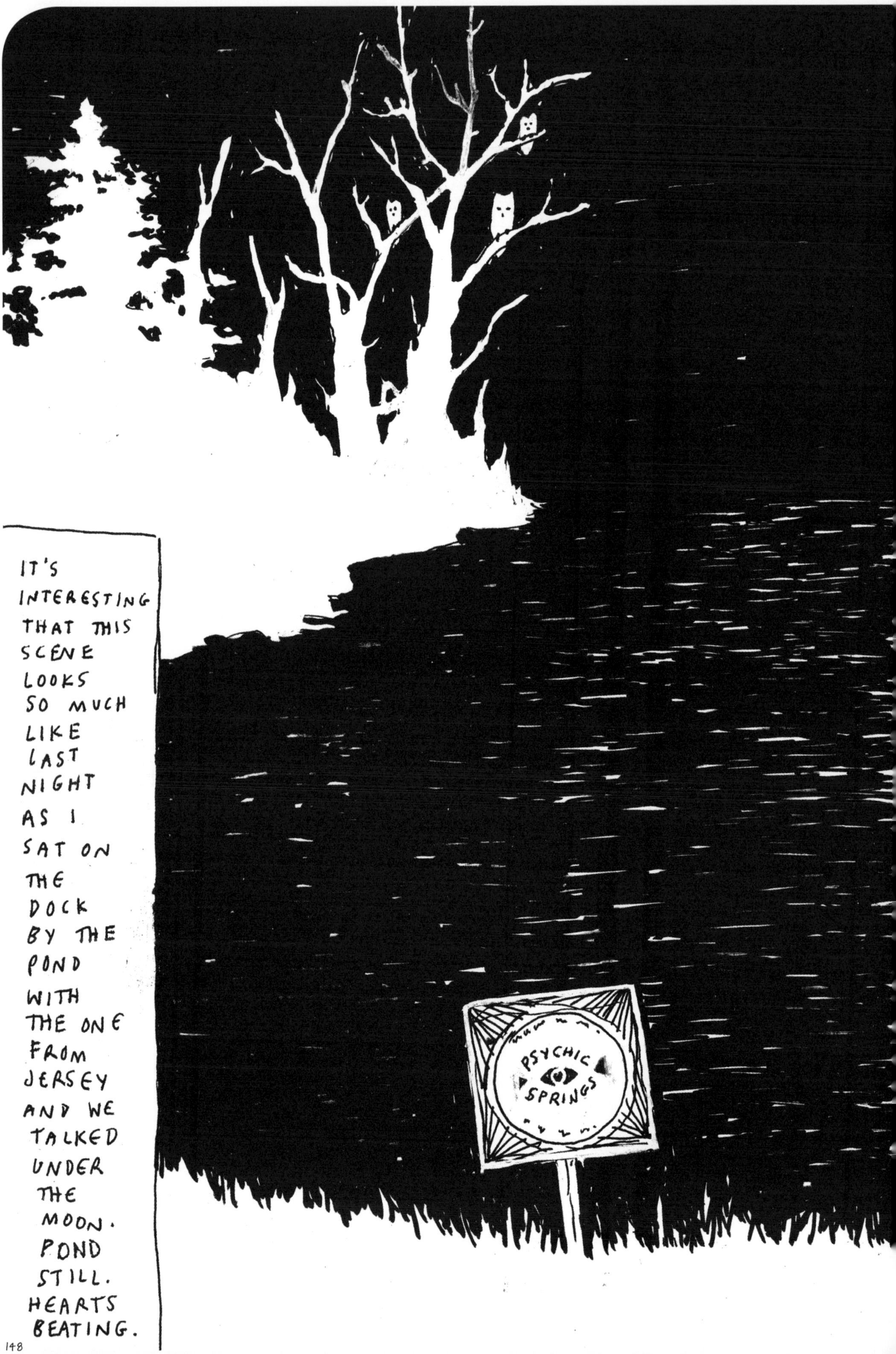
IT'S INTERESTING THAT THIS SCENE LOOKS SO MUCH LIKE LAST NIGHT AS I SAT ON THE DOCK BY THE POND WITH THE ONE FROM JERSEY AND WE TALKED UNDER THE MOON. POND STILL. HEARTS BEATING.
PSYCHIC SPRINGS

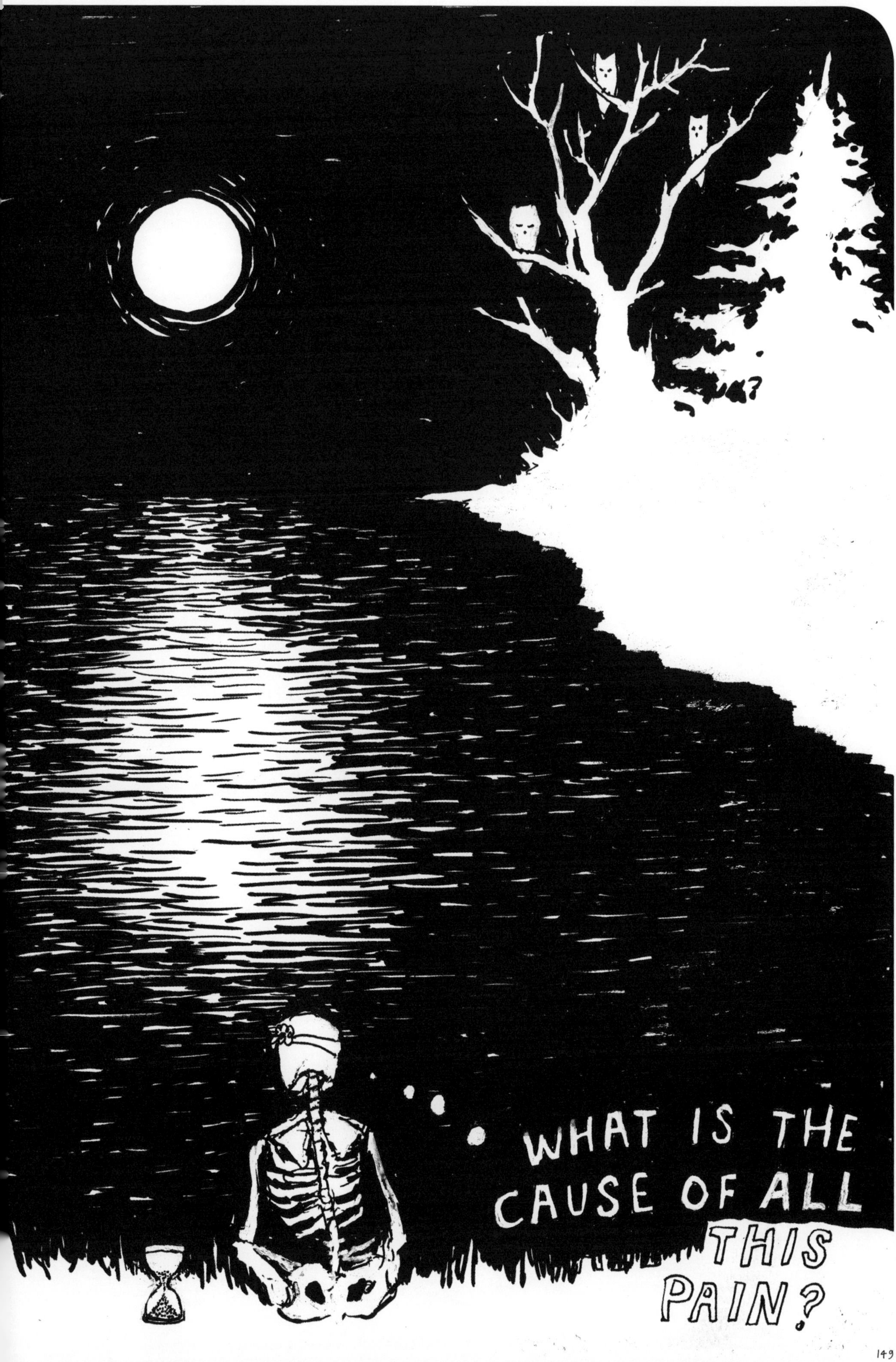
WHAT IS THE
CAUSE OF ALL
THIS
PAIN?

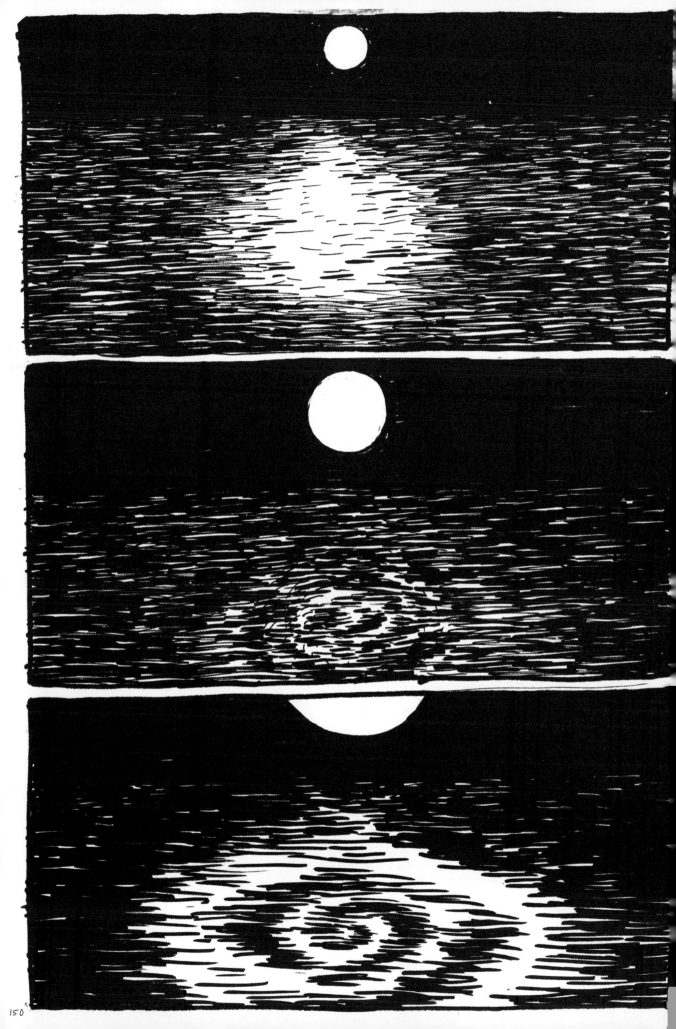

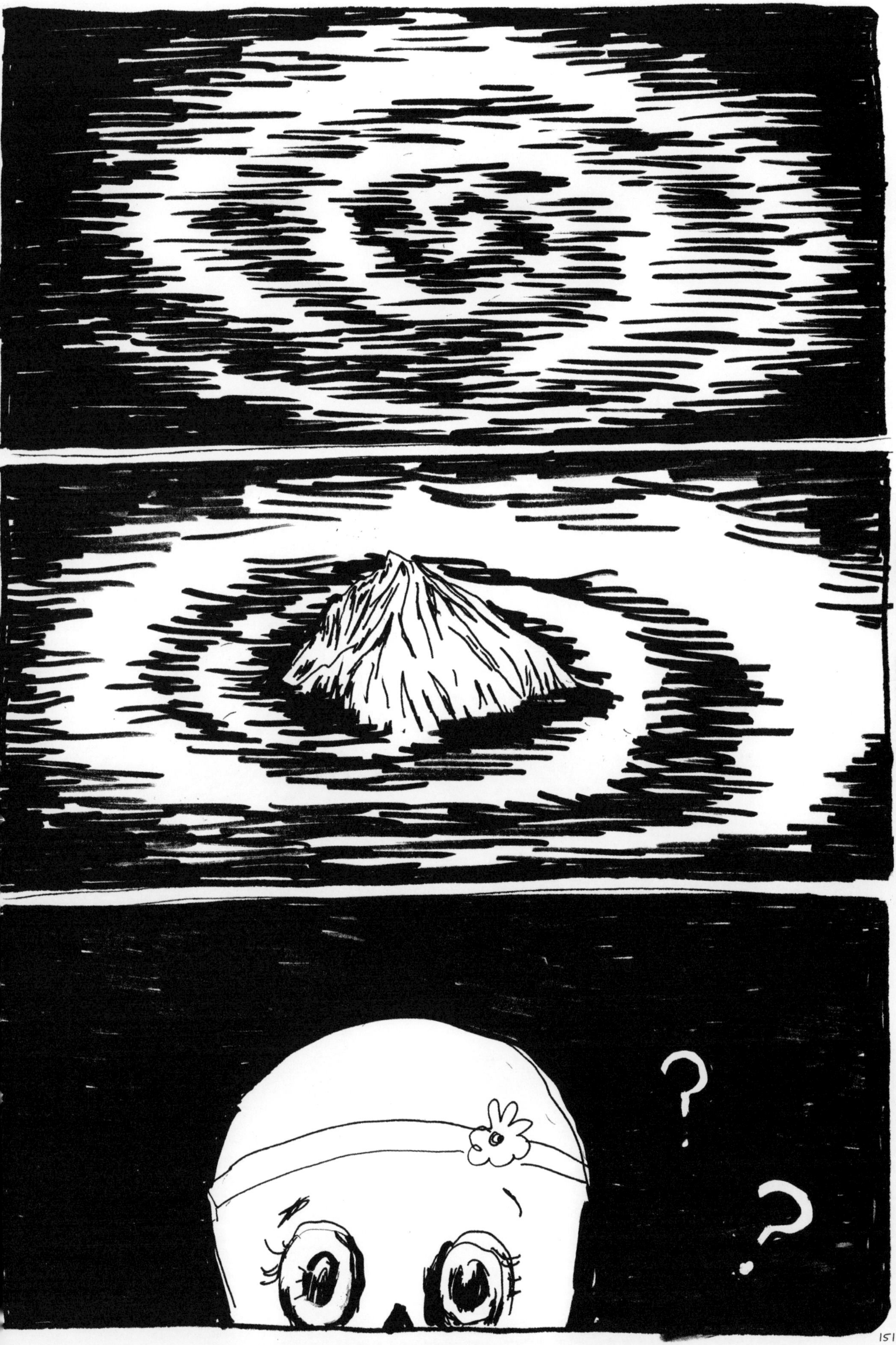
?
?

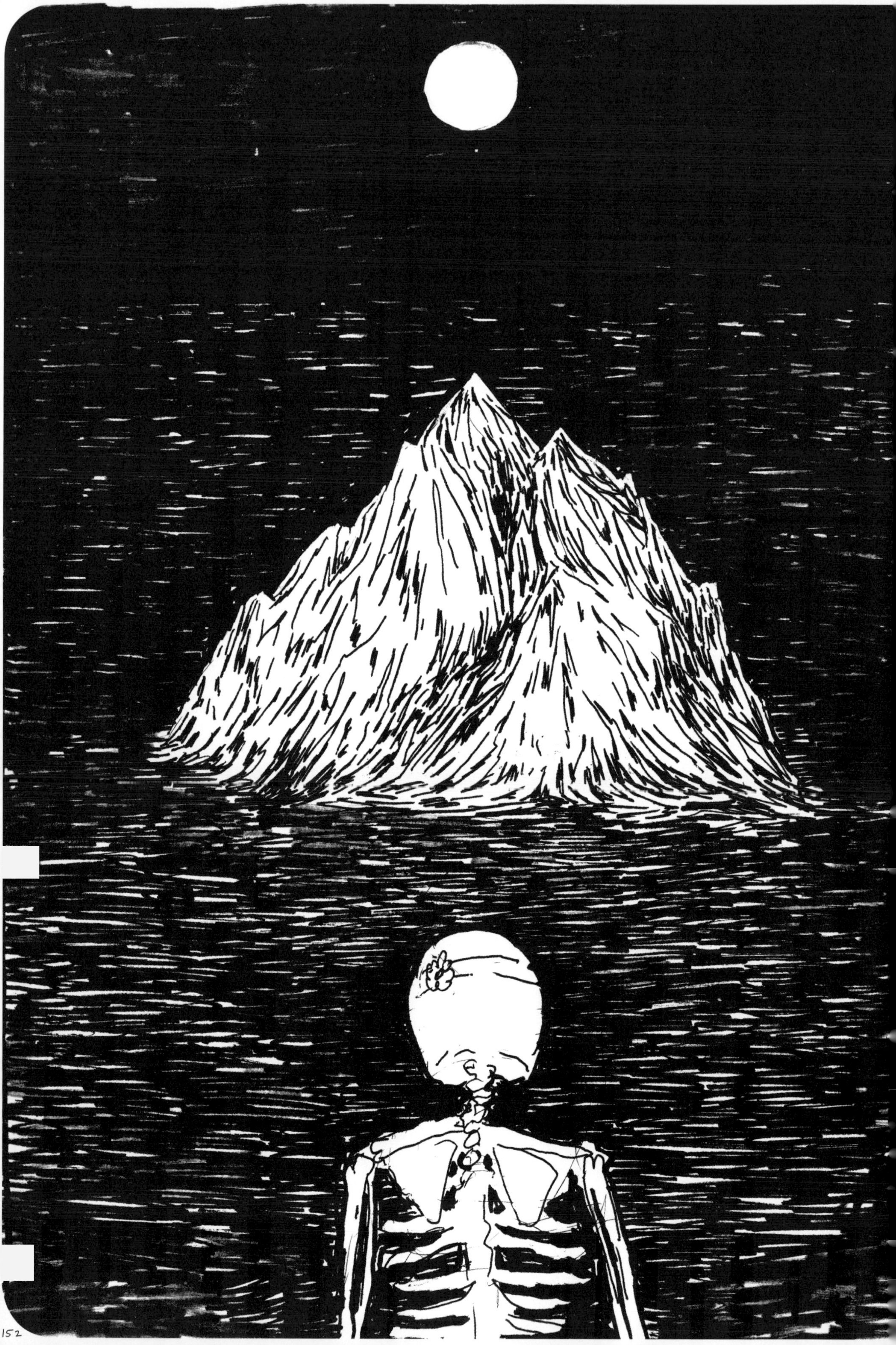

I AM THE MOUNTAIN OF PERFECTION. I CAST A SHADOW ON THE WHOLE WORLD. I AM THE GRAND ILLUSION, THE MONUMENTAL PAIN-MAKER. YET I AM MERELY MOONLIGHT GLISTENING ON WAVES.

MAY 17, 2019 7AM

"DRAWING THE FEELING"

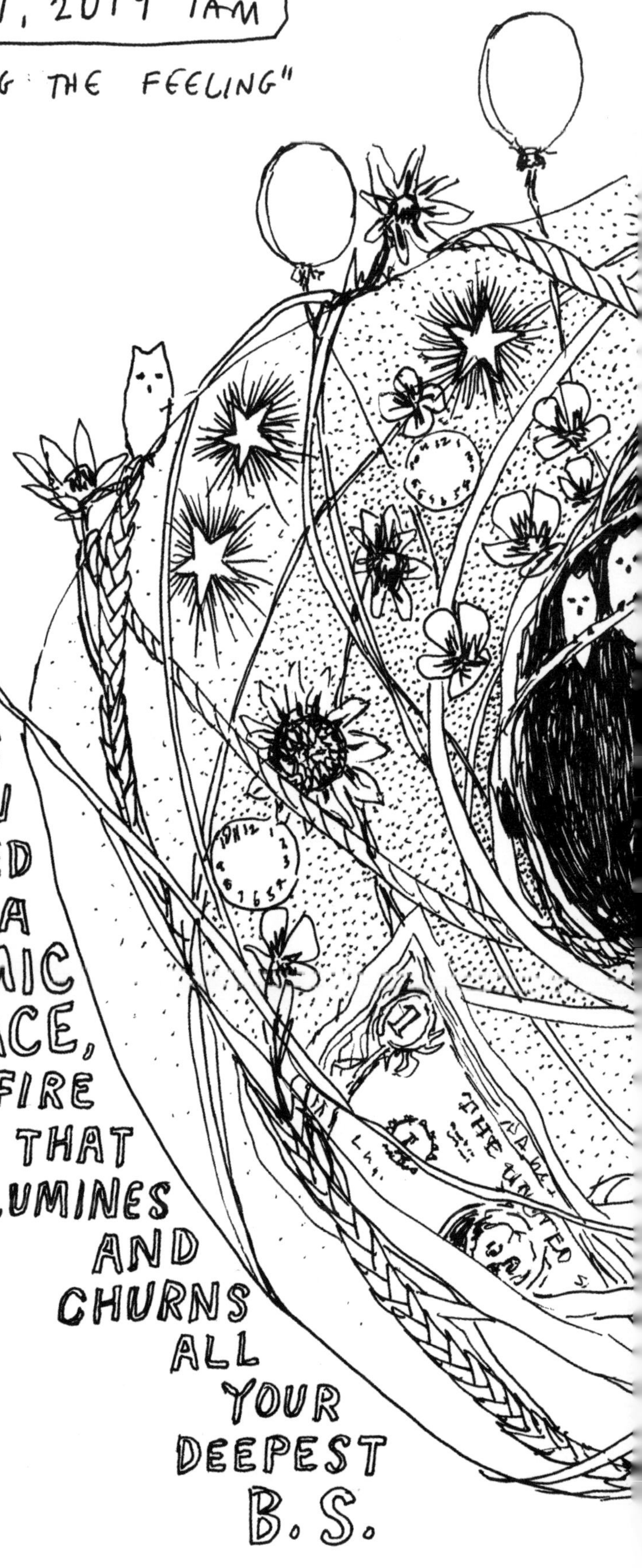

THOUGH THE ASHRAM SEEMS IDYLLIC, ESPECIALLY IN THESE PAGES, IT IS OFTEN CALLED A KARMIC FURNACE, A FIRE THAT ILLUMINES AND CHURNS ALL YOUR DEEPEST B.S.

FOR EXAMPLE, YESTERDAY AFTER FOUR
HOURS OF HAULING BRANCHES (KARMA YOGA)
A SORE BACK, SCRAPED LIP, & BLOODY NOSE...
I SAT IN THE SUN WONDERING:

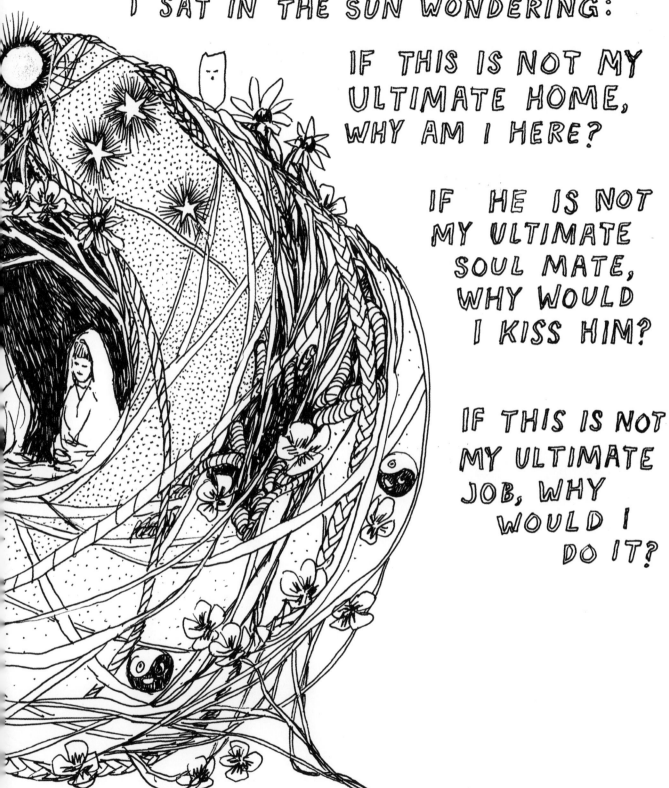

IF THIS IS NOT MY
ULTIMATE HOME,
WHY AM I HERE?

IF HE IS NOT
MY ULTIMATE
SOUL MATE,
WHY WOULD
I KISS HIM?

IF THIS IS NOT
MY ULTIMATE
JOB, WHY
WOULD I
DO IT?

I LOOK UP THE
ORIGIN OF THE
WORD "ULTIMATE"...

IT COMES
FROM
THE WORD
"*ultimare*"

WHICH
MEANS

TO

END.

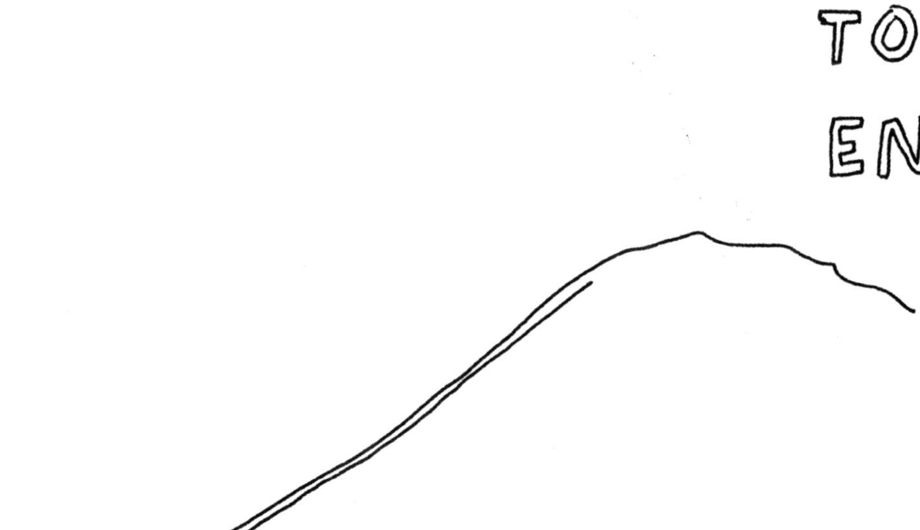

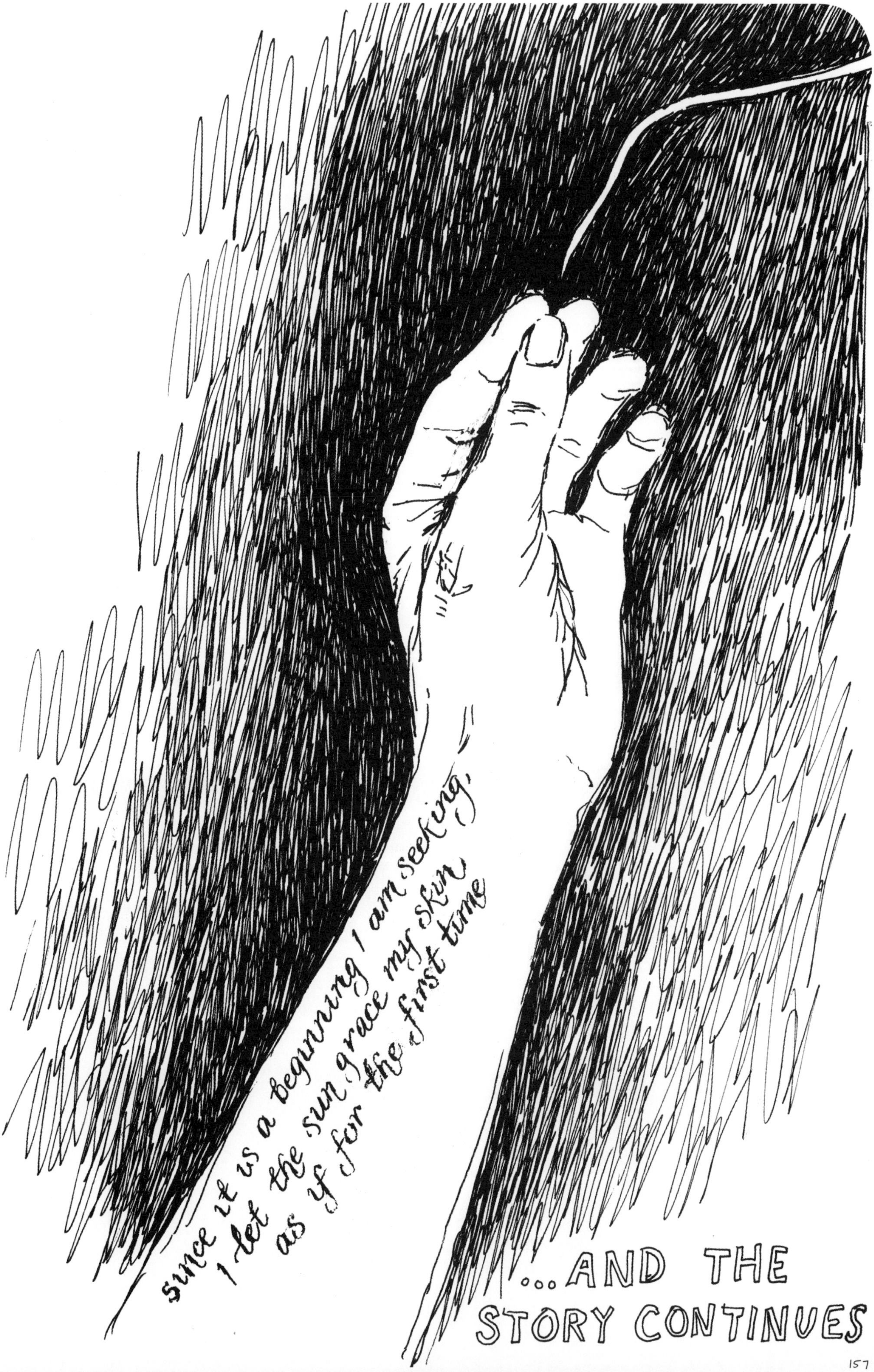
since it is a beginning I am seeking,
I let the sun grace my skin,
as if for the first time
...AND THE
STORY CONTINUES

MAY 18, 2019 4pm
I'M RUNNING OUT OF TIME

WHAT IS THE REMEDY FOR THE MOUNTAIN OF PERFECTION?

TIME

WHAT? BUT I DON'T HAVE ENOUGH!

MAKE FRIENDS WITH IT.

HOW?

BE STILL. WAIT.

THEN WHAT?

THE MOUNTAIN SOFTENS
TIME TURNS ON ITS HEAD
THE TRUE REMEDY APPEARS

WHEN?

JUST FLIP IT!
NOW.
YEAH DUH

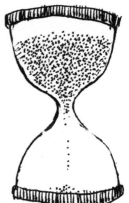

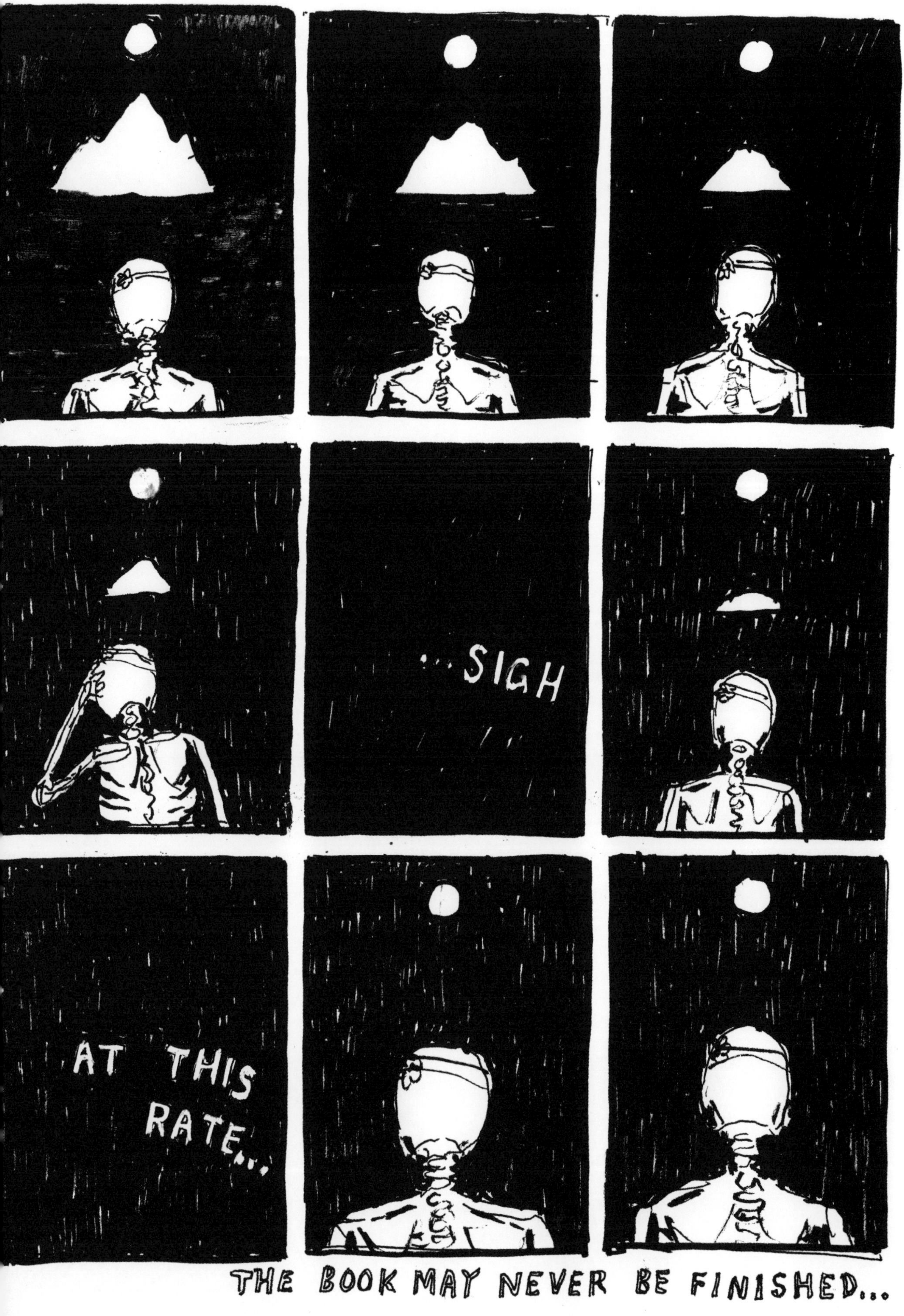
...SIGH
AT THIS RATE...
THE BOOK MAY NEVER BE FINISHED...

MAY I BEFRIEND THE FORCES OF TIME,

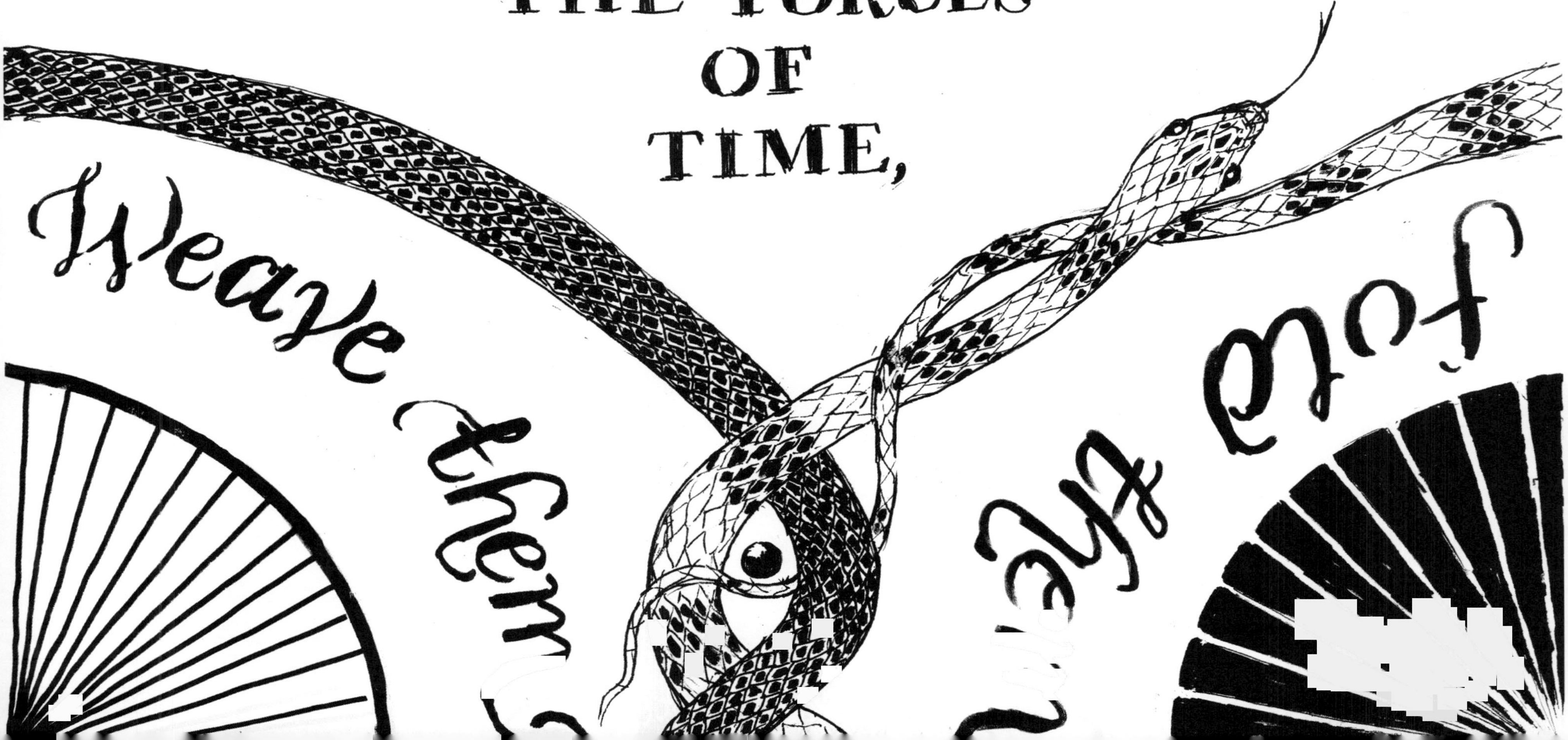
Weave them

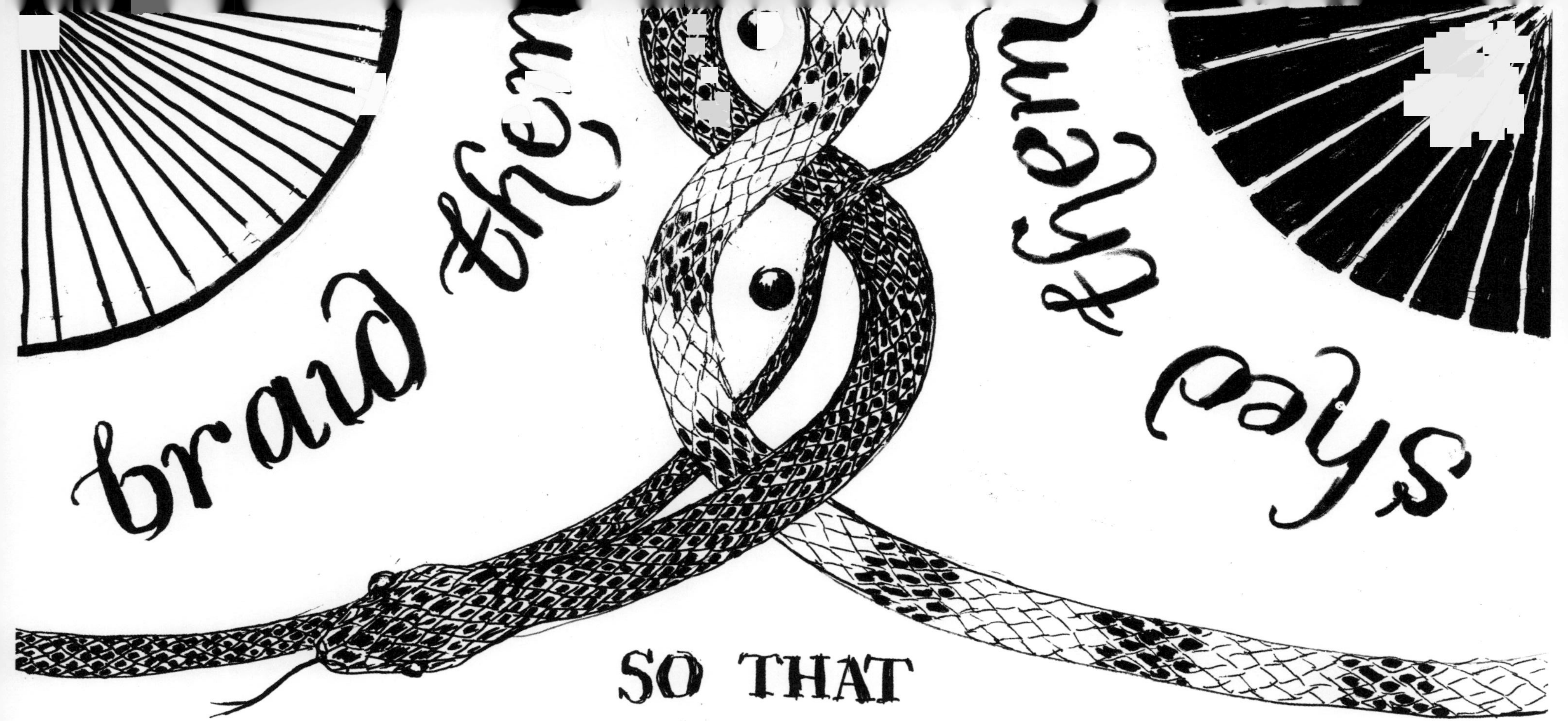
braid them
shed them

SO THAT
I, LIKE THE SERPENT,
MAY COMPLETE
WHILE BECOMING

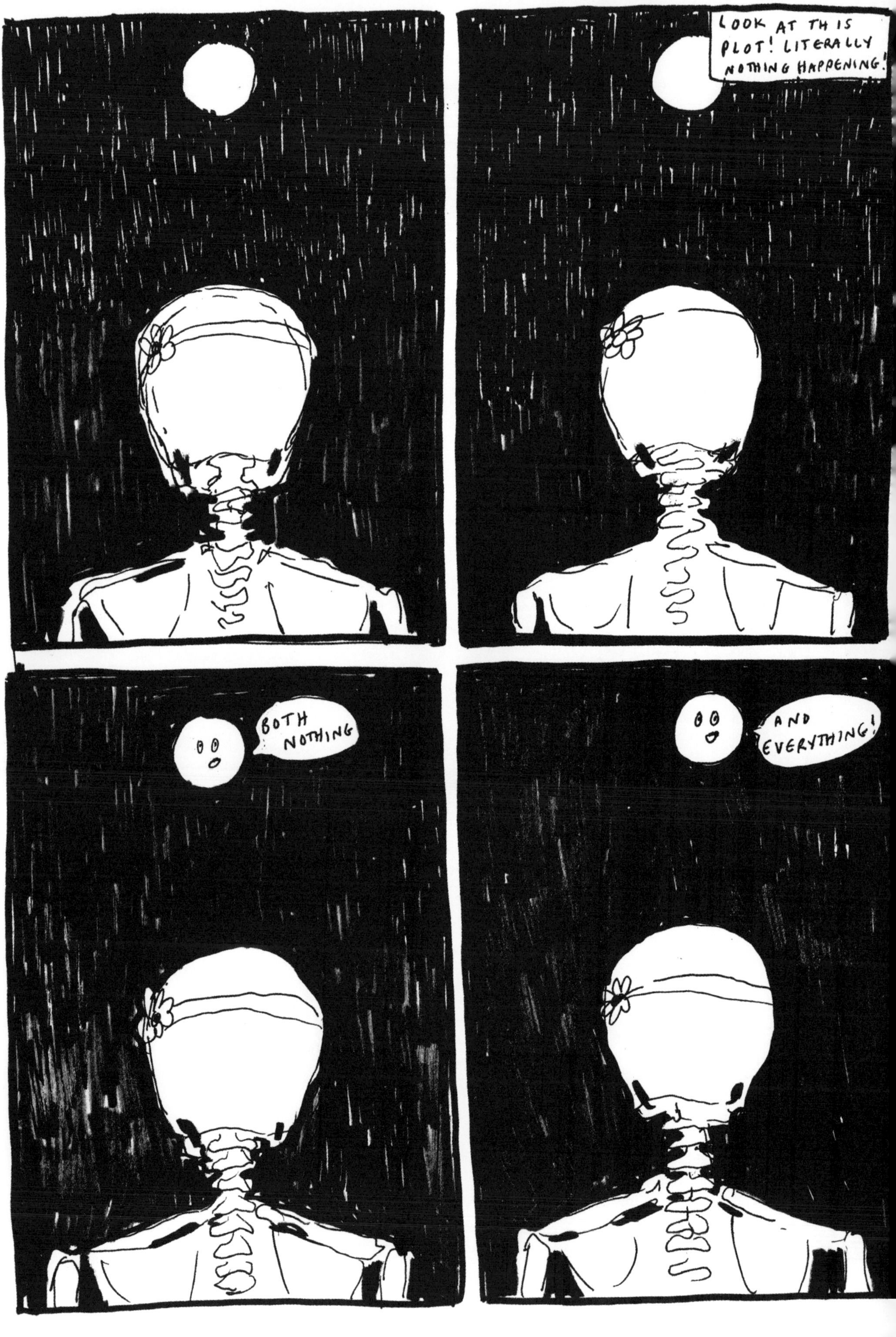
LOOK AT THIS PLOT! LITERALLY NOTHING HAPPENING!
BOTH NOTHING
AND EVERYTHING!

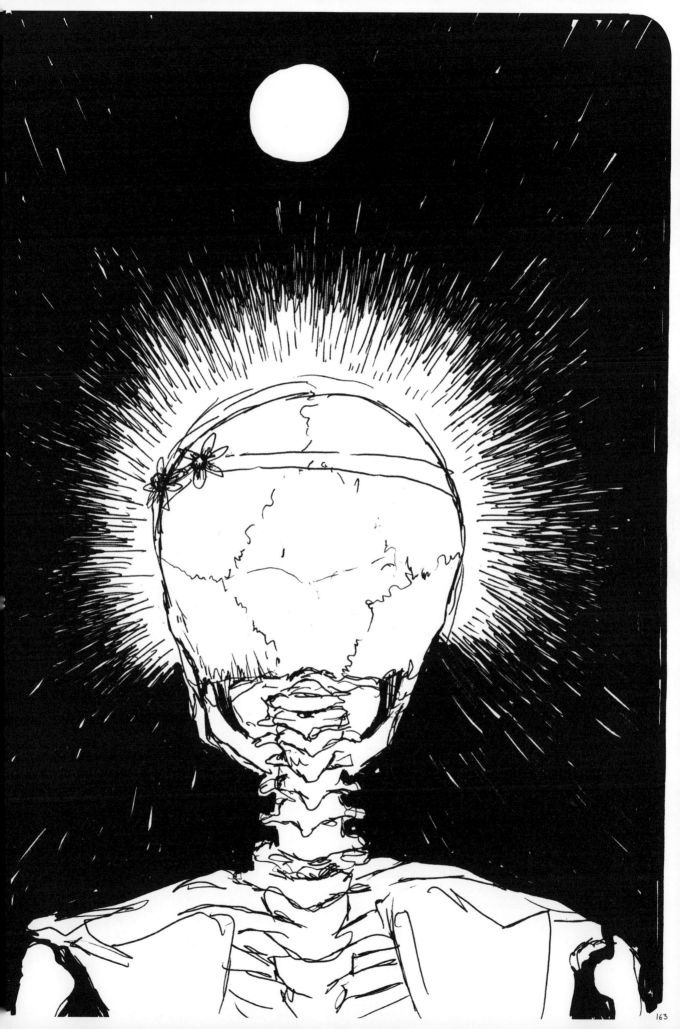

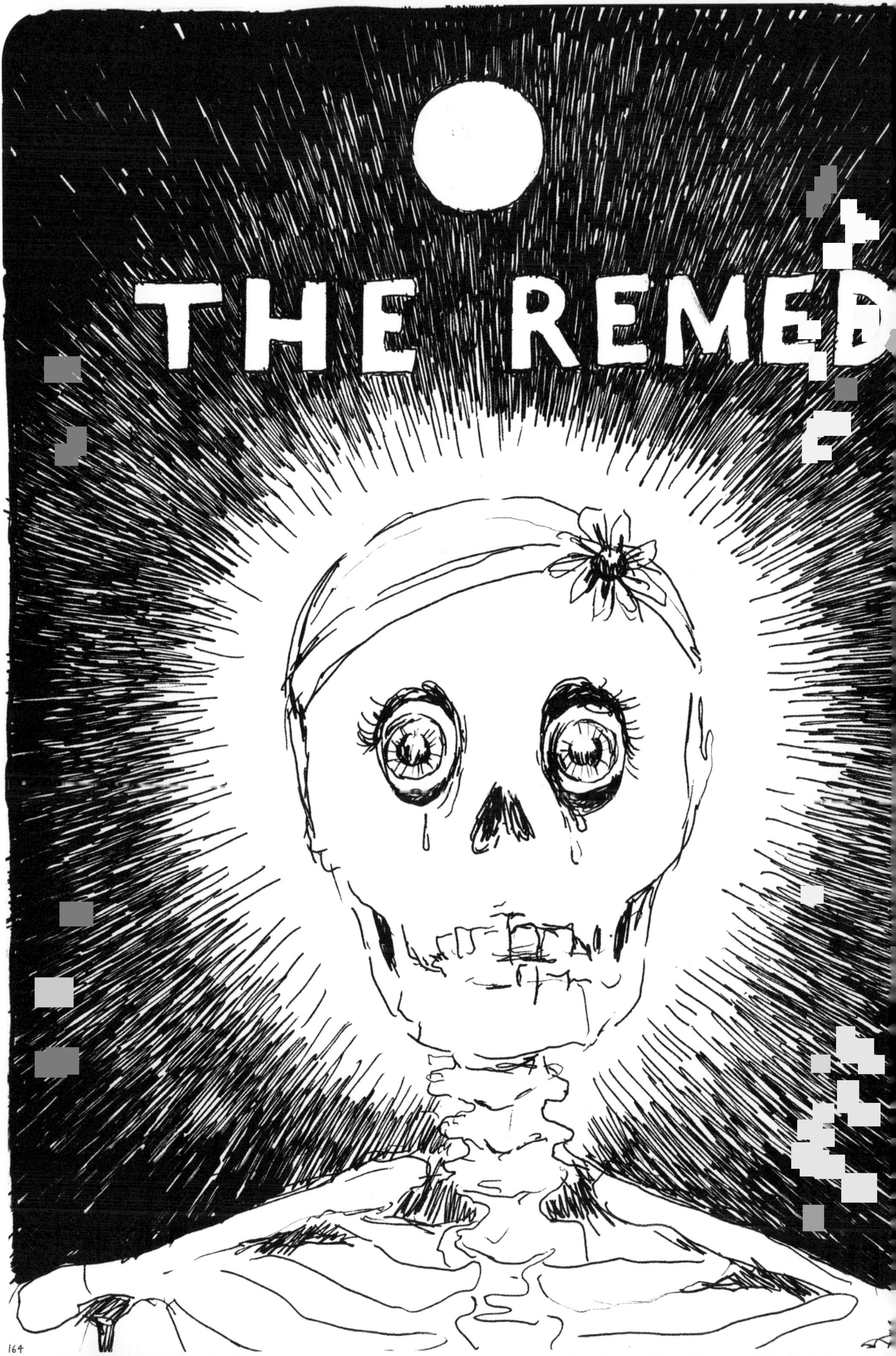
THE REMED

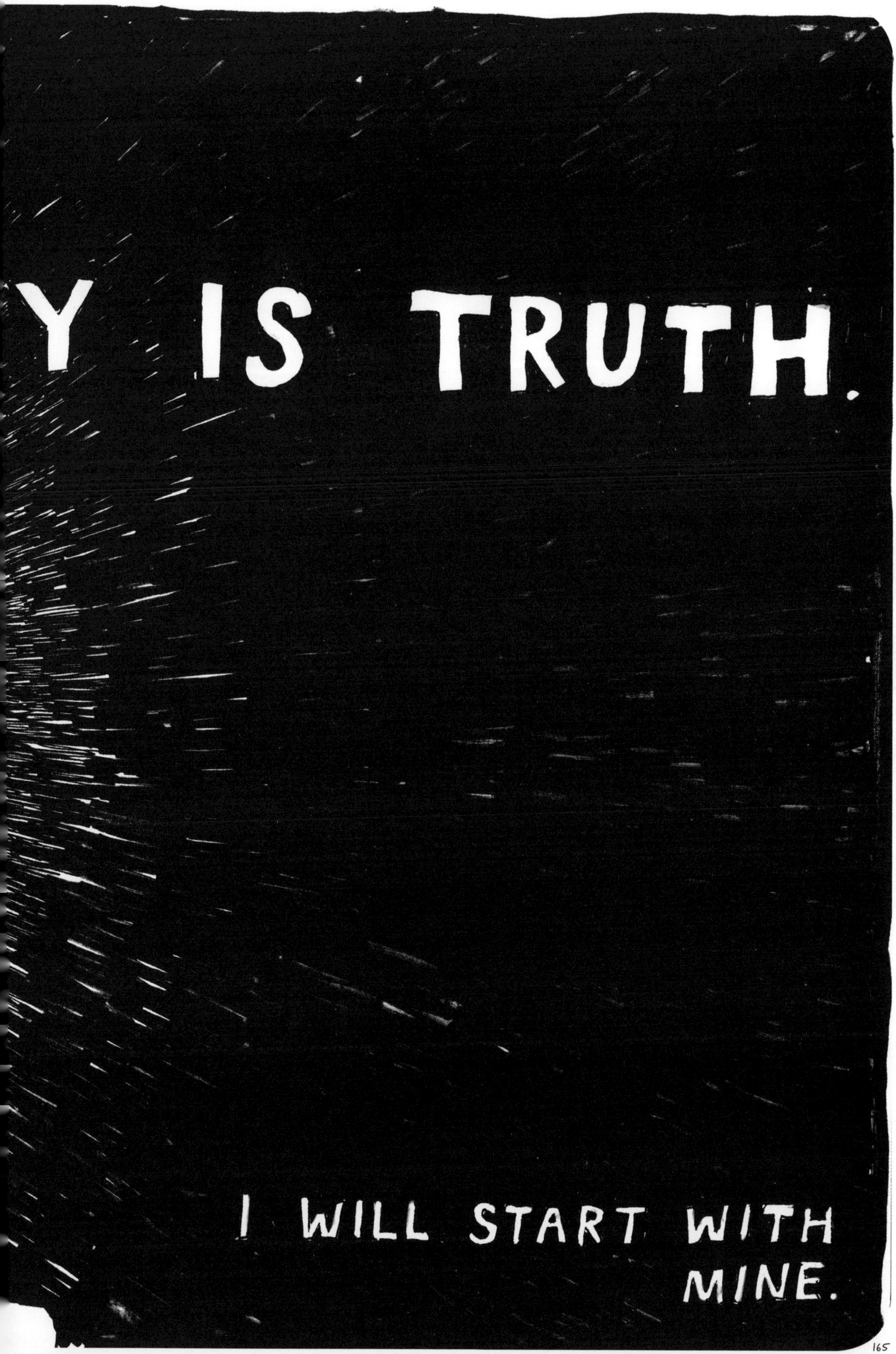
Y IS TRUTH.
I WILL START WITH MINE.

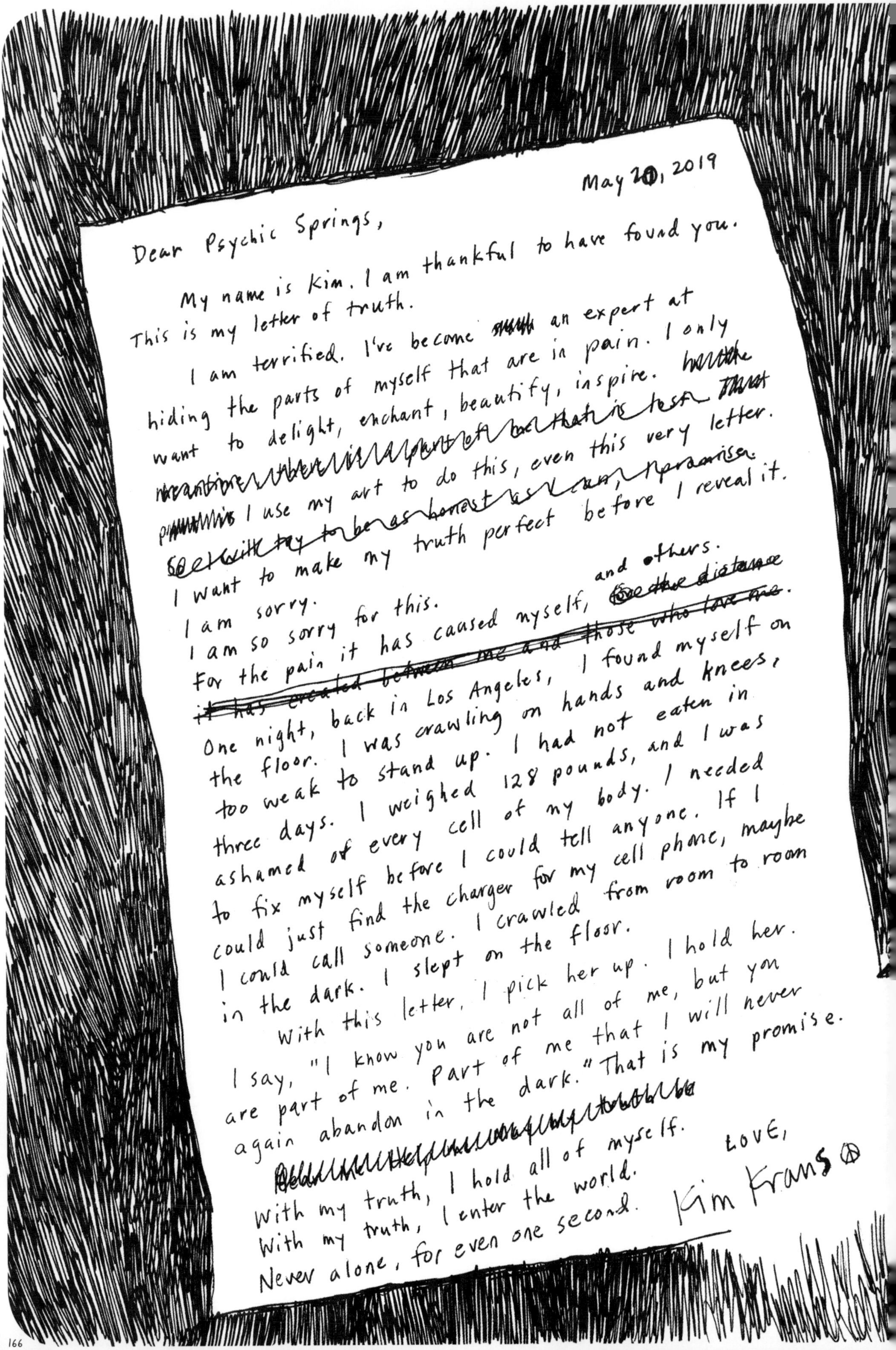

May 20, 2019

Dear Psychic Springs,

My name is Kim. I am thankful to have found you. This is my letter of truth.

I am terrified. I've become ~~such~~ an expert at hiding the parts of myself that are in pain. I only want to delight, enchant, beautify, inspire. ~~but the~~ ~~meantime~~ ~~that is test that~~ ~~I use my art to do this, even this very letter.~~ I use my art to do this, even this very letter. ~~so will try to be as honest as I can, I promise.~~

I want to make my truth perfect before I reveal it.

I am sorry.

I am so sorry for this. and others. For the pain it has caused myself, ~~for the distance~~ ~~it has created between me and those who love me.~~

One night, back in Los Angeles, I found myself on the floor. I was crawling on hands and knees, too weak to stand up. I had not eaten in three days. I weighed 128 pounds, and I was ashamed of every cell of my body. I needed to fix myself before I could tell anyone. If I could just find the charger for my cell phone, maybe I could call someone. I crawled from room to room in the dark. I slept on the floor.

With this letter, I pick her up. I hold her. I say, "I know you are not all of me, but you are part of me. Part of me that I will never again abandon in the dark." That is my promise. ~~Hold with my truth, I hold all of myself.~~

LOVE,

With my truth, I hold all of myself. With my truth, I enter the world. Never alone, for even one second.

Kim Krans

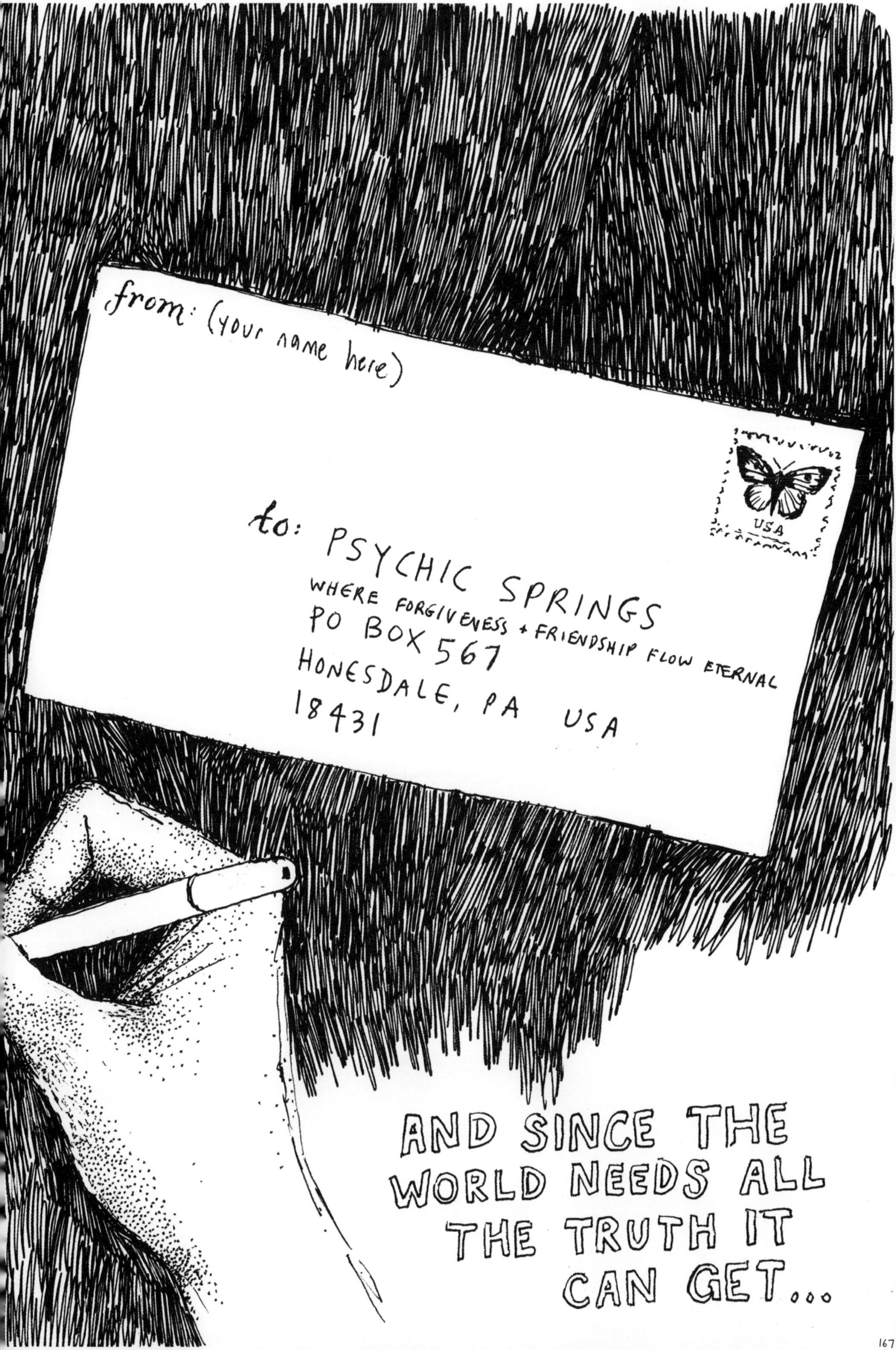
from: (your name here)
to: PSYCHIC SPRINGS
WHERE FORGIVENESS + FRIENDSHIP FLOW ETERNAL
PO BOX 567
HONESDALE, PA USA
18431
USA
AND SINCE THE WORLD NEEDS ALL THE TRUTH IT CAN GET...

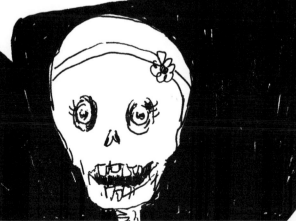

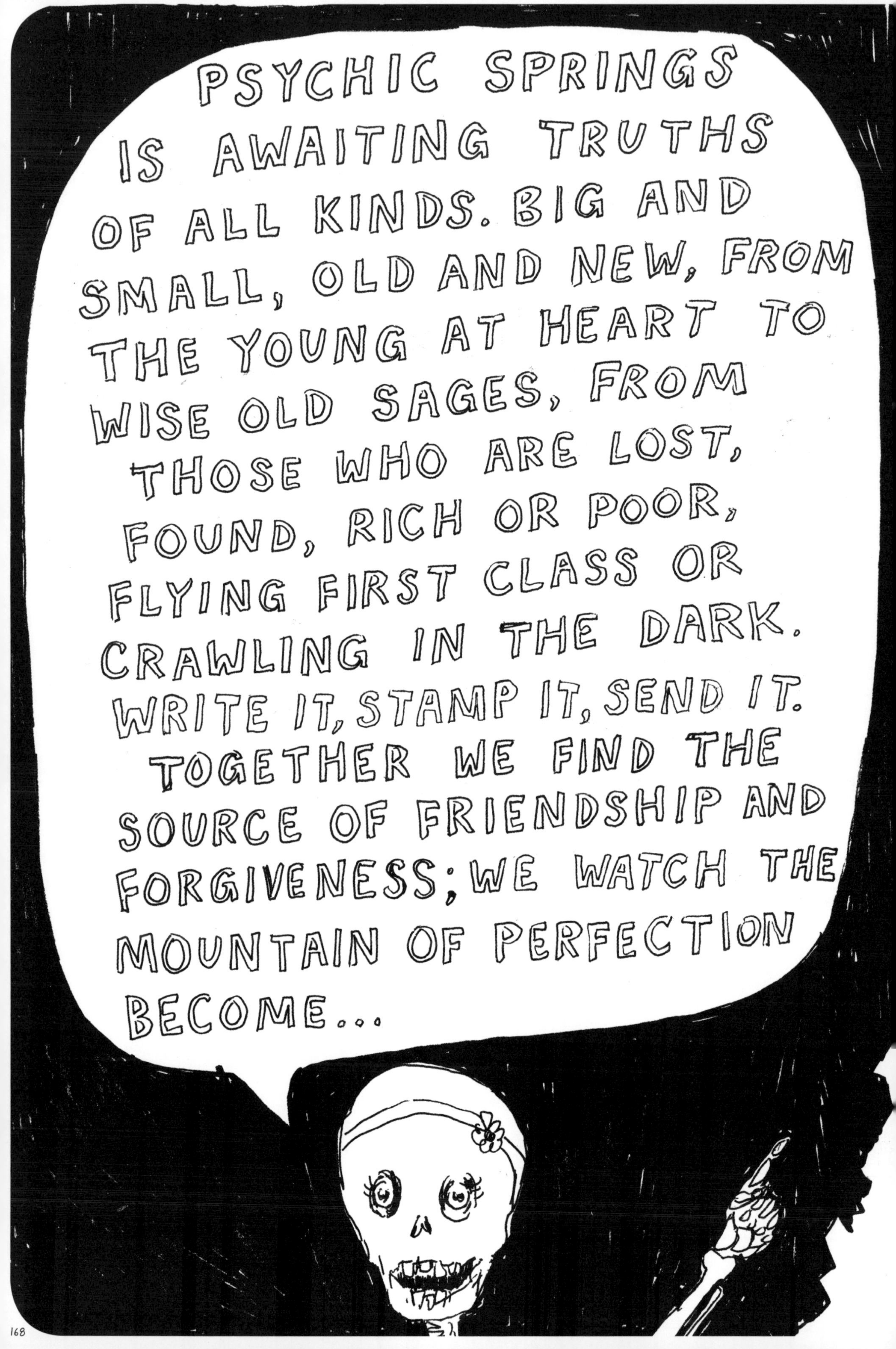

PSYCHIC SPRINGS IS AWAITING TRUTHS OF ALL KINDS. BIG AND SMALL, OLD AND NEW, FROM THE YOUNG AT HEART TO WISE OLD SAGES, FROM THOSE WHO ARE LOST, FOUND, RICH OR POOR, FLYING FIRST CLASS OR CRAWLING IN THE DARK. WRITE IT, STAMP IT, SEND IT. TOGETHER WE FIND THE SOURCE OF FRIENDSHIP AND FORGIVENESS; WE WATCH THE MOUNTAIN OF PERFECTION BECOME...

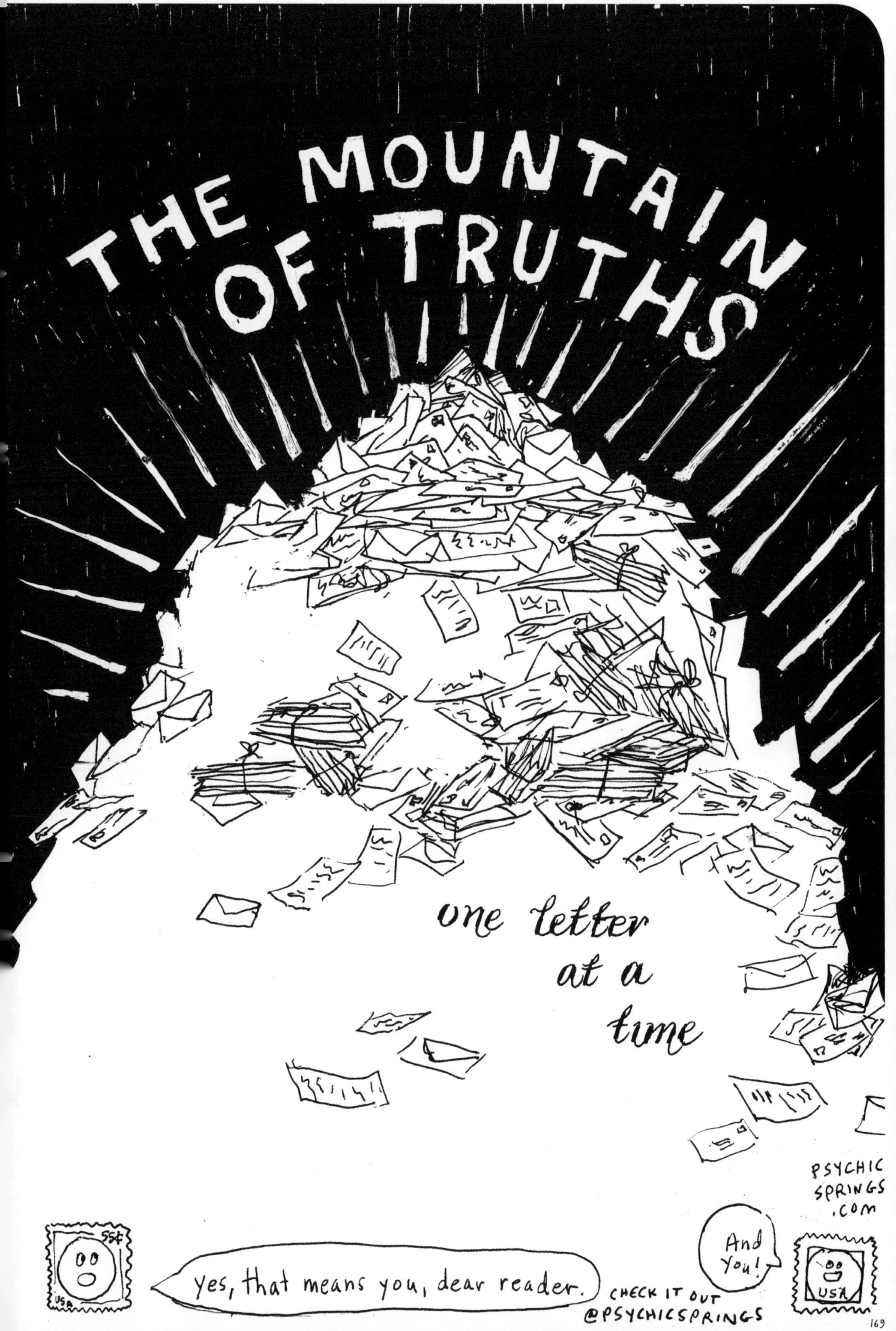
THE MOUNTAIN OF TRUTHS
one letter at a time
PSYCHIC SPRINGS .COM
55¢
USA
yes, that means you, dear reader.
And You!
USA
CHECK IT OUT @PSYCHICSPRINGS

"DRAW THE FEELING" MAY 21 2019 7am

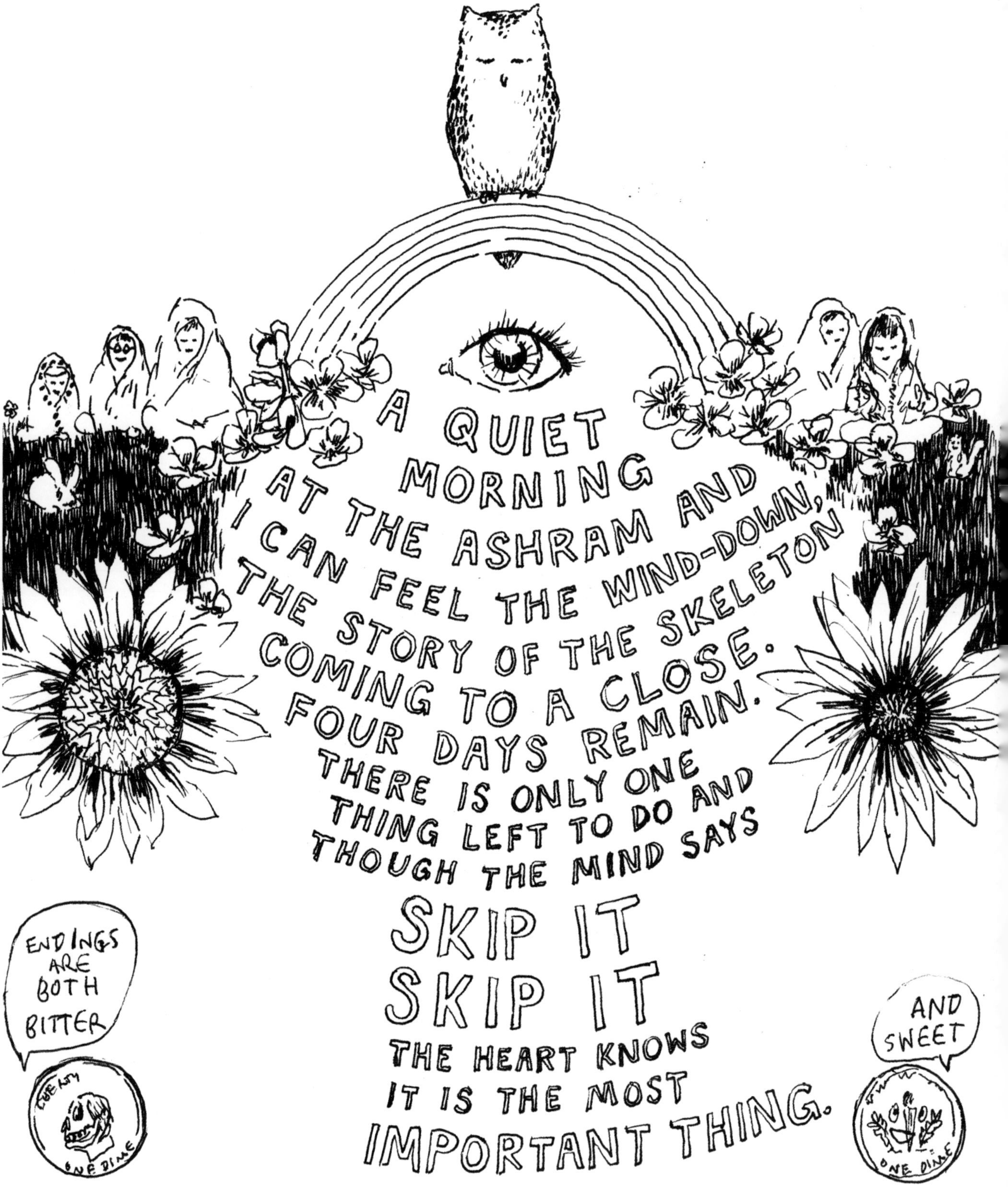
A QUIET MORNING AT THE ASHRAM AND I CAN FEEL THE WIND-DOWN, THE STORY OF THE SKELETON COMING TO A CLOSE. FOUR DAYS REMAIN. THERE IS ONLY ONE THING LEFT TO DO AND THOUGH THE MIND SAYS
SKIP IT
SKIP IT
THE HEART KNOWS IT IS THE MOST IMPORTANT THING.
ENDINGS ARE BOTH BITTER
AND SWEET

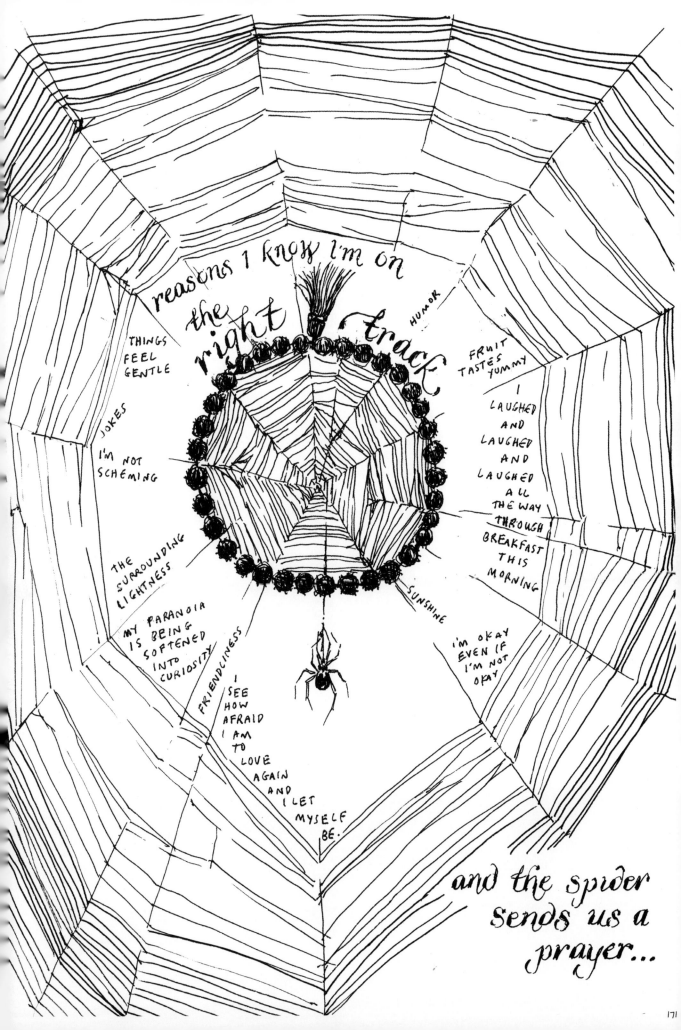

reasons I know I'm on the right track

THINGS FEEL GENTLE

JOKES

I'M NOT SCHEMING

THE SURROUNDING LIGHTNESS

MY PARANOIA IS BEING SOFTENED INTO CURIOSITY

FRIENDLINESS

I SEE HOW AFRAID I AM TO LOVE AGAIN AND I LET MYSELF BE.

HUMOR

FRUIT TASTES YUMMY

I LAUGHED AND LAUGHED AND LAUGHED ALL THE WAY THROUGH BREAKFAST THIS MORNING

SUNSHINE

I'M OKAY EVEN IF I'M NOT OKAY

and the spider sends us a prayer...

171

PRAYER FOR LIFE ON EARTH & THE WORLD WIDE WEB (AKA THE SPIDER'S PRAYER)

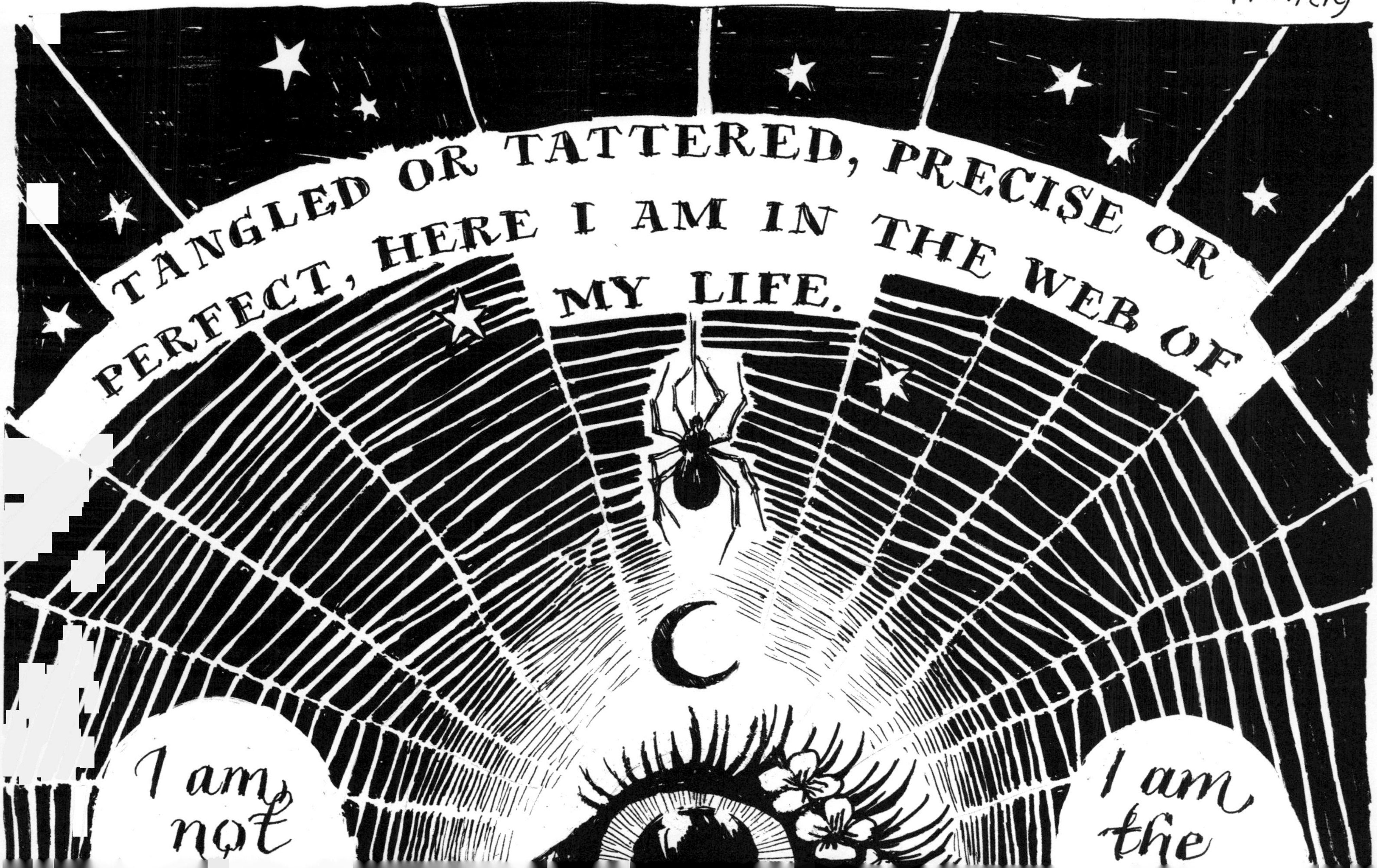
TANGLED OR TATTERED, PRECISE OR PERFECT, HERE I AM IN THE WEB OF MY LIFE.
I am not
I am the

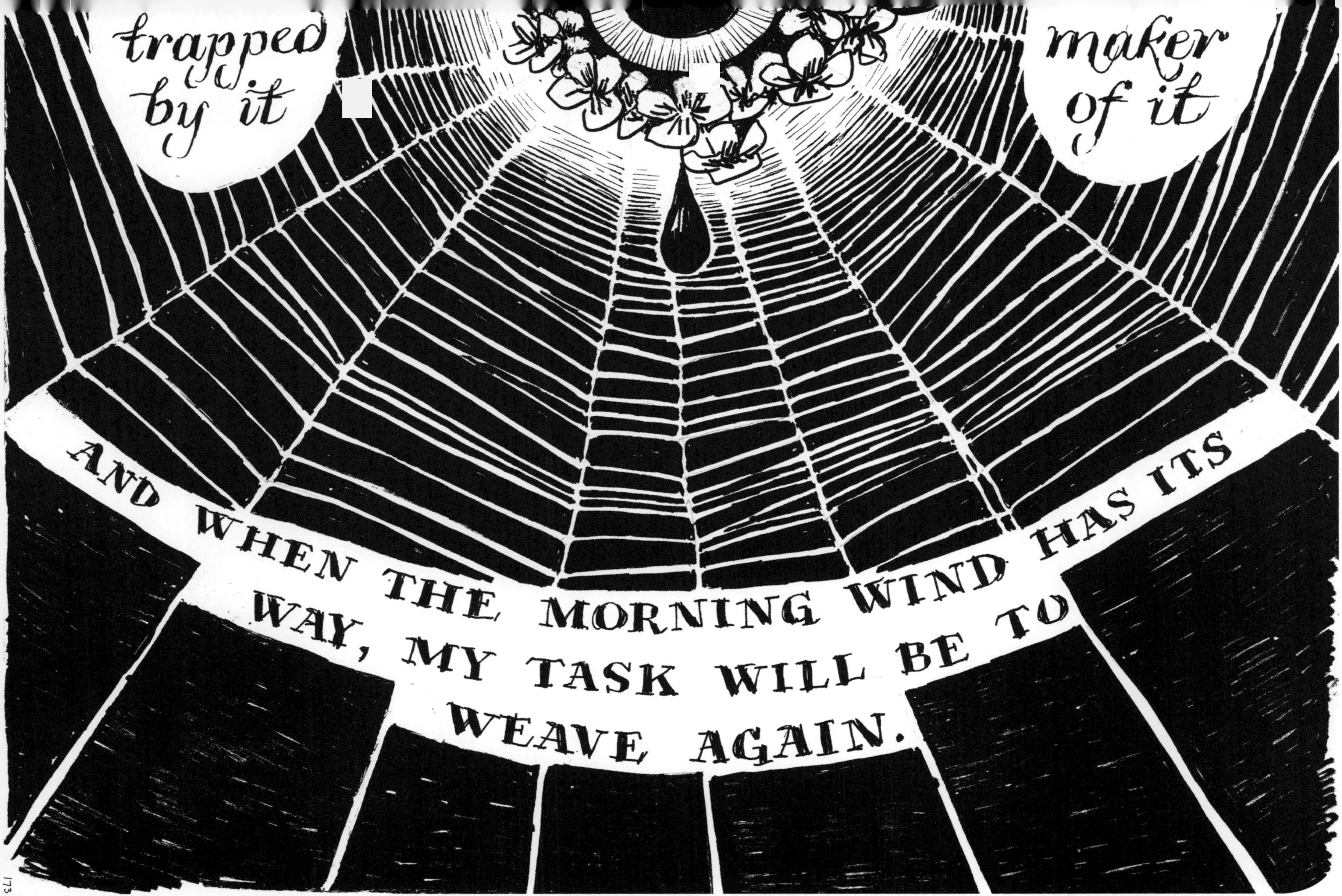
trapped by it
maker of it
AND WHEN THE MORNING WIND HAS ITS WAY, MY TASK WILL BE TO WEAVE AGAIN.

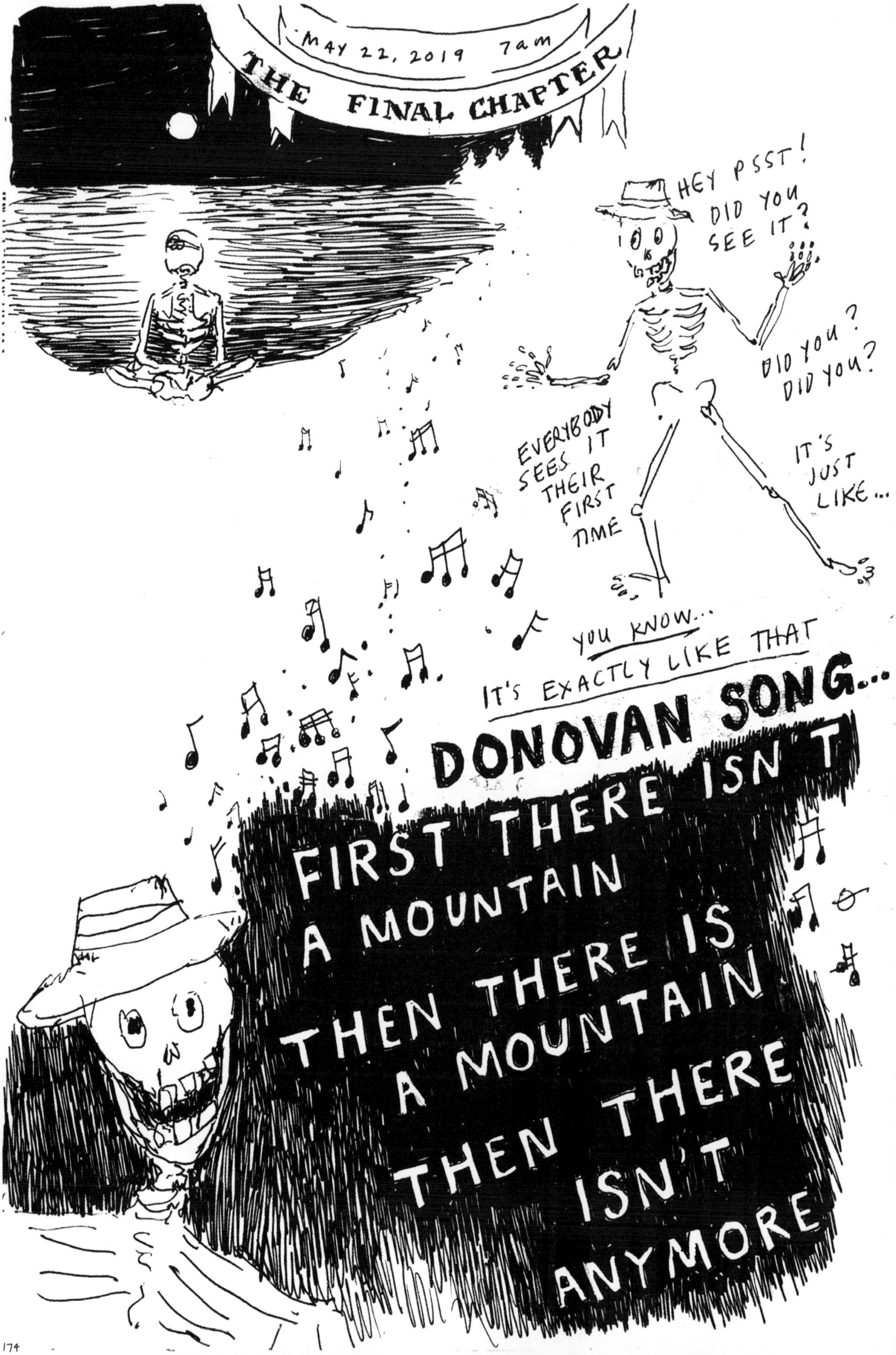

MAY 22, 2019 7am
THE FINAL CHAPTER
HEY PSST! DID YOU SEE IT?
DID YOU? DID YOU?
EVERYBODY SEES IT THEIR FIRST TIME
IT'S JUST LIKE...
YOU KNOW...
IT'S EXACTLY LIKE THAT
DONOVAN SONG...
FIRST THERE ISN'T A MOUNTAIN
THEN THERE IS A MOUNTAIN
THEN THERE ISN'T ANYMORE

UMMM... SUNNY... I DON'T THINK THAT'S QUITE HOW THE LYRICS GO...

OF COURSE IT IS! IT'S A ZEN THING, VERY PHILOSOPHICAL.

QUITE SURELY DONOVAN VISITED PSYCHIC SPRINGS AT SOME POINT BECAUSE IT'S A PRECISE LYRICAL DEPICTION OF A VERY ADVANCED LEVEL OF CONSCIOUSNESS THAT IS ONLY OBSERVED WHEN THE EGO HAS RELINQUISHED ITS GRIP ON THE SELF AND THE IMAGE RATHER BEING DUAL IS NON DUAL...

SUNNY!
SHEESH.
IT'S TIME TO GO.

AND

I HAVE NEWS

I KNOW
MY NAME

OH. YES. OKAY. YES IT IS.

YES? YES?

I'M ELKE! ELKE THE SKELETON.

OH MY DEAR ELKE. HOW VERY LOVELY TO OFFICIALLY MEET.

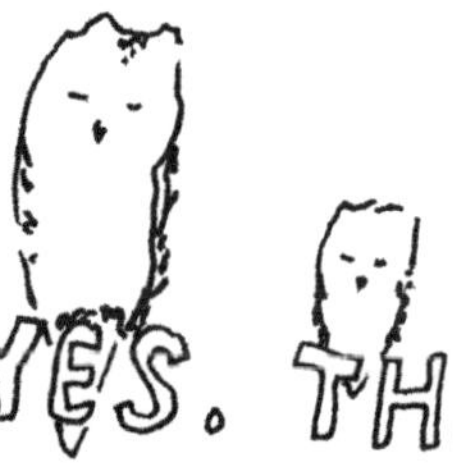

ELKE, YOU ARE RIGHT.
WE MUST MAKE HASTE.
I HAVE TO GET YOU BACK
TO THE WORLD.

AH YES. THE WORLD.

AND I MUST TEND TO
THE MARQUEE.

AH, THE MARQUEE.

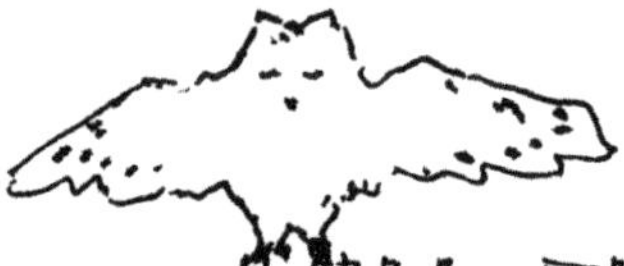

SO I WILL WALK YOU AS
FAR AS THE WHITE TREE,
THEN WE PART WAYS TILL
NEXT TIME.

WILL THERE BE
A NEXT TIME?
CAN I COME BACK HERE?

YOU MUST. YOU MUST. OTHERWISE
IT GOES TO SHAMBLES, LIKE IT
WAS WHEN YOU ARRIVED. THIS
PLACE USED TO BE SPARKLY AND
SHIMMERY, ALIGHT WITH LIFE!
NOW... WELL, IT'S GONNA TAKE
SOME TIME...

BUT THE
FLOWERS
ARE
COMING
BACK,
SEE

THEY ARE. THEY WILL.
AND SOON WILL THE
BUNNIES AND
DEER AND
THE SUN
ITSELF.

HOW
LONG
WILL
IT
TAKE?

IT
DEPENDS.

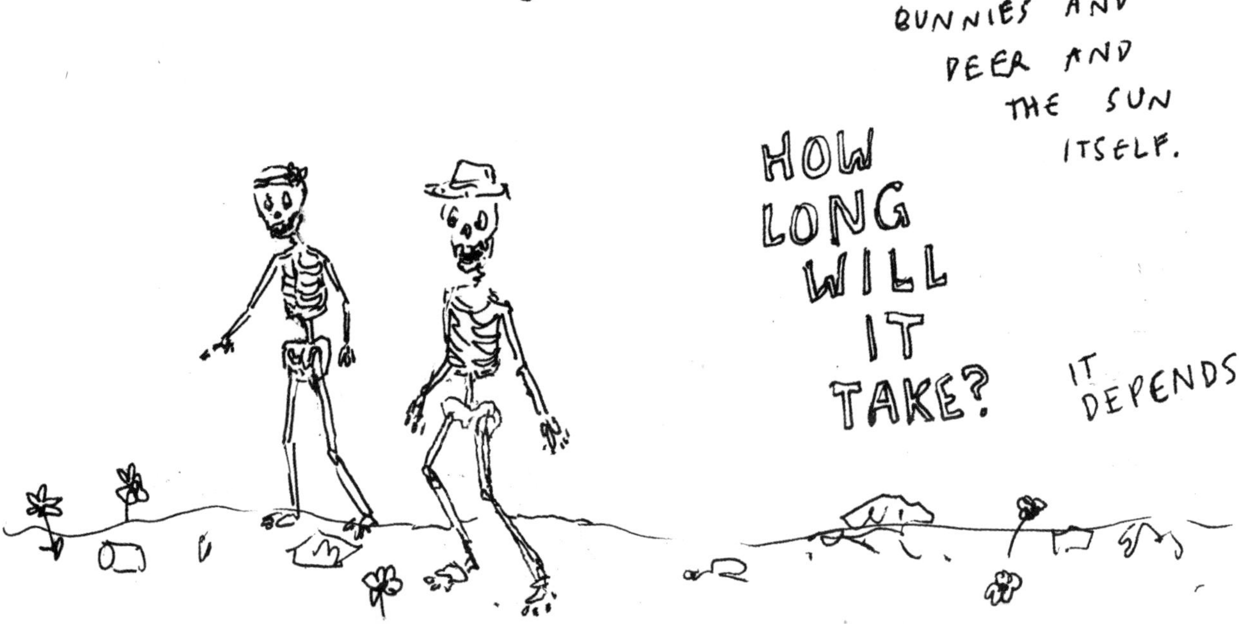

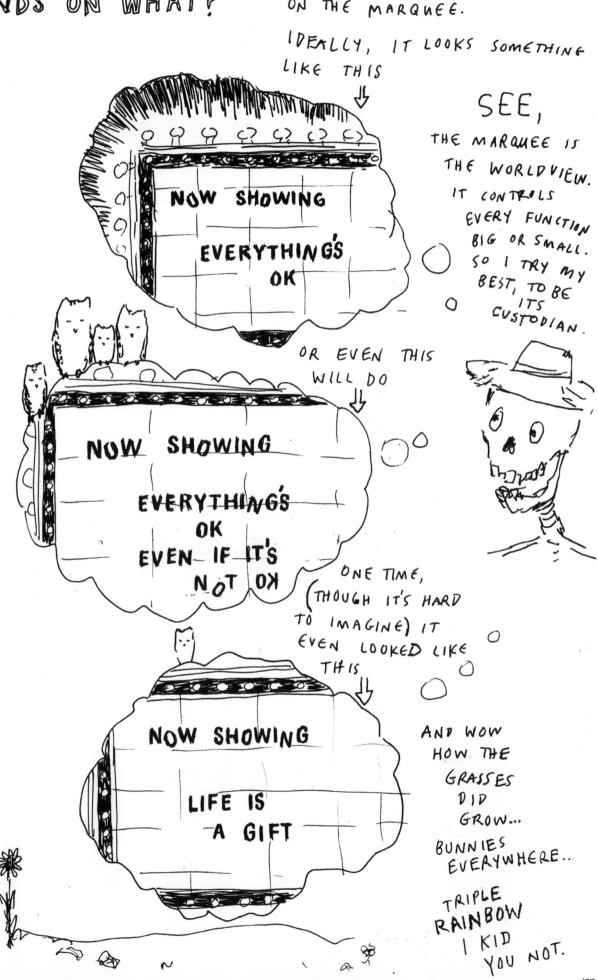

DEPENDS ON WHAT?

ON THE MARQUEE.

IDEALLY, IT LOOKS SOMETHING LIKE THIS

NOW SHOWING

EVERYTHING'S OK

SEE, THE MARQUEE IS THE WORLDVIEW. IT CONTROLS EVERY FUNCTION BIG OR SMALL. SO I TRY MY BEST, TO BE ITS CUSTODIAN.

OR EVEN THIS WILL DO

NOW SHOWING

EVERYTHING'S OK EVEN IF IT'S NOT OK

ONE TIME, (THOUGH IT'S HARD TO IMAGINE) IT EVEN LOOKED LIKE THIS

NOW SHOWING

LIFE IS A GIFT

AND WOW HOW THE GRASSES DID GROW... BUNNIES EVERYWHERE...

TRIPLE RAINBOW I KID YOU NOT.

PRAYER FOR THE TRIPLE RAINBOW

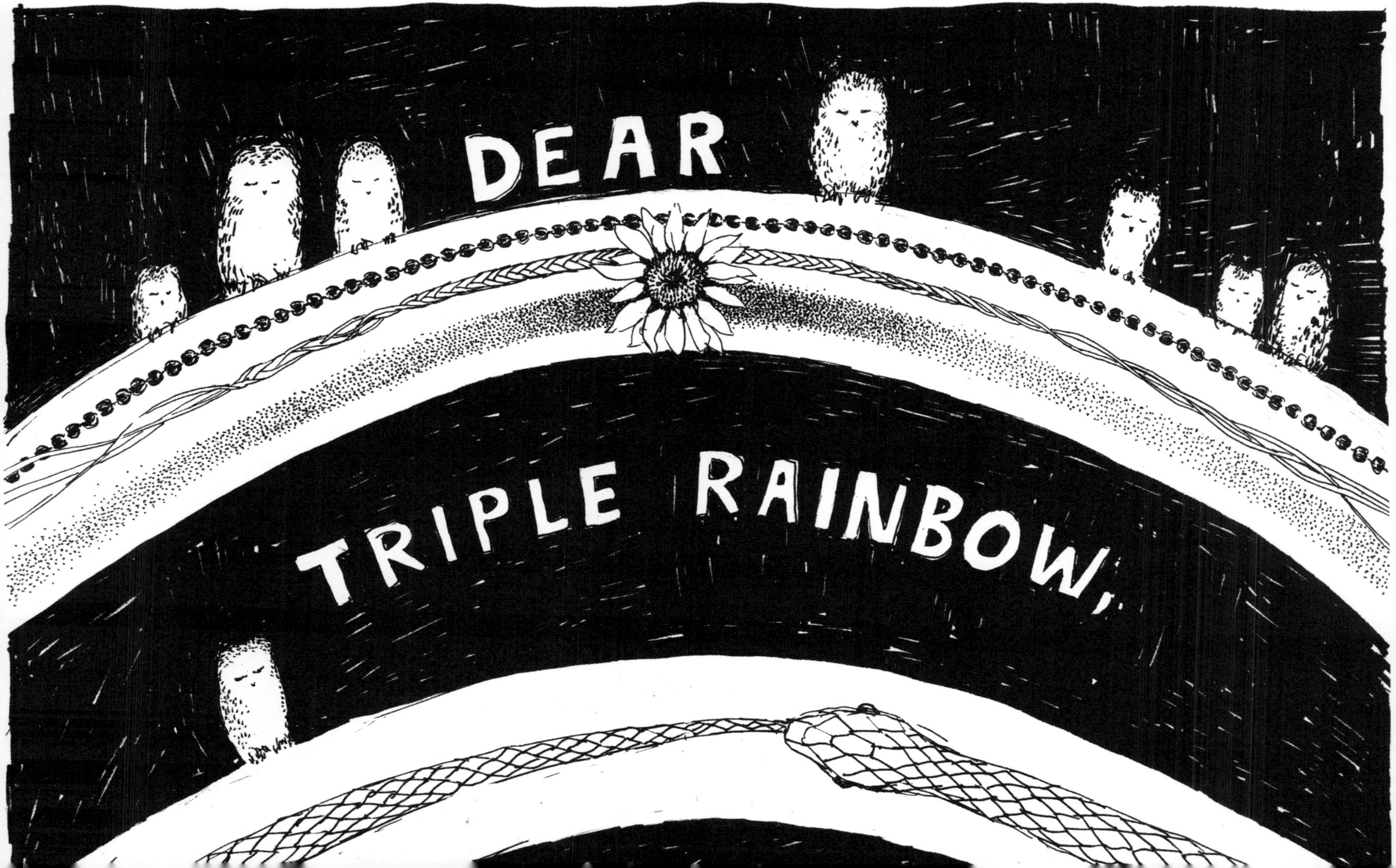
DEAR
TRIPLE RAINBOW,

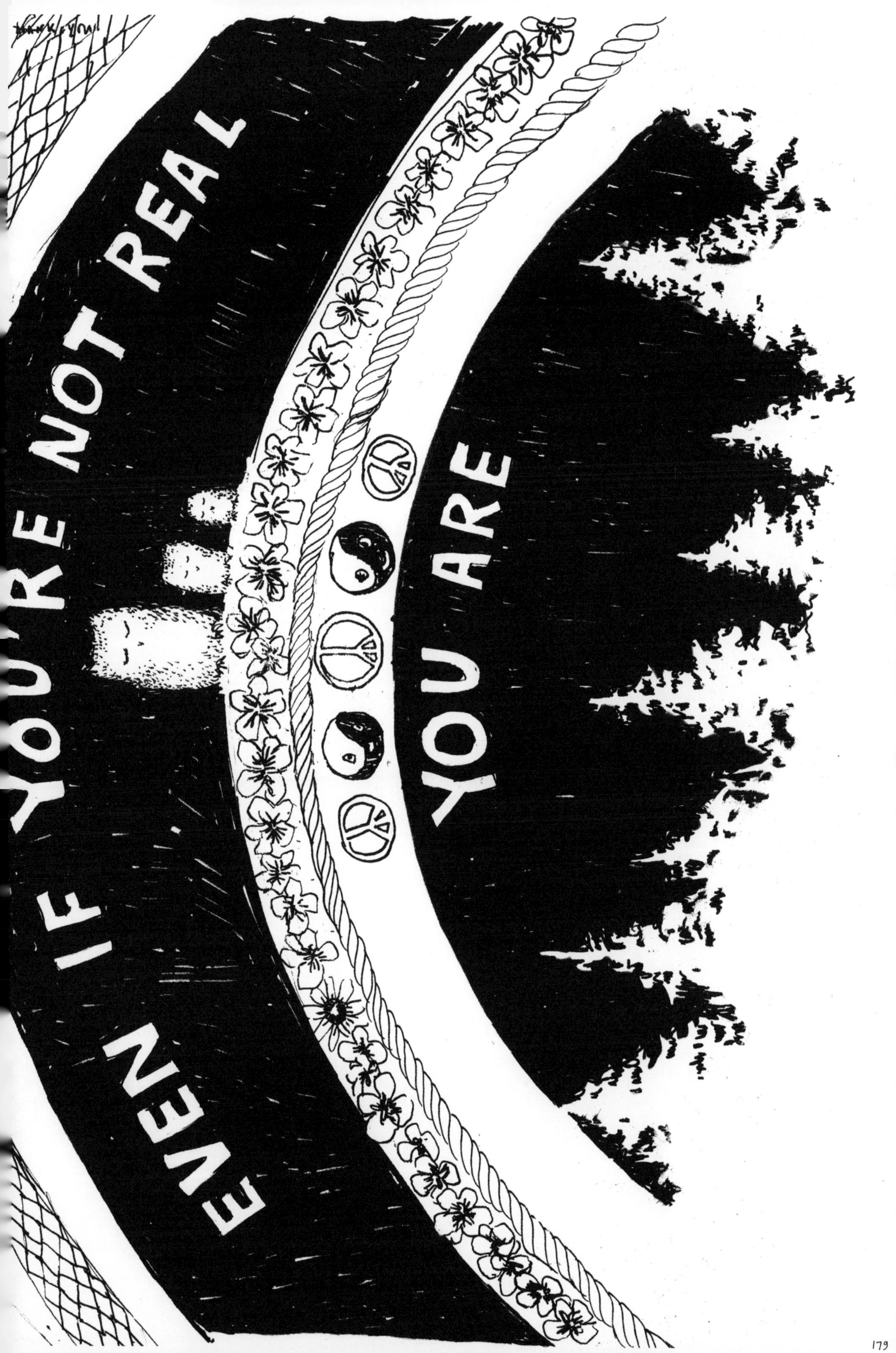
EVEN IF YOU'RE NOT REAL
YOU ARE

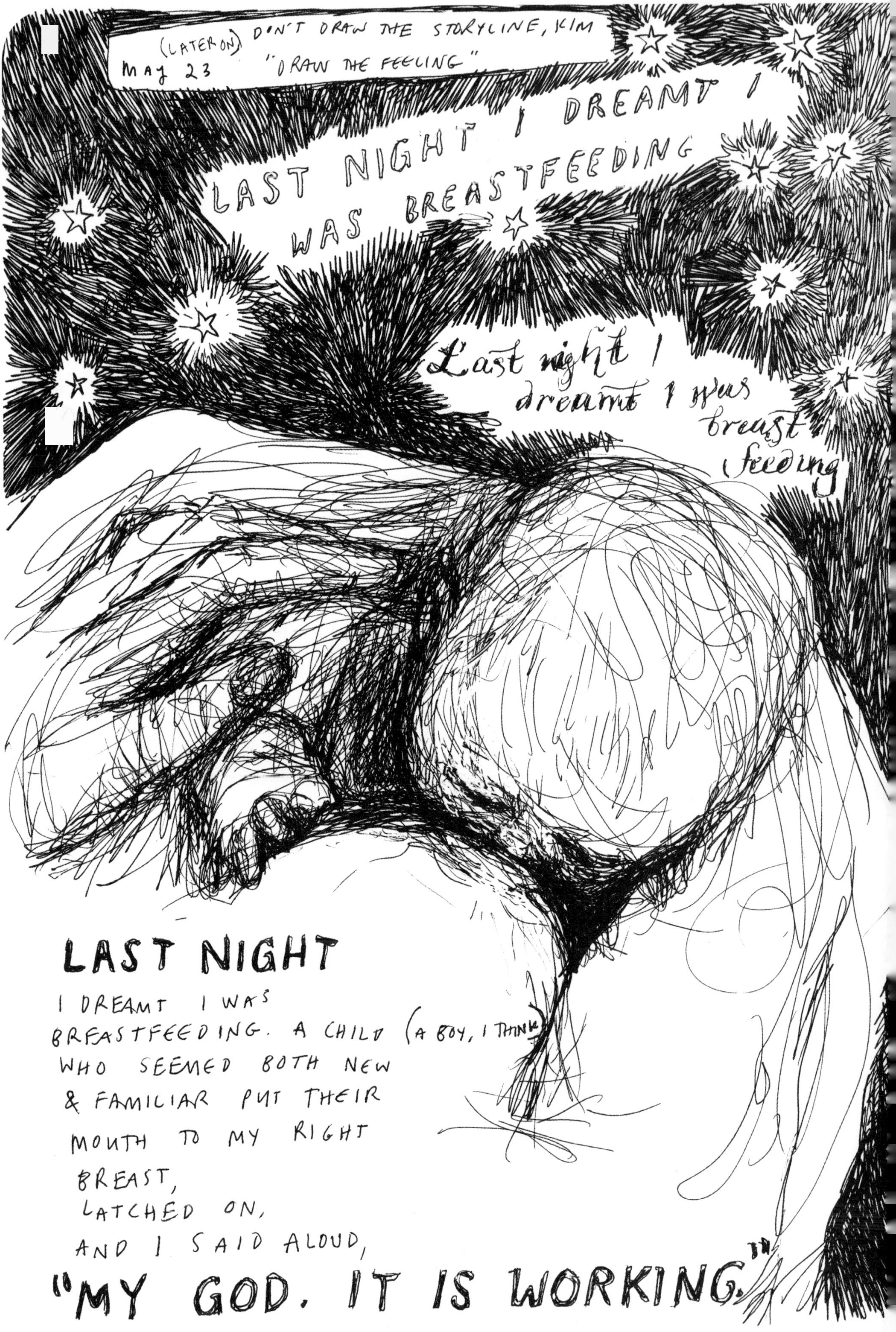
(LATER ON) DON'T DRAW THE STORYLINE, KIM
May 23 "DRAW THE FEELING"
LAST NIGHT I DREAMT I WAS BREASTFEEDING
Last night I dreamt I was breast feeding
LAST NIGHT
I DREAMT I WAS BREASTFEEDING. A CHILD (A BOY, I THINK) WHO SEEMED BOTH NEW & FAMILIAR PUT THEIR MOUTH TO MY RIGHT BREAST, LATCHED ON, AND I SAID ALOUD,
"MY GOD. IT IS WORKING."

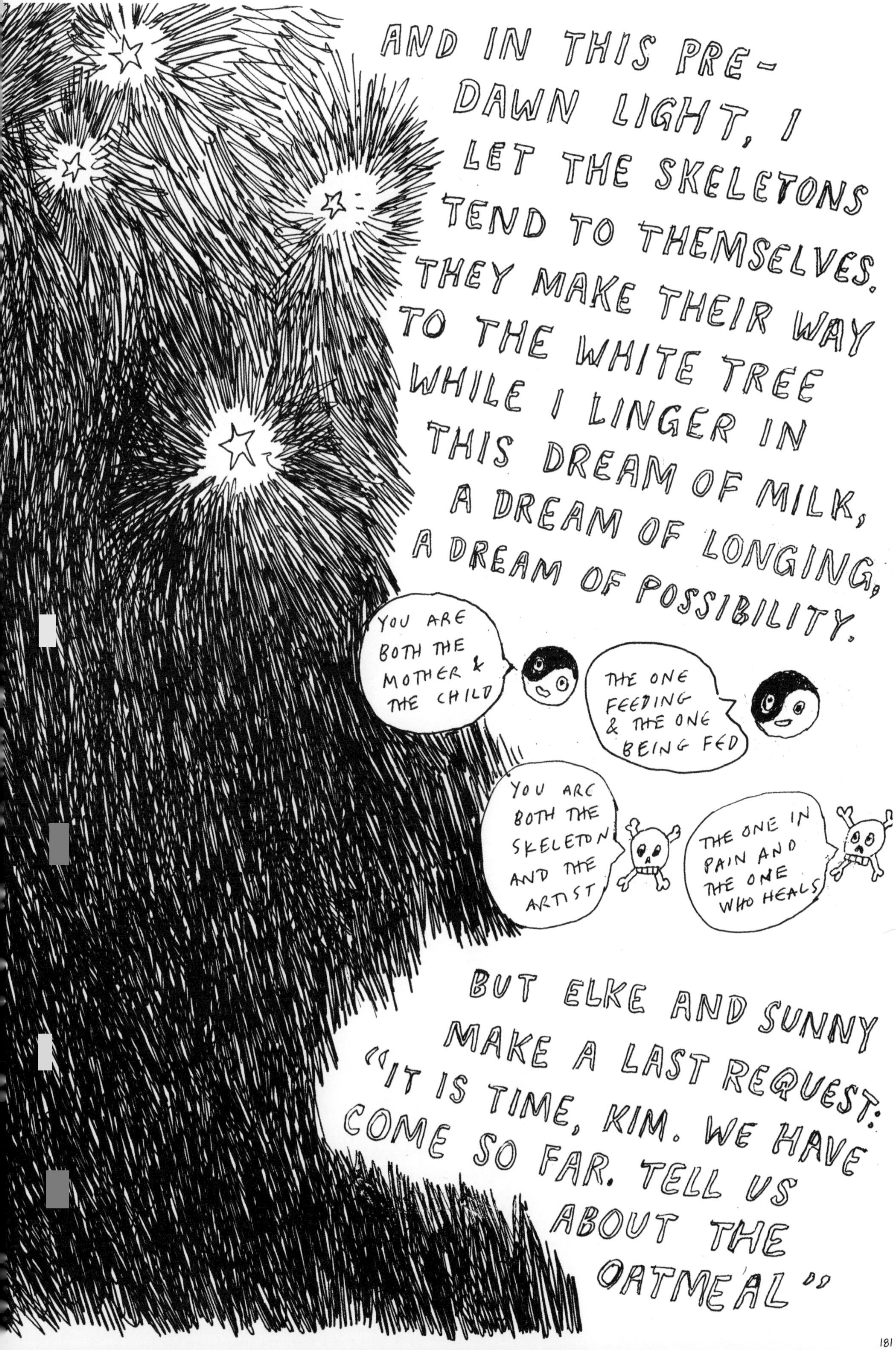
AND IN THIS PRE-DAWN LIGHT, I LET THE SKELETONS TEND TO THEMSELVES. THEY MAKE THEIR WAY TO THE WHITE TREE WHILE I LINGER IN THIS DREAM OF MILK, A DREAM OF LONGING, A DREAM OF POSSIBILITY.
YOU ARE BOTH THE MOTHER & THE CHILD
THE ONE FEEDING & THE ONE BEING FED
YOU ARE BOTH THE SKELETON AND THE ARTIST
THE ONE IN PAIN AND THE ONE WHO HEALS
BUT ELKE AND SUNNY MAKE A LAST REQUEST: "IT IS TIME, KIM. WE HAVE COME SO FAR. TELL US ABOUT THE OATMEAL"

WHEN OATMEAL REPRESENTS MUCH BEYOND ITSELF

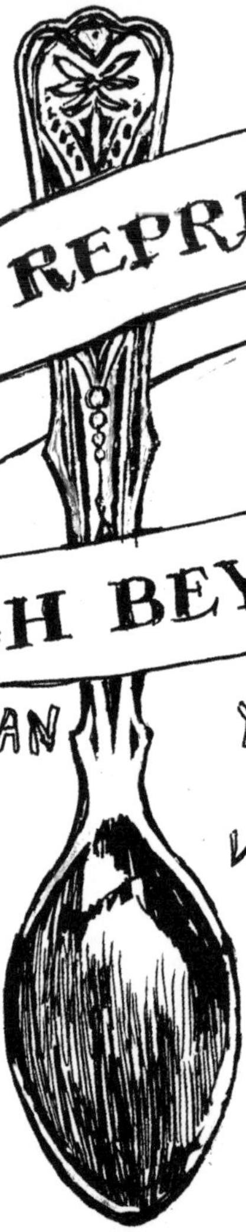

I WAS MARRIED TO ARJAN FOR 12 YEARS. THAT MAKES ABOUT 4,380 MORNINGS THAT WE SPENT TOGETHER, DOING WHAT MARRIED COUPLES DO. AND SOMEWHERE ALONG THE LINE HE FELL INTO THE HABIT OF MAKING US BREAKFAST. OATMEAL, IN FACT. EVERY MORNING (WELL, NEARLY) WHETHER HUNGOVER, HAPPY, FIGHTING, FUCKING, BROKE, BEAUTIFUL, BORED OR BICKERING... THERE IT SAT AT 8 AM (ON THE NOSE)

AND IT WASN'T YOUR TYPICAL OATMEAL. IT WAS MAGICAL.

AND NO MATTER HOW DISTRACTED I'D ALREADY BE BY DRAWING, WORKING, MEDITATION, FASHION OR FINANCES, THE POT WOULD SIT, COVERED, WARM ON THE TABLE, WAITING.

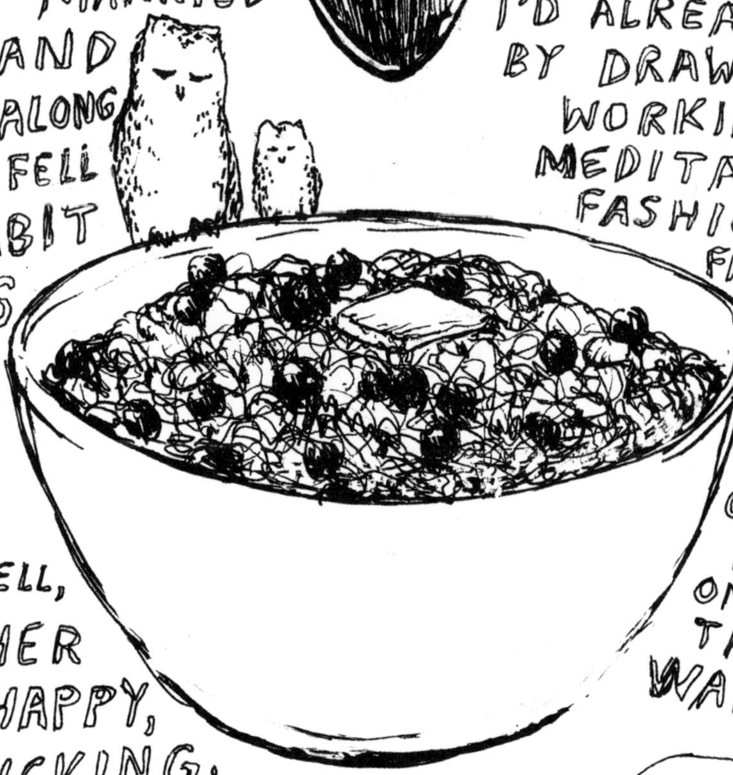

THE IMAGE HAUNTS ME.

WHEN I THINK OF OUR MARRIAGE, IT'S ALL I SEE. WHEN I ENVISION A REMEDY FOR LONELINESS, IT'S ALL I SEE.

AND I REALIZE NOW, I HAVE NEVER PROPERLY THANKED HIM. AND SINCE THERE SEEMS TO BE NO BETTER PLACE, AND NO BETTER MOMENT, I'LL TAKE THESE LAST PAGES TO TRY, IN MY OWN BELATED WAY, TO ACKNOWLEDGE THE YEARS, MONTHS, WEEKS, DAYS, HOURS, MOMENTS OF KINDNESS THAT PASSED BETWEEN US.

DEAR ARJAN,

THANK YOU FOR MAKING OATMEAL FOR US EVERY MORNING. IF MY MATH IS CORRECT, ESTIMATING YOU DID SO 5 OUT OF 7 MORNINGS ON AVERAGE, THIS WOULD EQUAL A LITTLE OVER 3,000 POTS OF OATMEAL. SEEMS CRAZY, BUT IT'S TRUE.

I BETTER GET STARTED...

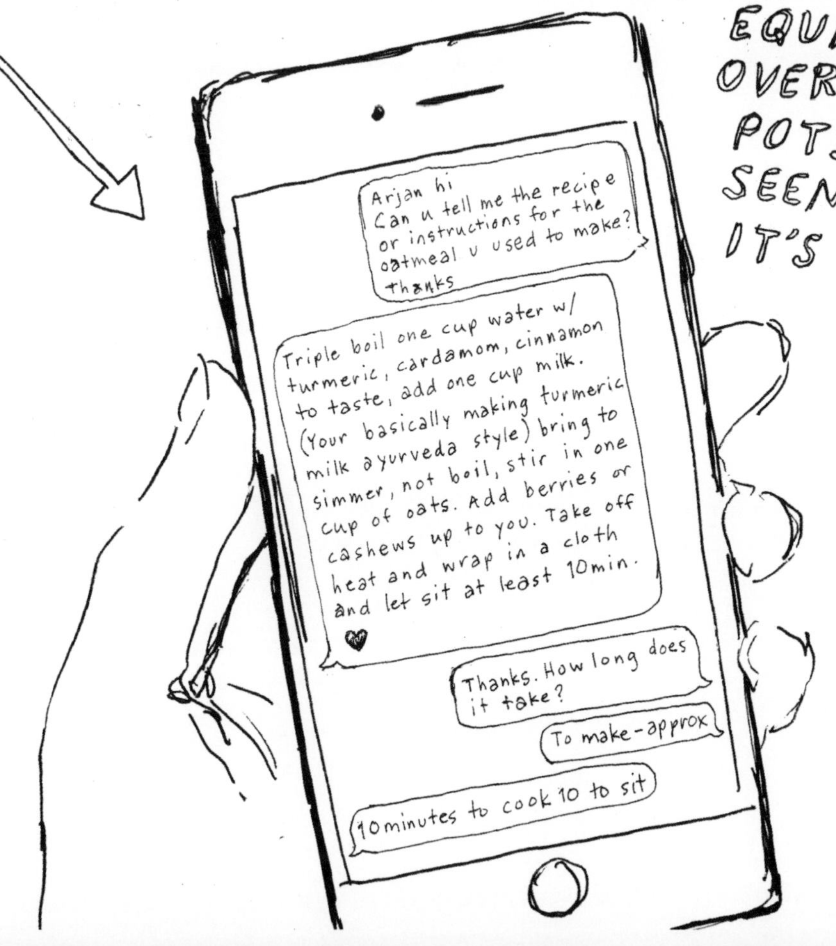
Arjan hi
Can u tell me the recipe or instructions for the oatmeal u used to make? thanks
Triple boil one cup water w/ turmeric, cardamom, cinnamon to taste, add one cup milk. (Your basically making turmeric milk ayurveda style) bring to simmer, not boil, stir in one cup of oats. Add berries or cashews up to you. Take off heat and wrap in a cloth and let sit at least 10min.
Thanks. How long does it take?
To make-approx
10minutes to cook 10 to sit

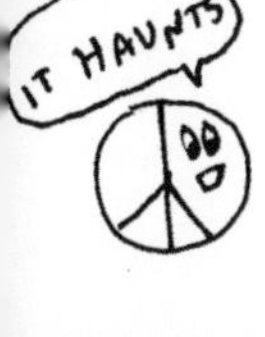
IT HAUNTS

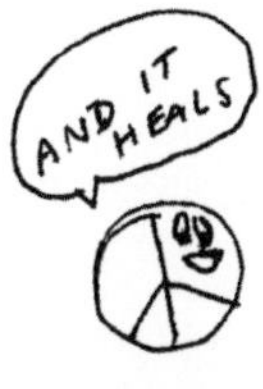
AND IT HEALS

MAY 24 2019

1. THANK YOU
2. THANK YOU
3. THANK YOU
4 THANK YOU
5. THANK YOU
6. THANK YOU
7. THANK YOU
8 THANK YOU
9. THANK YOU
10. THANK YOU
11. THANK YOU
12 THANK YOU
13 THANK YOU
14 THANK YOU
15 THANK YOU
16 THANK YOU
17 THANK YOU
18 THANK YOU
19 THANK YOU
20 THANK YOU
21 THANK YOU
22 THANK YOU
23 THANK YOU
24 THANK YOU
25 THANK YOU
26 THANK YOU
27 THANK YOU
28 THANK YOU
29 THANK YOU
30 THANK YOU
31 THANK YOU
32 THANK YOU
33 THANK YOU
34 THANK YOU
35 THANK YOU
36 THANK YOU
37 THANK YOU
38 THANK YOU
39 THANK YOU
40 THANK YOU
41 THANK YOU
42 THANK YOU
43 THANK YOU
44 THANK YOU
45 THANK YOU
46 THANK YOU
47 THANK YOU
48 THANK YOU
49 THANK YOU
50 THANK YOU
51 THANK YOU
52 THANK YOU
53 THANK YOU
54 THANK YOU
55 THANK YOU
56 THANK YOU

57. THANK YOU
58 THANK YOU
59 THANK YOU
60 THANK YOU
61 THANK YOU
62 THANK YOU
63 THANK YOU
64 THANK YOU
65 THANK YOU
66 THANK YOU
67 THANK YOU
68 THANK YOU
69 THANK YOU
70 THANK YOU
71 THANK YOU
72 THANK YOU
73 THANK YOU
74 THANK YOU
75 THANK YOU
76 THANK YOU
77 THANK YOU
78 THANK YOU
79 THANK YOU
80 THANK YOU
81 THANK YOU
82 THANK YOU
83 THANK YOU
84 THANK YOU
85 THANK YOU
86 THANK YOU
87 THANK YOU
88 THANK YOU
89 THANK YOU
90 THANK YOU
91 THANK YOU
92 THANK YOU
93 THANK YOU
94 THANK YOU
95 THANK YOU
96 THANK YOU
97 THANK YOU
98 THANK YOU
99 THANK YOU
100 THANK YOU
101 THANK YOU
102 THANK YOU
103 THANK YOU
104 THANK YOU
105 THANK YOU
106 THANK YOU
107 THANK YOU
108 THANK YOU
109 THANK YOU
110 THANK YOU

111 THANK YOU
112 THANK YOU
113 THANK YOU
114 THANK YOU
115 THANK YOU
THANK YOU
THANK YOU
THANK YOU
THANK YOU
THANK YOU
THANK YOU
THANK YOU
THANK YOU
THANK YOU
THANK YOU
THANK YOU
THANK YOU
THANK YOU
THANK YOU
THANK YOU
THANK YOU
THANK YOU
THANK YOU
THANK YOU
THANK YOU
THANK YOU
THANK YOU
THANK YOU
THANK YOU
THANK YOU
THANK YOU
THANK YOU
THANK YOU
THANK YOU
THANK YOU
THANK YOU
THANK YOU
THANK YOU
THANK YOU
THANK YOU
THANK YOU
THANK YOU
THANK YOU
THANK YOU
THANK YOU
THANK YOU
THANK YOU
THANK YOU
THANK YOU
THANK YOU

THANK YOU
THANK YOU
THANK YOU
THANK YOU
THANK YOU
THANK YOU
THANK YOU
THANK YOU
THANK YOU
THANK YOU
THANK YOU
THANK YOU
THANK YOU
THANK YOU
THANK YOU
THANK YOU
THANK YOU
THANK YOU
THANK YOU
THANK YOU
THANK YOU
THANK YOU
THANK YOU
THANK YOU
THANK YOU
THANK YOU
THANK YOU
THANK YOU
THANK YOU
THANK YOU
THANK YOU
THANK YOU
THANK YOU
THANK YOU
THANK YOU
THANK YOU
THANK YOU
THANK YOU
THANK YOU
THANK YOU
THANK YOU
THANK YOU
THANK YOU
THANK YOU
THANK YOU
THANK YOU
THANK YOU
THANK YOU
THANK YOU
THANK YOU
THANK YOU
THANK YOU
THANK YOU
THANK YOU
THANK YOU
THANK YOU
THANK YOU

THANK YOU
THANK YOU
THANK YOU
THANK YOU
THANK YOU
THANK YOU
THANK YOU
THANK YOU
THANK YOU
THANK YOU
THANK YOU
THANK YOU
THANK YOU
THANK YOU
THANK YOU
THANK YOU
THANK YOU
THANK YOU
THANK YOU
THANK YOU
THANK YOU
THANK YOU
THANK YOU
THANK YOU
THANK YOU
THANK YOU
THANK YOU
THANK YOU
THANK YOU
THANK YOU
THANK YOU
THANK YOU
THANK YOU
THANK YOU
THANK YOU
THANK YOU
THANK YOU
THANK YOU
THANK YOU
THANK YOU
THANK YOU
THANK YOU
THANK YOU
THANK YOU
THANK YOU
THANK YOU
THANK YOU
THANK YOU
THANK YOU
THANK YOU
THANK YOU
THANK YOU
THANK YOU
THANK YOU
THANK YOU
THANK YOU
THANK YOU
THANK YOU
THANK YOU
THANK YOU
THANK YOU

THANK YOU
THANK YOU
THANK YOU
THANK YOU
THANK YOU
THANK YOU
THANK YOU
THANK YOU
THANK YOU
THANK YOU
THANK YOU
THANK YOU
THANK YOU
THANK YOU
THANK YOU
THANK YOU
THANK YOU
THANK YOU
THANK YOU
THANK YOU
THANK YOU
THANK YOU
THANK YOU
THANK YOU
THANK YOU
THANK YOU
THANK YOU
THANK YOU
THANK YOU
THANK YOU
THANK YOU
THANK YOU
THANK YOU
I'M SORRY
THANK YOU
THANK YOU
THANK YOU
WE TRIED
SO HARD
TO MAKE
IT WORK
THANK YOU
THANK YOU
THANK YOU
THANK YOU
THANK YOU
AS ANY
TWO PEOPLE
DO I GUESS
THANK YOU
THANK YOU
THANK YOU
THANK YOU
THANK YOU
WHEN THEY
KNOW THE
PERSON IN
THANK YOU
THANK YOU
FRONT OF
THEM IS
PRECIOUS
BUT THEY
DON'T KNOW
HOW TO
LOVE WITHOUT
GRIPPING
THANK YOU
THANK YOU

THANK YOU
THANK YOU
THANK YOU
THANK YOU
THANK YOU
THANK YOU
THANK YOU
THANK YOU
THANK YOU
THANK YOU
THANK YOU
THANK YOU
THANK YOU
THANK YOU
THANK YOU
THANK YOU
THANK YOU
THANK YOU
THANK YOU
THANK YOU
THANK YOU
THANK YOU
THANK YOU
THANK YOU
THANK YOU
FOR BEING
THERE ~~FOR~~
WHEN YOU
COULD, AS
YOU COULD
SUNRISE
THANK YOU
THANK YOU
THANK YOU
THANK YOU
THANK YOU
THANK YOU
THANK YOU
THANK YOU
THANK YOU
THANK YOU
THANK YOU
THANK YOU
THANK YOU
THANK YOU
THANK YOU
THANK YOU
THANK YOU
THANK YOU
THANK YOU
THANK YOU
THANK YOU
THANK YOU
THANK YOU
THANK YOU
THANK YOU
THANK YOU
THANK YOU
THANK YOU
THANK YOU
THANK YOU
THANK YOU
THANK YOU
THANK YOU
THANK YOU
THANK YOU
THANK YOU
THANK YOU

THANK YOU
THANK YOU
THANK YOU
THANK YOU
THANK YOU
FOR ADDING
THE CASHEWS
THAT ALWAYS
MADE IT
SO YUMMY
THANK YOU
THANK YOU
THANK YOU
THANK YOU
THANK YOU
THANK YOU
THANK YOU
THANK YOU
THANK YOU
THANK YOU
THANK YOU
THANK YOU
THANK YOU
THANK YOU
THANK YOU
THANK YOU
THANK YOU
THANK YOU
THANK YOU
THANK YOU
THANK YOU
THANK YOU
THANK YOU
THANK YOU
THANK YOU
THANK YOU
THANK YOU
THANK YOU
THANK YOU
THANK YOU
THANK YOU
THANK YOU
THANK YOU
THANK YOU
THANK YOU
THANK YOU
THANK YOU
THANK YOU
THANK YOU
THANK YOU
THANK YOU
THANK YOU
THANK YOU
THANK YOU
THANK YOU
THANK YOU
THANK YOU
THANK YOU
THANK YOU
THANK YOU
THANK YOU
THANK
YOU

THANK YOU   THANK YOU   THANK YOU   THANK YOU   THANK YOU   TO INTEGRATE   THANK YOU   THANK YOU
THANK YOU   THANK YOU   EACH AND   THANK YOU   THANK YOU   THANK YOU   THANK YOU   THANK YOU
THANK YOU   THANK YOU   EVERY   THANK YOU   WITH THE   THANK YOU   THANK YOU   THANK YOU
THANK YOU   THANK YOU   MORNING   THANK YOU   WHITE TOWEL   TO SOAK   THANK YOU   THANK YOU
THANK YOU   BECAUSE IN   THANK YOU   THANK YOU   THANK YOU   AND SETTLE   THANK YOU   THANK YOU
THANK YOU   MY CONSTANT   THANK YOU   THANK YOU   TO KEEP IT   THANK YOU   THANK YOU   THANK YOU
THANK YOU   THANK YOU   FOR TWELVE   THANK YOU   THANK YOU   THANK YOU   THANK YOU   THANK YOU
THANK YOU   AND RELENTLESS   THANK YOU   THANK YOU   WARM UNTIL   THANK YOU   THANK YOU   THANK YOU
THANK YOU   THANK YOU   THANK YOU   THANK YOU   THANK YOU   THANK YOU   THANK YOU   THANK YOU
THANK YOU   SEARCH   THANK YOU   THANK YOU   I WAS   THANK YOU   THANK YOU   THANK YOU
THANK YOU   THANK YOU   YEARS.   THANK YOU   THANK YOU   THANK YOU   THANK YOU   THANK YOU
THANK YOU   FOR WHAT I   THANK YOU   THANK YOU   READY TO   THANK YOU   THANK YOU   THANK YOU
THANK YOU   THOUGHT WAS   THANK YOU   THANK YOU   THANK YOU   THANK YOU   THANK YOU   THANK YOU
THANK YOU   A PERFECT   THANK YOU   THANK YOU   EAT.   THANK YOU   THANK YOU   THANK YOU
THANK YOU   LIFE   THANK YOU   THANK YOU   THANK YOU   THANK YOU   THANK YOU   THANK YOU
THANK YOU   THANK YOU   THANK YOU   THANK YOU   THANK YOU   INTO EACH   THANK YOU   THANK YOU
THANK YOU   THANK YOU   THANK YOU   THANK YOU   THANK YOU   OTHER   THANK YOU   THANK YOU
THANK YOU   THANK YOU   THANK YOU   THANK YOU   THANK YOU   THANK YOU   THANK YOU   THANK YOU
THANK YOU   THANK YOU   THANK YOU   THANK YOU   THANK YOU   THANK YOU   THANK YOU   THANK YOU
THANK YOU   THANK YOU   THANK YOU   THANK YOU   THANK YOU   THANK YOU   THANK YOU   THANK YOU
THANK YOU   THANK YOU   THANK YOU   THANK YOU   THANK YOU   THANK YOU   THANK YOU   THANK YOU
THANK YOU   THANK YOU   THANK YOU   THANK YOU   THANK YOU   THANK YOU   THANK YOU   THANK YOU
THANK YOU   THANK YOU   THANK YOU   THANK YOU   THANK YOU   THANK YOU   THANK YOU   THANK YOU
AND SOMETIMES   THANK YOU   THANK YOU   THANK YOU   THANK YOU   THANK YOU   THANK YOU   THANK YOU
AFTERWARDS   THANK YOU   THANK YOU   THANK YOU   THANK YOU   THANK YOU   THANK YOU   THANK YOU
WE WOULD GO   THANK YOU   THANK YOU   THANK YOU   THANK YOU   THE HEAT   THANK YOU   THANK YOU
FOR A WALK   THANK YOU   THANK YOU   IT NEVER   THANK YOU   JUST ENOUGH   THANK YOU   THANK YOU
THANK YOU   THANK YOU   THANK YOU   TASTES   THANK YOU   THANK YOU   THANK YOU   THANK YOU
THANK YOU   THANK YOU   THANK YOU   QUITE   THANK YOU   TO SOFTEN   THANK YOU   THANK YOU
THANK YOU   THANK YOU   THANK YOU   LIKE   THANK YOU   THANK YOU   THANK YOU   THANK YOU
OUT IN   THANK YOU   AND BELIEVE   THANK YOU   THANK YOU   THANK YOU   THANK YOU   THANK YOU
THE SUN   THANK YOU   ME, I'VE   THANK YOU   THANK YOU   THANK YOU   THANK YOU   THANK YOU
THANK YOU   THANK YOU   TRIED TO   THANK YOU   THANK YOU   THANK YOU   THANK YOU   THANK YOU
THANK YOU   THANK YOU   MAKE THE   THANK YOU   THANK YOU   THANK YOU   THANK YOU   THANK YOU
THANK YOU   THANK YOU   THANK YOU   THANK YOU   THANK YOU   THANK YOU   THANK YOU   THANK YOU
THANK YOU   I FORGOT   THANK YOU   THANK YOU   THANK YOU   THANK YOU   THANK YOU   THANK YOU
THANK YOU   TO SEE   THANK YOU   THANK YOU   YES MAYBE   THANK YOU   THANK YOU   THANK YOU
THANK YOU   THE PERSON,   OATMEAL   THANK YOU   THANK YOU   THANK YOU   THANK YOU   THANK YOU
THANK YOU   THANK YOU   THANK YOU   THANK YOU   THANK YOU   THANK YOU   THANK YOU   THANK YOU
THANK YOU   THANK YOU   THANK YOU   THANK YOU   THE SECRET   THANK YOU   THANK YOU   THANK YOU
BUT MOST   THE MAN,   MYSELF   THANK YOU   THANK YOU   THANK YOU   THANK YOU   THANK YOU
TIMES WE   THE GENTLE   THANK YOU   THANK YOU   THANK YOU   THANK YOU   THANK YOU   THANK YOU
WOULD WORK   BEING IN   THANK YOU   THANK YOU   WAS IN HOW   AND BLEND   THANK YOU   THANK YOU
THANK YOU   FRONT OF   THANK YOU   YOUR   YOU WRAPPED   THANK YOU   THANK YOU   THANK YOU
THANK YOU   ME   THANK YOU   MAGIC   IT THANK YOU   THANK YOU   THANK YOU   THANK YOU
WORK AND   THANK YOU   SINCE THE   OATMEAL   SWADDLED IT   THANK YOU   THANK YOU   THANK YOU
WORK AND   THANK YOU   THANK YOU   THANK YOU   THANK YOU   ALL THE   THANK YOU   THANK YOU
WORK YOU   THANK YOU   MORNING   THANK YOU   THANK YOU   ELEMENTS   THANK YOU   THANK YOU
AND I   THANK YOU   I LEFT   THANK YOU   THANK YOU   INTO ONE   THANK YOU   THANK YOU
THANK YOU   THE ONE WHO   THANK YOU   THANK YOU   AND LET   THANK YOU   THANK YOU   THANK YOU
THANK YOU   LOVED ME   NEARLY   THANK YOU   IT BE   THANK YOU   THANK YOU   THANK YOU
THANK YOU   AS BEST   EIGHTEEN   THANK YOU   THANK YOU   THANK YOU   THANK YOU   THANK YOU
THANK YOU   HE COULD   MONTHS AGO   THANK YOU   THANK YOU   THANK YOU   THANK YOU   THANK YOU
THANK YOU   THANK YOU   WITH   THANK YOU   THANK YOU   THANK YOU   THANK YOU   THANK YOU
AND I CAN'T   IN THE WAY   CHEMO AND   IN THE   THANK YOU   THANK YOU   THANK YOU   THANK YOU
HELP BUT   HE COULD   HORMONES   GREEN   THANK YOU   THANK YOU   THANK YOU   AND
APOLOGIZE   THANK YOU   THANK YOU   POT   THANK YOU   THANK YOU   THANK YOU   ALTHOUGH
FOR THIS   THANK YOU   AND THE   THANK YOU   THANK YOU   THANK YOU   THANK YOU   THANK YOU
THANK YOU   THANK YOU   FINAL   THANK YOU   THANK YOU   THANK YOU   THANK YOU   THANK YOU
THANK YOU   THANK YOU   MISCARRIAGE   WRAPPED   THANK YOU   THANK YOU   THANK YOU   THIS MAY
THANK YOU   THANK YOU   THANK YOU   THANK YOU   ALL THE   THANK YOU   THANK YOU   THANK YOU
THANK YOU   THANK YOU   LEAVING MY   THANK YOU   INGREDIENTS   THANK YOU   THANK YOU   SEEM
THANK YOU   THANK YOU   BODY, BUT   THANK YOU   THANK YOU   HAVING TIME   THANK YOU   THANK YOU
THANK YOU   THANK YOU   THANK YOU   THANK YOU   THANK YOU   THANK YOU   THANK YOU   CRAZY

185

THANK YOU
THANK YOU
THANK YOU
THANK YOU
TO WRITE
THIS OVER
AND OVER
AND OVER
THANK YOU
THANK YOU
THANK YOU
IT [illegible] COMES
NOWHERE
NEAR THE
CRAZINESS
OF THREE
THOUSAND
THANK YOU
THANK YOU
THANK YOU
THANK YOU
THANK YOU
THANK YOU
THANK YOU
THANK YOU
THANK YOU
THANK YOU
POTS OF
WARM AND
BEAUTIFUL
THANK YOU
THANK YOU
MAGIC
OATMEAL
THAT TOTAL
IF MY MATH
IS CORRECT
(3,000 x 10 minutes)
THANK YOU
THANK YOU
THANK YOU
THANK YOU
THANK YOU
THANK YOU
THANK YOU
THANK YOU
THANK YOU
THANK YOU
THANK YOU
SIXTY TWO
AND A HALF
DAYS SPENT
THANK YOU
THANK YOU

OATMEAL
MAKING
THANK YOU
THANK YOU
THANK YOU
THANK YOU
THANK YOU
THANK YOU
THANK YOU
THANK YOU
THANK YOU
THANK YOU
THANK YOU
THANK YOU
THANK YOU
THANK YOU
[illegible]
THANK YOU
THANK YOU
THANK YOU
THANK YOU
THANK YOU
THANK YOU
THANK YOU
THANK YOU
THANK YOU
THANK YOU
THANK YOU
THANK YOU
THANK YOU
THANK YOU
THANK YOU
THANK YOU
THANK YOU
THANK YOU
THANK YOU
THANK YOU
THANK YOU
THANK YOU
[illegible]
THANK YOU
THANK YOU
THANK YOU
THANK YOU
THANK YOU
THANK YOU
THANK YOU
THANK YOU
THANK YOU
THANK YOU
THANK YOU
WITHOUT
ASKING
ANYTHING
IN RETURN
THANK YOU
THANK YOU
THANK YOU
THANK YOU
THANK YOU
THANK YOU

THANK YOU
THANK YOU
THANK YOU
THANK YOU
THANK YOU
THANK YOU
THANK YOU
THANK YOU
THANK YOU
THANK YOU
THANK YOU
THANK YOU
THANK YOU
THANK YOU
THANK YOU
THANK YOU
THANK YOU
THANK YOU
THANK YOU
THANK YOU
THANK YOU
THANK YOU
THANK YOU
THANK YOU
THANK YOU
THANK YOU
THANK YOU
THANK YOU
THANK YOU
THANK YOU
THANK YOU
THANK YOU
THANK YOU
THANK YOU
THANK YOU
THANK YOU
THANK YOU
THANK YOU
THANK YOU
THANK YOU
THANK YOU
THANK YOU
AND YOU
KNOW HOW
I AM
THANK YOU
THANK YOU
THANK YOU
THANK YOU
THANK YOU
A FORCE
TO RECKON
WITH
THANK YOU
THANK YOU
RELENTLESS
THANK YOU
THANK YOU

THANK YOU
THANK YOU
THANK YOU
TIRELESS
THANK YOU
THANK YOU
THANK YOU
THANK YOU
DETERMINED
THANK YOU
THANK YOU
THANK YOU
THANK YOU
THANK YOU
ABSOLUTELY
SET ON
PROVING
THAT I CAN
REACH
THREE
THOUSAND
THANK YOUS
THANK YOU
THANK YOU
THANK YOU
THANK YOU
THANK YOU
THANK YOU
THANK YOU
THANK YOU
THANK YOU
THANK YOU
THANK YOU
[illegible]
[illegible] IN NO
TIME AT
ALL
THANK YOU
THANK YOU
THANK YOU
THANK YOU
THANK YOU
THANK YOU
THANK YOU
SO QUICK
TO FORGET
THAT EACH
OF THESE
THANK YOUS
THANK YOU
THANK YOU
THANK YOU
THANK YOU
THANK YOU
THANK YOU
THANK YOU
THANK YOU
THANK YOU
THANK YOU
THANK YOU
THANK YOU

REPRESENTS
THANK YOU
THANK YOU
THANK YOU
AN ENTIRE
MORNING
THANK YOU
THANK YOU
THANK YOU
THANK YOU
THANK YOU
THANK YOU
THANK YOU
THANK YOU
THANK YOU
A SUNRISE
THANK YOU
THANK YOU
THANK YOU
THANK YOU
THANK YOU
THANK YOU
THANK YOU
THANK YOU
THANK YOU
THANK YOU
THANK YOU
THANK YOU
THANK YOU
THANK YOU
THANK YOU
THANK YOU
THANK YOU
THANK YOU
THANK YOU
THE BEGINNING
OF A DAY
IN WHICH
WE TRIED
AS BEST
WE COULD
THANK YOU
THANK YOU
TO DO
THE BEST
WE COULD
THANK YOU
THANK YOU
THANK YOU
THANK YOU
THANK YOU
THANK YOU
THANK YOU
THANK YOU
THANK YOU
THANK YOU
THANK YOU
THANK YOU
THANK YOU

THANK YOU
THANK YOU
THANK YOU
THANK YOU
THANK YOU
THANK YOU
THANK YOU
THANK YOU
THANK YOU
THANK YOU
AND IF
THEY CALL
ME CRAZY
THANK YOU
THANK YOU
THANK YOU
WHICH IT'S
LIKELY
THANK YOU
THANK YOU
THEY WILL
DO
THANK YOU
THANK YOU
IT MAY
AS WELL
BE FOR
SAYING
THANK YOU
THANK YOU
THANK YOU
THANK YOU
THANK YOU
THANK YOU
THANK YOU
THANK YOU
THANK YOU
THANK YOU
TO A MAN
I ONCE
LOVED
THANK YOU
THANK YOU
THANK YOU
THANK YOU
THANK YOU
AND IN
MANY WAYS
THANK YOU
WILL ALWAYS
LOVE
THANK YOU
AND PLUS
THANK YOU
THANK YOU
THANK YOU
THANK YOU
THANK YOU

THANK YOU
THANK YOU
THANK YOU
I CAN FEEL
IT THANK YOU
IN MY
WHOLE
BODY
THANK YOU
THANK YOU
THAT THREE
THOUSAND
THANK YOUS
THANK YOU
THANK YOU
THANK YOU
THANK YOU
THANK YOU
THANK YOU
THANK YOU
THANK YOU
THANK YOU
THANK YOU
COULD
[illegible] PUT
AT EASE
THANK YOU
THE MOST
RESTLESS
HEART
THANK YOU
THANK YOU
THANK YOU
THANK YOU
THANK YOU
THANK YOU
THANK YOU
THANK YOU
THANK YOU
THANK YOU
THANK YOU
THANK YOU
AND
SOFTEN
THANK
YOU
THANK
YOU
THANK
YOU
THANK
ALL
THE
EDGES
THANK
YOU

THANK YOU THANK YOU
THAT WE
DEVELOP
THANK YOU
THANK YOU
THANK YOU
TO SHIELD
OURSELVES
THANK YOU
THANK YOU
THANK YOU
THANK YOU
FROM THE
HEARTBREAK
THANK YOU
OF ~~THE~~ THIS
WORLD
THANK YOU
THANK YOU
THANK YOU
THANK YOU
THANK YOU
THANK YOU
THANK YOU
THANK YOU
THANK YOU
THANK YOU
THANK YOU
THANK YOU
THANK YOU
THANK YOU
THANK YOU
THANK YOU
THANK YOU
THANK YOU
THANK YOU
THANK YOU
THANK YOU
THANK YOU
THANK YOU
THANK YOU
THANK YOU
THANK YOU
THANK YOU
THANK YOU
THANK YOU
THANK YOU
THANK YOU

THANK YOU
THANK YOU
THANK YOU
THANK YOU
THANK YOU
THANK YOU
THANK YOU
THANK YOU
THANK YOU
THANK YOU
THANK YOU
THANK YOU
THANK YOU
THANK YOU
THANK YOU
THANK YOU
THANK YOU
THANK YOU
THANK YOU
THANK YOU
THANK YOU
THANK YOU
THANK YOU
THANK YOU
THANK YOU
THANK YOU
THANK YOU
THANK YOU
THANK YOU
THANK YOU
THANK YOU
THANK YOU
AND
NOW
THANK YOU
THANK YOU
I LET THE
THANK YOUS
BECOME
THEIR OWN
PULSE
THANK YOU
THANK YOU
OR SONG
THANK YOU
AND I STOP
COUNTING
THANK YOU
AND COMMENTING
THANK YOU
OR TRYING
TO PROVE
ANYTHING

THANK YOU
THANK YOU
THANK YOU
THANK YOU
AND I LET
THE PHRASE
DRIFT
THANK YOU
THANK YOU
THANK YOU
THANK YOU
THANK YOU
IN AND OUT
THANK YOU
BECOMING
OTHER
PHRASES
AND SOUNDS
THANK YOU
AS I CAN
FEEL IT
WANTS TO
BECOME
THANK YOU
THANK YOU
THANK YOU
THANK YOU
THANK YOU
THANK YOU
THANK YOU
THANK YOU
THANK YOU
THANK YOU
THANK YOU
THANK YOU
THANK YOU
THANK YOU
THANK YOU
I'M SORRY
I'M SORRY
I'M SORRY
I'M SORRY
I'M SORRY
I'M SORRY
I'M SORRY
I'M SORRY
I'M SORRY
I'M SORRY
I'M SORRY
~~FORGIVE ME~~

I'M SORRY
I'M SORRY
I'M SORRY
I'M SORRY
I'M SORRY
I'M SORRY
I'M SORRY
I'M SORRY
I'M SORRY
I'M SORRY
I'M SORRY
I'M SORRY
I'M SORRY
I'M SORRY
I'M SORRY
I'M SORRY
I'M SORRY
I'M SORRY
I'M SORRY
I'M SORRY
I'M SORRY
I'M SORRY
I'M SORRY
I'M SORRY
I'M SORRY
I'M SORRY
I'M SORRY
I'M SORRY
I'M SORRY
I'M SORRY
I'M SORRY
I'M SORRY
I'M SORRY
I'M SORRY
I'M SORRY
I'M SORRY
I'M SORRY
I'M SORRY
I'M SORRY
I'M SORRY
I'M SORRY
I'M SORRY
I'M SORRY
I'M SORRY
I'M SORRY
I'M SORRY
I'M SORRY
I'M SORRY
I'M SORRY
I'M SORRY
I'M SORRY
I'M SORRY
I'M SORRY
I'M SORRY

I'M SORRY
I'M SORRY
I'M SORRY
I'M SORRY
I'M SORRY
I'M SORRY
I'M SORRY
I'M SORRY
I'M SORRY
I'M SORRY
FOR ALL
OF MY
SHORTCOMINGS
AND ALL
THE WAYS
I HURT YOU
EITHER
TRIVIAL
OR MONUMENTAL
AND THIS
LIFE, OH
THIS LIFE
THIS LIFE
THIS LIFE
THIS LIFE
THIS LIFE
THIS LIFE
THIS LIFE
THIS LIFE
THIS LIFE
THIS LIFE
THIS LIFE
THIS LIFE
THIS LIFE
THIS LIFE
THIS LIFE
THIS LIFE
THIS LIFE
THIS LIFE
THIS LIFE
THIS LIFE
THIS LIFE
THIS LIFE
THIS LIFE
THIS LIFE
THIS LIFE
THIS LIFE
THIS LIFE
THIS LIFE
THIS LIFE
THIS LIFE
THIS LIFE
THIS LIFE
THIS LIFE

THIS LIFE
THIS LIFE
THIS LIFE
THIS LIFE
THIS LIFE
THIS LIFE
THIS LIFE
THIS LIFE
THIS LIFE
THIS LIFE
SO PRECIOUS
SO PRECIOUS
SO PRECIOUS
SO PRECIOUS
SO PRECIOUS
SO PRECIOUS
SO PRECIOUS
SO PRECIOUS
AND
THIS HEART
THIS HEART
THIS HEART
THIS HEART
THIS HEART
THIS HEART
THIS HEART
THIS HEART
THIS HEART
THIS HEART
THIS HEART
THIS HEART
THIS HEART
THIS HEART
THIS HEART
THIS HEART
THIS HEART
THIS HEART
THIS HEART
THANKS YOU
AND IT
THANKS YOU
AND IT
THANKS YOU
AND IT
THANKS YOU
AND IT
THANKS YOU
AND IT
THANKS YOU
AND IT
THANKS YOU
AND IT
THANKS YOU
AND IT
THANKS YOU
AND IT
MISSES YOU

AND MISSES YOU
AND MISSES YOU
AND MISSES YOU
AND MISSES YOU
AND MISSES YOU
AND MISSES YOU
AND MISSES YOU
AND MISSES YOU
BUT I LET
THE WAVE
WASH OVER
ME, OVER
US, OVER
ALL OF THOSE
WHO ARE
BRAVE
ENOUGH TO
HAVE THEIR
HEARTS
BROKEN
AND ALL
THERE IS
LEFT TO
SAY TO
ANYONE WHO
HAS GONE
THROUGH IT
IS THANK YOU
THANK YOU
THANK YOU
thank you
thank you
thank you
thank you
thank you
thank you
thank you
thank you
thank you
thank you
thank you
thank you
thank you
thank you
thank you
thank you
thank you
thank you
thank you
thank you
thank you
thank you
thank you
thank you

thank you
thank you
thank you
thank you
thank you
thank you
thank you
thank you
thank you
thank you
thank you
thank you
thank you
thank you
thank you
thank you
thank you
thank you
thank you
thank you
thank you
SUNRISE
thank you
thank you
DAWN
thank you
thank you
thank you
thank you
thank you
thank you
thank you
thank you
thank you
thank you
thank you
thank you
thank you
thank you
thank you
thank you
thank you
forces of
change

thank you
thank you
thank you
thank you
thank you
thank you
thank you
thank you
thank you
thank you
thank you
thank you
thank you
thank you
thank you
thank you
thank you
thank you
thank you
thank you
thank you
thank you
thank you
thank you
thank you
thank you
thank you
thank you
thank you
thank you
thank you
thank you
thank you
thank you
thank you
thank you
thank you
thank you
thank you
thank you
thank you
thank you
thank you
thank you
thank you
thank you
thank you
thank you
thank you

thank you
thank you
thank you
thank you
thank you
thank you
thank you
thank you
thank you
thank you
thank you
thank you
thank you
thank you
thank you
thank you
thank you
thank you
thank you
thank you
thank you
thank you
thank you
thank you
thank you
thank you
thank you
thank you
thank you
thank you
thank you
thank you
thank you
thank you
thank you
thank you
thank you
thank you
thank you
thank you
thank you
thank you
thank you
thank you
thank you
thank you
thank you
thank you
thank you
thank you

thank you
thank you
thank you
thank you
thank you
thank you
thank you
thank you
thank you
thank you
thank you
thank you
thank you
thank you
thank you
thank you
thank you
thank you
thank you
thank you
thank you
thank you
thank you
thank you
thank you
thank you
thank you
thank you
thank you
thank you
thank you
thank you
thank you
thank you
thank you
thank you
thank you
thank you
thank you
thank you
thank you
thank you
thank you
thank you
thank you
thank you
thank you
thank you
thank you
thank you
thank you
thank you

thank you
thank you
thank you
thank you
thank you
thank you
thank you
thank you
thank you
thank you
thank you
thank you
thank you
thank you
thank you
thank you
thank you
thank you
thank you
thank you
thank you
thank you
thank you
thank you
thank you
thank you
thank you
thank you
thank you
thank you
thank you
thank you
thank you
thank you
thank you
thank you
thank you
thank you
thank you
thank you
thank you
thank you
thank you
thank you
thank you
thank you
thank you
thank you
thank you
thank you

thank you
thank you
thank you
thank you
thank you
thank you
thank you
thank you
thank you
thank you
thank you
thank you
thank you
thank you
thank you
thank you
thank you
thank you
thank you
thank you
thank you
thank you
thank you
thank you
thank you
thank you
thank you
thank you
thank you
thank you
thank you
thank you
thank you
thank you
thank you
thank you
thank you
thank you
thank you
thank you
thank you
thank you
thank you
thank you
thank you
thank you
thank you
thank you
thank you
thank you

thank you
thank you
thank you
thank you
thank you
thank you
thank you
thank you
thank you
thank you
thank you
thank you
thank you
thank you
thank you
thank you
thank you
thank you
thank you
thank you
thank you
thank you
thank you
thank you
thank you
thank you
thank you
thank you
thank you
thank you
thank you
thank you
thank you
thank you
thank you
thank you
thank you
thank you
thank you
thank you
thank you
thank you
thank you
thank you
thank you
thank you
thank you
thank you
thank you
thank you

thank you
thank you
thank you
thank you
thank you
thank you
thank you
thank you
thank you
thank you
thank you
thank you
thank you
thank you
thank you
thank you
thank you
thank you
thank you
thank you
thank you
thank you
thank you
thank you
thank you
thank you
thank you
thank you
thank you
thank you
thank you
thank you
thank you
thank you
thank you
thank you
thank you
thank you
thank you
thank you
thank you
thank you
thank you
thank you
thank you
thank you
thank you
thank you
thank you
thank you

thank you
thank you
thank you
thank you
thank you
thank you
thank you
thank you
thank you
thank you
thank you
thank you
thank you
thank you
thank you
thank you
thank you
thank you
thank you
thank you
thank you
thank you
thank you
thank you
thank you
thank you
thank you
thank you
thank you
thank you
thank you
thank you
thank you
thank you
thank you
thank you
thank you
thank you
thank you
thank you
thank you
thank you
thank you
thank you
thank you
thank you
thank you
thank you
thank you
thank you

thank you
thank you
thank you
thank you
thank you
thank you
thank you
thank you
thank you
thank you
thank you
thank you
thank you
thank you
thank you
thank you
thank you
thank you
thank you
thank you
thank you
thank you
thank you
thank you
thank you
thank you
thank you
thank you
thank you
thank you
thank you
thank you
thank you
thank you
thank you
thank you
thank you
thank you
thank you
thank you
thank you
thank you
thank you
thank you
thank you
thank you
thank you
thank you
thank you
thank you
thank you
thank you
thank you
thank you

thank you
thank you
thank you
thank you
thank you
thank you
thank you
thank you
thank you
thank you
thank you
thank you
thank you
thank you
thank you
thank you
thank you
thank you
thank you
thank you
thank you
thank you
thank you
thank you
thank you
thank you
thank you
thank you
thank you
thank you
thank you
thank you
thank you
thank you
thank you
thank you
thank you
thank you
thank you
thank you
thank you
thank you
thank you
thank you
thank you
thank you
thank you
thank you
thank you
thank you
thank you
thank you
thank you
thank you

thank you
thank you
thank you
thank you
thank you
thank you
thank you
thank you
thank you
thank you
thank you
thank you
thank you
thank you
thank you
thank you
thank you
thank you
thank you
thank you
thank you
thank you
thank you
thank you
thank you
thank you
thank you
thank you
thank you
thank you
thank you
thank you
thank you
thank you
thank you
thank you
thank you
thank you
thank you
thank you
thank you
thank you
thank you
thank you
thank you
thank you
thank you
thank you
thank you
thank you
thank you
for all
of it
thank you
every
single
part
of it
thank you
thank you
thank you
thank you

thank you
thank you
thank you
thank you
thank you
thank you
thank you
thank you
thank you
thank you
thank you
thank you
thank you
thank you
thank you
thank you
thank you
thank you
thank you
thank you
thank you
thank you
thank you
thank you
thank you
thank you
thank you
thank you
thank you
thank you
thank you
thank you
thank you
thank you
thank you
thank you
thank you
thank you
thank you
thank you
thank you
thank you
thank you
thank you
thank you
thank you
thank you
thank you
thank you
thank you
~~thank you~~
~~thank you~~
~~thank you~~
~~thank you~~
~~thank you~~
thank you
thank you
thank you
thank you
thank you
thank you
thank you

there is
nothing
else to
say.
really
thank you
everything
else
thank you
thank you
seems
~~thank you~~
to
fall
short
thank you
thank you
thank you
thank you
thank you
thank you
thank you
thank you
thank you
thank you
thank you
thank you
thank you
thank you
thank you
thank you
thank you
thank you
thank you
thank you
thank you
thank you
thank you
thank you
thank you
thank you
thank you
thank you
thank you
thank you
thank you
thank you
thank you
thank you
for the
gift
of forgiveness.
Kim

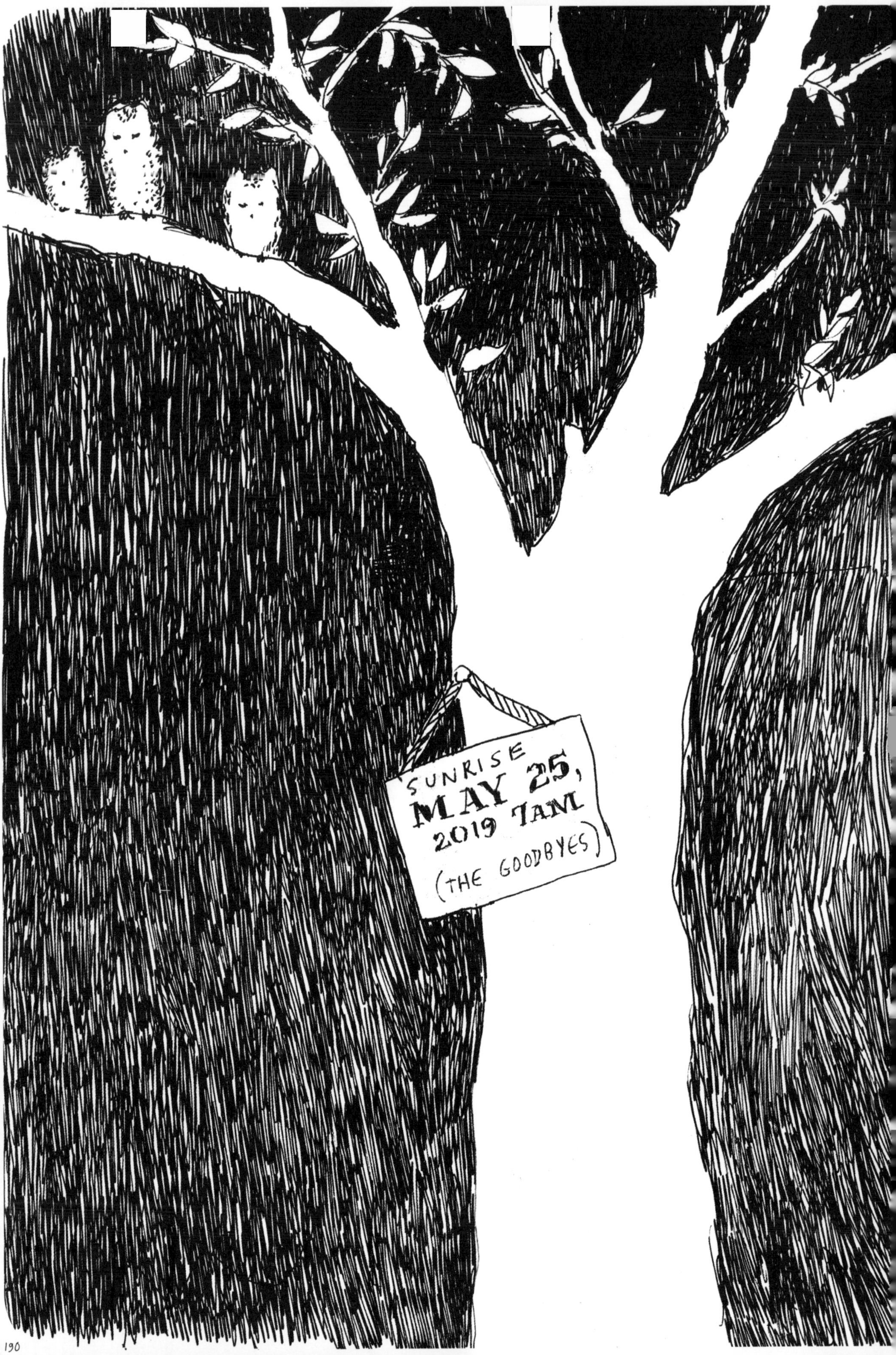
SUNRISE
MAY 25,
2019 7AM
(THE GOODBYES)

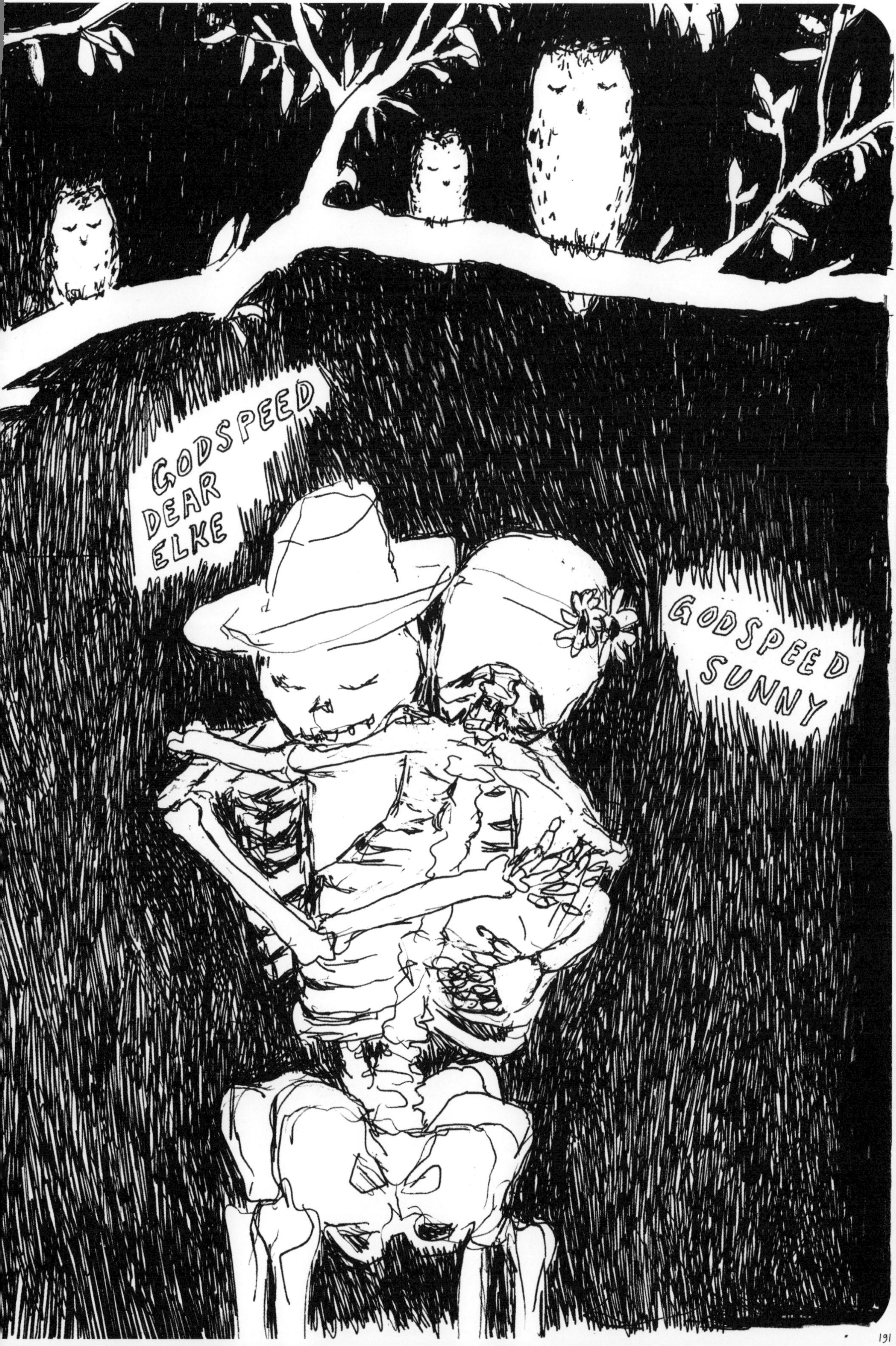
GODSPEED
DEAR
ELKE
GODSPEED
SUNNY

ELKE, TAKE THIS FOR JOURNEY.
KEEP IT CLOSE.
YOU WILL NEED IT WHERE YOU ARE GOING.
THE BOOK OF NAMES
THANK YOU, SUNNY

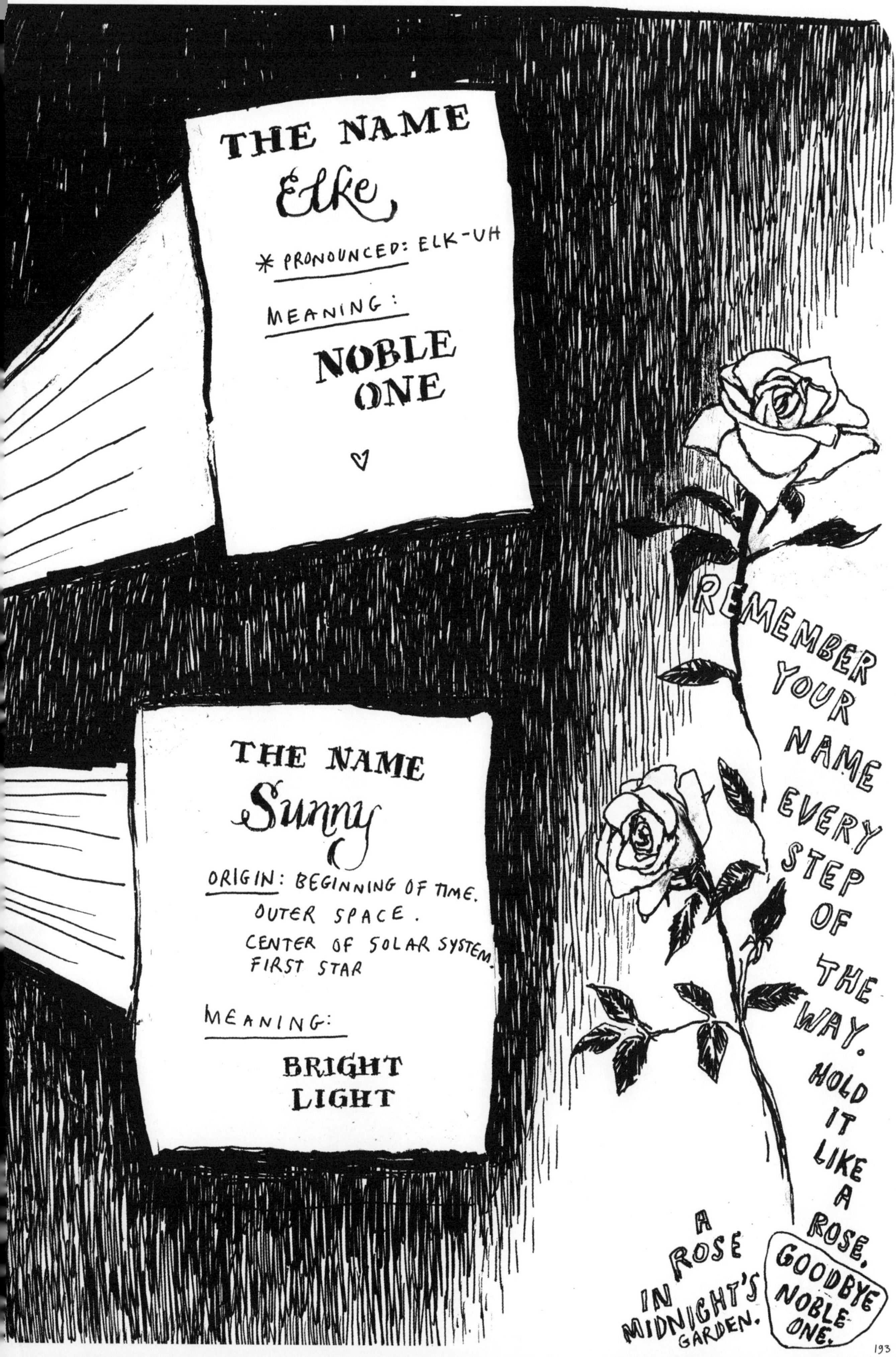
THE NAME
Elke
* PRONOUNCED: ELK-UH
MEANING:
NOBLE ONE
THE NAME
Sunny
ORIGIN: BEGINNING OF TIME.
OUTER SPACE.
CENTER OF SOLAR SYSTEM.
FIRST STAR
MEANING:
BRIGHT LIGHT
REMEMBER YOUR NAME EVERY STEP OF THE WAY.
HOLD IT LIKE A ROSE.
A ROSE IN MIDNIGHT'S GARDEN.
GOODBYE NOBLE ONE.

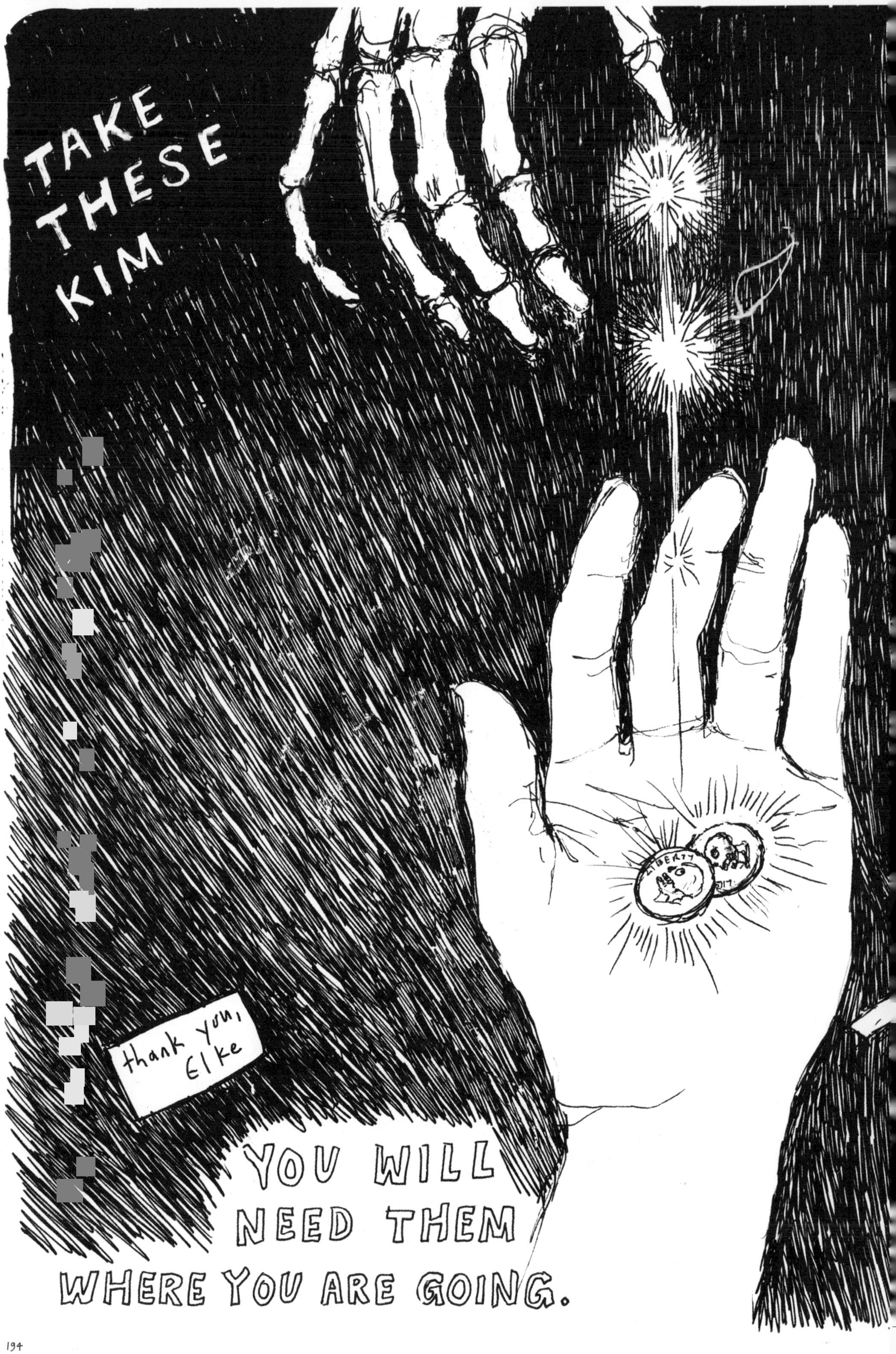
TAKE THESE KIM
thank you, Elke
YOU WILL NEED THEM WHERE YOU ARE GOING.

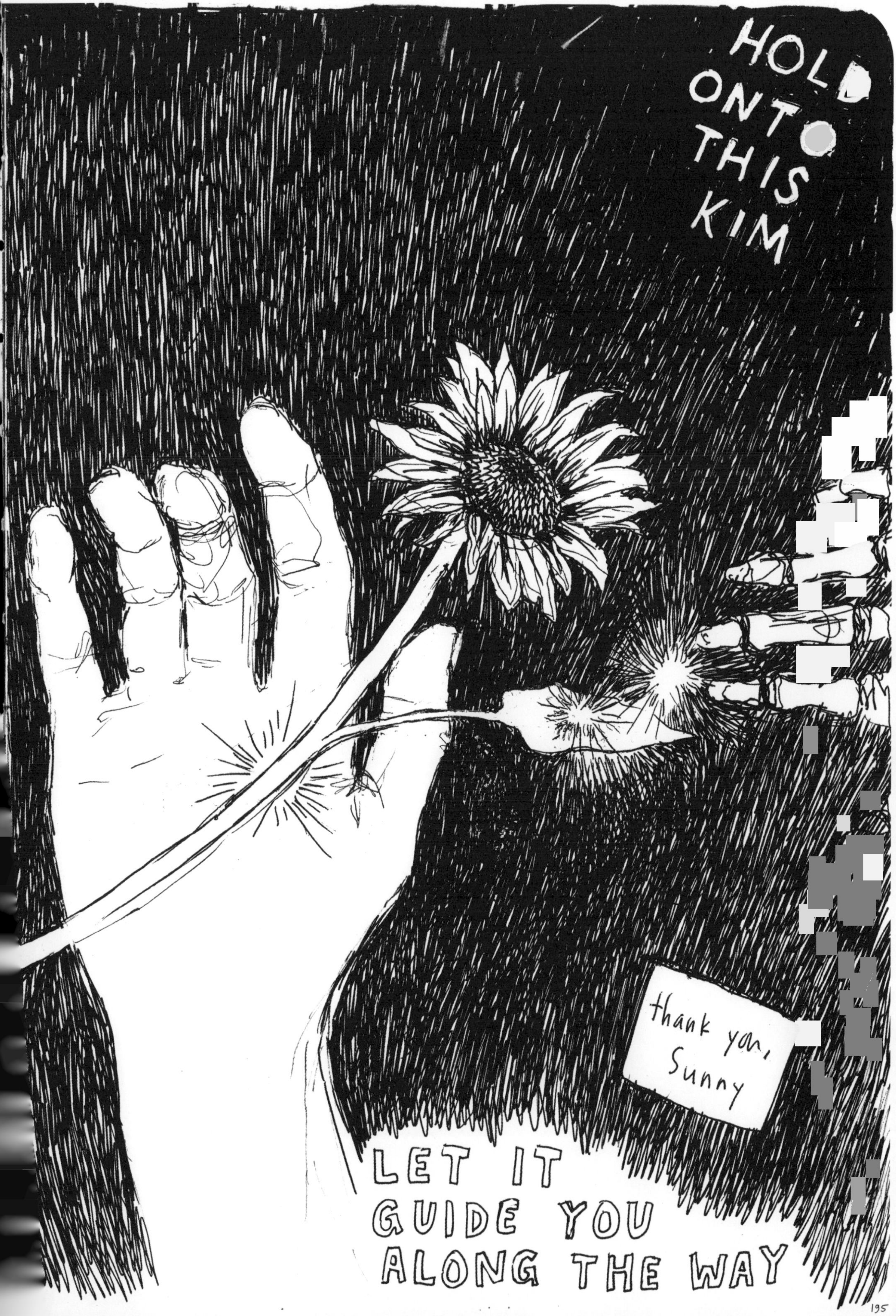
HOLD ONTO THIS KIM
thank you, Sunny
LET IT GUIDE YOU ALONG THE WAY

I CLOSE MY

EYES AND SAY

A SINGLE

THANK YOU

TO ALL
THAT IS

AND ALL
THAT IS
YET TO
BE.

AND I
OPEN
MY
EYES

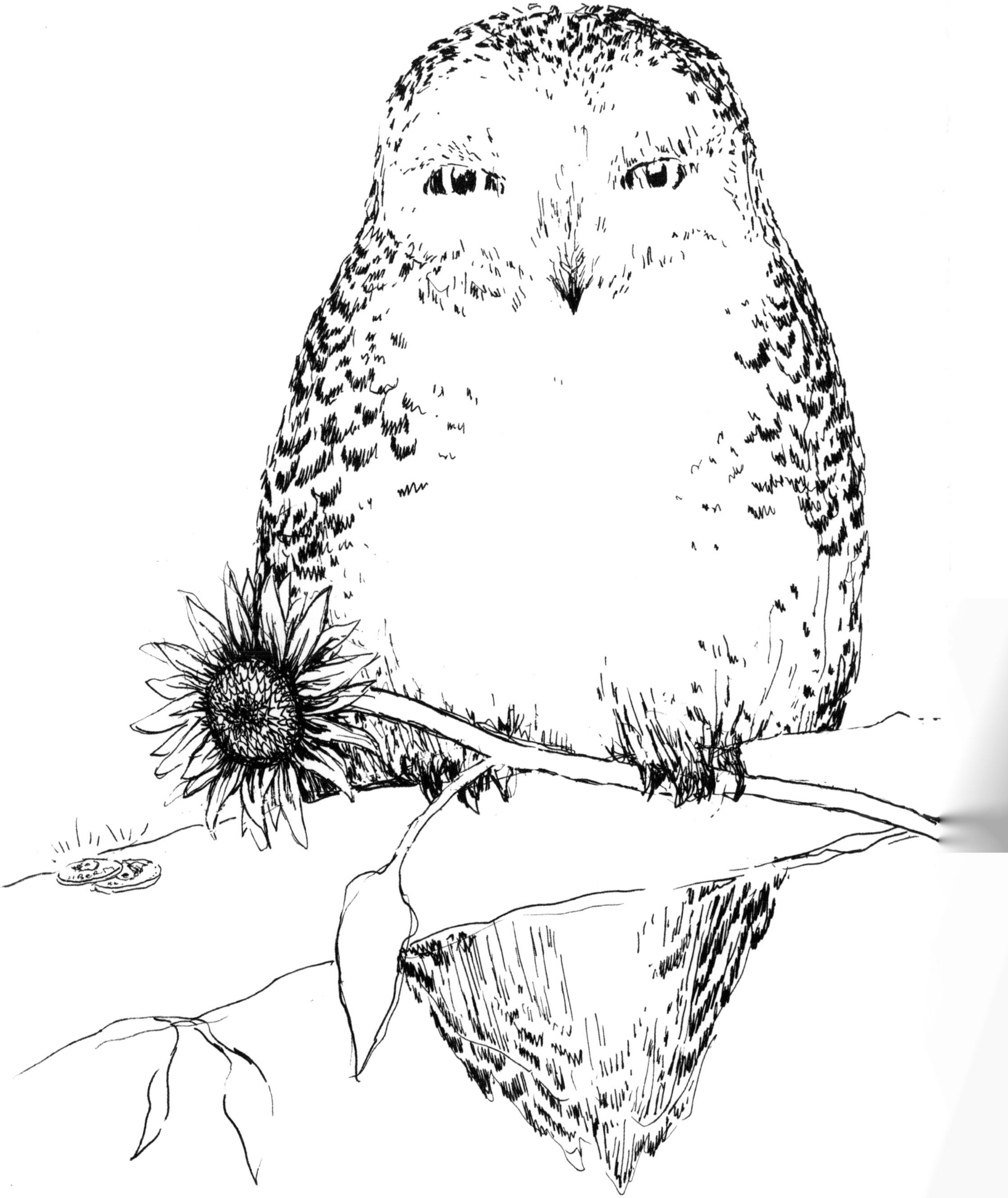

TO THE SOFT WINDS
OF SUMMER.

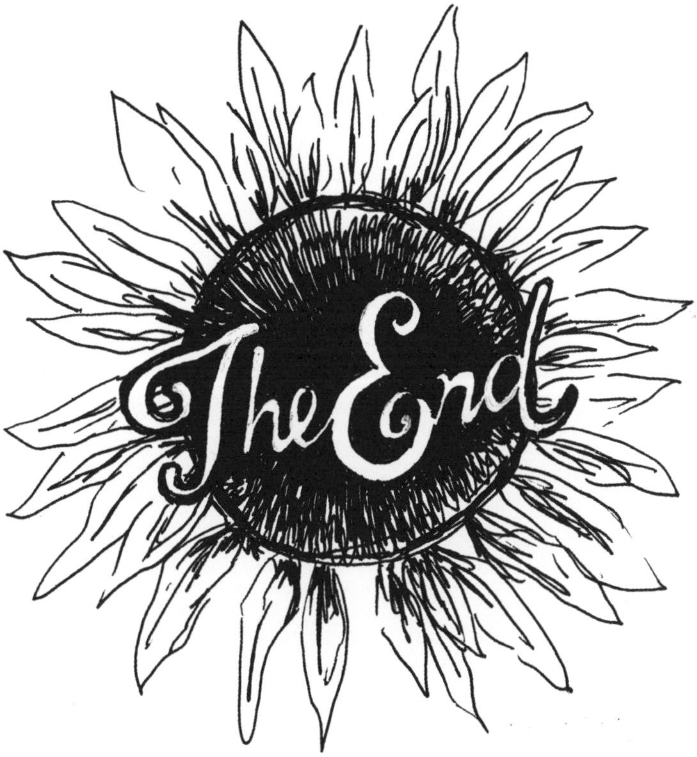
The End

I WILL GIVE

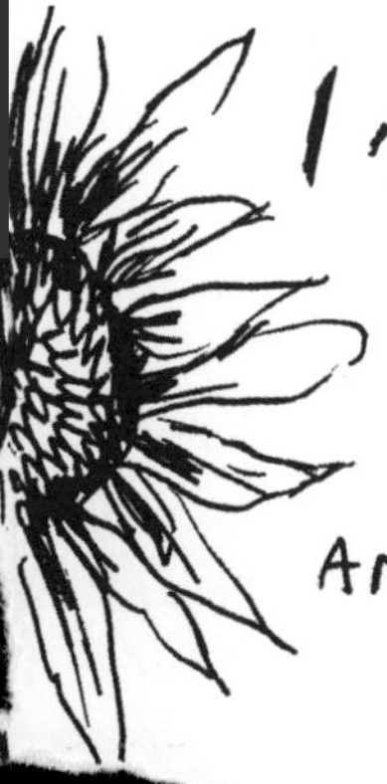

AFTERWORD

♡ JUNE 19, 2019

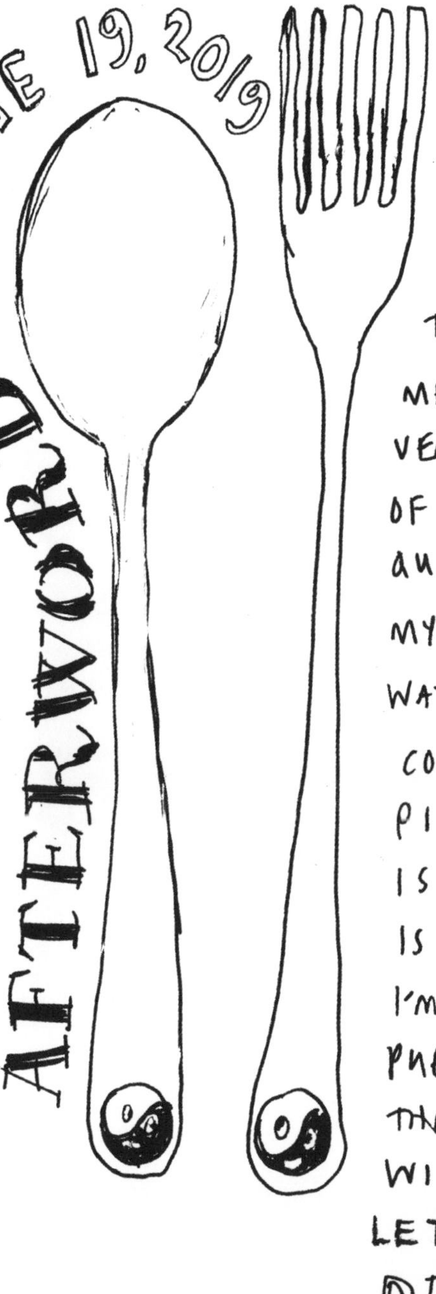

I hope someday, dear reader, that you and I will share a meal.

NOW THAT BLOSSOMS & BONES IS COMPLETE, AND IT WILL SOON FIND ITS WAY INTO THE HANDS OF BOTH STRANGERS AND MY DEAREST FRIENDS, I REALIZE WE NEED ONE FINAL PRAYER.

SEE, NOW THAT I'VE LET THE EATING DISORDER OUT OF THE BAG THERE'S A NEW LAYER OF PARANOIA AROUND THE TABLE. EVERYONE WATCHES ME LIKE A HAWK BUT TRIES VERY HARD NOT TO. BY VIRTUE OF HOW SHAME TRAVELS SO QUICKLY & CONTAGIOUSLY, SOON MY TABLE COMPANIONS START WATCHING THEIR PORTION CONTROL. WE SIT AROUND PICKING LIKE BIRDS. NO ONE IS HUNGRY HERE? THIS FOOD IS YUMMY, PEOPLE! COME ON! I'M ANTICIPATING THAT WITH THE PUBLICATION OF THIS BOOK THAT THE TABLE PARANOIA WILL ONLY INCREASE, SO LET'S USE A PRAYER TO

DISPEL THE MEAL FEAR.

SHRINE, PLEASE SEND US A SWEET ONE. I PROMISE TO SPEAK IT BEFORE EACH MEAL.

T A SPIN THIS EVE... IT'S PIZZA NIGHT AT THE ASHRAM. ☮

I AM NEITHER PERFECT NOR IMPERFECT

YOU ARE NEITHER PERFECT NOR IMPERFECT

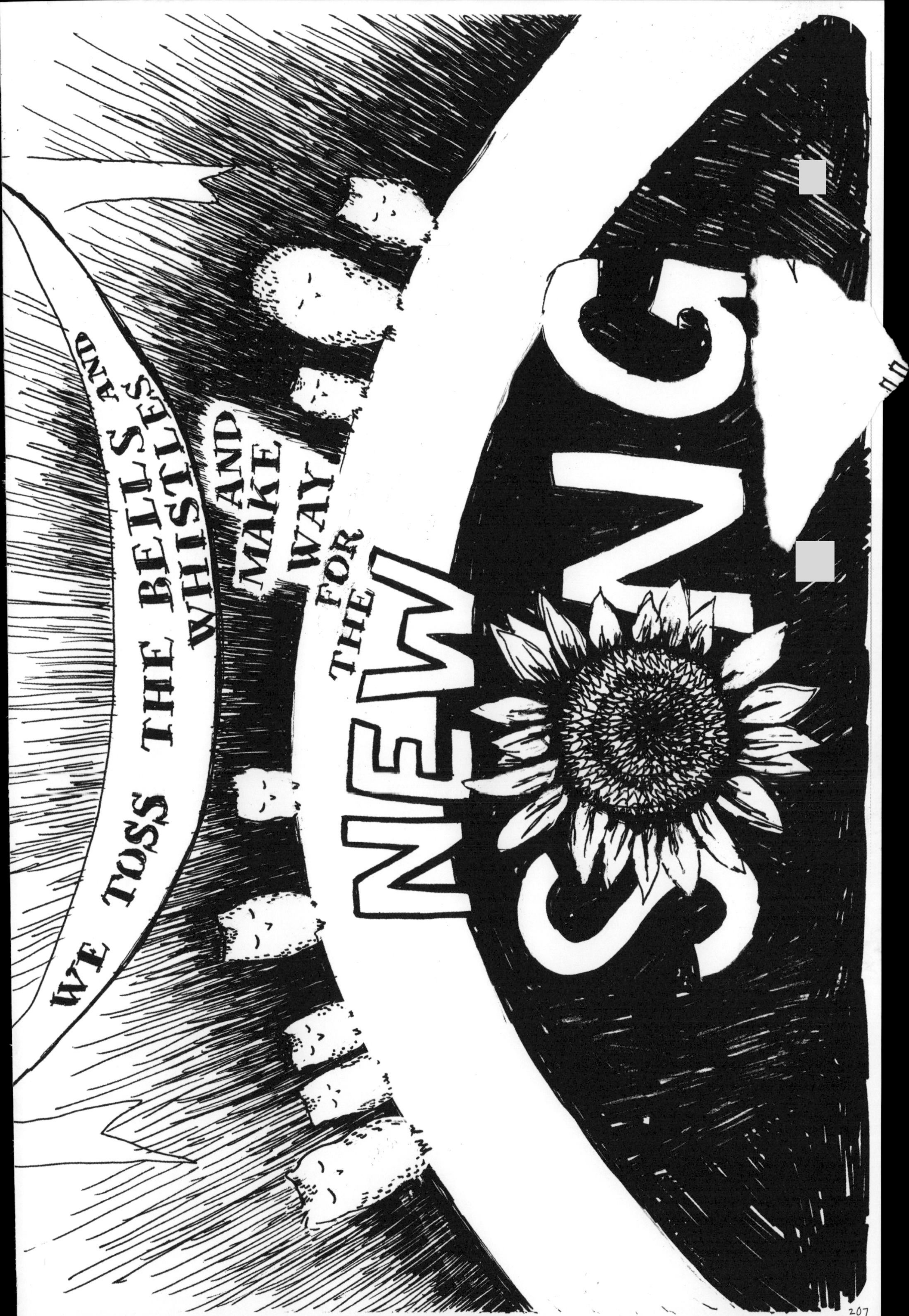
WE TOSS THE BELLS AND WHISTLES AND MAKE WAY FOR THE
NEW
SONG

Thank You

TO

THE HIMALAYAN INSTITUTE
IN ALLAHABAD, INDIA AND IN
HONESDALE, PENNSYLVANIA FOR
PROVIDING THE NURTURING EN-
VIRONMENT IN WHICH A BOOK
OF THIS NATURE COULD BE
BORN. TO YOUR FOUNDERS, FAC-
ILITATORS, RESIDENTS, TEACHERS,
& GLOBAL COMMUNITY I OFFER
MY INFINITE PRANAMS.

Love,

Kim Krans
7/5/19

P.S.

IN PARTICULAR,
TO MY DEAR
FRIEND SEAN COREY,
I THANK YOU FOR
BRINGING THE
BLOSSOMS TO
WHAT WAS ONCE
ONLY BONES.

sat nam ☮

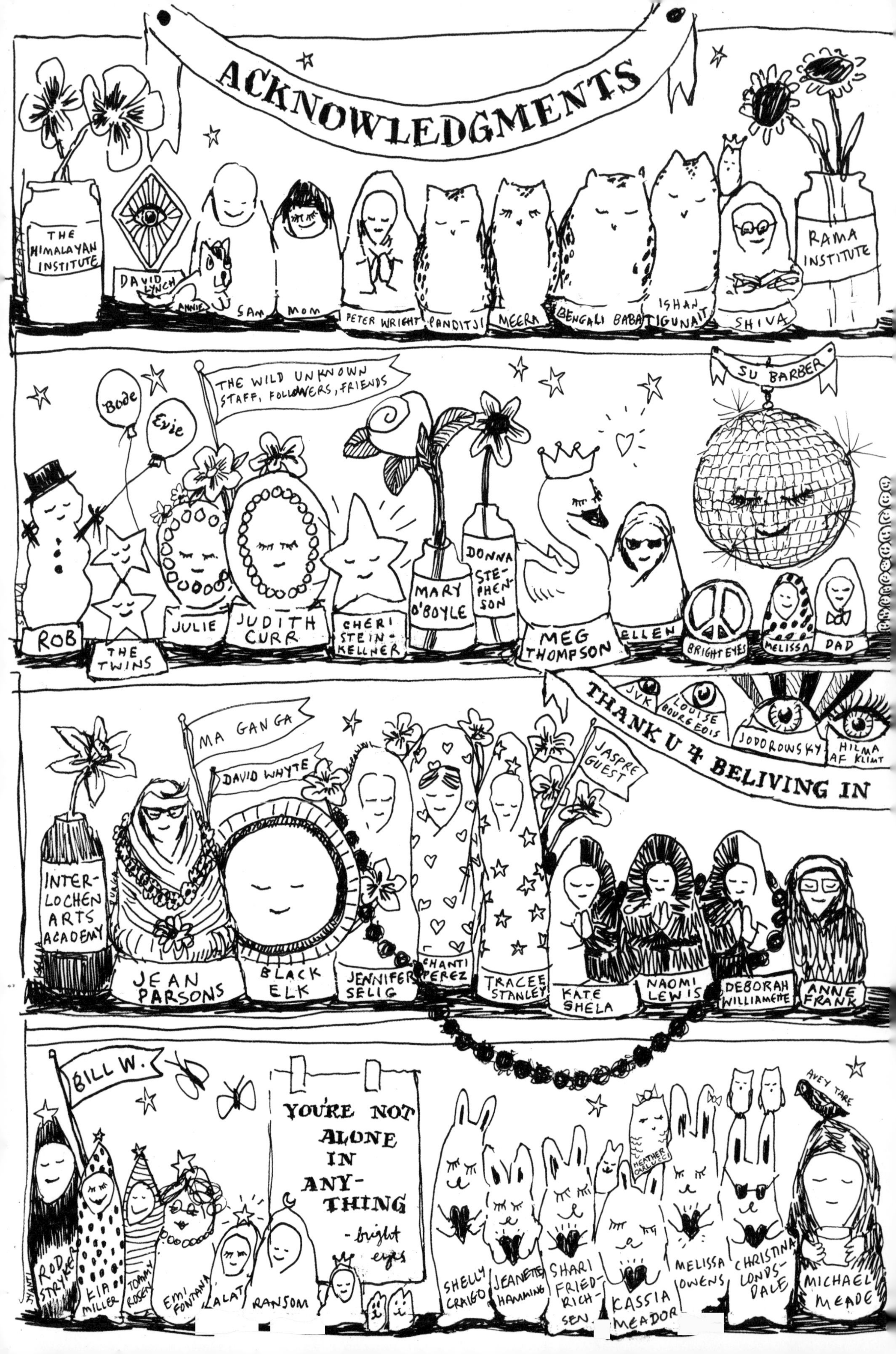
ACKNOWLEDGMENTS
THE HIMALAYAN INSTITUTE
DAVID LYNCH
ANNIE
SAM
MOM
PETER WRIGHT
PANDITJI
MEERA
BENGALI BABA
ISHAN TIGUNAIT
SHIVA
RAMA INSTITUTE
Bode
Evie
THE WILD UNKNOWN STAFF, FOLLOWERS, FRIENDS
SU BARBER
ROB
THE TWINS
JULIE
JUDITH CURR
CHERI STEIN-KELLNER
MARY O'BOYLE
DONNA STEPHENSON
MEG THOMPSON
ELLEN
BRIGHT EYES
MELISSA
DAD
THANK U 4 BELIVING IN
JVK
LOUISE BOURGEOIS
JODOROWSKY
HILMA AF KLIMT
MA GANGA
DAVID WHYTE
JASPRE GUEST
INTERLOCHEN ARTS ACADEMY
JEAN PARSONS
BLACK ELK
JENNIFER SELIG
CHANTI PEREZ
TRACEE STANLEY
KATE SHELA
NAOMI LEWIS
DEBORAH WILLIAMETTE
ANNE FRANK
BILL W.
YOU'RE NOT ALONE IN ANY-THING
- bright eyes
AVEY TARE
HEATHER CARLUCCI
RODE STRYKER
KIA MILLER
TOMMY ROSEN
EMI FONTANA
LALAT
RANSOM
SHELLY CRAIGO
JEANETTE HAMMING
SHARI FRIED-RICH-SEN
KASSIA MEADOR
MELISSA OWENS
CHRISTINA LONDSDALE
MICHAEL MEADE